This first scholarly edition of a major Renaissance text is edited and introduced by John Henry Jones, a leading expert on the Faust legend. The English translation of the best-selling *German Faust Book* of 1587 has long been known as Marlowe's principal source for *Doctor Faustus*. The earliest surviving edition of this translation, published in 1592, is here presented complete, in modern spelling and with a line register for reference, together with full details of all alterations and omissions from the German source. Textual comparisons with *Doctor Faustus* and with later editions of *The English Faust Book* provide crucial information on the development of the Faust theme in England and Germany. In an introduction making full use of hitherto unpublished research, Dr Jones offers new arguments both on the dating of Marlowe's play, and on the personal history and probable identity of the original translator of *The German Faust Book*, known only as 'P. F. Gent'.

THE ENGLISH FAUST BOOK

THE ENGLISH FAUST BOOK

A critical edition based on the text of 1592

edited by
JOHN HENRY JONES

Published by the Press Syndicate of the University of Cambridge
The Pitt Building, Trumpington Street, Cambridge CB2 1RP
40 West 20th Street, New York NY 10011–4211, USA
10 Stamford Road, Oakleigh, Victoria 3166, Australia

First published 1994

Printed in Great Britain at the University Press, Cambridge

A catalogue record for this book is available from the British Library

Library of Congress cataloguing in publication data

Historia von Doctor Johann Fausten. English
The English Faust Book : a critical edition based on the text of
1592 / edited by John Henry Jones
p. cm.
Includes bibliographical references and index
ISBN 0 521 42087 3
1. Faust, d. ca. 1540 – Legends I. Jones, John Henry II. Title
PT923.E5 1994 833′.4–dc20 93–8594 CIP

ISBN 0 521 420873 hardback

Contents

Plates

Figure

Preface

Despite its crucial role in the transmission and development of the Faust legend, both in England and, indirectly, in Germany, the English Faust Book has received little scholarly attention in comparison with either its German precursor or its immediate (and ultimately eclipsing) offspring, Marlowe's *Doctor Faustus*. As a translation it has escaped consideration either as an English prose romance or as a literary creation in its own right, perhaps because the author's achievement in rendering and modifying his German source has not been fully appreciated. Nor has it been much honoured as the starting point for other literary developments, notably the prose romance of 'Friar Bacon', source for Greene's play and much of Prospero's magic. And while there have been a number of 'modern' reprintings of Orwin's 1592 edition, annotations and critical assessments have been modest and the bibliography wholly ignored. Only Rohde (1910) and D'Agostini & Silvani (1978) have attempted to discover sources for the author's departures from the German text and only the former has given serious attention to the identity of the author. The date of the lost first edition, crucial as a *terminus ab quo* for *Doctor Faustus*, has been the subject of often ill-founded speculation; and the printing history has been muddled by Greg's partisan interpretation of the evidence. The present edition attempts to redress this situation.

In my edition of William Empson's *Faustus and the Censor* (Basil Blackwell, 1987) I promised as forthcoming a parallel-text edition of the German and English Faust books in which the EFB would have been printed in parallel with an exact translation of the German Faust Book of 1587. In the event, this proved too ambitious a publication project. However, its aims are met by the present edition which clearly indicates which parts of the EFB text deviate substantially from the German and supplies exact translations of the German passages excluded, thus managing to convey the contents of both works. I hope that this will also reveal the skill of the English author and the extent of his commitment to the work.

In 1989, a Research Fellowship from the Leverhulme Trust enabled me to investigate the bibliography of the early editions of the EFB, its printing history and its relationship to the prose romance of 'Friar Bacon'. My findings, hitherto unpublished except for a note on Marlowe's source, are incorporated in the textual notes and in my introduction to the text, which thus contains a great deal of 'new' material. The effect is a swing in favour of an early date for the publication of the EFB and the composition and performance of *Doctor Faustus*, though I cannot suppose that contrary arguments will die. The recognition of a late text of 'Friar Bacon' as representative of the common source for Greene's *The Honourable History of Friar Bacon and Friar Bungay* and some parts of *The Tempest* is crucially significant for dating the EFB and I trust this justifies the space I have accorded it and the 'shoulder of mutton' incident. In any case, it is interesting material and deserves exposure.

With regard to the identity of the EFB author, the elusive 'P. F. Gent', I make no extravagant claim for the candidate I propose. It is quite probable that no absolute proof will ever be discovered, but the man has the right initials, crops up at the right time in the right place and has precisely the right smell. I have enlisted the help of many German and Polish archivists and librarians in an attempt to trace him in Europe, but without success. Nevertheless, those kind helpers have provided many significant details relating to the EFB travel chapter which are incorporated in the commentary. Whoever 'P. F.' was, he deserves far greater recognition than he has been accorded, and it is a great pity that he did not extend his literary activities.

Possibly in response to the 400th anniversary of Marlowe's death, a number of other books concerning *Doctor Faustus* are currently either in preparation or in the press. Routledge are issuing a volume on Marlowe's sources, edited by William Tydeman and Vivien Thomas, and incorporating an edition of the EFB (I thank Ms Thomas for showing me her introduction to this part and for some stimulating correspondence). Regrettably Eric Rasmussen's *A Textual Companion to 'Doctor Faustus'* (Manchester University Press, 1993) had not appeared when the present work was ready for the press. Also forthcoming in the Revels Plays series is Greene's 'Friar Bacon', edited by David Kastan of Columbia University.

In the context of recent publications on *Doctor Faustus*, I hope I may be excused for securing this opportunity to refute certain charges. Empson's *Faustus and the Censor* inevitably raised a lot of flak and there is sure to be more. Recently some of this has been directed at me as his editor; in particular, Richard Dutton (*Yearbook of English Studies* 23 (1993), p. 11) has unwarrantedly accused me of complicity in Empson's censorship thesis. I wish to make it clear that my involvement with the essay was strictly editorial; I had no hand in its composition and I do not support, nor ever have, Empson's contentions, though I do not regret promoting the publication of such a stimulating example of Empson at his most entertaining.

It is a pleasure to acknowledge the very willing cooperation of the many persons who have aided me in my researches. My especial thanks go to Dr Heeg-Engellart of the Würzburg Staatsarchiv, O. A. Targiel, City Archivist at Frankfurt on the Oder, Professor Dr Jan Pirozyński of the Biblioteka Jagiellońska, Krakow, and Dr Władysław Stępniak, Director of the Archiwum Głowne Akt Dawnych, Warsaw, for topographical and historical details; to Mr James Lawson, Librarian of Shrewsbury School Library, for supplying me with a facsimile of the Shrewsbury fragment and information regarding its provenance; and to Ms Frances Palmer of the Horniman Museum, London, for help in identifying Elizabethan instruments. I am also grateful to Dr P. J. Becker of the Berlin Staatsbibliothek, Christian Hogrefe of the Herzog August Bibliothek, Wolfenbüttel, and Professor Dr Zbigniew Nowak of the Biblioteka Gdanska, for their cooperation in respect of editions of the German Faust Book. I should also like to express my sincere appreciation of the courtesy and assistance rendered to me by librarians and staff at the many libraries I have visited or contacted, especially at the British Library, where most of the work was done.

I am indebted to Kevin Taylor of Cambridge University Press for his kindness and determined commitment, and to the reader, commissioned by the Press, for his painstaking checking of the text and his helpful suggestions, of which many have been implemented.

Finally, I wish to thank Dr John Haffenden for his tireless encouragement, constructive criticism and ever open ear, and Hetta, Lady Empson, for her unfailing friendship and support. The last word should go to William Empson who first awakened my interest in Faustus.

Principal abbreviations

(For critical apparatus see p. 89, and for additional abbreviations and symbols used in the commentary, see p. 185.)

Agrippa	*Henry Cornelius Agrippa, of the Vanitie and Uncertaintie of Arts and Sciences*, Englished by Ja. Sa[nford]. Gent, London 1575
Arber	E. Arber: *A Transcript of the Register of the Company of Stationers of London 1554–1640 AD*, London 1875
Bennett	H. S. Bennett: *English Books and Readers 1558–1603*, Cambridge University Press 1965
Butler *Magus*	E. M. Butler: *The Myth of the Magus*, Cambridge University Press 1948
Butler *Rit.*	E. M. Butler: *Ritual Magic*, Cambridge University Press 1949
COT	G. Braun and F. Hohenberg: *Civitas Orbis Terrarum*; facs. edn, Cleveland & New York (World Publishing Co.) 1966. 5 vols. The publication dates of the 1st Latin edn of each volume are: I: 1572; II: [1575]; III: [1581]; IV [*c.* 1588]; V: [1598]
D'Agostini	Maria Enrica D'Agostini, Giovanna Silvani (eds.): *Analisi comparata delle fonti inglesi e tedesche des Faust dal Volksbuch a Marlowe*, Napoli (Tullio Pronti) 1978. (This work is a comparison of the texts of the Wolfenbüttel MS, the Spies *Historia* and the EFB, Orwin 1592)
Dee	John Dee: *The Private Diary*, ed. James O. Halliwell, Camden Society Publications, Vol. 19, London 1842
Dr F	Marlowe's *Doctor Faustus*, see Greg. References are by line number to the Greg edition, prefixed with A or B to indicate 1604 and 1616 texts respectively.
E	EFB present text. In citations, e.g. [E: 1027], the numbers

	indicate the line number of the present text
EFB	English Faust Book
Empson	William Empson: *Faustus and the Censor*, ed. John Henry Jones, Oxford (Basil Blackwell) 1987
Eyre	*A Transcript of the Registers of the Worshipful Company of Stationers, from 1640–1708*, ed. G. E. Briscoe Eyre, London 1913
French	Peter J. French: *John Dee. The World of an Elizabethan Magus*, London (Routledge, Kegan Paul) 1972
Fulvius	*L'antichita di Roma di Andrea Fulvio ... con le aggiuntioni e annotationi di Girolamo Ferrucci Romano.* Venetia 1588
G	*Historia von D. Johann Fausten...* Frankfurt am Main (Spies) 1587. [edn princeps]. cf. Henning *Historia*. In citations, e.g. [G: 37], the numerals refer to the pagination of the Spies edition
GFB	German Faust Book, see G, and Henning *Historia*
Greg	*Marlowe's 'Doctor Faustus' 1604–1616. Parallel Texts*, ed. W. W. Greg, Oxford (Clarendon Press) 1950
Greg & Boswell	W. W. Greg & E. Boswell: *Records of the Court of the Stationers' Company 1576–1602*, London 1930
Henning *Bib.*	Hans Henning: *Faust bibliographie*, Berlin (Aufbau) 1966 etc.
Henning *Historia*	*Historia von D. Johann Fausten. Neudruck des Faustbuches von 1587*, hrsg.u.eingeleitet von Hans Henning. 2.Aufl., Leipzig (Bibliographisches Institut) 1982
Hon. Hist.	Robert Greene: *The Honourable History of Friar Bacon and Friar Bungay*, see Ward
Hoby	'The Travels and Life of Sir Thomas Hoby 1547–1564', *The Camden Miscellany*, Vol. x, London (Historical Society of Great Britain) 1902: an edition of the previously unpublished MS (British Library: Egerton MS 2148), *c.*1555. The descriptions of Italy refer to 1549
Johnson 1945	Francis R. Johnson: 'Marlowe's "Imperiall Heaven"', *ELH* 12 (1945), pp. 35–44
Johnson 1946	Francis R. Johnson: 'Marlowe's Astronomy and Renaissance Skepticism', *ELH* 13 (1946), pp. 241–54
Kirschbaum	Leo Kirschbaum: 'Is *The Spanish Tragedy* a leading case?', *Journal of English & Germanic Philology*, 37 (1938) pp. 501–12
Logeman	*The English Faust-book of 1592*, ed. Henry Logeman: *Recueil de travaux publiés par la faculté de philosophe et lettres de l'université de Gand*, fasc. 24, Gand / Amsterdam, 1900. This edition is the basis for the printing in Palmer & More.
OED	*The Oxford English Dictionary*, Oxford (Clarendon Press) 1933

*OED*²	*OED*, 2nd edn, Oxford 1989
Palmer & More	P. M. Palmer and R. P. More: *The Sources of the Faust Tradition*, New York (Oxford University Press) 1936, repr. 1966
Petsch	*Das Volksbuch vom Doktor Faust. Nach der 1. Ausgabe 1587*, hrsg. v. Robert Petsch, Halle a. S. (Niedermeyer) 1911
RCP Ann.	Annals of the Royal College of Physicians. MS, transcript and translation: London, The Royal College of Physicians
Rohde	Richard Rohde: *Das Englische Faustbuch und Marlowes Tragödie*, Halle a. S. 1910 (L. Morsbach: *Studien zur Englische Philologie*, Heft 43)
Scot	Reginald Scot: *The Discoverie of Witchcraft*, London 1584
SCR	Stationers' Company Register, see Arber, Eyre
STC	*A Short-Title Catalogue of Books Printed in England, Scotland & Ireland and of English Books Printed Abroad 1475–1640*, compiled by A. W. Pollard & G. R. Redgrave, revised and enlarged by W. A. Jackson, F. S. Ferguson and Katharine F. Pantzer, London (Bibliographic Soc.) 1986
STC(w)	*A Short-Title Catalogue ... 1641–1700*, compiled by Donald Wing, 2nd edn, revised and enlarged, New York 1972
Thomas	William Thomas: *The historie of Italy*, London (T. Marsh) 1561.
Thoms	W. J. Thoms: *Early English Prose Romances*, London (Routledge) 1827–8
Tilley	Morris Palmer Tilley: *A Dictionary of the Proverbs in England in the Sixteenth and Seventeenth Centuries*, Ann Arbor, 1950
Tisch.	The *Tischreden* of Martin Luther, in *Martin Luthers Werke, Kritische Gesamtausgabe*, Weimar, 1912 etc., Part 2: *Tischreden* (6 vols.)
Turler	*The traveiles of Ierome Turler divided into two bookes.* Imprinted at London by William How, for Abraham Veale, 1575
w	Text of the Wolfenbüttel MS: *Historia vnd Geschicht Doctor Johannis Faustj*, Wolfenbüttel, Herzog-August-Bibliothek, Signatur: 92 Extravagantes, folio; as printed in *Das Faustbuch nach der Wolfenbüttler Handschrift*, ed. H. G. Haile, (Philologische Studien u. Quellen, Hft. 14) Berlin (Erich Schmidt) 1963
Ward	A. W. Ward (ed.): *Marlowe: 'Tragical History of Dr Faustus'; Greene: 'Honourable History of Friar Bacon and Friar Bungay'*, Oxford (Clarendon) 1901 (4th edn). The first edition (1868) does not contain Fleay's appendices on the dating of the plays, present from the 2nd edn (1886–7) onwards
Widman	Georg Rudolf Widman: *Warhafftige Historia von... D. Iohannes*

Faustus, Hamburg 1599 (three parts with separate pagination), available as facsimile with a postscript by Gerd Wunder, Schwäbisch Hall (Oscar Mahl) 1978

Yates — Frances A. Yates: *Giordano Bruno and the Hermetic Tradition*, London (Routledge & Kegan Paul), University of Chicago Press 1964

Introduction

THE FAUST BOOKS AND THE FAUST LEGEND

The 'History of the Damnable Life and Deserved Death of Doctor John Faustus', commonly known as the English Faust Book (EFB), was published perhaps as early as 1588, but the earliest extant edition, the basis of the present text, is that printed by Thomas Orwin 'to be sold by Edward White' (London 1592) (see Plate 6. p. 90), which survives as a unique copy.[1] The work of an obscure but brilliant translator whose identity, cloaked by the cipher 'P. F. Gent', remains uncertain,[2] it is probably[3] the earliest 'foreign' translation of the enormously successful anonymous German Faust Book of 1587 (see Plate 1, p. 2).[4] It brought the Faust story to post-Armada England at a time of intense dramatic and literary activity, invigorated by the University Wits; Christopher Marlowe snapped it up. There can rarely have been a more felicitous timing or a more apposite engagement.

The undoubted immediate and enduring popularity of the EFB is not surprising since it exhibited within a single work many of the characteristics of already popular genres of prose fiction. But in mingling the racy, episodic treatment of prose romance and jest book with an intellectual plot of signal relevance to the age, it transcended all, providing a work at once novel and disturbing, comprehending popular aspirations and their attendant anxieties. Faustus' insatiable curiosity for all things in heaven and earth stamp him as a man of the Renaissance, his zest for world-wide travel (the EFB expands his horizons on the German) and interest in antiquities and sights reflect the contemporary passion for 'chorography'[5] and the educative Grand Tour. Yet such curiosity awakened misgivings, and above all else, the Faust book is a cautionary tale. The majority of its readers would have accepted the story as horrifyingly true;[6] the sympathy which the more liberal-minded readers, who

HISTORIA
Von D. Johan
Fausten/dem weitbeschreyten
Zauberer vnnd Schwartzkünstler/
Wie er sich gegen dem Teuffel auff eine be-
nandte zeit verschrieben/ Was er hierzwischen für
seltzame Abentheuwer gesehen/selbs angerich-
tet vnd getrieben/biß er endtlich sei-
nen wol verdienten Lohn
empfangen.
Mehrertheils auß seinen eygenen hin-
derlassenen Schrifften/allen hochtragenden/
fürwitzigen vnd Gottlosen Menschen zum schrecklichen
Beyspiel/abscheuwlichen Exempel/vnd treuw-
hertziger Warnung zusammen gezo-
gen/vnd in den Druck ver-
fertiget.
IACOBI IIII.
Seyt Gott vnderthänig/widerstehet dem
Teuffel/so fleuhet er von euch.
CVM GRATIA ET PRIVILEGIO.
Gedruckt zu Franckfurt am Mayn/
durch Johann Spies.
M. D. LXXXVII.

1 Facsimile of title page of the Spies Faust Book of 1587

were later to love Falstaff, felt for the lusty, sociable, fun-loving protagonist who could box the Pope's ears and hoodwink the Great Turk, must have made the tragedy the more poignant. The book is undeniably ambivalent in combining exemplary moral exhortation with heroic fashioning, though the extent of the latter depended on the reader's viewpoint: to a Puritan, the pleasurable excesses of the table and the lusts of the flesh were equally reprehensible signs of Faustus' possession, his mock heroism a diabolic satire.

Much of this applies *a fortiori* to the German original, but the more emphatic reception of the Faust book in Germany, compared with that in England, was due to the very different socio-religious milieu of its publication. In the first place, while new to England, the legendary Faustus was already firmly seated in the German national consciousness; the process had begun within the lifetime of the historical 'George' (Jörg) Faustus (died *c.* 1539), seed for the legend propagated most influentially by his contemporary, Luther, and later, with commanding authority, by Philip Melanchthon. In fact, the legend took over so quickly and so absolutely that it is difficult to extricate the historical Faustus, even in contemporary notices.[7] He was an astrologer, physician and natural philosopher, always on the move (often in flight), always provocative, boasting miraculous abilities and a mastery of the seven liberal arts (occult practices), even claiming to be the fount of necromancers. From his first notice (1508) to the peak of his fame (mid-1530s) he attracted the scorn of the Humanists (Trithemius, Mutianus, Camerarius) and the enmity of civic authorities (Ingolstadt, Nuremberg, Wittenberg), yet he enjoyed the patronage of Franz von Sickingen, the Bishop of Bamberg and the von Hutten family, and had influential friendships at Erfurt and Würzburg. Progressively outlawed, feared by many, respected by others for his 'science', he became famous throughout the land yet remained the classic outsider, rootless, a will o' the wisp, passing, like Socrates and Jesus Christ, without a personally written legacy to assert his true identity.[8] Of such are legends made.

Luther, who never actually met Faustus, regarded him as a sorcerer, aided by the devil, and predicted he would earn the devil's reward, i.e. the devil would kill him as soon as he had outlived his usefulness. This comes as no surprise in view of Luther's conservatism with regard to 'new' science, his hostility to astrology and his obsession with the ubiquitous presence of the devil, a heritage to be bequeathed to all Protestant Germany in the well-thumbed pages of the *Tischreden*,[9] the second bible of the reformed faith. Here Faustus is an occasional table topic: 'Much was spoken of Faustus who had a familiar spirit...', offering a platform for Luther's attacks on 'the devil's brother-in-law'.[10] By the time these words were read by all who could read, Luther's prediction had been confirmed: Faustus had died obscurely (it was rumoured, violently) in South Germany, probably at Staufen in Breisgau.[11] The first published account of his death, by the Basel Protestant pastor Johannes Gast,[12] reported that he had been found lying near his bed with his face twisted to the ground, a direction it stubbornly maintained upon the bier even after the head had three times been turned to the fore. Philip Melanchthon in his perennial lectures at Wittenberg[13] was more explicit: 'He was killed by the devil in a small village in Wurtemberg', and he provides a detailed biographical sketch of 'Johann' Faustus, 'born at Knittlingen', in which the magician's life and deeds are interpreted as devil-dealing; his dog, his horse, are familiar spirits, and he himself is 'a sewer full of devils'.

With this foundation, there could be nothing to arrest the royal progress of the legend. During the following decades it accreted a host of anecdotes from all parts of Germany, especially Upper Saxony, and the deeds of other magicians were fostered upon Faustus: the tale of Trithemius raising the spirit of Mary of Burgundy before the emperor Maximilian becomes one of Faustus raising Alexander the Great and his paramour before Charles V, the miraculous garden of Albertus Magnus blooms at Faustus' door.[14] Some of these short tales began to appear in collections of moral histories in the 1570s[15] testifying to the gathering impetus, but what principally fuelled the public interest in Faustus during this period was the climactic intensification of the German witch craze.

Neither its horrors nor its scale require any rehearsal: it affected everyone. The devil was on every tongue and spawned a specialist genre, the *Teufel-literatur*, in which specific devils (including the *Zauber Teufel*) were allocated to every kind of sin or immorality, and which was later to besiege the presses of Frankfurt with such publications as the *Theatrum de Veneficis* and the *Theatrum Diabolorum*, themselves collections of numerous works devoted to witchcraft and diabolic possession.[16] Even those, such as Weyer[17] and Lercheimer[18], who were courageously outspoken against the burnings, proclaimed their belief in the ubiquitous devil luring mankind to destruction, feeding the imaginations of the enfeebled witches so that they thought themselves capable of supernatural powers but were in reality the victims of melancholic delusions. The pacts which these unfortunates claimed to have made with the devil, usually 'a dark man', were part of their delusion, but neither Weyer nor Lercheimer questioned the ability of an adept magician, versed in the *grimoires*,[19] to conjure the devil and make a pact with him; Faustus and his ilk earned their full condemnation, though the humane Lercheimer, a crypto-Calvinist, limited his suggested punishment to exile from the community.

All these writings made explicit what was implied in Luther's 'devil's reward': Faustus had made a pact with the devil. With this decisive and completing extension, the Faust legend joins common ground with other well-known legends of the past, the Catholic legends of Cyprian of Antioch and Theophilus of Adana, and Luther's tale of a student who had made a pact.[20] The Theophilus story is the most pertinent, with its emphasis on the contract, written in blood, denying God, Christ and the Holy Ghost, and handed to the devil. Theophilus is saved through the intercession of the Virgin Mary who miraculously recovers the contract; such a salvation was no longer available in Protestant Germany, but in any case, Faustus' damnation was a foregone conclusion from the inception of the legend.

All the ingredients for a fully developed account of the legendary Faustus were now to hand: the 'historical' elements of Faustus' learning and studies, the anecdotal material telling of his feats of magic, and the all-important framework of his pact with the devil and his 'fetching' at the end of his allotted term. Given the furore of public interest and the eagerness of publishers for such a guaranteed success, a 'life of Faustus' was inevitable; the only surprise is that it should have come so late. Johann Spies,[21] the Lutheran publisher of the German Faust Book, indicates the ripeness of public expectation in his preface to the work:

> Everywhere, at parties and social gatherings, there is great inquiry for a history of this Faustus. Indeed, a number of modern writers have touched here and there upon the subject of this magician, his diabolic art and frightful end, but I have often wondered that, as yet, no one has presented this terrible tale in an orderly fashion and published it as a warning to the whole of Christendom. I inquired amongst scholars and learned men as to whether perhaps someone had already written such a work but I was unable to discover anything for certain until recently I received a manuscript from a good friend at Speyer.[22]

Spies is describing public interest in the period just prior to the summer of 1587 when he must have received his manuscript, for there is no doubt that he would have published just as soon as it came to his hands: he rushed out the first edition in time for the Frankfurt fair in September.[23] Thus it is probable that the work was actually written in 1586 or later. (A surviving MS of the Faust book, the so-called Wolfenbüttel MS,[24] itself clearly a dictated copy, cannot be dated precisely but there are indications that it did not long precede publication.[25]) If this date of composition is correct then there were two major factors which may have triggered the writing and shaped the inner theme of the work. One was the publication, in 1585, of Lercheimer's *Christlich Erinnerung von Zauberei*, ('Christian Commentary on Magic')[26] with its emphasis on the assaults of the devil and the particular mode of assault employed to take advantage of particular failings, including intellectual pride. The other was the late flowering in Northern Europe of Renaissance hermetism and the presence in Saxony of the two most famous and most suspect magicians of the age, John Dee and

Giordano Bruno.[27] Dee was in Leipzig in May 1586, in diplomatic retreat from Prague where suspicions of necromancy had made his presence increasingly uncomfortable and insecure (see below, p. 30).[28] As for Bruno, he arrived in Wittenberg in the late summer of the same year and lectured there until 1588, enthusiastically received by the Lutheran scholars.[29] Both these men were world famous in academic circles, both for their prodigious learning and their advanced hermetic ideas; both were representative of an extension of philosophic inquiry into areas which possibly transgressed the divinely prescribed limits of human knowledge, Dee with his persistence into 'angelic communication', Bruno with his mysticism involving decan images and 'star demons'. It is just this caution which the unknown, but in all probability Saxon, author of the Faust book has seized upon in his exemplary story and which Marlowe was to pin-point so exactly:

> 'Faustus...
> Whose fiendful fortune may exhort the wise
> Onely to wonder at unlawfull things,
> Whose deepeness doth intice such forward wits,
> To practise more than heavenly power permits.'
> *Dr F*: [A1513–7; B2117–21],

for the Faust book is no simple statement of the legend dressed with a Lutheran tendency; it incorporates within that framework the parable of the learned scholar who finds all his gifts inadequate to satisfy his vain curiosity (*Fürwitz*[30]) concerning the secrets of the cosmos and is led to seek the aid of the devil. His consequent despair in God deprives him of the power to repent; his sin against the Holy Ghost denies him divine grace; he is damned.

The raising of Helen of Greece before the students and Faustus' subsequent cohabitation with her appears to confirm this reading. For beyond the classical allusion (the destructive power of beauty) lay the esoteric identification of Helen with the consort of Simon Magus whom he worshipped as Sophia, the divine wisdom.[31] In his *Oratio Valedictoria* (1588), Bruno extols 'Sophia, Wisdom itself, beautiful as the moon, great as the sun, . . . Her have I loved and sought from my youth, and desired for my spouse, and have become a lover of her form. . . and I prayed. . . that she might be sent to abide with me. . .'[32] These words post-date the Faust book but they may convey an earlier sentiment known in Wittenberg circles, the precise milieu the author chose for his setting of Faustus' life.

Detailed analytical speculation on the process whereby the Faust book achieved its final shape lies outside the scope of this introduction, but the work is generally regarded as a multi-stage production,[33] perhaps beginning with a

Latin original dealing with the principal theme of the devil's entrapment of Faustus, later translated and expanded to include the anecdotal material of the central parts and the three great journeys: through the heavens, into hell, and throughout the known world. There can be little doubt that some of this material, probably including Faustus' pact, was circulating piecemeal amongst the students and thus available to the author/revisionist. Certainly there was more than one Faust book. The Spies Faust book (henceforth *Historia*) makes two clear references[34] to a life of Faustus supposedly written by his house-boy Christopher Wagner and takes pains in the story to allow for its production.[35] This 'pseudo-Wagner' work (which is not the later 'Wagner book' (see below, p. 10, n. 51)) is lost, but its one-time existence is corroborated in yet another life of Faustus which was being written in 1587, the 'Authentic Life' by the Halberstadt lawyer Georg Rudolf Widman.[36] This was not published until 1599, well after the author's death, but Widman began his work before Spies published his Faust book (he probably knew the *Historia* in a manuscript version). His extended 'biography' relies heavily on this source but includes much extra material he claims to have collected from the students and much from the account of 'Johannes Wäiger', as he names the house-boy. Thus Widman supplies information on material available to the author of the *Historia* and illuminates the fashioning of the most complex character in that work, the spirit Mephostophiles.

This fascinating creation probably started life as the brain-child of 'pseudo-Wagner', but as a Mephostophiles quite different from the one depicted in the *Historia*. In Widman's work, this proto-Mephostophiles is the spirit sent to Faustus in fulfilment of the conditions of the pact, a pact there made with the devil in person.[37] It is an essentially friendly spirit whose great mischance it is to be subject to Lucifer. 'You should not fear me', Mephostophiles tells Faustus, 'for I am no devil but a familiar spirit; we are amicable to men and gladly associate with them.'[38] His friendly concern for Faustus' interests even extends to yoking the oxen to the cart and bringing in the harvest lest his master, Faustus, should incur suspicion by continuing to live a life of luxury while neglecting his estates.[39] And there is a touching domesticity about a conversation between Faustus and his spirit while Wäiger is present, recording everything verbatim.[40] Although this Mephostophiles has clearly been briefed as to what questions he may and may not answer, he never threatens Faustus or attempts to terrify him; that role is left to Lucifer himself.

It is surprising that Widman should have accepted this characterization, for he was an ardent Lutheran, and to Luther all spirits were devils. Certainly it would not do for the author of the *Historia* who makes Mephostophiles the prime diabolic mover of the action, though once in a while the proto-

Mephostophiles glimmers through.[41] The resultant fusion of roles of servant and gaoler, friend and betrayer, tempter and executioner, converts the simple moralistic tale of the precursors (I include Widman) into a subtle psychological drama in which a major component is the revelation of Mephostophiles' true nature, both to Faustus and the reader. The devil incarnate is still brought in to terrify Faustus on occasion, but he is used more as Mephostophiles' ultimate weapon rather than as a tyrannous and unappeasable master. By the time Faustus' moral fibre has been sufficiently eroded by his self-indulgent living, Mephostophiles is quite capable of cowing him into submission himself by threatening to tear him in pieces on the spot.

The *Historia* burdens Mephostophiles with yet another function: he must justify the ways of God, in particular, the damnation of Faustus. The reader is to be reminded that the devil is God's instrument. In a chapter enumerating the manifold assaults of the devil on mankind,[42] Mephostophiles details the process whereby he possessed Faustus and exonerates himself: 'Why not? For as soon as we saw your heart and what you had in mind and how none but the devil could further your aims, we set to work and made your thoughts and fancies still more insolent and daring.'[43] And in a later chapter, absent from the EFB as it has come down to us,[44] he goes further and berates Faustus in tones more appropriate to Luther than the devil, justifying the punishment which is about to be exacted:

> 'Because you knew full well what is written in the bible, that you should pray only to God, serve Him and love no other gods but him... and because you have not done this but have tested your God, fallen away from Him and committed yourself to us, body and soul, now you must keep your promise... You despised the skills God gave you, you were not satisfied with them but invited the devil to be your guest... In all your dealings you have called yourself the devil's friend, so now prepare yourself. For God is Lord, the devil but abbot or monk... You should not have put so much trust in the devil, for he is God's ape, a murderer and a liar.'[45]

For the author of the *Historia*, Faustus' great sin is self-reliance: in his arrogance, he has despaired in God, without whose support his reason is perverted and his judgments are false. When, finally, he sees the fruits of his folly, this same arrogance denies him God's mercy by placing false limitations upon it. Repeatedly we are told that 'like Cain, he thought his sins too great to be forgiven', thus depriving himself of the ability to repent. Superficially this is all very well, but it ignores Mephostophiles' part in the proceedings, for it is he who drives Faustus to this despair, reiterating Cain's example, and chanting 'Too late!', besides actively preventing good thoughts by bringing in succubae or threatening him with immediate dismemberment when he is on the verge of repentance. One might reasonably question the justice of a God who permits His agent such licence, but the message comes through clearly: the man who ceases to rely on God and makes himself the judge of what may be known or attempted, in that instant, crosses the brink of an inescapable maelstrom.

The *Historia* uses all its varied source material to present a structured account of Faustus' subsequent deterioration. In the carefully manipulated dialogues, Faustus' curiosity is turned into an obsession with hell, which only serves to reveal to him his folly and his plight. His desire to marry to satisfy his increased libido is thwarted and he is prompted to embark upon a life-long debauchery with succubae. His travels show him a distant glimpse of Paradise but it is wholly unapproachable. His grand acts at the courts of emperor and prince shrink to fraudulent ploys on peasants and party tricks to impress his student companions. Eventually he becomes a gibbering wreck writing vain lamentations but still unable to repent. The spiritual, mental and physiological breakdown culminates ultimately in the battered and dismembered body lying on a dung heap.

This then supplies the broad design of the Faust book, largely retained in the EFB which, despite additions and omissions, is essentially faithful to the German author's intentions. That the *Historia* lacks artistry in implementing this design is perhaps to be expected considering its peculiar genesis and the varied source material, used rough-hewn and indiscriminately. The language is for the most part barren, many of the episodes are bathetic, Faustus vacillates between the heroic and the abject, sometimes flesh, sometimes paste-board. Yet by some strange magic, the character of Faustus remains a whole, defying fragmentation and absorbing every distortion, just as the Faust book preserves its nightmare unity. The public loved it.

As Spies had doubtless surmised, demand for the *Historia* was instant and widespread. The first edition was sold out within a couple of weeks and three more editions and two new recensions, each with additional chapters of anecdotes, appeared during the same year.[46] All in all, at least fourteen editions of the *Historia* were published to 1593, twenty to the end of the century, including a version in Low German (1588).[47] At Tübingen a group of students made a version in rhymed doggerel, published there in 1588 without permission, provoking the first documented example of authoritarian disapproval of the Faust book: the students and publisher were sent to gaol and received a good whipping for their temerity.[48] But in Frankfurt, Spies continued to flourish, protected by the heavily scored piety of his design to present the story 'as a terrible example and a warning to all Christendom to resist the assaults of the devil'.[49] He and the other Faust-book publishers were the target for a stinging rebuke by Lercheimer in the third edition of his 'Christian Commentary' (1597),[50] greatly concerned by the slander to his alma mater,

Wittenberg, sanctified hearth of the Reformation, and the influence on the curious-minded young whom he thought might be tempted to copy Faustus; but his words came far too late to be effective other than to register protest and distance himself from probable association with the Faust book. By then his compatriots were eagerly enjoying a sequel to the Faust book, the 'Wagner book' of 1593,[51] an account of the deeds of Wagner and his spirit Auerhahn after the death of Faustus. This remained popular well into the seventeenth century when the series was augmented by the satirical *D. Johann Fausten Gauckeltasche* ('Dr Faustus' Conjuring Bag') (1607).[52] The publication of Widman's ponderous tome (1599) coincided with a decline in demand for the *Historia* which received no further reprintings until the nineteenth century and had quite disappeared from view by Goethe's time. His knowledge of Faust derived from an expanded (!) treatment of Widman,[53] a slight, fanciful Faust story called the *Faustbuch der Christenden Meinenden* (1725),[54] Marlowe's *Doctor Faustus* and, possibly his prime inspiration, the German folk play of Faust, a favourite item in the repertoire of the puppet theatres.[55] The origins of this Faust play are obscure but in all likelihood it evolved from tailored versions of Marlowe's play as performed by English actors, 'die Englischen Comedianten', touring in Germany in the late sixteenth/early seventeenth centuries.[56] If so, this reimportation of Faustus into Germany at a time when the first wave of public interest was nearly spent was of great consequence for the continental development of the theme.

In such a process, the English Faust Book clearly plays a crucial role. None of the other early translations (Danish (1588), Dutch (1592), French (1598), Czech (1611))[57] initiated comparable developments, nor did they show the same imaginative flair – and although the seminal success of the EFB is very much due to place and timing, the author should be allowed much credit both in arresting Marlowe's attention and supplying him with unique material; nor was the influence confined to Marlowe: Greene and Shakespeare owe indirect debts via the prose romance of 'Friar Bacon', itself directly modelled on the EFB in an attempt to share the lucrative market (see below, pp. 55ff). The early printing history of the EFB is rendered problematic by the non-survival of the first (and possibly, second) edition or any manuscript; but from 1592 until the eighteenth century the EFB was never long out of print,[58] attesting to an abiding popularity of the work, far outliving that of the *Historia* in Germany, and penetrating the Enlightenment, both in its original form and in a number of cheap abridgments. A verse treatment was extant from c. 1633,[59] and a Faust ballad, *The Just Judgment of God upon … John Faustus*, to the tune of 'Fortune My Foe', proved a good money-spinner for the seventeenth century ballad syndicates ('Fortune My Foe' became equally well known as 'Faustus', sure indication of a hit).[60] And just as

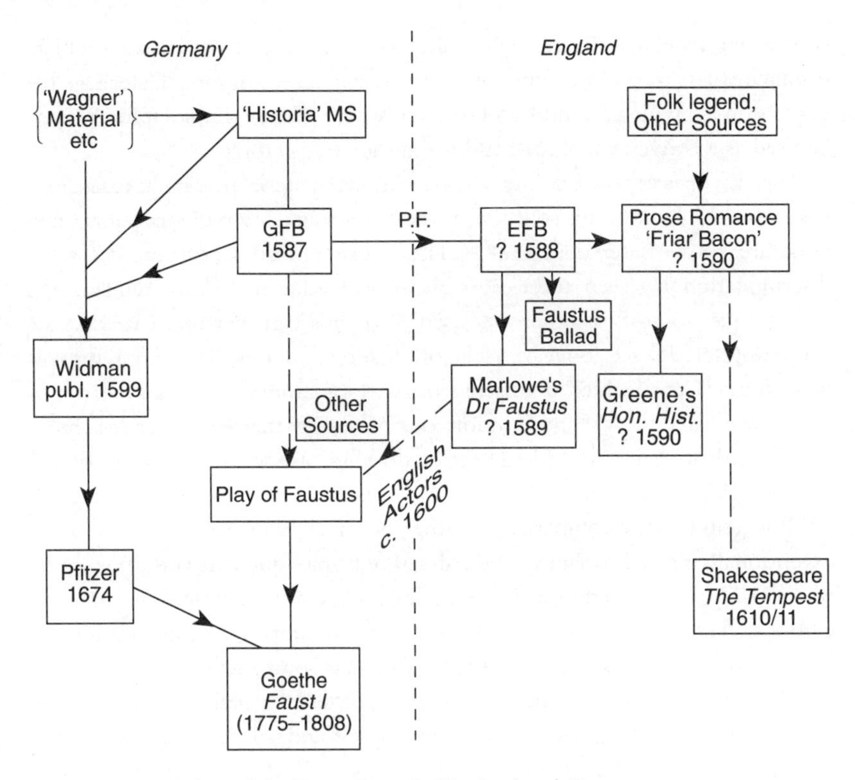

Fig. 1 Transmission of the Faust theme in England and Germany

the *Historia* had its sequel, so too the EFB: *The Second Report of Doctor John Faustus* (1594);[61] this 'English Wagner Book' is no translation of the German, but an independent satirical and highly amusing work, written much in the style of Nashe by an unknown author, 'an English gentleman, student in Wittenberg ... University'. This too had a long following.

All these developments, including those in Germany, are summarized in the accompanying scheme (Fig. 1), which charts the literature of the Faust theme from its inception to the time of Goethe and demonstrates the seminal importance of the *Historia* and the EFB.

THE EFB AND ITS AUTHOR

The title pages of the Orwin and subsequent early editions of the EFB allege that it was 'translated into English by P. F. Gent', 'according to the true copy' (i.e. authentic edition) 'printed at Frankfurt'. Although 'Gent' is a known surname of the period, here it is an abbreviation for 'Gentleman', as indicated by the contrasting typefaces (Roman and Italic) for 'P. F.' and 'Gent', besides which, instances of Elizabethans with two Christian names are rare. Deferring the discussion of his identity until later (see below, p. 29ff), the simple cipher PF may be used as a convenient short-hand for author/translator.

Since PF does not include any of the additional material present in recensions B and C of the *Historia*, his source must have been an edition of recension A and none are known later than 1588.[62] The translation does not permit further discrimination between these possible source editions. There remains the vexing question of whether he used a manuscript version such as the Wolfenbüttel MS (see above, p. 5); he omits some (but not all) passages present in the Spies *Historia* which are absent from W,[63] sometimes hints at knowledge of matter exclusive to W,[64] and in numerous places his translation accords more closely with W than with Spies,[65] yet he does not use W to make sense of a (? haplographic) omission in Spies.[66] As it is ludicrous to contemplate PF indulging in textual comparisons, either he must have been gifted with an exceptionally fine editorial eye and subbed out Spies' pietistic additions, or he was working from an edition,[67] no longer extant, closer to W than all surviving editions. This question cannot be resolved but imposes some caution on interpretations of PF's lesser departures from his source text.

PF's translation is by no means exact. Like other Elizabethan translators, he felt free, even impelled, to improve on the original and tailor it to his own design in a manner which would be unthinkable today. But his handling is rarely cavalier; his paraphrasings show a concern for the intention of the source text and, apart from a few clear mistranslations, all his amendments are deliberate, their nature dictated by the gravity of the particular material. Thus while he is prone to paraphrase the short anecdotal tales which probably held little interest for him, his renderings of the dialogues and what he considered significant matter are often exact; his departures from his source in these weightier sections are motivated by his own beliefs or incredulities and by a strongly developed dramatic sense which informed some important remodelling. His interest rarely flags; taken as a whole his translation is a work of earnest commitment.

PF possessed three qualities notably lacking in the German author: a flair for pungent expression, a vivid visual imagination and a taste for ironic humour; in combination they served to exalt the humble Faust book to a work of considerable art. Except in Mephostophiles' poetic outburst ('Wherefore learn of me...' etc. [789–839]),[68] there is no attempt at a high style. The language is that of Stowe's *Survey of London*, Scot's *Discovery of Witchcraft* and Giles Fletcher's *Russian Commonwealth*: vigorous descriptive prose, informed by mental precision, startlingly fresh, and inevitably quickening the characters of Faustus and Mephostophiles by improving their rhetoric. One example, taken from Mephostophiles' description of hell, will serve to show PF's skill when he chooses to be exact:

'And mark Faustus, hell is the nurse of death, the heat of all fire, the shadow of heaven and earth, the oblivion of all goodness, the pains unspeakable, the griefs unremovable, the dwelling of devils, dragons, serpents, adders, toads, crocodiles and all manner of venomous creatures; the puddle of sin, the stinking fog ascending from the Stygian lake, brimstone, pitch and all manner of unclean metals, the perpetual and unquenchable fire, the end of whose miseries was never purposed by God.' [635–42],

for which the original reads:

'Unnd mercke, daß die Helle ist ein Helle deß Todes, ein Hitz deß Feuwers, ein Finsternuß der Erden, ein Vergessung alles Guten, der Enden nimmermehr von Gott gedacht, sie hat Marter und Wehe, und ewig unerleschlich Fewer, ein Wohnung aller Hellischen Drachen, Würme und Ungeziffer, Ein Wohnung der verstossenen Teuffel, Ein Stanck vom Wasser, Schwefel unnd Pech, unnd aller hitzigen Metall.' [G: 55, u/v normalized]

Besides using such arresting phrases as 'the nurse of death', 'the puddle of sin' and 'unclean metals', PF has remodelled the passage by repositioning to the end what, for him, is of transcendental importance, the notion of perpetuity. What, in the German, is a clumsy catalogue of horrors becomes, under PF's hand, a carefully structured peroration. Even here he is unable to restrain himself from additions (the extra venomous creatures, the Stygian lake) but they are not wanton, they serve a masterful rhetoric, seen at its best, perhaps, in Faustus' peroration (for which there is no German counterpart) to his *Oratio* to the students: 'Thus, even thus, (good gentlemen, and my dear friends) was I enthralled in that satanical band, all good desires drowned, all piety banished, all purpose of amendment utterly exiled, by the tyrannous threatenings of my deadly enemy' [2894–8]. Here controlled alliteration and assonance isolate and link the successive privations, building to the appalling wail of 'utterly exiled', a most forceful description of Faustus' condition as he sees it and as, in fact, it is.

With such skills at his command, it is not surprising that PF improves whatever he touches, however prosaic. Thus,

[Padua] ist mit einer dreyfächtigen Mawer befästiget, mit mancherley Gräben, unnd umblauffenden Wassern [G: 102]

is rendered:

[Padua] is fenced about with three mighty walls of stone and earth, betwixt the which runneth goodly ditches of water. [1298ff]

And here is a final example of a greatly improved close approximation to the German text, this time reflecting PF's frequent use of direct speech to replace the reported speech of the original. After Faustus has spent a week in the harem of the Grand Turk making love to his wives in the guise of Mahomet, the emperor questions them as to his prowess and whether he had made love as ordinary men do. The German text continues:

Ja antworten sie, es were also zugangen, er hett sie geliebet, gehälset und were mit dem Werck wol gestaffiert, sie wolten solches alle Tage annemmen, Zu deme, so were er nackendt bey jnen geschlaffen... [G: 119]

for which PF supplies:

'Yea my lord,' quoth one, 'as if you had been there yourself, you could not have mended it, for he lay with us stark naked, kissed and colled us, and so delighted me that for my part, I would he came two or three times a week to serve me in such sort again.' [1669–73]

This is not only better, it is also amusing in a way which the German is not. The nakedness, thrown in as an afterthought in the German, is very properly at the forefront of the imaginative scene PF has presented so economically.

'[K]issed and colled us' is but one of many felicitous phrases with which PF has enlivened his text. Helen 'of Greece' has 'amorous coal-black eyes' [2367] and she looks around her 'with a rolling hawk's eye' [2371], rendering *mit gar frechem und bübischem Gesicht* [G: 173]. The incarcerated duke of c. 32 is not merely 'troubled' [*betrübt*, G: 146], he is 'stricken into an exceeding dump' [1995f]. Other notable inventions include 'the fodines of precious stones' [830], the 'insatiable speculator' [1295], the Pope's 'fat abbey lubbers' [1363] and the seminal 'ravished his mind' [297] and 'ravished with delight' [959].

But PF's imagination transcends linguistic invention. It is clear that to him translation was a re-description, in English, of the scenes represented to his imagination. He 'sees' each encounter enacted in his mind's eye and these mental reconstructions furnish additional touches of realism. Thus, when Charles V decides to look for the distinguishing wart on the neck of Alexander's paramour, he does not go directly as in the German, but first 'took Faustus by the hand without any words' [1903f]. In the following episode (c. 30) PF invents a mechanism to make the emperor see the horned knight trapped in the casement: he is drawn there by the mocking laughter of the courtiers [cf. 1922–4]. In c. 7, PF, misled by a reference to Wagner in the Spies text [G: 25], assumes the 'unhappy wag' is present during Mephostophiles' magic show, and imagines him terrified at the fiery proceedings, 'but being hardened by his master, he bad him stand still and he should have no harm' [276f]. At Wittenberg, before the thunder storm, Faustus is not just 'standing' in the market place, as in the German, but 'jesting merrily' with his friends [1821f]. All these minor touches contribute to a tale well told, spiced too with a gentle irony reminiscent of Scot's

Discovery of Witchcraft (1584); the heavy-handed, shocked piety of the GFB is banished by PF's wink: 'no doubt there was a virtuous house-keeping' [312f], 'these sweet personages' [2639], 'this pleasant beast' [117], and 'I think he could crack nuts too like a squirrel' [893f].[69]

Nevertheless, except where PF chooses to make his intervention plain there is no interruption in the flow: exact translation is fluently commingled with paraphrasings, inventions and asides and no distinction would be apparent to a reader who did not know the original. In the present edition, all substantial (longer than half a line) or significant departures from the German are printed in bold type and a full listing is included in the commentary which includes my translations of all passages omitted from the German.

PF's major departures from his source may conveniently be discussed under two heads: (a) omissions and replacements, (b) additions. They serve to illuminate two different but linked questions, the politico-theological sensitivity of the material and the persona and identity of the writer. Obviously the latter, particularly PF's precise confessional flavour, determines the extent of 'in-house' sensitivity, but the possibility of external censorship cannot be ruled out and there is some evidence for an extensive revision in MS (see below, pp. 50f).[70]

Some of the omissions are simply good subbing. Thus PF refuses G c. 36 since it is virtually a repeat of the shorter G c. 40 (EFB c. 35) set in a different town. A set of doggerel verses [G c. 7] following Faustus' pact, stressing the dangers of playing with fire, is discarded as clutter, as are many of Spies' moralistic asides, including the exculpation of Faustus' parents for sparing the rod [G: 2f] (though PF may have felt they were not entirely blameless).[71] The cosmological chapters [GFB c. 19–21] are skilfully condensed into a single chapter [c. 18] including a brilliant addition [789–839, see below, pp. 21ff]. But apart from these purely literary improvements there are two major exclusions, at least one of which was motivated by religious sensitivity, not necessarily PF's.

Chapter 19 of the EFB [840 etc] begins as a translation of G c. 22: Faustus is displeased with Mephostophiles for withholding information and failing to satisfy his curiosity; defending itself against these charges, his spirit begs Faustus to ask whatever he wishes. Emboldened by this charitable offer, Faustus asks how God created the world. All this is faithfully rendered, but now comes an abrupt change. In the GFB, Mephostophiles answers Faustus' question with a heretical creation myth, beginning with the Aristotelian concept of an eternal world (for a full translation, see the commentary to 840). Spies takes great care to protect himself (and his readers) by stating that this is a wicked falsehood and prints in the margin: 'Devil, you lie! God's word teaches otherwise' [G: 75]. At the conclusion of the report, Faustus rejects it in favour of Moses' version, but does not openly quarrel with his spirit. The next (quite unrelated) episode (G c. 23) begins with the unsolicited visit of Belial,[72] 'Faustus' prince and proper master' [G: 77], who explains that he has read Faustus' night-thoughts and is here to satisfy his wish to see the principal spirits of hell. There is a beast-book parade of therioform devils but there is no sense of threat to Faustus. He witnesses their transformations and is given a book to enable him to do likewise. When he asks who made the insects, he is told they were created to plague mankind after his fall, a cue for the devils to transform themselves into swarms of insects which drive Faustus out of his study and then disappear. Mephostophiles is not mentioned throughout the entire chapter.

PF makes his first significant change in the phrasing of Faustus' question to Mephostophiles which included a demand to be told about the birth of mankind [G: 75], rendered as 'why man was made after the image of God' [860f]. The spirit immediately flies into a rage and vanishes, leaving Faustus in terrified anticipation of instant destruction; his fears seem to be confirmed when Lucifer, 'the chiefest devil', arrives with an ugly crew, accuses him of back-sliding and determines to show him some 'hellish pastimes' to 'draw and confirm thy mind a little more steadfast unto us' [880–3]. The parade of the seven principal spirits largely accords with that in the GFB, but when a host of spirits have assembled, filling the hall to capacity, there is a fearful thunderclap 'upon which every monster had a muckfork in his hand, holding them towards Faustus as though they would have run a tilt at him' [921–3]. This reminds Faustus that Mephostophiles had told him how the souls in hell were tormented by 'being cast from devil to devil upon muckforks' [925], an earlier PF addition [652f] in the chapter on hell (c. 15).[73] However, this moment of terror passes without further incident; the continuation proceeds much as in the German but with the inclusion of Mephostophiles as a fiery dragon, and a more dramatic persecution by the insects, in which Mephostophiles does not respond to Faustus' cries for assistance. Finally Lucifer mocks his victim: '"Ho, ho, ho Faustus, how likest thou the creation of the world?"', and Faustus is left alone, only to be 'ravished with delight' at 'the sweetest music that ever he heard before', and wishing he had seen more of the devils' 'pastime'.

This is excellent invention, born of the necessity to censor the heretical creation myth (even censorship can be beneficial) and contains hidden subtleties. The provocative questions asked by PF's Faustus are not only an indication of his wish to renege on his pact, they are a double insult to the infernal powers: it was accepted dogma that the devil could create nothing but illusions, and no devil would wish to be reminded of this or that man was stamped in God's image. In the subsequent terrorization of Faustus he is shown the image, or rather, the multiform images, of the devil. God's unity and constancy is contrasted with the devil's multiplicity and mutability. The threat of the muckforks (PF presumably took his inspiration from a Judgment painting, or a morality play) is a variant working of a motif recurring throughout the Faust book, that of tossing. In c. 7 Faustus is charged by a bull [289]; in his journey to hell (c. 20) he is tossed out of his pig-a-back chair [1005f]; the gullible Jew tosses Faustus' leg into a ditch [2054f]; the birds Faustus catches are flung to the students who 'lightly pulled the necks off them' [2296]; and in the gruesome final scene the devil dashes Faustus 'from one wall against another' [2927] and his carcass lands on the dung-heap. All these tossings are but a single metaphor for the vacillating mind of Faustus which deprives him of any constant purpose; Marlowe's antiphonal Good and Evil Angels are employed to the same end. PF's two separate additions of the muckforks are powerful reinforcements of this metaphor.

The second major exclusion from the source text is that of a curious chapter (G c. 65; W c. 68) placed there within the sequence of Faustus' lamentations; had it been included in the EFB, it should have followed c. 60. Mephostophiles appears and mocks Faustus while he is in the throes of despair, taunting him with a prolonged barrage of proverbs – 'every sausage has two ends', 'there is more to the dance than a pair of red shoes', etc. (for a full translation, see Appendix 2). And half-smothered within this froth of saws there lies that justification for Faustus' damnation, already quoted (see above, p. 8).

It is unlikely that PF omitted this chapter because he found it too difficult to translate;[74] there are one or two difficult passages but these are insufficient to have deterred PF from paraphrase or substitution if he had wished to include it. He may have found it unattractive on stylistic grounds or because it creates a structural hiccup just as the climax is approaching, but it is equally likely that the exclusion is motivated by sensitivity, for there are indications that PF's translation of this chapter featured in the MS, if not in the first edition. The bibliographic evidence (see pp. 50f) is slender, but a line from the B-text of *Doctor Faustus* (B1993: 'What weep'st thou? 'tis too late, despaire, farewell,') appears to echo Mephostophiles' doggerel in the excluded chapter: 'Bewail your wretched fate to none. / It is too late, despair of God,' [Appendix 2, lines 11f] (*Dein Unglück keinem Menschen klag. / Es ist zu spat, an Gott verzag.* [G: 210]). This parallel can scarcely be fortuitous, but since the B-text line (of disputed authorship) arguably derives directly from the German, it is no conclusive proof of an existing translation lost to censorship. Nevertheless given adequate grounds for sensitivity, such a premise merits entertainment.

One possible ground is Mephostophiles' sermon justifying the divine pleasure and identifying the devil as the servant of God, His 'abbot or monk', utterances which are theologically suspect: the attempt at justification is inherently presumptive in suggesting that man is capable of encompassing God's understanding, and the devil was considered God's agent only insofar as God was thought to permit (but not to will) the devil to commit evil in the furtherance of His designs, the evil remaining exclusively the responsibility of the devil. Is it then by God's design that Faustus is damned? (That such questions were unwelcome is indicated by the exclusion of '"Yea," quoth Mephostophiles, "Why should we not help thee forwards?"' [551f] from the 1618 edition.) However, a much more cogent ground for sensitivity surfaces when the material is considered in relation to the fierce pressures operating during the period of production of the EFB. In a later section (pp. 52ff) I shall argue that the translation was made during the summer of 1588 and was published late the same year. If so, it would have been presented for licence in the full furore of the Marprelate controversy (Marprelate's 'Epistle' was in circulation by mid-October, the 'Epitome' in late November[75]). Under such circumstances, when any potentially subversive literature was submitted to the keenest scrutiny, the very style of this chapter with its mocking tone, coarse language, and juxtaposition of gravity and jest, would have rendered it suspect: although the writing lacks Marprelate's mordant sarcasm, sustained argument and personally directed invective, it carries the same mood of scurrility which, in Marprelate's case, even discomfited many a Puritan. In such a context, a censor might readily have extrapolated from the devil as 'God's ape' and the devil as 'abbot or monk' to the devil as bishop, a recurrent Marprelate motif. It would have been surprising if the chapter had survived.

These considerations detract from Rohde's view[76] that the omission indicates PF's refusal to countenance any mockery of Faustus, showing that he esteemed him more highly than the German author did. Rohde enlists support from a set of subtle but consistent departures from the source text concerning the root of Faustus' transgression.[77] In the German, the accent is upon pride, arrogant presumption and wantonness (*Übermut*), whereas in the EFB it is shifted towards 'speculation' [44f, 74], 'devilish cogitation' [169] and a contempt for a pious vocation [46f, 233f, 553f], the latter in particular demonstrating a Calvinist tendency prominent elsewhere in the EFB in its condemnation of intemperance. Compare, for example, Mephostophiles' GFB justification for possessing Faustus (quoted on p. 8, above) with PF's version: 'For so soon as we saw thy heart, how thou didst despise thy degree taken in divinity and didst study to search and know the secrets of our kingdom, even then did we enter into thee' [552–5]. 'Had I not desired to know so much I had not been in this case' exclaims Faustus [562f, exclusive to EFB]. For all this, it is difficult to sustain Rohde's argument that Faustus' failings in the EFB are less ignoble than in the GFB, for there too, 'vain curiosity' (*Fürwitz*) is a principal cause of Faustus' defection from God.[78]

One other sensitivity displayed consistently throughout the EFB centres upon a refusal to entertain the notion of succubae. As Empson has noted,[79] the women Mephostophiles procures for Faustus in recompense for his enforced 'celibacy', or to distract him from pious thoughts, are all real in the EFB, whereas in the German text they are explicitly devils or succubae [cf. 396f, 398f, 408, 705f and commentary thereto]. This principle extends to the seven most beautiful women whom Faustus collects to satisfy his passions towards the end of his term [EFB c. 53], although PF's 'sweet personages' [2639; G: 197: *Teuffelischen Weibern*] hints that they may not be what they appear. Helena is a special case; obviously she cannot be real, yet must be included. PF leaves her as an undefined 'spirit', but when she becomes pregnant, he feels impelled to add 'to his [i.e. Faustus'] seeming', adhering to the dogma that the devil can create nothing. Despite this, I suspect that PF's credulity did not extend to succubae, just as he seems to have baulked at explicit invisibility [cf. commentary to 1976, 1982–4, 2597].

Before proceeding with the principal additions (which reveal a great deal about PF) there is one other significant change demanding attention, namely the EFB treatment of Mephostophiles. Here the main distinction from the German is occasioned by one of PF's rare mistranslations: at line 145f, Faustus is informed that Lucifer 'hath notwithstanding a legion of devils at his commandment *that we call the Oriental Princes*'; the clause here italicized is an attempt to render the German *den wir den Orientalischen Fürsten nennen,* [G: 13], continuing *denn seine Herrschafft hatte er im Auffgang*, i.e. 'we call him the Prince of Orient since he has his dominion in the East'. Later [217], when Mephostophiles lists his credentials to Faustus, PF remains faithful to his error and makes him a '"prince but servant to Lucifer: and all the circuit from *septentrio* to the meridian, I rule under him"', and Faustus is 'inflamed to hear himself to have gotten so great a potentate to be his servant'. Apart from this flattery to Faustus' vanity, Mephostophiles' ennoblement has no subsequent effect and the princely image is soon effaced by the humble Franciscan habit. Marlowe noted it, however: 'Now Faustus, thou art conjurer laureate / That canst command great Mephostophilis.' [A276f, absent from B]. Since, at this point in the play, there has been no communication between the spirit and Faustus, we are to assume that Marlowe's Faustus already knew of Mephostophiles' high degree, though in the conjuration preceding the above quote, it is Beelzebub who is addressed as *Orientis Princeps* and requested *ut appareat, et surgat Mephostophilis.* This is but a slight departure from the EFB:

'Then began Doctor Faustus to call on Mephostophiles the spirit and to charge him in the name of Beelzebub to appear there personally without any long stay' [83–5]. The 'English' Faustus is here more knowledgeable than his 'German' counterpart; in the GFB, Faustus 'conjured the devil' [G: 7] and there is no immediate mention of Mephostophiles – in fact, Faustus does not learn the name of his spirit until G c. 5, after all the preliminary negotiations have been concluded. When, in response to Faustus' query, the spirit tells him he is called Mephostophiles, this is the first occurrence of the name in the GFB and all published literature. The name probably derives from tortured Greek: 'no friend to light', punning also on 'no friend to Faust',[80] i.e. it was invented to fit the Faust legend and was not on the recognized stock list of spirits which an adept might attempt to conjure.

While there is nothing gained by holding back the name of the spirit until its relations with Faustus have become more intimate, there seems little to have recommended blurting it out immediately as in the EFB. But having done so, it is wholly crass for Faustus to ask Mephostophiles his name later, in faithful rendition of the German. '"My name is, as thou sayest, Mephostophiles"' responds the embarrassed spirit [216f], perhaps wondering whether the magician has already lost his wits. But such a clumsy fudging is grossly inconsistent with PF's editorial care to ensure the smoothness of his interventions, his mental visualization of every scene and his willingness to jettison unnecessary text. It carries the hall-mark of a late revision.

Of course, none but the most reckless of magicians would have attempted to conjure by calling on the 'devil', as in the GFB. It was both practical and more salutary to command the appearance of a specific spirit, such as Lucifuge Rofocale, of the type inclined to make pacts, one moreover, of limited powers, who could be arrested by the conjurer's threats and blasted into submission with a rod, ritually sanctified with holy water in the name of Jehovah and half the heavenly host.[81] To call up a principal devil would be tantamount to suicide. So the EFB version in which Faustus calls specifically for Mephostophiles 'in the name of Beelzebub' is not without point and indicates that Faustus is no lunatic amateur, nor is his action such a blatant rejection of God as that implied in the GFB. However, these are not considerations which would leap to the mind of the average Elizabethan reader, or editor, without a prompt and it is not wildly improbable that that prompt was *Doctor Faustus*. Marlowe was faced with the need for an on-stage conjuration (a *sine qua non*) couched in awesome verbiage, with ringing phrases and fear-inspiring names, hence *Orientis Princeps Beelzebub*, hence *Acheron*, hence *ut appareat et surgat Mephostophilis*, mingling the familiar with the new. Faustus' error in invoking the wrong devil is put to good use later, when he is able to question Mephostophiles, 'Tell me, what is that

Lucifer thy Lord?' [A307, B288], leading on naturally to the discussion on hell. Then again, the immediate introduction of 'Mephostophilis' to the audience dispenses with the need for fumbling queries later. Thus there are strong dramatic advantages in adopting this treatment, whatever the early edition of the EFB may have supplied. If the extant text of the EFB does involve reverse borrowing, the mechanism would require a performance of *Doctor Faustus* before mid-1592.

To come now to PF's principal additions, one is a poetic enticement to occult learning and powers, one obfuscates a cosmological problem, and the remainder are extensions of the topographical descriptions of Faustus' 'Grand Tour' (EFB cc. 22f).

The first occurs in chapter 18 [789–839]. It is virtually a paean to the spirit of the Renaissance and lifts the Faust book momentarily to a higher plane of literature; at the same time it solves a delicate problem which the German author failed to address. Faustus has given his soul in return for the disclosure of secret wisdom unattainable by ordinary means [cf. 246–52], but the information supplied to him, at such great cost, by his spirit, is frankly disappointing, both to Faustus ('I cannot have any diligence of thee further than thou list thyself' [851f]) and to the curious reader. The only subject Mephostophiles seems to know much about is hell, and even what he knows about that could have been gleaned from the Sunday fire-sermon. When the inquiries turn to astronomy and cosmology (G cc. 19–21), matters of very keen interest to contemporary readers, Mephostophiles responds with extracts from Elucidarius[82] which would scarcely satisfy a school-boy. The author is in a dilemma: he needs to expatiate on what he cannot know; necessarily his Mephostophiles is bridled by the same constraint. Marlowe solves the problem by making his Faustus expostulate at the puerility of Mephostophilis' answers and his failure to deliver the goods: 'These slender questions Wagner can decide: / Hath Mephostophilis no greater skill? [B618f (A678f)] ... These are fresh men's questions' [B625 (A685)], to be followed by Faustus' exasperated, "Well, I am answered" [A694, B636]. PF, however, chose a different and original course, skilfully turning the material into a cornucopia of exciting promises by an 'experienced' spirit who knows all the answers: '"Wherefore Faustus, learn of me: I will teach thee the course and recourse of [the planets], the causes of winter and summer, the exaltation and declination of the sun ... herein there is nothing hidden from me ... Yea, Faustus, I will teach thee the secrets of nature ... I will make thee as perfect in these things as myself"' [789–829], and he tosses in some tit-bits: '"that the snow should be of so great virtue as the honey; and the Lady Saturnia, ♓ in *occulto*, more hotter than the sun in *manifesto*" – pure mumbo-jumbo to whet the appetite of the scientifically curious. One feels that Faustus has not been cheated, especially when the spirit extends his promises to powers: '"learn now of me to make thunder, lightning,... the clouds to rent ...[83] to fly like myself... to run through walls, doors and gates ... to nourish thyself in the fire... to go invisible, to find out the mines of gold and silver, the fodines of precious stones"'. It is a brilliant speech, ringing throughout with the spirit's enthusiasm to spring Faustus from his dull disputations: '"Thy time Faustus, weareth away, then why wilt thou not take thy pleasure of the world? Come up, we will go visit kings..."'.

There is a passionate intensity in this superb peroration that is unsurpassed in Elizabethan prose literature and it confirms the writer as one of very considerable talent, one moreover, who cannot have been a stranger to the temptation of fantastic longings. The magical powers offered to Faustus go far beyond those accredited to ordinary witches, such as control of the weather, or those manifested in Faustus' subsequent adventures (for which, incidentally, this speech provides an advance programme). They accord most nearly with those attributed to Simon Magus in the *Clementine Recognitions* (Book II, c. 9)[84]: 'I am able to render myself invisible to those who wish to lay hands on me and again visible when I am willing to be seen. If I wish to flee, I can dig through the mountains and pass through rocks as if they were clay.' Were he to throw himself from a high mountain he would be 'borne unhurt to the earth, as if held up'; bound, he could untie his own bonds and tie up those who had bound him; he could open the gates of a prison, render statues animated, cause trees to spring up and sprout, pass unhurt through the fire, make his countenance unrecognizable, show two faces, change into a sheep or a goat, make beards grow on little boys; 'I shall ascend by flight into the air; I shall exhibit abundance of gold and shall make and unmake kings. I shall be worshipped as a God... Whatever I wish I shall be able to do.' It is difficult to believe that the Faust-book writer was not influenced by these passages; if so, the veiled allusion foreshadows the later association of Faustus with Simon Magus in the Old Man's attempt to convert him [2471f]. What effect such a passage may have had upon credulous contemporaries it is impossible to assess. Was it this which inspired the notorious empiric, Simon Forman, to begin conjuring in 1588?[85]

The cosmology of this passage, as in the German, is the modified Aristotelian (geocentric) system of concentric spheres as expounded in contemporary textbooks,[86] with seven planetary spheres and an eighth sphere of the fixed stars, bounded by a non-mobile heaven which was the abode of God and the blessed. In addition there were three (four including the earth) elementary spheres within the lowest planetary sphere, that of the moon, of which the uppermost was the *coelum igneum* or 'fiery heaven'. In translating and adapting the German,

PF betrays his very limited comprehension of the system. Thus he speaks of ‘the fiery sphere above ♄ and the signs of the zodiac’ [819f], translating the German ‘fewrige’ directly, yet it is clear from the GFB text that this is the German author’s expression for the *coelum empyreum*, the outermost, non-mobile heaven.[87] PF immediately proceeds to confuse this ‘fiery heaven’ with the *coelum igneum* of the sub-lunar sphere: ‘the fiery sphere . . . doth not burn the whole face of the earth, being hindered by placing the two moist elements [i.e. air, water] between them’ [819–22]. (It is this *coelum igneum* which Marlowe’s Mephostophilis rejects as fabulous [B630f].)

A similar sense of confusion, allied to a strongly authoritarian tone, characterizes PF’s second major addition. This comes in the middle of chapter 21 in which Faustus writes to a former colleague, describing his journey through the heavens, so until PF intervenes on his own behalf, the narrator is supposed to be Faustus. The departures from the German text begin at line 1156 with the omission of: ‘The movement of the firmament in the heavens is so forceful that it always moves from East to West, carrying the stars, sun and moon along with it, causing them to move, as we see, from their rising to their setting’ [G: 97f], which is consistent with the geocentric cosmology of the GFB. PF replaces this by an elaborate and confusing explanation for the observed movement of the sun and planets which seems both to take account of the heliocentric theory and to deny it. Still speaking as Faustus, he writes: ‘we think that the sun runneth his course and that the heavens stand still; no, it is the heavens that move his course and the sun abideth perpetually in his place; he is permanent and fixed in his place, and although we see him beginning to ascend in the orient . . ., setting in the occident . . ., yet he moveth not. It is the axle of the heavens that moveth the whole firmament . . . wherein are placed the sun and the rest of the planets, turned and carried at the pleasure of the spirit of God, which is wind’ [1163–77], and this conclusion is repeated later: ‘even so the firmament wherein the sun and the rest of the planets are fixed, [is] moved, turned, and carried with the wind, breath or spirit of God, for the heavens and the firmament are movable as the chaos but the sun is fixed in the firmament. ‘[1205–9]. PF seems determined to have his cake and eat it. For him, the firmament is a ‘chaos or confused thing’ and he likens it to a soap bubble moved ‘at pleasure of the wind’, an analogy for the breath of God. As for the sun, ‘the body substantial is but little in compass’ but ‘by reason of the thing wherein it is placed’ it emits beams making it visible over the whole world.

Empson interpreted this passage as bravely partisan, a championing of the Copernican theory.[88] But while there are undeniable heliocentric elements, they are not presented with any understanding; there is a confusion between the apparent diurnal motion of the sun and stars, caused by rotation of the earth, and the apparent annual motion of the sun against the background of the fixed stars, caused by the earth's revolution about the sun. In fact, neither cause is stated and the sun appears to be 'fixed' only in so far as it is fixed in a movable firmament as a speck on a soap bubble, and the agent of its movement is variously 'the axle of the heavens' or 'the breath of God'.

The impression conveyed is that of an enthusiast who does not understand what he is talking about. As Johnson[89] has indicated, the Copernican theory was not seriously propagated in contemporary expositions of cosmology, and certainly not widely accepted before Galileo's discoveries in the early seventeenth century. Even amongst astronomers many regarded it essentially as an alternative mathematical model and few of these could reconcile the notion of a rotating earth with its evident immobility. PF has fastened upon an imperfectly received notion of a 'fixed' sun and has interpreted it in terms of a geocentric cosmology. More important for him was the divine regulation of the heavens; hence his insistence that the movement of the chaos is directed by the breath of God. It is this which provokes him suddenly to breach the framework of the story and thunder forth in person: 'Yea Christian Reader, to the glory of God and for the profit of thy soul, I will open unto thee the divine opinion touching the ruling of this confused chaos, far more than any rude German author, being possessed with the devil, was able to utter' [1177–81], and he proceeds with an exegesis of the first chapter of Genesis, designed to prove 'some of my sentence before to be true' [1181], i.e. that the heavens are moved by the wind or breath of God. His argument could scarcely have been put in the mouth of Faustus, the 'rude German author', without totally betraying his characterization. By referring to 'my sentence before' and repeating the soap bubble simile, 'like as I showed before' [1203], PF tells the reader that the passages prior to his personal intervention are also his own, and not part of Faustus' letter, though the reader is not to know at what point the transition from Faustus to PF takes place. This dismisses any idea that the confused cosmology represents the imperfect understanding of the 'rude', i.e. unlettered, Faustus; PF is accepting full responsibility for whatever he has written, translation or not. His deprecation of Faustus' learning suggests he held his own in high esteem, though 'rude' coupled with 'German' may indicate nothing more than nationalistic contempt, a trait apparent in PF's several condemnations of German drinking habits, e.g.: 'after the manner of Germany, where it is counted no feast unless all the bidden guests be drunk' [2208ff]. Marlowe leaves the whole business well alone; the spheres 'all iointly move upon one axletree' [A669 (B610)] about a 'centricke earth' [A666, B606] and 'move from East to West in twenty-four houres upon the poles of the world'

[A675f, B615f]. Any involvement in the heliocentric debate would have disrupted his plot.

Finally, there are the topographical additions. The German version of Faustus' journey throughout the known world (G cc. 26f) is tedious reading, and, based largely on Hartmann Schedel's *Weltchronik* of 1493,[90] it was far from up-to-date in 1587, though not gravely anachronistic for a tour supposedly made in the 1520s. PF does his best to rectify both these faults, both by updating the information and by including more interesting 'sights' for Faustus to admire. In so doing he produced perhaps the most lively brief travelogue of the sixteenth century, with sufficient detail to intrigue the reader but never so much as would stay his relentless passage; it must have contributed greatly to the popularity of the work.

PF adds at least a touch to most of the descriptions of the cities visited by Faustus, and some of his additions, notably those concerning Naples, Venice and Rome, are source material for *Doctor Faustus* (here at least, the direction of borrowing is not in question); in the case of Faustus' dealings with the Pope [1349–80], the divergence from the German extends to the action (Faustus 'smites' the Pope whereas in the GFB he merely blows in his face, the visiting cardinal is named, and PF ends the episode with a dramatic coda as, beneath fulminating skies, Faustus drops his plate amidst the procession of bare-foot friars) and this too is grist for Marlowe [A878–929, B1071–1126]. But beyond amplifying the topographical detail, PF considerably extends Faustus' itinerary, both in the preliminary 25-day lightning tour [1237–51], embracing the New World as well as the Old, and in the main tour, by including Bologna, Sienna, Breslau, Sandetz, Leipzig and Hamburg. Throughout, PF manifests a keen interest in 'modern' geography, showing himself conversant with contemporary atlases, such as Munster's *Cosmographia*,[91] and likes to display his knowledge of routes, as in his quiet mockery of the tomb of the Three Kings at Cologne, supplying a detailed itinerary for the bodies of the Magi in their passage from Palestine to their present supposed resting place [1414–20]; since it is Faustus who provides the commentary here, PF's self-indulgence is quite in character for such an experienced, wide-ranging traveller. Such characterization is rarely out of sight in the material PF has chosen to include, for, apart from describing wonders which no tourist would have missed, he introduces features of distinct interest (or moral application) to Faustus, particularly curiosities with magical associations. Thus, at Naples Faustus sees the 'highway' that Virgil, the magician,[92] cut through a 'mighty hill of stone in one night' [1272–4]; at Prague, he finds the cursed sepulchre of a notable conjurer, a 'monument which might have been a mirror to himself' [1537–40], and at

Würzburg 'an altar where are engraven the four elements and all the orders and degrees in heaven, that any man of understanding whosoever that hath a sight thereof, will say that it is the artificiallest thing that ever he beheld' [1483–6]. Breslau, although providing a geographical link between Prague and Cracow, seems to be included expressly to rehearse the description of the brazen virgin [1559–71] 'made to do execution upon those disobedient town-born children that be so wild that their parents cannot bridle them'; they end up 'stamped in small morsels', a warning to Faustus of the ultimate consequence of his own disobedience.

Such implicit characterization may have come easily to PF if, as it appears, his own interests and curiosities coincided with those imagined for his protagonist. His enthusiasm for the Würzburg altar presents him as a 'man of understanding' of the heavens and confirms him as a man who thought highly of his own learning (see above, p. 24). Other curiosities which excite him are natural phenomena (the ice bell at Salzburg, the well of Zipzar, the barnacle goose and the black salt of Cracow), works of engineering (the Grotto di Posilippo, the harbour at Naples, the obelisk and conduits of Rome), folk-lore (the tales of the basilisk, the brass virgin of Breslau, the dragon of Cracow) and any remarkable work of artifice (the strange weaponry of the Castel St Angelo, the great barrel of Leipzig, the steeple of Strasbourg cathedral). The question is, whether these undoubted enthusiasms reflected his own experiences as a wide-eyed traveller or whether they are 'armchair' enthusiasms bred from a reading of published and MS accounts, supplemented by travellers' tales. Purely as a characteristic of the age, assuming that his title, 'Gent.', has any factual basis, he is as likely to have travelled as not. Foreign travel was part of a young gentleman's education, allowing him to learn languages and customs, and fit him for diplomatic service; certain professions, such as medicine and law, warranted periods of study at foreign centres of excellence, such as Padua and Bologna. And if PF was no young man in 1587, he might well have been nurtured amongst the Marian exiles in Strasbourg or Geneva.[93] In fact, there were Englishmen scattered throughout every major city in Europe, as travellers' accounts testify, many of them long-term residents – agents, merchants and trade factors, churchmen, scholars, diplomats and spies. Both by inclination and necessity, a new English visitor would seek out his fellow-countrymen, to gain life-saving information and impart his own news and experiences. The result was a communication nexus in which there was exchange not only of vital information, but of sights seen, tales heard, customs and abuses. Such wide-ranging information supplemented and up-dated what the tourist had already read in contemporary cosmographies too bulky (and too valuable) to be part of his luggage. Doubtless the information would have been accurate regarding vital matters, but the casual reminiscences, as ever, would have been prone to error, compounded at second hand by the vagaries of memory. Thus the inaccuracies of PF's additions (and there are many) do not, as Logeman suggests,[94] preclude the possibility of his being a traveller. On the contrary, they support the idea, for if he had copied from published sources the errors would not have been so numerous. Then again, contemporary published or manuscript sources fail to provide many of the accurate details incorporated in PF's additions although, of course, they duplicate some of the information. Logeman, who did not pursue his researches very far, posits a 'lost' cosmography,[95] a very dubious proposition since such works had a much greater lifetime than a small quarto such as the Faust book, and were held in more respect. In fact, it is doubtful that PF had any major cosmography to hand when he made his translation, for although some of his additional information was available in works such as the *Civitates Orbis Terrarum*,[96] there is almost no evidence of direct copying or verbal influence; the only instance I have discovered is the description of the barnacle goose [1713–15], where the source is clearly identifiable as *A Brief Collection ... out of Munster*,[97] an eminently portable little book. The cosmographic works I have cited in the commentary are thus not so much sources as parallels, serving to establish the extent of published contemporary knowledge.

Faced with this lack of direct sources, Rohde's hypothesis,[98] that PF travelled extensively and reported on sights he himself had seen, becomes very attractive. In determining PF's probable itinerary, his errors are important as indicators of places he is unlikely to have visited (Rome, Florence, Basel), whereas a combination of accuracy with a sense of immediate experience (his effusive praise of the Würzburg altar, for example) may indicate his presence. On this basis, he would appear to have visited Leipzig, Würzburg, Prague and Cracow, and possibly Strasbourg, Padua and Venice. At Leipzig he describes the 'new churchyard', i.e. the cemetery, lavishly praised as the finest in Europe in a Leipzig publication of 1587,[99] but without the detail of PF's description; he also mentions the huge barrel and tells how 'you must go upon a ladder...', etc. (cf. [1691f]: 1608/10 ed., probably retaining the original). At Padua, PF evinces a familiarity with the twice-daily passage-boat to Venice and compares it with the ferry to Greenwich; this observation apart, he is solely concerned with the university and has Faustus enroll himself 'under the German Nation' as 'the insatiable Speculator'. Was this inclusion prompted by the recollection of his own enrolment under the English nation? Regrettably the documents for the relevant period have not survived. If he had spent some time at Padua, then a journey South is not out of the question: many students took the opportunity to go to Naples and one or two were brave enough to don a Catholic disguise and visit Rome.[100] But PF's garbled accounts of Florence and Rome would seem to discount his presence there. Certainly, if he had seen the 'pyramid', i.e. the obelisk, 'La Guglia', he must have realized that his dimensions are ludicrous, unless the figures show errors of transmission.[101] As for Naples, although, with the possible exception of the 'windmill in the sea', the data appears to be correct, there is no true immediacy in the account. The same might be said for PF's additions to the description of Prague which are largely correct but lack a convenient source: there *were* two important churches on the Königsburg (the cathedral of St Veit and the romanesque basilica of St George), the 'sepulchre of a noted conjurer' is probably the tomb of the Holy Nepomuk, who was credited with many miracles, there *was* a royal menagerie and, of course, the Jewish community was a well-known feature, though the numbers of Jews, both here ('thirteen thousand') and at Cracow ('twenty-five thousand'), are grossly exaggerated, in the latter case by a factor of ten.[102] As to Cracow, despite PF's error in placing the 'Casimir' (Kasimierz) or Jew's Town, on the wrong side of the River Vistula [1582f], the details bespeak an eye-witness: the mammoth bones of 'the dragon who kept the rock' are still on view, though moved from their EFB location, the 'silver altar' can be identified as that above the tomb of St Stanislav; but what convinces most is the description of the Wielickza salt mines, including the intensely visual impression that 'the salt is as black as the Newcastle coals' [1588].

The inclusion of Sandetz (Nowy Sącz), not exactly a tourist attraction, is decisive, although its significance has escaped previous commentators through their failure to identify 'Don Spiket Jordan', 'the captain' of the town [1591f]. Here, 'captain' is PF's word for the Polish *starost*, no mere platoon commander but a plenipotentiary regional governor of considerable military and political importance. Spytek Wawrzyniec Jordan (d. 1596),[103] a powerful Catholic nobleman, became *starost* of Nowy Sącz on the 20 July 1584 and held this office until 22 January 1590. In the power struggles following the death (12 December 1586) of King Stephen Batory, Jordan supported the Zborowski (pro-Austrian) faction against Jan Zamoyski; however, he took no part in the siege of Cracow (winter 1587–8), nor in the decisive battle of Byczyna (24 January 1588) in which Zamoyski defeated the imperial forces, but remained entrenched in his stronghold of Nowy Sącz. In the following year, at the cost of a huge fine, he made his peace with the new monarch Sigismund, retaining his seat in the Diet (*Seym*) and continuing to oppose Zamoyski and promote Catholic interests.

PF's leisurely sight-seeing in the EFB is apt to present the reader with the false picture of a secure world, when in fact he was travelling in troubled times. The naming of Jordan and the inclusion of Sandetz suggests that PF was present in Cracow in 1587, perhaps shortly before the siege ('[the castle] is full of all manner of munition, and hath always victual for three year to serve 2000 men'

[1580f]) when the whole country was anxiously waiting to see how this powerful magnate would comport himself in the coming offensive. The actual description of Sandetz is full of confusions: the monastery of 'St Dioclesian' [1596] (a nonsense), i.e. the convent of Poor Clares (a retreat for aristocratic ladies, as PF correctly observes), was located not in the 'new town' but in Old Sandetz (Stary Sącz); the 'tomb of Christ' cannot be substantiated.[104] I suspect PF gathered these details from his informant at Cracow rather than by direct experience, but they would never have been included if he had not been to Cracow.

To summarize these indications, PF would appear to have spent some time in Italy, probably at Padua, possibly with a trip to Naples, and, not necessarily at the same period of his life, to have visited Strasbourg, Northern Germany, Franconia and Bohemia, and to have penetrated Poland at least to Cracow, perhaps in the immediate aftermath of the death of King Stephen, i.e. early to mid-1587. His knowledge of German (unusually good for an Englishman of that time) and his contempt for German drinking habits (see above, p. 24) proclaim his familiarity with the country. If the thesis of his travels is accepted, then the logistics of the importation of the Faust book into England[105] are simplified by assuming he was in Germany at the time of publication. This would imply his presence there at least until September 1587 or, if he were staying in Leipzig, possibly until the Easter fair there in 1588. Such a time-table is consistent with my suppositions regarding his stay in Cracow, and with the limits for the period of translation. I shall argue later that the EFB was first published in late 1588; if so, PF must have made his translation and returned home in the summer of that year. He would have taken ship from Hamburg or Stade, and perhaps this is why Hamburg gets its mention in his Faust book.

PF's self-exposure in deviating from his source text allows a limited profile of the man. He is confident in his abilities, both as author and a 'man of understanding', at times boldly assertive and contemptuous of ignorance. There is a Calvinist tendency apparent in his dislike of intemperance, his emphasis on the seductive power of music and his regard for the sanctity of vocation, yet he is quick-spirited and never ashamed to indulge his sense of humour. He is a man of the world gifted with an acute visual imagination, a man no stranger to the dreams which tempted Faustus, and like Faustus, his curiosity is insatiable; he has some mangled knowledge of astronomy and a fair occult vocabulary which he spins with ease. Like Faustus, he is a traveller; in the midst of his travels he falls upon the Faust book and is so taken by it that he performs a labour of love; I cannot doubt that he felt a strong affinity for his protagonist.

Rohde, extrapolating from these characteristics and the likelihood that PF had travelled to Prague and Cracow, suggested a tentative identification with Dr John Dee, treating the cipher P. F. as a blind.[106] This hypothesis is surely untenable: not only is Dee's prose style markedly different from PF's (and totally lacking in humour), he could not have written such bad science. It is also a grave misjudgment of Dee's character to imagine he would have considered the Faust book worthy of his attention, let alone his labour, even supposing his German was good enough to read it, or that it came to his hands. Nor would it have been politic for Dee, a suspected nigromancer, to popularize a notorious magician. Nevertheless, Dee's presence in Poland deserves to be noted, since it might have occasioned PF's presence there. As a younger man, Dee had travelled extensively on the continent, but his lengthy stay in Eastern Europe, accompanied by Edward Kelly and both families, began in late 1583.[107] He was in Cracow until the summer of 1584 (when Jordan became *starost* of Nowy Sącz), then moved to Prague. He visited Cracow again in April 1585 and was received by King Stephen.[108] Returning to Prague, he pursued his 'angel magic' and alchemy with Kelly, making brief trips to Kessel and Erfurt, but by May 1586 suspicion against him at the Imperial Court had become intense and he retired to the safety of Leipzig; when Papal influence persuaded Rudolph II to banish him from his dominions, Dee accepted the protection of the Bohemian Count Rosenberg and moved to Trebona, where he remained until, belatedly obeying his queen's request, he began his return home (January 1588/9), leaving Kelly to the emperor's mercy. Travelling via Nuremberg, Frankfurt on Main (26 March 1589) and Bremen, where he stayed about eight months, he arrived at Gravesend in early December.[109] Dee's account of this period in his private diary is very incomplete but there is ample testimony to the number of Englishmen who were coming and going around him, and the interest of the avaricious (including Boris Godunov) in the outcome of his alchemical experiments. There are no P. F. s here, nor any reference to Faust or the Faust book, neither here nor in the remainder of the diary (to 1601); nor does he ever mention Marlowe, not even his death, which he probably would have done had he known him.

Any search for PF has to be based on the assumption that 'P. F.' are the true initials. There is no reason to suppose that, in using this cipher, the author was trying to hide his identity (this could have been easily achieved by an anonymous publication); the use of initials was fairly common, especially for 'debut' works, combining modesty with, perhaps, a concession to family honour, to spare embarrassing connections. A disadvantage lies in the possibility for typographical error. Although all the early editions of the EFB carry the initials 'P. F.', they are changed to 'P. P.' in the 1622 edition, then to 'P. R.' in 1636,[110] and this change is transmitted to all subsequent seventeenth-century printings. However, the insecurity must surely attach to the 1622 and 1636 variants, when the identity of the author was probably no longer known, rather than to that of the early editions, when both the author and his MS were probably to hand.[111]

Fortunately the initials P. F. are a relatively rare combination. Logeman consulted the *National Dictionary of Biography* and discovered only three candidates which all proved inadmissible on other grounds[112] and *STC* lists no other known publications by the same author bearing this cipher.[113] The title 'Gent' could indicate membership of an armigerous family, but it was frequently assumed without such foundation[114] and was also a privilege of university graduates. There are no P. F. s amongst persons granted licences to pass beyond the seas, though the records are very incomplete and would not, in any case, have included persons on diplomatic or state missions.[115] A search through the matriculation records of the Universities of Oxford and Cambridge, and of the Inns of Court, yields another score of potential candidates,[116] but since most of them sink into relative obscurity on leaving the university the task of elimination is no easy matter; nor does P. F. have to be among them – he might have received further education abroad. Indeed, the candidate I have to offer escapes this net:

At a meeting of the Comitia (i.e. the governing council) of the Royal College of Physicians on 30 September 1588 the case of Paul Fairfax (Farfax) was discussed, as recorded in the Annals:[117]

> Paul Fairfax of London, a travelled man, gave out in the market places pamphlets full of arrogance and ostentation describing the admirable properties of a water which he called his 'Aqua Coelestis',[118] with which he had cheated the people of their money. He confessed that he had practised medicine in London for four months: and that he had cured the son of Mr Treen of Southwark, suffering from dropsy, also the daughter of Mr Spagman [see note 120], afflicted with a pain in the head, and many others by this distilled water and other divers potions and pills.
>
> It was decided that for his previous practice he should pay five pounds to the College as a fine: and give his bond that he would not practise medicine in future. If he refused or did otherwise, he would be imprisoned.

Such cases of unlicensed practitioners occur frequently in the RCP annals and show how rigorously the College defended its privileges and maintained control of standards. It was not unusual for the 'quack' to appeal to the Privy Council and there are several letters from Sir Francis Walsingham on behalf of such persons, begging the College to reconsider their verdict in view of the good cures they had achieved. With a single exception, the College replied, very politely, that His Lordship was misinformed, that the person concerned was ignorant of all good medicine and was a grave menace to health, and that the decrees of the College would stand. Thus the sequel to the 30 September decision is not unexpected. Apparently Fairfax appealed to Sir Henry Carey, Lord Hunsdon, the Lord Chamberlain, who duly wrote to the College on his behalf. The letter is not extant but an answer was formulated, read and unanimously approved at the College Council meeting of 23 December:

Right honourable and our very good Lord, having received a letter from your Lord in the behalf of one Paul Fairfax for the liberty of his practice in physic here in London: and understanding by the contents of the same that your honour hath been misinformed as well of the quality of the man as also of our dealings towards him: we most humbly beseech your good Lord to accept of our answer which we here present in most dutiful wise. Touching the man, albeit by some travel he seemeth to have gotten some kinds of language and therewithal hath boldly put himself into some empirical practice, most dangerous in truth to the patient than in any wise commendable to the practitioner: yet, upon just examination, we find the man very weak in the substance of all kinds of good learning and rather to be pitied for his fantastical conceits, and well weening of his own ignorance, than any wise to deserve toleration in so dangerous a function: a man never trained up in any good school of learning, ignorant in the very principles of the art; and for lack of other good matter, furnished with certain ridiculous terms and childish phrases, invented only to entertain the simple hearer and to delude the unlearned multitude withal.

And whereas he layeth some challenge to a doctorship, he hath indeed showed unto us his letters testimonial for the same. Yet we, being better acquainted with the course of universities than he, have a better opinion of Frankfurt than to think that, wittingly and willingly, they would commit so foul an error as to admit either him or the like. And having made good survey of the letters, find by evident proof that they are vehemently to be suspected, to have been rather by some sinister means devised, than by any ordinary course obtained.

Touching us and our hard using of him, as he termeth it to your Lord, as well by imprisoning his body as by exacting the payment of money to his great impoverishing: may it please your good Lord to understand, that as yet he hath paid no one penny, but standeth bound in deed, and that for a very small sum, considering the quality of his offence and the straitness of our laws in that behalf; and yet for the payment thereof hath as long a day as himself requested. And as for his imprisonment, it was rather procured by his own indiscreet frowardness than meant by us at all, if he had showed any conformity in time. For being a gentleman, as he himself sayeth, and having so good acquaintance, as he protested: being offered to be set at liberty if he would have put in but any one sufficient surety (a matter of great ease for him to us, if the rest of his talk had been to be credited), he, as one rather contemning us and our friendly dealing, more upon stomach than discretion, made choice of imprisonment.

Thus have we delivered unto your good Lord a truth, beseeching your Honour so to interpret of our dealing toward him and all other in the like degree, as of men altogether abhorring from all extremity, but enforced to do that little which we do, even by the very duty that we owe to our laws and good orders, and by the consideration of our strict, solemn oath and conscience in that behalf. . . [119]

This letter, subscribed 'The President and Society of the College of Physicians in London', is dated 'this last of January 1588'. Presumably the annalist did not write up the minutes of the Comitia until some time after the event and has inserted the date (31 January 1588/9) on which the letter was sent, although the delay is so long that 'January' is possibly an error. There are no further recorded developments in the case and no further mention of Fairfax in the Annals.

Here then is a P. F., who claimed to be a 'gentleman' with influential friends, present in London from early June 1588 and still resident there, albeit in the Wood Street Counter, at the end of December. The 'travelled man' in the notice of 30 September is a translation for the original *circumforaneus* (the Annals were written mainly in Latin, but with letter drafts in English), i.e. an itinerant pedlar, going from one market to another, but the letter to Carey also mentions 'some travel' and 'kinds of language, which, coupled with Fairfax's claim to a doctorship at Frankfurt, seem to imply foreign travel, presumably in Eastern Germany. Of the two Frankfurts, only that on the Oder could then boast a university and medical faculty. I am assured by the city archivist that there is no record of any Paul Fairfax (or variant spellings) receiving any degree whatsoever at Frankfurt on the Oder, so the RCP's suspicions regarding the authenticity of his testimonials seem to be justified. But presumably Fairfax did not choose Frankfurt at random, and it would not be over-rash to infer that he had travelled in Eastern Europe and had returned to London, shortly before beginning to practise, in June of this Armada year, a sequence of activities which essentially coincides with the programme projected for PF. If he had been trading in German markets, he must have spoken German. But what is impressive about Fairfax in relation to PF is his arrogant self-assurance and self-esteem, his 'fantastical conceits' and his 'well-weening of his ignorance', i.e. thinking highly of his (superficial) knowledge. The letter reads much like the early, contemptuous reports of the historical Faustus by Humanists such as Trithemius and Mutianus; here was Fairfax behaving just like Faustus, advertising his 'waters' and cures and wandering from one locality to another. Such persons were anathema to the RCP in their campaign against unlicensed 'empirics' and Fairfax's high-handedness could certainly have worked against a fair hearing; the qualities grudgingly admitted in the (exceptionally long) letter must therefore be granted extra weight: this is no illiterate, common pedlar, but a proud man capable of putting a good case to Sir Henry Carey. Until, hopefully, more is discovered,[120] the case for identifying Paul Fairfax with PF remains slender, but what is revealed by Fairfax's single emergence into the spot-light is highly suggestive and he must be considered the most promising candidate to date for the authorship of the English Faust Book. If he is the man, the astrological mumbo-jumbo of Mephostophiles' 'learn of me' speech, the half-baked cosmology of chapter 21 and the brutally interpolated exegesis of Genesis, with its idiot insistence upon the distinction between God's Works and God's Words, are wholly in character. Above all, this identification would explain the affinity of the author for his protagonist and the motivation for his labours.

BIBLIOGRAPHIC ANALYSIS AND PRINTING HISTORY OF THE EARLY EFB EDITIONS

Full bibliographic descriptions of sixteenth and seventeenth-century editions of the English Faust Book, and a concordance with relevant entries in the Register of the Stationers' Company, are presented in Appendix 1. The present discussion is concerned with variants among the early editions and is directed to elucidating a genetic scheme. For these purposes the following summary of the extant early editions, all small quarto, published in London, will suffice:

STC[121]	*Abbrev.*	*Date*	*Printer and publisher*
(10711)	S	[?1592]	[Edward Allde, ? for Edward White]
10711	O	1592	Thos. Orwin, to be sold by Edward White
10712	'08	1608	John Windet for Edward White
10712.5	'10	1610	E. Allde for Edward White
10713	'18	1618	Edw. Allde for Edward White
10713.5	'22	1622	William Jones for T. P[avier] and J. W[right]
10714	'36	1636	for John Wright
2151	'48	1648	for Edward Wright

All the editions from 1608 onwards suffer from three separate line omissions (one a double-line omission) with respect to O, indicating that the latter could not have been used as a basis for any of the post-1608 editions; indeed, other indications show that it was apparently unknown or not available to editors from 1608 inclusive. Following 1610, each edition derives successively from its extant predecessor, possibly via lost editions; thus '18 and later editions are scarcely of value in determining the nature of the first edition. With this regard, the textual notes supply a complete collation of substantive variants for S, O, '08 and '10 only, plus collation of these variants with '18, '22, '36 and '48.

Of the four early editions of interest, it is uncertain whether S was actually published or even completed, since it survives only as a fragment, of unknown provenance, in the library of Shrewsbury School;[122] it is incorrectly collated in *STC* as identical with O. This 'Shrewsbury fragment' is a single sheet, uncut, printed both sides, representing the inner and outer formes of signature A (Plate 2, p. 36). Unfortunately it is imperfect, lacking the catch-words at one end and some 3½ cm of text (including the imprint on A1) at the other. The lower half of the printer's device is missing, but it is still clearly recognizable as McKerrow 290 (see Plate 3a, p. 38), one of a number used by Edward Allde from 1592 to 1626.[123] This alone would not be sufficient proof that Allde was the printer since devices were sometimes transferred from one printer to another. However, confirmation is provided by the decorated initial I (of 'Iohn Faustus') on sig. A2 (see Plate 3c). Although this initial is very similar to that used by Orwin (see Plate 3b), there are marked differences in detail; but the identical initial is used on sig. D1 of an edition of Greene's *Philomela, The Lady Fitzwaters Nightingale* (*STC* 12296), which, according to the colophon, was printed by 'E. A.' for Edward White in 1592.[124] It is thus virtually certain that the fragment is an Allde printing, nor is this surprising in view of White's frequent use of this printer. What is curious is that White should have switched from Allde to Windet and back again, for there can be no doubt that the Shrewsbury fragment antedates the 1608 edition (see below); possibly Allde was too busy for the 1608 printing. Windet did a very bad job and it is little wonder that White reverted to Allde for the 1610 edition.

The page-breaks of S are identical with those of '08 and '10, and distinct from those of O, and it is clear that it is a page-for-page copy of a precursor which did not have the large decorated initial on sig. A2, since in S this is a 41-line page, in contrast to the, otherwise universal, 40-line format: the extra line was necessary to incorporate all the text on that page and such a procedure would only have been adopted in making a page-for-page copy.

The 1592 (Orwin) edition (the basis for the present text) is well set and cleanly printed, with unique page-breaks; it is also the only paginated edition and the only one with a register of contents. The large (9 line) decorated initial at the beginning of the text (sig. A2), similar to that in S (see Plate 3), is replaced in both '08 and '10 by a smaller factotum. Of these two later editions, '08 is typographically slovenly and the only extant copy includes a misfold (sig. H); some pages show that lines of type had come loose and were hastily (and incorrectly) reset before imposition.[125] By contrast, '10 is a careful production, on a par with Orwin's. At first sight this is a page-for-page reprint of the Windet printing but a closer study shows that Allde has 'corrected' Windet's typos in a number of places, giving in each case the text of O, although it is clear from the inclusion of all the other '08 variants (including line omissions) that Orwin's edition was not used as a reference text. The most significant 'repair' is on sig. K3: '08: a pittifulle sight] '10 (as O): a pitifull & fearfull sight [cf. 2928]. Clearly '10 is not copying from '08 but from a precursor, conveniently labelled [z],

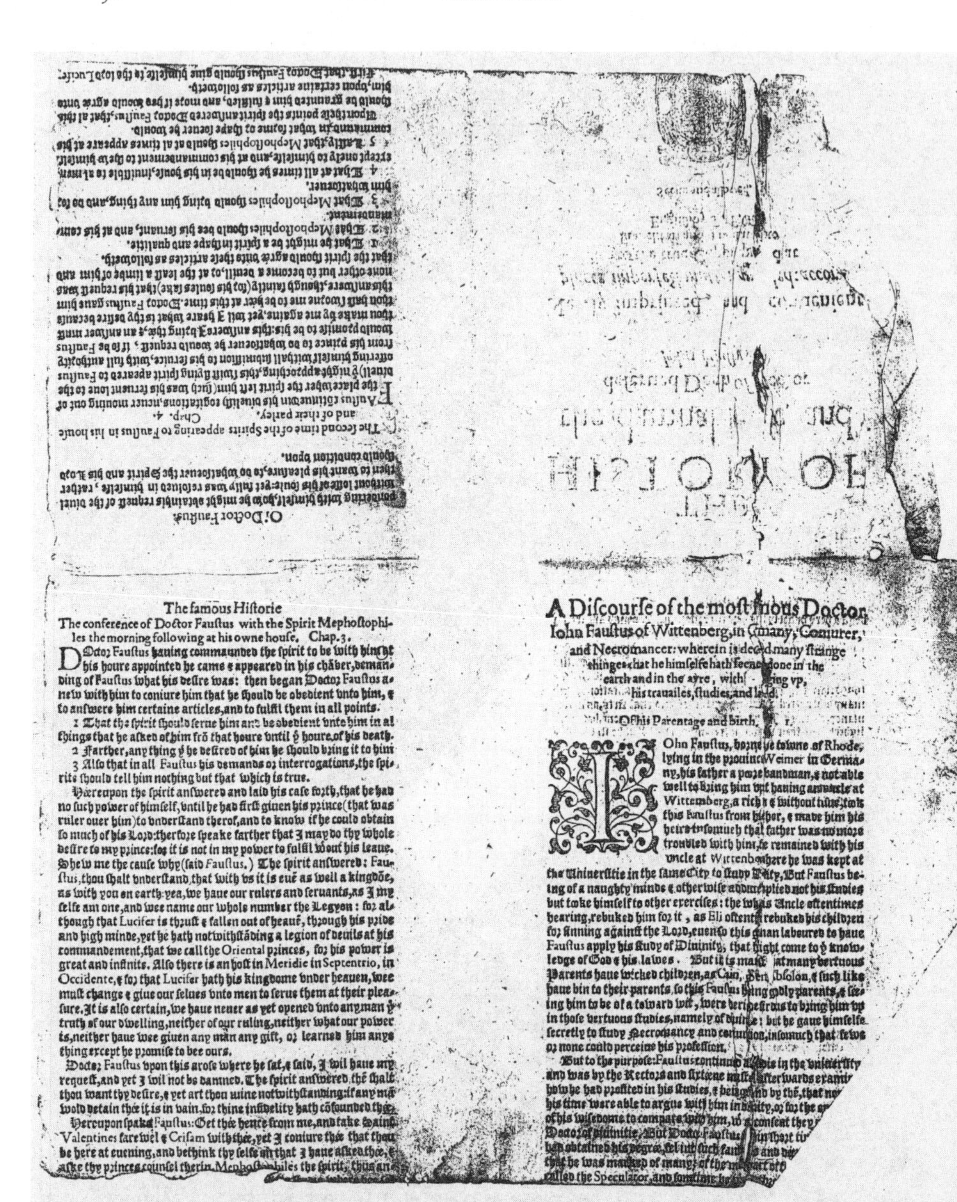

Of Doctor Faustus.

The famous Historie

The conference of Doctor Faustus with the Spirit Mephostophiles the morning following at his owne house. Chap. 3.

Doctor Faustus hauing commaunded the spirit to be with him at his houre appointed he came & appeared in his chāber, demanding of Faustus what his desire was: then began Doctor Faustus anew with him to coniure him that he should be obedient vnto him, & to answere him certaine articles, and to fulfil them in all points.

1 That the spirit should serue him and be obedient vnto him in al things that he asked of him frō that houre vntil ẏ houre of his death.

2 Farther, any thing ẏ he desired of him he should bring it to him

3 Also that in all Faustus his demands or interrogations, the spirits should tell him nothing but that which is true.

Hereupon the spirit answered and laid his case forth, that he had no such power of himself, vntil he had first giuen his prince (that was ruler ouer him) to vnderstand therof, and to know if he could obtain so much of his Lord: therfore speake farther that I may do thy whole desire to my prince: for it is not in my power to fulfil w out his leaue. Shew me the cause why (said Faustus.) The spirit answered: Faustus, thou shalt vnderstand, that with vs it is euē as well a kingdōe, as with you on earth: yea, we haue our rulers and seruants, as I my selfe am one, and wee name our whole number the Legyon: for although that Lucifer is thrust & fallen out of heauē, through his pride and high minde, yet he hath notwithstāding a legion of deuils at his commandement, that we call the Oriental princes, for his power is great and infinite. Also there is an host in Meridie in Septentrio, in Occidente, & for that Lucifer hath his kingdome vnder heauen, wee must change & giue our selues vnto men to serue them at their pleasure. It is also certain, we haue neuer as yet opened vnto any man ẏ truth of our dwelling, neither of our ruling, neither what our power is, neither haue wee giuen any mān any gift, or learned him any thing except he promise to bee ours.

Doctor Faustus vpon this arose where he sat, & said, I wil haue my request, and yet I wil not be damned. The spirit answered, thē shalt thou want thy desire, & yet art thou mine notwithstanding: if any mā wold detain thee it is in vain, for thine infidelity hath cōfounded thee.

Hereupon spake Faustus: Get thee hence from me, and take Saint Valentines farewel & Crisam with thee, yet I coniure thee that thou be here at euening, and bethink thy selfe on that I haue asked thee, & aske thy princes counsel therin. Mephostophiles the spirit, thus an-

A Discourse of the most [illegible] Doctor Iohn Faustus of Wittenberg, in [illegible], Coniurer, and Necromancer: wherein is de[illegible] many strange thinges that he himselfe hath seene [illegible] done in the earth and in the ayre, with [illegible] ging vp, his trauailes, studies, and la[illegible].

Of his Parentage and birth. [illegible] 1.

Iohn Faustus, borne [illegible] towne of Rhode, lying in the prouince Weimer in Germany, his father a poore husbandman, & not able well to bring him vp: but hauing an vncle at Wittemberg, a rich [illegible] & without issue, took this Faustus from his father, & made him his heire, insomuch that his father was no more troubled with him, he remained with his vncle at Wittenb[illegible] where he was kept at the Vniuersitie in the same City to study [illegible], But Faustus being of a naughty minde & otherwise addicted, applied not his studies but tooke himself to other exercises: the which his Vncle oftentimes hearing, rebuked him for it, as Eli oftentimes rebuked his children for sinning against the Lord, euen so this man laboured to haue Faustus apply his study of Diuinity, that he might come to ẏ knowledge of God & his lawes. But it is manifest that many vertuous Parents haue wicked children, as Cain, [illegible] Absolon, & such like haue bin to their parents, so this Faustus hauing godly parents, & seeing him to be of a toward wit, were very desirous to bring him vp in those vertuous studies, namely of diuinitie: but he gaue himselfe secretly to study Necromancy and coniuration, insomuch that fewe or none could perceiue his profession.

But to the purpose: Faustus continued [illegible] in the vniuersity and was by the Rectors and sixteene [illegible] afterwards examined how he had profited in his studies, & being [illegible] by thē, that no[illegible] his time were able to argue with him in diuinity, or for the [illegible] of his wisedome to compare with him, w[illegible] consent they [illegible] Doctor of Diuinitie. But Doctor Faustus [illegible] that ti[illegible] had obtained his degree, fel into such fan[illegible] and [illegible] that he was marked of many, of the m[illegible] called the Speculator, and sometime [illegible]

2 Facsimile of the Shrewsbury Fragment

The famous Historie

then Faustus should be fetched away, & if he should hold these Articles & conditions, that then he should haue al whatsoeuer his heart would wish or desire, & that Faustus should quickly perceiue himselfe to be a spirit in all maner of actions whatsoeuer. Heerupon Doctor Faustus his mind was so inflamed, that he forgot his soule, and promised Mephostophiles, to hold al things as he had mentioned them: he thought the diuel was not so black as they vse to paint him, nor hell so hot as the people say. &c.

The third parley betweene Doctor Faustus and Mephostophiles about a conclusion. Chap. 5.

After Doctor Faustus had made his promise to the deuill, in the morning betimes he called the spirit before him & commaunded him that he should alwaies come to him like a frier, after the order of Saint Fraun̄cis, with a bell in his hand like Saint Anthonie, and to ring it once or twise before he appeared, ẏ he might know of his certain comming. Then Faustus demaunded of his spirit, what was his name? The spirit answered, my name is as thou saist Mephostophiles, and I am a prince, but seruant to Lucifer, and all the circuit from Septentrio to the Meridian, I rule vnder him. Euen at these words was this wicked wretch Faustus inflamed, to hear himself to haue gotten so great a potentate, to be his seruant, forgetting the lord his maker & Christe his Redeemer, became an enemie to all mankind, yea worse the Giaunts whō the poets faine to climb ẏ hils to make war w the gods: not vnlike ẏ enemy of God & his Christ, that for his pride was cast into hel: so likewise Faustus forgot ẏ ẏ high climbers catch ẏ greatest fals, & that ẏ sweetest meat requires ẏ sowrest sauce. After a while Faustus promised Mephostophiles to write & make his obligation, with ful assurance of the articles in the chapter before rehearsed. A pittifull case, (Christian Reader) for certainly this Letter or obligation was found in his house after his most lamentable end

THE HISTORY OF the damnable [illegible]fe, and deserued Deah of [D]octor Iohn Fa[u]st[us].

Newly imprinted, a[n]d conuenient places imperfect matter a[mended]: according to the true Coppie p[rinted] at Franckfort and Translated into English by P. F. G[ent.]

Seene and allowed.

3(a) Printer's device used by E. Allde: McKerrow 290 (from R. B. McKerrow: *Printers' and Publishers' Devices in England and Scotland, 1485–1640*, London 1913)
(b) Decorated initial from sig. A2 of Orwin 1592
(c) Decorated initial from sig. A2 of the Shrewsbury Fragment

common to both '08 and '10, of which these editions are page-for-page copies. This is not only of some significance for the number of lost editions, but it absolves the compositors of these editions from blame with regard to line omissions, etc. : since these are common to both editions, they must have been features of their common precursor [z].

The Orwin text runs from sig. A2–L2v, compared with sig. A2–K3v for the later editions; the discrepancy is largely due to the extra space Orwin has given in the chapter headings, greatly enhancing the appearance of his text, rather than to the slight difference in format (O: 40 lines of 103mm; '08: 40 lines of 102mm). '08 and '10 are flooded with contractions, especially the macron contraction for n or m, and this constitutes a major and significant distinction from the Orwin edition. The contrast is greatest in the list of countries on Faustus' itinerary [1237–50], at the beginning of chapter 22: Orwin does not use a single contraction, '08 uses 22. Possibly many of these were copied direct from manuscript into the first edition and were transmitted to the 1608 edition without modification. This is supported by the probability that many of the variants in '08 result from MS misreads (see below). Unlike the Orwin edition, neither the Windet nor the Allde printings are paginated. One would not expect such a cheap publication to be paginated and if the MS did not supply a register (but see below, p. 51), there would have been no necessity for such a troublesome refinement. The presence of a register in the 1592 edition testifies to the care expended on this revision. (For Orwin's pagination errors, see below, pp. 41f).

Certain errors of omission in '08/10 (in c. 18) would appear to be due to an inadequate fount for astrological signs. Thus in Orwin's edition (sig. C4v) the planets are listed (correctly) as ♄ . ♃ . ♂ . ○ . ♀ . ☿ and ☾ [cf. 790], given in '08 and '10 as ♃♃ . ⚥ . ○ . ☿ & ☾ . This list is partially corrected (to ♄ . ♃ ♀ . ☉☿) in the 1618 edition (also Allde) and there are similar errors in later editions. On the same page Orwin prints 'the spheare above ♄ and' [cf. 819f] and 'Saturnia, ♓ in Occulto' [cf. 827]. The later editions omit both ♄ and ♓ and the sense is lost to all subsequent editors, showing that none of them worked from either a MS or the Orwin edition or showed any knowledge of either. Clearly these errors were present in [z].[126]

The line omissions are of much greater significance. Both '08 and '10 omit (the same) lines of text with respect to O, and the lost text is not recovered in any subsequent edition. As I have shown, these omissions must have featured in [z]. In each case, the text of O is substantiated by parallel passages in the GFB, so there is no question of the material having originated in O. The three instances are cited below; line endings are indicated by the slash, and the text omitted is printed in bold:

(i) O sig. B4 [cf. 484f]: an angell of / **God, he sate on the Cherubins, and sawe all the wonderfull works of** / God, yea he was
'08/10 sig. B4r: an angel of God, yea hee / was

(ii) O sig. D4v [cf. 1095–7]: the heauens. / Beholde, **being in these my muses, sodainly I heard a great noyse, in / so much that** I thought
'08/10 sig. D3v: the heauens. Beholde / I thought

(iii) a double line omission:
O sig. L1v [cf. 2872–4]: bad **Christian; a good Chri/stian, for that I am heartely sorry, and in my heart alwayes praye / for mercy, that my soule may be deliuered; a bad** Christian, for that I / know
'08/10 sig. K2v: bad christiā, for that I know /

These are common haplographic errors, easily made in copying a MS or type-setting from copy: the compositor's eye has jumped to the second of a repeated set of words in his copy text, or jumped a line at a line-ending. In all three cases the lengths of the omitted lines are equal to those of the printed text, so if the omissions were made direct from MS, then the latter would have the same line-length as the printed text, a distinct possibility. However, while line-omissions made during sequential composition or MS copying pass undetected by the type-setter or copyist, those made during the composition of a page-for-page copy result in page shortening. On reaching the end of his page, the compositor would be aware that he had made an error; the quickest and least troublesome remedy was to insert a line of leading to make up the deficit. This is precisely what has happened with omissions (i) and (ii). The standard page length of '08/10 (and hence of [z]) is forty lines, excluding header and catchword; sig. D3v (omission (ii)) is only thirty-nine lines, and although sig. B4 (omission (i)) appears to be forty lines, an extra line of leading has been incorporated in the heading to chapter 13 on that page.[127] So sig. B4 is effectively a thirty-nine-line page. Thus omissions (i) and (ii) were made during the composition of a page-for-page copy; since they must have featured in [z], this edition must itself have been a page-for-page copy, even if these omissions were made during its production. Omission (iii) cannot have been made during the composition of a page-for-page copy, since sig. K2v of '08/10 is a forty-line page[128]; it was made during the production either of a MS copy or of a sequentially composed edition.

There are 306 substantive variants in '08, as collated against O, of which six are revealed as '08 typos by collation with the Allde 1610 edition. None of these variants is such as to produce a radical alteration of the basic text and the majority involve single words, the longest (a gross exception) half a line [cf. 2798]. Most of the variants are purely stylistic and non-diagnostic in the sense that they do not allow the revision to be located in one or other of the editions. However, 132 variants either show a clear superiority of one of the texts or supply the literal translation from the German in one text, modified in the other. Of these, the O reading is superior in sixty cases, that of '08 in seventy-two. This at once demonstrates that O and [z] derive either from a common precursor or from distinct manuscripts; certainly they cannot be linearly related.

'08/10 supply literal translations from the German in seven cases [cf. 87, 223, 904, 1057, 2390, 2613, 2675], O in four [cf. 377f, 1337, 1615, 2045], so O represents an improved text relative to '08/10. O appears not to transmit any MS misreads, while '08/10 transmits five: 'mocked' for 'marked' [44], 'Althar' for 'Alchar' [1137, 1674], 'came' for 'ranne' [1282], 'pittie' for 'pietie' [2896], and the highly significant 'Trēt' for 'Trier' [1255] (see below, pp. 43f).

The presence of all misreads in [z] and none in O suggests that Orwin had recourse to a superior MS, one free from the haplographic omissions which feature in [z]. Although, owing to his use of extra leading in the chapter titles, Orwin's page-breaks differ from those in all the other early editions, including S, his line-breaks are frequently identical, and rarely distant from, those of '08/10, and the conformity with those of S is even greater.[129] Orwin is clearly avoiding the preparation of a sequentially composed edition, with its extra expenditure of time and type, by marking his MS or copy with line-breaks from an available edition; by casting off type, he is then able to work as if he were preparing a page-for-page edition.

The evidence presented thus far can be interpreted by three possible genetic schemes:

(1) involving a single MS:

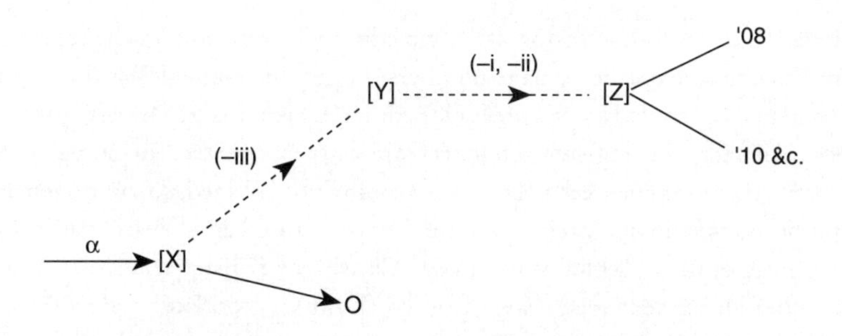

where [x] is the *editio princeps*. The sequentially composed edition, [y], is required to account for omission (iii); on this scheme, the omission could not have been made in [x] without loss of material to o.

(2) involving two MSS, a 'bad' MS α, and a superior MS β.

(a) direct incorporation of β-readings in o:

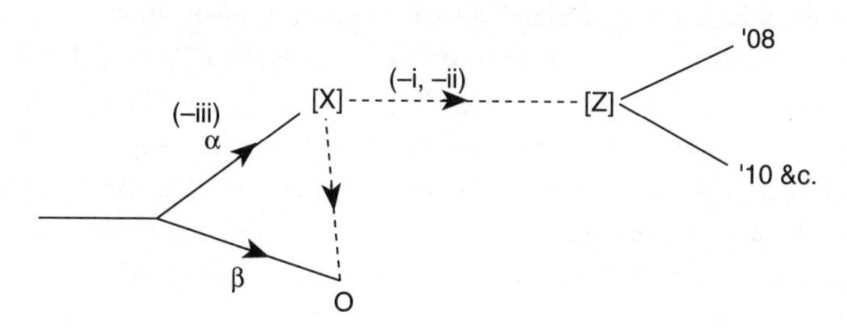

On this scheme, omission (iii) was made during the production of MS α and did not feature in MS β. It is attractive in explaining why all the misreads are located in [z], and does not require the sequentially composed edition [y] of scheme 1.

(b) a sequentially composed edition [w], prepared from MS β, as precursor for o:

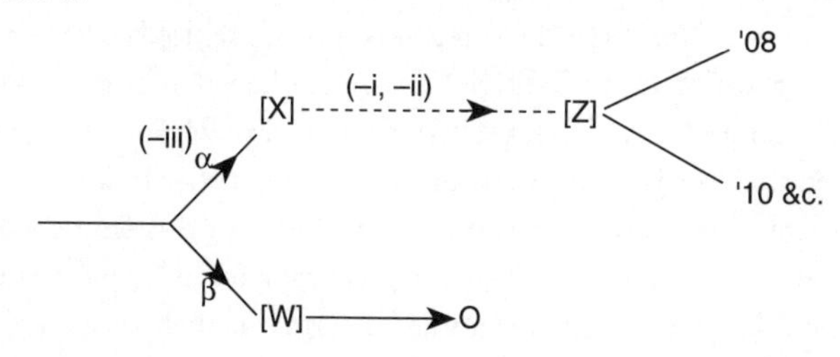

The difficulties associated with this scheme will become apparent in the discussion of the printing history (see below, pp. 45ff). However, Logeman has argued that o was based on a paginated precursor;[130] his inference rests upon the partly inaccurate observation that although there are several errors of pagination in o (cf. description of Orwin edition in Appendix 1), the register of contents cites the corrected page numbers. Logeman assumed that the register of contents was copied from a precursor edition which was free from pagination errors. In fact, the register references are only corrrected for some of the chapters, those for chapters 17 and 18 remaining uncorrected, so, on Logeman's hypothesis, a paginated precursor would have featured an identical pagination error in signature C, which is not likely. Clearly the register was made from o itself after all the text sheets were printed and it was too late to alter the text pagination; Orwin will have discovered his errors and rectified the register references where possible. Unfortunately he could not refer to the correct page numbers for chapters 17 and 18 (20 and 21 respectively) since his text contained no pages bearing these numbers, so here he was forced to retain the references to the incorrect paginations (23 and 23 respectively). Thus there is no case for a paginated precursor for o.

To pass now to a consideration of s, this fragment shows twenty-four substantive variants with respect to o, '08/10, or both; of these, eleven supply the o reading, twelve the '08/10 reading and one is specific to s. Of the o readings, seven are inferior, two are equivocal and two superior, including 'marked' [44] ('08/10 has the misread 'mocked'). Of the '08/10 readings, five are inferior (including one literal: ye enemy [cf. 223]), five are equivocal and two superior, but in both the latter cases Orwin appears to have made a questionable edit: 'this I. Faustus' [cf. 23], where the 'I.' is an insert, and 'call for Mephostophiles' for 'call on Mephostophiles' [83].

These results show that s cannot have derived from o or '08/10 but is closer to the *editio princeps* than either. The inclusion of 'marked' [44] locates it on the 'good' side of [x], either as a direct precursor of o, or as a copy of one, depending on the interpretation of its unique variant. This occurs on sig. A2v: 'worldly pleasures than the ioy to come'; o offers '... pleasure... ioyes...', '08/10 '... pleasures... ioyes...' [cf. 65]. The three versions of the double variant here are equivocal as to the direction of edit, but it is quite likely that both Orwin and the editor of [z] changed 'ioy' to 'ioyes' (the other variants in s suggest that its editor, Allde, made little or no revision of his copy text). It would be rash to invoke a common precursor for o and s on the basis of this single variant, but equally insecure to propose s as a direct precursor for o when it is uncertain whether the edition was completed. What is certain is that s is a page-for-page copy of a precursor with page-breaks conforming to '08/10; at the same time it is typographically very close to o, as the close conformity of line-breaks shows. Thus s may be inserted in any of the three schemes, either on the direct line from [x] (schemes 1, 2a) or [w] (scheme 2b) to o, or as a spur on that line:

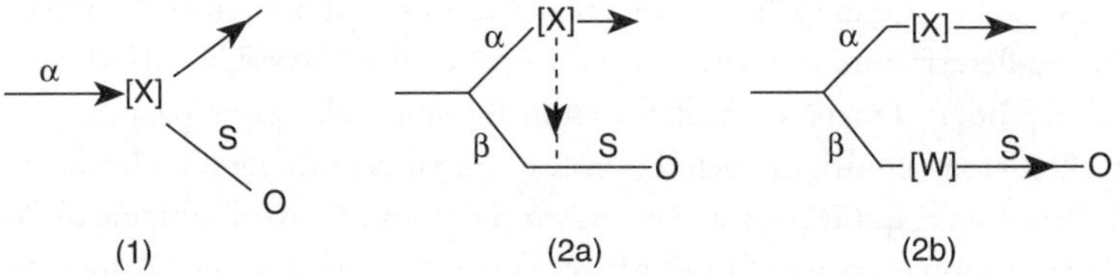

α [X] s o

(1)

α [X] β s o

(2a)

α [X] β [W] s o

(2b)

where the indeterminate placing of s reflects the uncertainty concerning its role as a direct precursor for o.

Of the three schemes proposed, 2b must be abandoned because of the improbability of an edition [w] (see below, p. 50), and 1 does not satisfactorily explain why all the misreads are located in [z] and none in s or o. Further grounds for discarding scheme 1 relate to the misread 'Trēt' ('08/10) for 'Trier' (o, cf. [1255]), which is of direct consequence for Marlowe's *Doctor Faustus*.[131] In both the latter (A and B texts) and in the GFB, Trier is the first stop on Faustus' Grand Tour. PF translates the passage with little change: 'Trier . . . but there he saw not many wonders, except one fayre Pallace . . ., and also a mighty large Castle that was built of bricke, with three walles and three great trenches, so strong, that it was impossible for any princes power to win it' (o sig. E2v, [cf. 1256–60]). In *Doctor Faustus* (probably Marlowe here) the passage is interpreted thus (A823ff):

> . . . the stately towne of Trier,
> Inuirond round with ayrie mountaine tops,
> With walles of flint, and deepe intrenched lakes,
> Not to be wonne by any conquering prince,

This is rather different from the EFB, and although in the absence of any clues the inaccuracies (Trier is not surrounded by high mountains) might be attributed to poetic licence, they take on a very different perspective if the passage is viewed as a description, not of Trier but of Trent on the Adige. Marlowe was very interested in cosmography, and his pains over the geography of *Tamburlaine* indicate his scrupulous attention to detail. It is quite clear that, perhaps troubled by the Faust-book description, he turned to the obvious reference book: Braun and Hohenberg's *Civitates orbis terrarum*, where the description of 'Tridentum' [132] includes the following:

> Tridentum, civitas in finibus Venetiae provinciae, inter montes in planitie posita est, muris vallate lapideis. . . Influit placide in urbem per muros ab Oriente aquae rivus . . . *Montes circum se habet . . . et ita praealtos, vt dicas, coelum summa montium cacumina contingere*

The italicized phrases are evidently the source of A824, and 'muris vallate lapideis' yields 'walles of flint', rather than the 'brick' of both the EFB and GFB; the latter description, ultimately from Schedel's *Weltchronik*, is included in the *Civitates* under 'Treveris': 'Videtur enim ibi stupendi operis palatium, quod instar Babylonici muri, ex cocto latere factum, tantae firmitatis hodie manet, vt nulla arte frangi queat',[133] but there is no mention of any mountains or lakes.

Thus Marlowe's copy of the EFB contained 'Trent', not 'Trier', for only so could he have been led to introduce the description from the *Civitates*. His use of 'ayrie mountaine tops' is most apt since it projects Faustus' soaring flight. But Marlowe retained the impregnability of the place from the EFB. The 'Trier' of the received text of *Doctor Faustus* must therefore be seen as a post-1592 correction (either in performance or by an editor) and Marlowe's source cannot have been O; it must have been an earlier edition incorporating misreads. Apart from releasing *Doctor Faustus* from the 1592 *terminus ab quo* set by the Orwin edition, this finding suggests that the misreads were present in [X] (on the reasonable assumption that Marlowe used the first edition as his source). Their correction, in S and O, necessitates recourse to a MS and the printing history shows it is most unlikely that this could have been MS α.

These considerations leave only scheme 2a, which, modified to include S becomes:

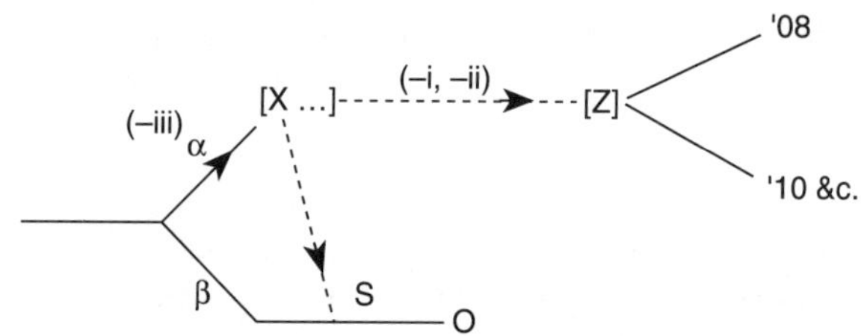

The Shrewsbury fragment must be regarded as the earliest printing to have survived, and since Allde appears not to have been a revising editor, it is probably very close to MS β. This MS may well have included authorial changes and corrections which have been incorporated into O, and this may have warranted the title-page description (common to all these editions) 'newly imprinted and in convenient places imperfect matter amended'. Having once appeared (in S or O), it would have been appropriated to later editions such as [Z], regardless of the 'imperfect matter' they still contained. However, the probability of editions intermediate between [X] and [Z] is high and the possibility of an edition [Y], cleared of sensitive material and bearing the notice of amendment, cannot be ignored; in such a case, [Y], rather than [X], would be the immediate typographic precursor for S and O. Such an edition would conveniently accommodate the small editorial changes required by any reverse borrowing from *Doctor Faustus* (see above, pp. 20f).

The main problem in presenting a secure printing history of the early editions of the EFB is posed by the lack of any relevant contemporary entry in the Register of the Stationers' Company. Despite Collier's statement[134] that the EFB was entered in 1588 (perhaps wishful thinking), there is no early entry for the *editio princeps*, nor for Orwin's 1592 edition. The earliest entry, in effect a copyright assignment for a work which had never previously been entered, is dated April 1596, when *The History of the Damnable Life and Deserued Death of Doctor JOHN FAUSTUS* was entered to Edward White 'he havinge thinterest of abell Jeffes thereto'.[135] However, the book had earlier been the subject of a copyright dispute between the printers Abel Jeffes and Thomas Orwin; it was settled in the Stationers' Company 'Court of Assistants' and recorded in the Court minutes under 18 December 1592:

Abell Ieffes / Thomas Orwin Yt is ordered: that if the book of Doctor Faustus shall not be found in the hall book entred to Richard Oliff before Abell Ieffes claymed the same which was about May last. That then the seid copie shall Remayne to the said Abell as his proper copie from the tyme of his first clayme which was about May last as aforesaid[136]

At first sight this is a puzzling minute and it is capable of more than one interpretation. There can be no doubt that the 'book of Doctor Faustus', considered in association with both Orwin and Abel Jeffes, particularly in respect of the copyright assignment of 1596, is the 'Damnable Life', i.e. the EFB. The 'hall book' is the Stationers' Company Register, and Richard Oliff (or Olive) was another stationer, a book-seller and occasional printer, whose involvement is relatively obscure but who had, apparently, possessed a 'copie' (i.e. a manuscript) before it was acquired by Orwin. There are no further references to this settlement in the Court minutes, but since the copyright clearly remained with Jeffes until he assigned it to White in 1596, no entrance to Oliff could have been found in the 'hall book', and the Court must have upheld Jeffes' claim.

The dispute evidently concerns Orwin's 1592 edition, 'to be sold by Edward White'. As Greg states:[137] 'The ground of Jeffes' claim is not stated, but, no entrance being alleged, it is difficult to see what it can have been if not an edition previous to Orwin's.' Indeed so, but Greg goes on to assume that the date of the claim is the date of Jeffes' edition, a wholly unwarranted assumption. Unfortunately Greg had accepted as axiomatic a late dating (1592–3) for the composition of *Doctor Faustus* and was transparently biased against any evidence suggesting publication of the EFB prior to mid-1592. As I shall argue in the concluding section (see below, p. 54ff), *pace* Greg, the book must have been published well before this date.

Greg's further interpretation is as follows: Orwin acquired a manuscript of the 'Damnable Life' from Oliff 'perhaps in 1592', assuming it had been entered in the Register. Meanwhile Jeffes 'somehow acquired another and inferior copy' and, about May 1592, printed an edition which has not survived. 'Regarding this edition as defective and unauthorized, Orwin proceeded to print and publish (through Edward White) his own superior copy (the extant edition). Against this action Jeffes complained to the Court of Assistants on 18 December.'

Setting aside the defects of this interpretation, the existence of the two MSS, of which Orwin's was superior, is supported by the bibliographic evidence given above, but that evidence also suggests that the superior MS was earlier available to Edward Allde, White's favourite printer, who used it to prepare the Shrewsbury fragment. Edward White is obviously a key figure here. He was one of the most prolific and successful of the publishers in this period and, like Orwin, was an influential member of the Livery of the Stationers' Company whereas Jeffes was a humble Yeoman. What Greg chose to ignore here is that throughout the summer of 1592 Jeffes and White were engaged in a piratical trade war, each publishing works of the other's copyright, and that from July Jeffes had been 'in ward' and was only released on the very day of the Court ruling of 18 December. It was not a case of Jeffes 'complaining' to the Court of Assistants on this day, but of his earlier complaint finally receiving attention. These circumstances radically affect the interpretation of the Court minute, and the whole background to the action, including Jeffes' pecuniary difficulties, demands careful consideration. The essential question is what motivated Jeffes' claim to the 'Damnable Life' in May 1592.

As the Jeffes/Orwin case is the only copyright dispute concerned with the EFB, and the verdict was given in favour of Jeffes, it is safe to assume that he was the printer of the lost *editio princeps*, though there is no reason to suppose this was in May 1592. Jeffes' failure to enter the book in the Register prior to publication is in no way remarkable (there are many similar cases), nor does it imply that the book was unlicensed for publication by the censoring authorities, although Jeffes was no stranger to such a misdemeanour (see below, pp. 47). It may merely represent an attempt to avoid paying registration fees (6d per title) at a time when he was particularly hard up, for there is plenty of evidence to show that Jeffes was often in severe financial difficulties. Thus, under 5 September 1586, the Register shows entry to Edward White of '*a sackfull of news* being an old copy, which the said Edward is ordered to have printed by Abell Jeffes',[138] and on the same date: 'allowed to Abell Jeffes a book: *pretie conceiptes etc.* to be printed for the company',[139] later published by Edward White as *The Booke of prittie conceites*.[140] Both Register entries indicate charitable intent on the part of the Company, which occasionally enforced distribution of available printing to relieve distress amongst underworked printers,[141] of whom Jeffes was clearly one.

At this stage of his career Jeffes, a Freeman of the Stationers' Company since 1580, was keeping two apprentices and is listed (23 June 1585) as having one press. He published five major works in 1587 (including the complete works of Gascoigne, Matthew Grove's *Pelops and Hippodamia* and a translation of Boccacio's *Philocopo*),[142] but 1588, the most probable date of issue of the EFB, is a complete blank, both in terms of his known printings and entries in the Stationers' Company Register. Around this time he moved premises from Fore Street beyond Cripplegate to Philips Lane within the city, continuing to trade beneath the sign of the Bell. In 1589 there are only two known Jeffes publications (Ascham's *Toxophilus* and *The Scholemaster*),[143] and very little known printing in 1590.[144] His activity seems to pick up in 1591,[145] by which time he had relocated his business to Paul's churchyard, at the great North door of Paul's, well-placed to oversee the doings of his near neighbour White, and in June of that year he took on his third apprentice.[146] 1592 was a bumper year: Jeffes printed works by Lodge, Nashe, Greene, Henry Roberts, and the 'History of Quintus Curtius',[147] but there were serious troubles on hand. In observance of the 1586 Star Chamber decree and under pressure from Archbishop Whitgift, the Stationers' Company had intensified their weekly searches of printing shops to discover what was on the presses, the size of editions and the number of apprentices.[148] In one such search towards the end of July 1592, Jeffes was caught doing some illicit printing; the minutes of the Assistants' Court for 7 August record:

> whereas Abell Ieffes about the [22nd] day of July last did resist the search which master Stirrop, warden, Th[omas] Dawson and Tho[mas Rente]man, renters, were appointed to make and would have made of his printing house according to the ordinances and decrees, and for that he contemptuously proceeded in printing a book without authority contrary to our master, his commandment, and for that he refused to deliver the bar of his press neither would deliver any of the books to be brought to the hall according to the decrees, and also for that he used violence to our officer in the search, it is now therefore ordered by a full court held this day, that... he shall be committed to ward.[149]

Whatever book was involved, the offence had been sufficiently serious to send John Wolfe, the Company Beadle, to Croydon[150] to inform Whitgift, and, despite Jeffes' vain resistance, the books were brought to the hall.

It is impossible to decide what degree of restraint was imposed on Jeffes following the 7 August. His committal did not prevent him entering *The second part of the Defiance to fortune* on 7 August [151] and three other works (including *the Spanish Tragedy*) on 6 October.[152] Was he allowed to continue printing? Greg originally thought not[153] but later revised this view,[154] claiming that Jeffes' first edition of *Pierce Penniless* was issued before 18 December, on what basis I do not understand (the two Jeffes editions dated 1592 must postdate the death of Greene (3 September) and the subsequent edition is dated 1593. Since the year did not end until March 25, there was ample time for Jeffes to print his first two editions after 18 December).

Following further visits of Wolfe to Croydon,[155] Jeffes made his submission (as directed by the Archbishop of Canterbury) at the Court of 18 December, humbly acknowledging 'his former offences and undutifulness, craving pardon and favour for the same and promising hereafter to live as becometh an honest man. . .'.[156] The minute of this submission is followed directly by that of the Jeffes/Orwin copyright ruling. Obviously with Jeffes in contempt, the case could not have been heard earlier and it must be assumed that Orwin and White took advantage of the interim to publish and sell their edition of the EFB. But this was not White's only injury to Jeffes: the minute of the copyright dispute directly precedes the following, under the same date:

> Whereas Edward White and Abell Ieffes have each of them offended. viz Edw White in having printed the spanish tragedy[157] belonging to Abell Ieffes and Abell Ieffes in having printed the tragedy of arden of kent[158] belonging to Edw White: it is agreed that all the books of each impression shall be as confiscated and forfeited according to the ordinances, disposed to the use of the poor of the Company for that each of them hath severally transgressed the ordinances in the said impressions.[159]

Additionally they were each fined ten shillings[160] but imprisonment was deferred, and it appears that they bought back their sequestered books before July 1593.[161]

The chronology of events here (1592) is important:

3 Apr:	entry to White of 'arden of kent'
May:	Jeffes claims copyright of EFB
before 22 July:	Jeffes publishes 'Arden of Faversham'
22 July:	search of Jeffes' printing shop
7 Aug:	Jeffes is committed to ward
3 Oct:	Jeffes enters 'The Spanish Tragedy'
Aug–Dec:	White publishes 'The Spanish Tragedy' and (?) the EFB
18 Dec:	Jeffes' submission; court ruling on EFB and on Jeffes' and White's misdemeanours.

For the elucidation of the full story, much hinges on the identity of the illicit book discovered in the search of 22 July. Although Whitgift was informed of the offence and was consulted before Jeffes' release, this does not necessarily imply that the book itself was reprehensible (Jeffes seems to have been punished as much for his 'contemptuous proceedings' and 'violence to our officer' as for his printing transgression – he had evidently been warned not to go ahead), but it may have been. There are two likely candidates.[162] One is 'Arden of Faversham' which Jeffes is known to have printed before 18 December, and probably before 22 July if he was unable to print while in ward. In this case White may have demanded severe action[163] at the time, though his later influence will have been undermined by his subsequent piracy of Jeffes' copyrights. The other (in my opinion more probable) candidate is Kyd's *The Spanish Tragedy*, for there was certainly a (no longer extant) Jeffes *editio princeps* of this work prior to White's late-1592 piracy: the title page of the latter bears the exceptional announcement 'Newly corrected and amended of such gross faults as passed in the first impression', as does Jeffes' 1594 edition. The 'gross faults' may have been matter for ecclesiastical censorship, which would explain Whitgift's involvement, and the announcements of amendment would then have become mandatory inscriptions. Jeffes and White evidently came to terms over *The Spanish Tragedy*, for Jeffes' 1594 edition is imprinted 'to be sold by Edward White'.

A possible scenario (endorsing much of Kirschbaum's view) is as follows: in May 1592 Jeffes learned that Allde was printing the 'Damnable Life' for White (the Shrewsbury fragment) and at once claimed copyright on the basis of his extant edition. Whether S was actually published or abandoned, Jeffes then avenged himself on White by printing *Arden of Faversham*. In July, despite warnings not to proceed, Jeffes printed an unlicensed edition of *The Spanish Tragedy*; this was discovered in the search, the books confiscated and Jeffes imprisoned. White took this opportunity for his own revenge by publishing the EFB (Orwin) and *The Spanish Tragedy* while Jeffes was in ward.[164] The whole back-log of disputes and misdemeanours was settled at the Court hearing of 18 December.

Jeffes' fortunes did not greatly improve following his release from prison; he was often sufficiently impoverished to pawn stock and receive loans from the Company.[165] Nevertheless it is noteworthy that, amongst other publications, he printed two editions of *The Second report of Doctor John Faustus* (the English Wagner book) for Cuthbert Burby in 1594. In the following year his publication of Giovanni Cipriano's *A wonderful Prophecy upon this troublesome World*,[166] a 'lewd' book, caused his final downfall: his press and letters were brought to the hall of the Stationers' Company and there defaced and made unserviceable, and he was once again imprisoned.[167] In the inevitable sale of his copyrights, White finally (April 1596) got what he wanted: Jeffes' 'interest' in the EFB. By 13 August 1599 all of Jeffes' copyrights had been assigned away[168] and no more is heard of him.

These interpretations provide a basis for dating some of the editions in the scheme on p. 44. S is to be seen as part of White's 1592 activities and I suggest that news of its production caused Jeffes to claim the EFB copyright in May. This would mirror his behaviour in respect of *The Spanish Tragedy* which he did not enter until 3 October and then, probably, as a protection against White's pirated edition. I would therefore date s as late-April/early-May 1592. The Orwin edition must date from August to mid-December of that year. [z] probably represents an Allde/White printing soon after White finally obtained copyright of the EFB in April 1596. It is interesting that [z] is based on Jeffes' earlier printing and not on Orwin's edition; presumably White was not allowed to do otherwise. By then Orwin was dead (d. 1593), and his manuscript, if it still survived, was the property of his industrious widow.

As for dating the *editio princeps*, the documented printing history affords no clues beyond a *terminus ad quem* of May 1592 (assuming my interpretations are correct), and other evidence (see below) must be brought to bear. Nor is there any clear evidence here for a censored version, though there are some bibliographic hints of censorship which now require brief consideration. However, the printing history does render an edition [w] (cf. scheme 2b, p. 43), sequentially prepared from MS β, highly improbable in view of Jeffes' keen interest in his rights.

As indicated in section II (p. 15ff), PF's translation, as it survives, makes two major exclusions from the German text: the heretical creation myth of GFB c. 22, and the curious GFB c. 65 in which Mephostophiles mocks the sorrowing Faustus with a barrage of proverbs. Both exclusions may be regarded as passive censorship but, in view of the uncertainties attending the early printing history, the question of active censorship of a first edition incorporating this material deserves consideration.

The bibliographic indications are slender and may be interpreted as coincidental errors, but they do affect those areas of the text which are under question. They are two-fold: a series of incorrect chapter numberings around the area where the heretical creation myth was to have been expected, and an error in Orwin's Register of Contents which relates to the sequence of Faustus' lamentations.

To take the latter first, the relevant section of the Register lists:

His talk with his servant. [p:] 74
Five complaints of Doctor Faustus before his end. [pp:] 75,76,77,
His miserable end, with his Oration to his friends. [pp. :] 78,79.

The correspondence with the chapters is as follows: 'Talk with servant': c. 57 (sig. K2v; p. 74); 'Complaints': c. 58 (sig. K3; p. 75), cc. 59,60 (sig. K3v; p. 76), [c. 61] (sig. K4; p. 77); 'Miserable end': c. 62 (sig. K4v; p. 78); 'Oration to his friends' (sig. L1; p. 81 (sic)). Clearly there are only four 'complaints', not 'five' as listed in the Register. This could well be interpreted as a simple slip on the part of whoever made the Register, but the absence of a chapter number (c. 61) in the Orwin text (the only such error in his edition) raises suspicion. Any EFB equivalent for the GFB c. 65 would have followed EFB c. 60 and all subsequent chapter numbers would have been advanced by 1. Orwin's Register error and numeral omission could be accounted for by supposing that the text of the Register was copied direct from MS β, itself copied from a censored original in which the Register had been left uncorrected and the original chapter number for the next lamentation had been cancelled.

Turning now to the chapter number errors of '08/10 (O's numbering is correct), these are listed in the following table which incorporates the correctly numbered chapters 19 and 24 to define the sequence:

'*1592*'	'*1608*'	'*1610*'	*chapter content*
19	19	19	Quarrel; Lucifer + 7 principal spirits
20	20	20	Faustus visits hell
21	19	19	Faustus' journey to the stars
22	—	—	Faustus' Grand Tour
23	34	34	Faustus' sight of Paradise
24	24	24	Comet
55	34	35	Faustus' cohabits with Helena

The last of these is probably without significance; '10's '35' (from [z]) may be seen as transmission of a misread for '55' in [z], compounded to '34' in '08 by Windet's error-prone compositor. But the errors '19' for '21' and '34' for '23' are difficult to explain, as also the failure to number chapter 22. They can be accounted for by the following speculative hypothesis: PF translated the GFB chapters 22 and 23 without substantial change, these appearing as chapters 19 and 20 of his MS. When someone (probably Jeffes) baulked at c. 19 (the heretical creation myth) PF was forced to rewrite this section, perhaps initially considering simple replacement of c. 19 by the 'journey to the stars', a natural continuation from Mephostophiles' promise (c. 18) to teach Faustus cosmology and to fly through the air. The consequent changes in chapter numberings were left largely uncorrected and pass into MS α. In the confusion, the 'Grand Tour' has lost its number altogether (perhaps an uncorrected cancellation like Orwin's failure to number c. 61). The '08/10 error of 34 for c. 23 (O) can then be seen as a misread for '24', PF's original numbering.

These arguments cannot claim much weight, particularly as '08/10 supply the correct chapter number for c. 61, omitted by Orwin. But at least they restrict the censorship, if there was any, to the manuscripts. There is no case for positing a published edition which fell foul of ecclesiastical censorship. The title-page announcement of amendments must therefore refer either to the slight improvements provided by MS β,[169] or to editorial changes in an edition [Y] (see above, p. 44)

FAUST IN ENGLAND: DATING THE EFB AND *DOCTOR FAUSTUS*

Internal evidence from the EFB shows that PF's source text was not post-1588,[170] and that, at the time of translation, Pope Sixtus V was still living, or believed to be (he died 27 August 1590, NS).[171] Both constraints are met by assuming the translation to have been made in the summer of 1588. Paul Fairfax had returned to London by July of that year, so, if the identification with PF is correct, he brought the GFB back with him.[172] As a returning traveller he is likely to have been short of funds and would have been anxious to capitalize on his labours quickly by selling his translation of what was known, in Germany at least, to be a best seller. Such considerations render a delayed publication most unlikely.

Certain English notices of Faustus indicate a detailed knowledge of the Faust-book story as early as 1589–90, and although this awareness may be interpreted as deriving from an EFB manuscript (or, much less likely, the German Faust-book or the German Faust tradition)[173] it is more probable that, as Kocher[174] advanced, it stems from a published edition. The earliest such notice is the SCR entry of 28 February 1588/9 to 'Ric. Iones' of 'a ballad of the life and deathe of Doctor Faustus the great Cunngerer',[175] allowed *inter alia* by the Bishop of London. Jones' publication has not survived and thus an identification of this with the late seventeenth century ballad 'The Judgment of God shewed upon one John Faustus' (entered 1 March 1674/5)[176] cannot be secure. However, this ballad, which Greg[177] admits to show a knowledge of the 'Damnable Life', was intended to be sung to the tune of 'Fortune my Foe', current by 1594, and by 1636 sufficiently closely associated with the Faust ballad to be known by its alternative name of 'Doctor Faustus'.[178]

Another Faust notice of the same year as the Jones ballad entry occurs in Gabriel Harvey's *An Aduertisement for Papp-hatchett* which is dated 'At Trinitie Hall: this fift of November: 1589' [179] and Greg dismisses it as follows: 'but it was first printed in *Pierce's Supererogation* in 1593, so that the evidence in this case is a little equivocal'.[180] 'Little' is the word! The *Advertisement* was a highly topical polemic written at the height of the Marprelate pamphlet campaign as a tilt against John Lyly's *Pappe with an Hatchet*.[181] It is most unlikely that Harvey would have rewritten it, inserting the Faustus allusion, for a 1593 publication, by which time his invective was directed against Greene and Nashe. Nor is Greg justified in contending[182] that 'the allusion may imply no more than a hearsay knowledge of the *Historia*', for the 'allusion' is not the mere 'incidental phrase "like another Doctor Faustus"' that Greg admits to, and even Kocher[183] failed to observe the significance of the continuation. To quote the relevant passages in full: 'As for that new-created Spirite [Harvey], whom double V [Lyly]. like another Doctour Faustus, threateneth to coniure upp at leysure, . . . were that Spirite disposed to appeare in his former likenesse, and to put the Necromancer to his purgation, he could peradventure make the coniuring wisard forsake the center of his Circle.' [184]

This shows much more than hearsay knowledge and the detail is worth examining. In the EFB [100], the spirit appears as a dragon, transforming to a fiery man and thence to a 'gray Frier'. During these transformations the EFB says expressly, 'Yet Faustus feared it not' [104]. But in *Doctor Faustus*, the sequence from Dragon to Friar is interrupted. The Dragon appears and goes; Faustus complains of delay ('Quod tu moraris?') and utters his second conjuration, which is effective: (A266) *Enter a Devil* / [Faustus]: I charge thee to returne and chaunge thy shape, / Thou art too vgly to attend on me. / Goe and returne an old Franciscan Frier . . .' and a little later Mephostophiles enters as a grey friar. The shock entry at A266 is meant to terrify, and presumably Faustus staggers, perhaps shaking his knees and clutching his bowels, stepping back almost out of his circle before he recovers his resolve. Perhaps this supplies the motive for his immediate self-gratulation (A275ff): 'Such is the force of Magicke and my spels' etc. It would appear to be this entry of the Devil which Harvey refers to as 'his former likeness' which 'put the Necromancer to his purgation'. Granted that the passage is susceptible to other interpretations, Harvey's Faust notice is suggestive of a performance of *Doctor Faustus* before (and not long before) 5 November 1589. (Harvey is thought to have been practising law at the Court of Arches in 1588–9, so he would have had opportunity to have seen the play if it were performed then.[185]) Although such a performance would have entailed Marlowe's intimate knowledge of the 'Damnable Life' well prior to this, it cannot be denied that he might have worked from a MS copy. But what is surely true is that in whatever form Marlowe found the EFB, whether as MS or published edition, he would have fastened upon it at once. He must have felt it was made for him, and at a time when the theatres were avid for new pieces and there was a sufficiency of hungry dramatists, any delay on his part would have given the prize to a rival. It is quite preposterous to suppose that if the EFB appeared in 1588 the play was not written until 1592. Thus, although an early date for the play does not necessitate an early printing of the EFB, the latter would imply an early date for the play.

To continue with the early notices, Harvey's marginalium ('if Doctor Faustus cowld reare Castles, & arme Diuels' etc.) in his copy of Morysine's 'The strategemes sleyghtes and polices of warre' (London 1539) cannot be dated unequivocally as prior to 1592,[186] although Hale Moore,[187] who first drew attention to the notice, supposed it written not later than 1591. It is a clear reference to the Faust book (English or German) rather than the play, but taken in association with the *Advertisement* allusion, it testifies to the impact the story made upon Harvey. A more securely dated early notice is provided in Henry Holland's *Treatise against Witchcraft* (Cambridge, 1590): p. 28: 'I will not denie ... but the deuill may delude his witches many waies in these transportations, & that many fabulous pamphlets* are published ...' [printed marginalium:] * Faustus. / Drunken Dunstan. / art. et in p. 156.' No one has yet discovered 'Drunken Dunstan' and the page reference is perplexing.[188] The context is aerial flight, a recurrent Faust-book motif, so Holland at least knew the content of the Faust book. Once again, Greg dismisses this as implying 'no more than a bare knowledge of the existence' of the GFB, which displays excessive scepticism. The notice is important in referring to a 'published' pamphlet, so here, for once, Greg's manuscript argument cannot be invoked.

Greg's attempted refutation of Kocher's hypothesis of a 1588–9 edition of the EFB demands that Jones, Harvey, Holland (and Marlowe, allowing for an early composition date for *Doctor Faustus*) obtained their information either from MS copies of the 'Damnable Life' or from knowledge of the German Faust Book. I submit this is no more probable than the existence of an early printing. The ballad notice especially commands attention, since the balladeer commonly traded on established public awareness of the plot material; the ballad provided a popular and entertaining gloss, recalling to mind the events of the story while the listeners' memories supplied the details. The subjects of the ballads were often recent, sensational events, such as notorious murders or daring escapades of war, but they also glossed on established romances and *de casibus* histories, and also on plays. The topical interest for such subjects guaranteed sales, and of this the balladeers and their publishers were keenly aware. Thus it is most unlikely that a ballad of Doctor Faustus would have been published until public interest had been awakened, and for that, neither a circulating MS, nor hearsay of the GFB, would have been sufficient.

Since Greg's manuscript argument precludes using *Doctor Faustus* to date the earliest EFB edition, such evidence as there is for an early composition and performance of the play may be set aside to be used as corroborative support. The evidence I shall present for a pre-1590 edition of the EFB is both new and more secure. It relates to the main source for Greene's *Honourable History of Friar*

Bacon and Friar Bungay,[189] namely the prose romance of Friar Bacon. I shall argue that this romance, although incorporating folk myths of Roger Bacon, is essentially a construct, modelled on the Faust book in direct imitation in an attempt to capture an established market. However, there is a major difficulty: Greene's source is not extant, nor is its existence documented.

Greene wrote his play in 1589 or 1590,[190] yet the earliest documentation for a published version of the prose romance is the Register entry under 12 January 1623/4 to Francis Grove for 'A booke called *the legend of Frier Bacon*'.[191] It is assumed that this refers to the book published by Francis Grove as *The Famous History of Frier Bacon*. . . ; the earliest dated extant edition is that of 1627,[192] but an undated edition in the Houghton Library, Harvard, is thought to predate this and has been assigned to *c.* 1625.[193] Numerous editions of this text appeared throughout the sixteenth century and later and it was reprinted by Thoms[194] from the 1629 edition, printed by E. A[llde] for F. Grove.

Possibly because of the late date of this representative text, it has received little close attention, though Ward[195] published lengthy extracts in his edition of Greene's 'Friar Bacon and Friar Bungay', and later editors have been content to accept and repeat his assessments. Subsequently the only critical examination has been that of Kerstin Assarsson-Rizzi[196] who emphasizes that the 'Famous History', although clearly representative of Greene's source, is unlikely to be in the exact form of the latter. In particular she demonstrates[197] that it includes a long extract from a work first published in 1597,[198] but failed to notice that the Grove editions (and their reprints) contain direct quotations from the English Faust Book (EFB) and Marlowe's *Doctor Faustus* (1604, etc.).[199] The Grove editions thus show extensive reworking of an original text, and incorporate material from the published EFB and *Doctor Faustus* then available.

Assarsson-Rizzi, in her bibliographic consideration of 'The Famous History', says: 'An abbreviated version of the romance does exist. First published more than a century after Greene's death, it is of no concern to the present study',[200] and in a note she lists the British Library classmark. It is most unfortunate she did not look at it: not only is it of concern, it is of paramount importance. Entitled *The Most Famous History of the Learned Fryer Bacon . . . also The Merry Waggeries of his man Miles* (see Plate 4, p. 56), it was printed at London for 'Tho. Norris at the sign of the Looking-glass on London Bridge'.[201] In the following discussion, all quotations from the text are taken from the BL copy; Grove's 1627 publication ('The Famous History' etc.) is designated by F, Norris's 'Most Famous History' by M, and Greene's lost source ('Bacon') by [B].

Although M may well be an abridgment (the last page of text refers to the 'full history at large',[202]) it is certainly not an abridgment of F. It omits the lengthy extract from the Bacon translation of 1597, and there are no direct quotations

The Most Famous
HISTORY
OF THE
Learned Fryer Bacon:
SHEWING
His Parentage and Birth. How he came to be a Scholar and to study Art-Magick; with the many wonderful Things he did in his Life-time, to the Amazement of the whole World; in making a *Brazen Head*, to have Walled all *England* with Brass: With his Penitent Death,
ALSO,
The Merry Waggeries of his Man *MILES*: And the Exploits of *VANDERMASTER*, a *German*, and *Fryer BUNGY*, an *English* Conjurer. With the manner of their woful Deaths, as a Warning to others.

Being all very profitable and pleasant to the Reader.

London: Printed by *Tho. Norris*, at the Sign of the *Looking-glass* on *London-Bridge*; And Sold by *M. Deacon* at the *Horse shoe* in *Giltspur-Street*.

4 Photograph of the title page of *The Most Famous History of the Learned Fryer Bacon*

from the EFB or *Doctor Faustus*; in fact, apart from a clear dependence on the EFB, it appears to be free of any material derivable from sources published post 1590. The language is more incisive and the songs are shorter. While these are characteristics to be expected for an abridgment of F, others are not. Thus, not only is there great disparity in detail, but M frequently includes more and, in particular, supplies motifs used by Greene which are notably absent in F. And although it could be argued that these derive from Greene, their context is different to that in the 'Honourable History' (*Hon. Hist.*) and they are integral to the development of the tale. If M is representative of Greene's source, then Greene's relocation of these motifs is wholly consistent with his treatment of sources. Additional support for regarding M as representative of a late sixteenth-century source derives from its inclusion (foreign to F) of passages clearly echoed in *The Tempest* (1610–11); indeed, as will become apparent, much of Prospero's magic is Baconic magic.

These points require considerable amplification but here I wish to indicate the direction of my argument. It is thus: that M is a representative text (or an abridgment of one) for a late sixteenth-century romance, current, either in MS or print, in 1590, on which Greene based his play of Friar Bacon and Shakespeare drew for the magic of *The Tempest*; further, that the Grove publication, F, is an expanded rewrite of this romance, in which, apart from inclusions from published sources, most of the names and much incidental detail have been changed, probably to avoid a copyright dispute such as that between Orwin and Jeffes. In addition, M uniquely transmits an allusion topical to the late sixteenth century, referring to an incident which can be dated precisely in March 1589/90 (see below, p. 62 et seq.), providing a close *terminus ab quo* both for this version of the romance and Greene's play. The correspondences of plot and incident between M and the EFB demonstrate that the romance was written in direct imitation of the latter, contrasting a national magician using 'good' magic for the benefit of his country with a wicked German magician, a parallel for Faustus, whose evil magic destroys him. Such an imitation must have been motivated by the known popularity of the EFB and hence, publication of the latter must have preceded 1590. This leaves no case for rejecting the theory that the early English Faustus notices derive from a printed edition, which I conclude to have been extant prior to February 1589.

As an important representative source both for Greene's play and *The Tempest*, the 'Most Famous History' warrants re-publication and careful critical attention. My excursions here must of necessity be brief, but within the limitations of available space, I shall now attempt to provide sufficient of the salient features to substantiate my argument.

The following précis, in note form, of the 'Most Famous History' (M), indicating significant variants in F, will provide a basis for discussion. For ease of reference, the material has been presented as nineteen numbered episodes, keeping to the sequence in M, to which the signature references apply. Details, etc., exclusive to M are printed in italics.

(1) (sig. A2r-A2v) (M: c. I; F: c. [1][203])
Birth of Roger Bacon in *Lancashire* (F: West of England), son of *Ralph* (F: unnamed, 'a wealthy farmer'); early indications of great intellect; schooling; parental opposition to further education; B. escapes to a monastery, becomes an *Augustinian* Friar; is sent to study at Oxford where he becomes a great and famous *proficient.*

(2) (sig. A2v) (M: ibid.; F: c. [2])
B.'s fame reaches King Edward III (F: unnamed; *Hon. Hist.*: Henry III) while on progress in Oxfordshire, holding court *4 miles from Oxford*; B. is sent for; the arrogant messenger, *a Gentleman of the Bed-chamber, Knight*, gives B. the lie; B.'s promise to the messenger, mentioning *Sir William Belton's place*; the messenger's return to court delayed *by a magic mist.*

(3) (sig. A3r) (M: ibid.; F: ibid.)
B. arrives at court and performs magic before the king and queen, designed to please each of the five senses (sources for *The Tempest*, echoes of EFB)

(4) (sig. A3r-A3v) (M: ibid.; F: ibid.)
The messenger returns, *scratched with bushes and briars* (F: quagmires, etc.); he attempts to avenge himself on B. (*sword in scabbard motif*, see below, p. 61), who publicly shames him with the *cook-maid, brought by a spirit at the window* (*shoulder of mutton motif*, cf. *Hon. Hist., Dr F*); the messenger warned; B. returns to *Brazen Nose College* (F: Oxford).

(5) (sig. A3r-A4r) (M: c. II; F: c. [3])
B.'s manservant, Miles, *'a merry droll and full of waggeries'*, pretends to keep Good Friday fast but secretly attempts to eat a black-pudding which sticks to his mouth. B. parades him before scholars and fastens him by the pudding to *the bar of the college gate* (F: a window) *with a set of verses on his back; a 4-hour penance.*

(6) (sig. A4r-B1r) (M: ibid.; F: c. [4])
A prodigal gent is saved from destitution by an old man (the devil) on condition he signs a contract *in blood* (echoes of EFB); the devil comes for him but is out-witted by B.; *the gent reforms and leaves his wealth to Brazen Nose College*

(7) (sig. B1v-B3r) (M: c. III; F: c. [5])
Introduces Friar Bungy, B.'s pupil and fellow magician; together they frame a brazen head which will enable them to wall all England with brass (*verbal parallels with Hon. Hist.*); they conjure a spirit to help them (*structural parallels with EFB*) and are instructed to watch the head for *two months* (cf. *Hon. Hist.*; F: one month); finally exhausted from lack of sleep, they set Miles to watch; when the head speaks, he fails to wake them and their labours are lost. *Miles fouls his breeches; better, funnier dialogue than in* F; B. charms Miles dumb for *two months* (F: one month).

(8) (sig. B3v-B4r) (M: c. IV; F: c. [6])
B. aids the king to capture a French town by means of a burning glass. *B. travels there by cloak-flight, echoing EFB*; (F includes the lengthy extract from the 1597 Bacon publication.)

(9) (sig. B4r-B4v) (M: ibid.; F. c. [7])
The French ambassador brings Vandermaster (F: Vandermast), a German magician, to the English court; V. performs a 'trial of art', raising Pompey the Great (*echoes of EFB*). B. raises Julius Caesar to vanquish Pompey. V. challenges B. to a magic duel, but B. passes the challenge to Bungy who raises the Hesperian Tree with Golden Apples, guarded by a dragon. V. raises Hercules, *clad in his lion skin* (cf. *Hon. Hist.*) to pick the apples, but B. intervenes, forcing Hercules to carry V. back to Germany. *The king makes a nationalistic comment.*

(10) (sig. B4v-C1r) (M: c. V; F: c. [8])
B. determines the inheritance of three brothers.[204]

(11) (sig. C1r-C2r) (M: ibid.; F: c. [9])
Three thieves attempt to rob B. in his study; he gives them each a bag of money which they are unable to put down; playing on an enchanted pipe, Miles leads them, dancing *to Sellengers Rounds* and beating each other with the bags, through '*quagmires, bogs and briars*' (cf. *Dr F*, B-text); when they finally drop in sleep, Miles recovers B.'s money *and takes the thieves' own money to spend with his hostess.*

(12) (sig. C2r-C2v) (M: ibid.; F: c. [10])
Vandermaster sends a villain (F: a Walloon soldier) to kill B., who, by his prescience, expects him; *when the villain draws his sword to strike, B. charms him motionless* (cf. *The Tempest*) and interrogates him; the villain does not believe in hell ('*a bugbear*', *etc.*, cf. *Dr F*), but B. raises *Julius Caesar* (F: Julian) the Apostate, *in a burning chair* (cf. *Dr F*, B-text), causing the villain to repent and join crusade to the Holy Land where he is slain.

(13) (sig. C2v-C3r) (M: c. [VI];[205] F: c. [11])
B. tricks a usurer, *Scrapegood* (F: Good-gatherer) out of £100 by 'blinding' him with a *pot of cockle-shells* (F: iron pot) which the usurer sees as gold pieces. B. distributes his gains amongst the poor scholars; when the charm dissolves, the usurer goes angrily to B. demanding restitution, but B. *laughs at him* (parallels with EFB).

(14) (sig. C3r-C3v) (M: ibid.; F: c. [12])
This tale, in which Miles pretends to conjure for food and drink, is adapted from a known source.[206] Named characters: *Goodman Delver* (F: unnamed), *Cutbeard the barber* (F: Goodman Stump the tooth-drawer); Miles' 'spirit': unnamed in M; F: Bemo.

(15) (sig. C3v) (M: ibid.; F: c. [15])
Miles steals one of B.'s conjuring books, takes it to the top of the house and reads some charms; the devil appears in a frightful shape, and, spitting fire, chases Miles over the leads; he falls, breaks his leg; B. dismisses the spirit, chastises Miles and sends for a surgeon (parallels with *Dr F*).

(16) (sig. C3v-C4r) (M: c. VII; F: c. [13])
This tale, extensively mined by Greene, shows parallels with EFB c. 50 [2542 etc.]: an Oxfordshire gent. successfully courts a young lady (unnamed in M; F: Millisant) but before they are married, her covetous father withdraws his consent at the suit of a rich knight whom the lady does not love. The knight hires Bungy to convey himself, the lady and her father to a chapel where Bungy will marry them. Meanwhile the disappointed suitor visits B. who, in his magic glass, sees the marriage already in progress at the chapel. B. and the suitor travel there by enchanted *gown* (F: chair; cf. EFB), B. strikes Bungy dumb, raises an opaque mist, rescues the maid and conveys the lovers to a distant chapel where he marries them. (F adds an extended description of the wedding feast, with unimaginative borrowings from EFB.)

(17) (sig. C4v) (M: ibid.; F: c. [14])
Vandermaster comes to England to seek revenge on B. through Bungy by challenging the latter to a magic duel. (F incorporates extra tit-for-tat incidents, partly borrowed from EFB, as a prelude to the duel.) They raise so many warring spirits that the magicians' circles are invaded and both men are *torn in a thousand pieces* (F: strangely burned by fire).

(18) (ibid) (M: ibid.; F: c. [16])
Two young gents ask B. to show them their fathers in his magic glass. They see them quarrelling *at a game of bowls*, then quarrel themselves and stab each other to death (cf. *Hon. Hist.*); at this, B. smashes his glass.

(19) (ibid) (M: ibid.; F: c. [17])
Soon after this, learning of the deaths of Bungy and Vandermaster, B. calls the scholars and declares he has long practised magic; he burns his books (cf. Prospero) and becomes an anchorite, digging his own grave with his nails, and dying a true penitent two years later. (F mentions B.'s remorseful meditations, paralleling Faustus' lamentations in EFB.)

This précis affords sufficient indications that M cannot be regarded as an abridgment of F, and more will surface in the quotations illustrating the discussion.

To consider first the sources for Greene's play absent from F, these are 'Brazen Nose College' (episodes 4, 6; *Hon. Hist.*: passim, e.g. scene ii), Hercules' lion-skin attribute (episode 9; *Hon. Hist.*: scene ix, s. d. l. 93) and a number of important motifs in episode 4 relating to the quarrel between Bacon and the royal messenger initiated in episode 2. There, having told the messenger that he would attend the court, Bacon 'bid him make great haste, or he should be there before him'. The messenger 'laughed, being well-mounted, saying scholars and travellers might lie by authority'. In answer Bacon promises not only to be at court before him 'but I will there show you the *cook-maid you lay with last, though now she is busy about dressing the dinner at Sir William Belton's, a hundred miles distant from this place*' (F: last wench that you lay withal). '"I doubt not but one will prove as true as the other"' replies the laughing messenger and gallops off, only to get lost in a magic mist. He eventually arrives at court (episode 4) 'all bemired and dirty, *his face and hands scratched with bushes and briars*' at the conclusion of Bacon's magic show. When the king questions him he curses 'Bacon and all his devils' and, in M only, continues: '"... *but here the dog is, and I'll be revenged on him"; whereupon he laid his hand on his sword, but Bacon waving his wand, charmed it in his scabbard that he could not draw it.*' Cautioning the messenger to be peaceful, Bacon explains the matter to the king. '"*Whilst he was speaking, in came the cook-wench, brought by a spirit at the window, with a spit and a roasted shoulder of mutton on it, being thus surprised as she was just taking it up*". *Spying her lover, she reminds him of his promise to provide her with linen, etc., "for our stolen pleasures has swelled, and I have but two months to reckon". He avoids her attempted embrace and she is carried out at another window to her master's house.*' (In F, Bacon 'pulled up the hangings, and behind them stood a kitchen-maid with a basting-ladle in her hand'; she does not speak and vanishes after Bacon has warned the messenger not to contemplate revenge.)

In Greene's play, the incident of the cook-maid is transferred to Bacon's cell at Brasenose (*Hon. Hist.* scene ii) and the character shamed is Burden. The stage direction at ii. 119 reads: 'Enter Hostess with a shoulder of mutton on a spit, and a devil.' Miles immediately refers to her as 'cook' (ii. 123) and at ii. 127, she claims to be 'Hostess at Henley, mistress of the Bell', though there is no suggestion that she is pregnant. Burden contents himself with 'A plague of all conjuring friars' (ii. 142); he is after all, an academic, not a courtier and swordplay would be out of character. But Greene does not waste the 'sword in the scabbard' motif, transferring it to scene v in which Prince Edward and his friends, in disguise, are mocked by Miles. The prince attempts to draw his sword: 'I strive in vain; but if my sword be shut / And conjur'd fast by magic in my sheath...' (v. 61f) He strikes Miles a box on the ear and Miles requests Bacon to 'conjure his hands too, that he may not lift his arms to his head' (v. 64f), which is precisely what Bacon does to the villain in M (episode 12), again absent from F. So here are three Bacon motifs used by Greene, supplied exclusively by M and in contexts which are quite evidently the original ones. It is wholly implausible that M is borrowing from Greene here.

Additional parallels between M and *Hon. Hist.* are to be found in episode 7 (the brazen head). In *Hon. Hist.*, Bacon tells Miles 'Bungay and I have watched these threescore days' (xi, 23), corresponding to M's 'two months' (Greene could have scanned his line equally well with 'thirty days'). The preceding line: 'And *girt* fair England with a wall of brass', perhaps echoes the source, transmitted, in M only, as 'all the *sea-girt* shores of England...'. While on this point, it is worth reflecting how the 'wall of brass' venture became associated with Friar Bacon, or, indeed, why the framing of the brazen head was an essential prelude to the undertaking. The brazen head is part of the folk myth of Friar Bacon (also attributed to Albertus Magnus, and allied to the automata of Virgilius,[207]) but the idea for the 'wall of brass' derives from the story of Merlin and is included in Spenser's *Faerie Queene*, Book III,[208] published 1590 and not available in England before late-1589.[209] It is, of course, just at this time that a wall of brass might have been considered a very desirable protection against an expected second Spanish enterprise. Perhaps, then, this feature was not part of the traditional myth of Bacon but injected from Spenser when the romance was written, a conjecture consistent with the dating I shall propose. (Spenser also exploits Merlin's 'magic glass', which has properties identical with Bacon's.) [210]

The obscure reference to Sir William Belton (episode 2), apparently echoed by Greene's 'Bell at Henley', is of much importance. There are no defensible identifications for a Sir William Belton from the late seventeenth or early eighteenth centuries, but a very secure one topical to 1590, namely Sir William Fleetwood (Fletewode), Recorder of the City of London, bibliophile and frequenter of St Paul's churchyard, a man noted for his eloquence and mighty voice (*bel tone*).[211] His life-history shows some remarkable coincidences with that of 'Friar Bacon', as reported in M: born in Lancashire, educated at Brasenose College, and resident during the period of his Recordership, at Bacon House,

No 24.

51

Right honorable and my singuler good lo: after yor lordships
speache used unto me in Fleetestreate, and the Readers was
assigned I repaired into the Arches, where with much adoe
I entred into two shoppes where one Robte Sweper butcher
killeth & selleth fleshe both muttons, veales, and lambes,
greate store. he doth it by vertue of a licence given
him, under the right honorable my verie good lord
the Earle of Essex his hande the which warrant if it be
well noted extendeth not soe farr as he therby is
to make any provision for my lo: owne mouthe but onlie
for his lo: householde. The which licence I doe send
unto yor lo: here inclosed, & some of the greatest Inholders
of the Shere have refused to assist me in this
service. after that they sawe such great mens hande
at their licences, May it please yor good lo: the said
Sweper at this tyme doth fayne himselfe ffrantick
and so kepeth his bedd his wief being honest he
doth cast her of he kepeth a harlott & placeth the
ruffyne in her place where he cometh he hath
a brother of much like condicion & dwelleth in
westm libertie, who (as I am enformed) is the
purveyor of sheepe, lambes, and calves that are
killed by vertue of this warrant but I cannot mete
with him as yet. I have sent two stubborne fellowes
to prison whom the said Sweper hath entertayned
for this lent tyme to be his slaughter men.
And thus beseching yor lo: to assist me in this
service I doe most humblie take my leave from
Bacon house the xxth of Marche 1589

Yor lo: most humblie bounden

W. Fleetewoode

5 Facsimile of Fleetwood's letter to Burghley, Lansdowne MS 62(24). fol. 51

Foster Lane![212] But what makes the identification secure is an affair in March 1590.

In 1589 and 1590 the Privy Council became particularly worried about transgressions of the Lenten Fast. This nationwide mortification was urged both in grateful response to the 'God-given' victory over the Armada, and as an observance calculated to avert a second attempted invasion and/or the plague, which was due (the motivation for *A Looking Glass for London*).[213] Accordingly, the Privy Council issued 'Orders for the restraint of the eating of Flesh in Lent', entered SCR 8 February 1588/9 and again on 22 February 1589/90.[214] Lord Burleigh seems to have been particularly concerned about the matter and spoke to Fleetwood about it, as appears from a letter of Fleetwood to Burghley dated '20th March 1589', [i.e. 1590] (see Plate 5):

Right honorable and my singular good lo: after yor lordships speache vsed vnto me in fflete streate ... I repaired in to the duchie, where wth much a doe I entered into two shoppes where one Robte Sweper butcher killeth & selleth fleshe both muttons, veales and lambes, greate store. he doth it by vertue of a Lycence given him, vnder the right honorable my verie good lord the Earle of Essex his hande the wch warraunt if it be well noted extendeth not soe farr as he thereby is to make any p[ro]vision for my lo: owne mouthe but onlie for his lo: howsholde. The wch licence I doe send vnto yor lo: here inclosed; some of the greatest Justices of the Sheire haue refused to assist me in this service after that they sawe such greate mens hande at theire licences, maie it please yor good lo: the said Sweper at this tyme doth fayne himselffe ffraunticke and so kepeth his bedd... he hath a brother ... who (as I am enformed) is the purveyor of sheepes, lambes, and Calves that are killed by virtue of this warraunt but I cannot mete wth him as yet. I haue sent two stubborne fellowes to prison whom the said Sweper hath entertayned for this lent tyme to be his slaughtermen... Bacon howse the xxth of Marche 1589 Yo^{r} lo: most humblie bownden W. Fletewarde.[215]

The Privy Council were swift to act. On 22 March they wrote to the Master of the Rolls and the Master of St Katharine's and the Recorder of London

requiring them by vertue thereof to call forthwith before them the butchers named in the enclosed scedule, and not onlie to see by what lycence they did pretende to kill and utter fleshe, but in her Majestie's name to commaund them to forbeare hereafter during the tyme of Lent to kill and utter any fleshe, unles thei were permytted to do the same by the cheefe officer of the libertie or liberties where thei did dwell; and after they had receaved that commaundement from them, yf they sould continewe still to utter or kill anie fleshe during Lent, they should cause the fleshe they had in their shoppes or howses to be taken from them and given to the poore prysoners, and lykewyse to cause them to be comytted to pryson, there to remaine untill theire Lordships shuld giue order for theire enlargement.[216]

There can be little doubt that the case made a stir: Fleetwood's 'with much a doe' implies some sort of affray, he sent 'two stubborne fellowes' to prison, and the Earl of Essex was scandalously involved. The allusion in M plays upon this incident: 'Sir William Belton's' place was Newgate prison, whither, by the ruling of the Privy Council, the confiscated meat was to be conveyed. Thus [B], the 1590 prototype of M, was in part a topical lampoon directed at Fleetwood, and, by implication, the Earl of Essex. Fleetwood was well known to the London Stationers, but not only as a bibliophile: he had been directly concerned with the formulation of the Statute regulating the printing and publication of books,[217] and was active in attempts to suppress the London theatres, both adequate grounds for an attack from the injured parties. He is likely to have seen [B], and would not have missed the allusion; he was scarcely a man to trifle with. In Grove's 1627 edition (F) the oblique references to Fleetwood and, possibly, Essex (the 'Gentleman of the Bed-chamber') are expunged, even to the removal of the 'shoulder of mutton'. Greene appears to have played safe by changing 'Sir William Belton's' to 'the Bell at Henley'.

The association of [B] with a time of sensitivity towards fasting in Lent is further underlined by the inclusion of episode 5 in which Miles, who 'loved his guts too much to pinch them' (M), breaks the Good Friday fast, surely no part of a folk legend. [B], then, is to be regarded as a novel fabrication, composed soon after March 1590, in which folk traditions of Friar Bacon are combined with elements of Merlinic magic derived from Spenser, incident (e.g. episode 5) reflecting topical concerns, and some borrowed tales (episodes 10, 14) to pad out the history. Considered as a source for Greene's play, the suggested composition date for [B] does not trespass upon the *terminus ad quem* for the play. The latter is known to have been performed on 19 February 1591/2 but in Henslowe's 'Diary' it is not marked 'ne'.[218] It is generally accepted that 'Faire Em' imitates the opening of Greene's 'Friar Bacon' and must therefore post-date it, and Greene makes sneering allusions to two passages in 'Faire Em' in an 'Epistle to the Gentlemen Students of both Universities'. This Epistle is prefixed to Greene's 'Farewell to Folly' in the earliest extant edition of 1591, and although this tract was registered 11 June 1587, the epistle cannot have been written then, since it contains allusions to 'Greene's Mourning Garment' (registered 1 July 1590 and first printed that year), and to the published 'Tamburlaine' (1590); so the Epistle may be dated 1590–1, antedated by both 'Faire Em' and 'Friar Bacon'.

Arguments in favour of 1589 as the year of composition of the play are found, upon inspection, to be specious. Fleay[219] considers the text line: (i, 136): 'Lacy, thou know'st next Friday is Saint James' (i.e. 25 July) and observes that this date fell on a Friday in 1578, 1589, and 1595: 'I have repeatedly shown that in such cases dramatic authors used the almanac for the current year, and not one instance has yet been adduced to the contrary.' This leads him to accept 1589 as the date of composition, the other two dates being out of the question. I submit that this is no firm ground for argument; why should Greene have bothered with such nicety for a play set in the reign of Henry III? and even if he did, he might, in 1590, have used the previous year's almanac and proved an exception to Fleay's rule. Fleay's other argument is based upon the form of Greene's motto appended to the end of the play: *Omne tulit punctum qui miscuit utile dulci*. 'This form of motto was only used by Greene until he issued his *Menaphon*, which was entered S. R. 23 August 1589; and then the shorter form *Omne tulit punctum* appears for the first time.' This argument is equally unconvincing since the evidence derives from a printed text, published after Greene's death (the *Historye of fryer BACON and ffryer BOUNGAY* is registered 14 May 1594, but the earliest extant edition is 1599); presumably the form of the motto, however it appeared in MS, was at the discretion of the publisher. Thus neither this argument, nor that based on St James' Day, carries much weight in comparison with those adduced for dating the source, and a summer 1590 composition-date is preferred.

The retention in M of all detail necessary to Greene's source suggests that M is closely representative of [B].[220] However, since M itself long post-dates the EFB, any argument that [B] is modelled on the latter must be based exclusively on structural and material (i.e. non-verbal) similarities between the romances. This proves to be no great constraint.

Setting aside the obvious disparity in content between the EFB and M, and the more serious theme of the former, the two stories have a great deal in common. In each, a gifted child of peasant stock shows great aptitude for learning, attains to excellence and becomes resident at a famous university (Oxford/Wittenberg). Both protagonists apply themselves to the study of magic, possess books of spells and become famous adepts; both keep a man/boy (Miles/Wagner) described as a wag. The central section of both histories is a series of episodes in which the magicians demonstrate their prowess at Royal courts (of Edward III/Charles V) and elsewhere, and both Faustus and Bacon defeat a rival magician (E: 2419 etc.; M: ep. 9). Each of them aids a pair of lovers (E: 2542 etc.; M: ep. 16), each is befriended by scholars whom they help and entertain, each is the object of attempted revenge by an enemy, each redresses injuries received and thwarts his enemies (E: 1942, 2446; M: eps. 4,12), each tricks a money-lender (Usurer/Jew). Both magicians are brought to lamentation, both give an oration to scholars and renounce their wicked lives (Bacon burns his books), both die, Bacon by natural causes, Faustus killed by the devil.

All the magicians in the two books utilize demonic magic and have many feats in common: Bacon and Faustus each raise a mist (E: 1640; M: eps. 2,16), strike people dumb (E: 2117; M: eps. 7,16) and paralyse them (E: 1618f; M: ep. 12), fly (and convey others) on a cloak, command music, food and drink, and dancers; each is adept at 'blinding' i.e. making a person see an object as other than it is (the Usurer's gold (M: ep. 13)/ the enchanted castle (E: 2170–2200). All the magicians raise dead (mostly classical) personages.[221] Both histories involve the conjuration of a demonic spirit (M: ep. 7) and a pact written in blood (M: ep. 6); both involve the destruction of a magician (Vandermaster, Bungy (M: ep. 17)/ Faustus) by demonic spirits.

The magic motifs exclusive to one or the other histories are very few: Bacon exhibits a limited prescience that derives from the romance of Merlin, whereas Faustus has to receive all his information from Mephostophiles. Bacon also makes much use of the power of magic attachment (also from 'Merlin': the sword in the stone) – the courtier's sword is fixed in its scabbard, Miles' pudding sticks in his mouth and subsequently the other end is charmed to the college gate, the thieves' money-bags are charmed to their hands. But Faustus arrests the Turkish emperor in his seat [1618f], fixes horns to the knights' heads and causes birds to cleave to a stick [2295]. In addition, Bacon possesses the all-important magic glass for seeing distant events (as does Merlin in 'The Faerie Queene', 1590); in the EFB, Faustus does not have one.[222] Powers exclusive to Faustus are the ability to transform himself (to a dragon, to Mahomet) and become invisible, also to raise himself up in the air. Faustus can also send flames of fire about a chamber [1616f] (Bacon produces fire with a burning glass (M: ep. 8), Vandermaster uses a dragon (M: ep. 17)) and produces thunder [1379]. Unlike Faustus, Bacon never makes a pact, bilateral or other, and he retains absolute control over the demonic spirits, to the extent that he can 'adopt' Vandermaster's Hercules and subjugate him to his will. At the same time this precludes him acquiring the nature of a spirit, a prime condition of Faustus' pact, conferring unique abilities.

The broad similarities outlined above suggest that the EFB provided a model for the romance of Friar Bacon. (Since the EFB is a translation from the German and 'Friar Bacon' appears not to have influenced the German Faust tradition, a reverse borrowing is out of the the question.) There are several explicit parallels which render this hypothesis virtually beyond doubt.

In the receptions accorded to Bacon and Faustus by their respective monarchs (Edward III, Charles V) the ruler has, in each case, learned of the fame of the magician, and, with great respect, asks for a demonstration of his art: 'then said the king, Worthy Bacon, having heard much of your fame, the cause of my sending for you, was to be a spectator of some fine curiosities in your art. The friar humbly excused at first: but the king pressing it, promising on his royal word, that no harm should come to him...' (M, sig. A3r, orthography modernized). Charles V's welcoming speech to Faustus [1848–53] is a close parallel and includes the promise of protection: 'I vow unto thee by the honour of mine imperial crown, none evil shall happen unto thee for so doing' [1852f]. Both promises of protection derive ultimately from Saul's promise to the witch of Endor[223] but whereas the promise to Faustus is expedient considering the period of the setting, the parallel promise to Bacon is an anachronism: he performs his magic openly and without any censure, and when ultimately he rejects it and burns his book it is not because he considers magic as intrinsically evil, but because he regards it as a vanity which has distracted him from his true vocation as a servant of God. It was not through fear of retribution that 'the friar humbly excused at first'. Like Faustus, Bacon requests silence before his performance begins, although Faustus is more insistent, stressing the danger of any utterance. Both magicians receive rewards, but pious Bacon will not accept money – only jewels.

In the subsequent displays of magic, M tellingly avoids the raising of a classical personage, which would have rendered the 'take-off' too transparent, and instead provides a sophisticated entertainment on a par with Faustus' feat before the Duke of Anholt [2165 etc.]. The Faustian motif of raising the spirit of a hero is reserved for the later display by the German Vandermaster: 'The King desiring to see Pompey the Great, Vandermaster raised him in Roman arms, so that he stalked majestically about the room as if he dared any one to the combat: when Bacon secretly raised the ghost of Julius Caesar, armed at all points in like manner' (M: sig. B4r). In Faustus' show, Alexander enters 'in all things to look upon as if he had been alive' and 'he had on a complete harness burnished and graven, exceeding rich to look upon' [1883–7]. The demeanour of Vandermaster's Pompey invites comparison with that of Helena, raised by Faustus for the students: 'she looked round about her with a rolling hawk's eye, a smiling and wanton countenance...' [2370f].

Just as in the EFB the command performance is immediately followed by the shaming (with horns) of a knight, so in M, there follows the shaming of the messenger (also a knight) by the appearance of the cook-maid; both mockeries have sexual implications, explicit in the latter case. In M, the messenger's attempted revenge is immediate and short-lived, whereas in the EFB there are two widely-spaced attempts, supplying an extended revenge motif, transferred in M to Vandermaster's plots against Bacon (episodes 12 and 17). One admirable feature of the 'Friar Bacon' remodelling of the shamed courtier incident is its presentation of a cause for the magician's antagonism, namely that the courtier had given him the lie (episode 2). Similar cause is given for Faustus' action in *Doctor Faustus* (A1084f, 1095), where, as in M, the knight is warned to 'speak well of' scholars in future (A1129, B1360f). (The relationship between [B] and *Doctor*

Faustus is difficult to interpret owing to uncertainties as to the date and authorship of individual portions of the received texts, and lack of space precludes further discussion here of this interesting aspect; the parallels are listed in Appendix 4a.)

Further parallels occur in the respective conjurations of the demonic spirits (EFB: cc. 2,3; M: eps. 7,17). When Vandermaster and Bungy conjure in episode 17: 'They made their circles, and Vandermaster raised a dragon, which running round Bungy's circle, threw . . . fire on him' (M sig. C4v), cf. the 'fiery man' of the EFB [117], which 'ran about the circle a great while'. More convincing is the parallel between the respective dialogues of Faustus and of Bacon (episode 7), with the spirit which has appeared. Thus, in M, Bacon and Bungy 'conjured up a spirit to enquire of the Infernal Council, whether it [the making of the brazen head] might be done, or not. The spirit however was unwilling to answer, till Bacon threatened with his charms to bind him in chains in the Red-Sea [etc.]. Terrified by this means, he said, of himself, he could not give them a positive answer, but must enquire of his Lord Lucifer. They hereupon granted him two days for an answer. . . '(sig. B1v). In the EFB the 'grey friar' [118] initially refuses Faustus' request that he appear the next morning at his house, and has to be brought to obedience by invoking the name of Beelzebub. When the spirit duly returns [127], Faustus makes his demands: 'Hereupon the spirit answered and laid his case forth, that he had no such power of himself until he had first given his prince. . . to understand thereof, and to know if he could obtain so much of his Lord [Lucifer]' [136–9]. He does not take two days as in M but returns the same evening; however, the notion that it takes a number of days for the infernal bureaucracy to work turns up later in the Faust book (c. 13) when Mephostophiles needs Ministerial permission to answer one of Faustus' questions: 'his spirit required him of three days' respite, which Faustus granted.' [480f] Thus 'Friar Bacon' parallels the Faust book in (i) the insubordination of the spirit, (ii) its subjugation by the magician, (iii) its claim that the request exceeds its mandate, (iv) Lucifer as Lord, (v) two or three days' respite for permissions.

The pact written in blood offers another parallel. Although Bacon does not himself make a pact with the devil, he comes to the aid of a distressed gentleman who does so (M: episode 4). The devil helps his potential victim to write the contract: 'O, said he, let me see, I'll prick your right vein: which he did, whilst the gentleman found an unusual trembling, and inward remorse in his mind: when, however, taking the bloody pen in his hand, he desperately subscribed, and sealed the writing' (M sig. A4v). Both of Faustus' pacts (EFB cc. 5,6; c. 49) are written in blood and it is one of the hindrances to his salvation at the last hour [2908f]. The gory details are given in c. 5: 'he took a small penknife and pricked a vein in his left hand, and for certainty thereupon were seen on his hand these words written, as if they had been written with blood: *O homo fuge*; whereat the spirit vanished, but Faustus continued in his damnable mind, and made his writing... [236–40]. Thus the detail of the parallel extends to (i) pricking the vein, (ii) a warning (inward remorse, amplified in Marlowe by the staying of the blood) and (iii) the 'desperate subscription'.

The 'crossed lovers' tale of M episode 16 is present, in germ, in the EFB (c. 50), beginning: 'In the City of Wittenberg was a student, a gallant gentleman, named N. N. This gentleman was far in love with a gentlewoman, fair and proper of personage. This gentlewoman had a knight that was a suitor unto her, and many other gentlemen, the which desired her in marriage...' [2543–6]. The continuation of the story is quite different from that in 'Friar Bacon', except that Faustus, like Bacon, aids the gentleman to marry his beloved, and the knight is thwarted. The similar beginning ('A gentleman in Oxfordshire being greatly enamoured of a young gentlewoman' (M: sig. C4r)), the 'rich knight', the young man's despair and his succour by the magician, are parallels too close to be ignored.

Finally there are the parallel 'orations to the students'. Friar Bacon's is tersely put: 'soon after hearing of the miserable ends of Vandermaster and Bungy, he called the scholars together, declaring he had a long time practised magic, burnt his books before them, to hinder others from doing it, shut himself up in a cell ... advising the scholars to study Holy things, and not mind the vanity of the world' (M: sig. C4v). In the more prolix EFB (c. 63), Faustus begins his oration: 'Forasmuch as you have known me this many years, in what manner of life I have lived, practising all manner of conjurations and wicked exercises, the which I have obtained through the help of the devil...' [2830–2] and exhorts them to 'let this my lamentable end to the residue of your lives be a sufficient warning, that you have God always before your eyes...' [2855–7]. Faustus does not burn his books (he has already bequeathed them to Wagner (EFB c. 57)) but Marlowe's Faustus offers to do so in his final monologue.

This exhausts the explicit parallels between the two books. Taken together, in conjunction with the common theme and shape of the two stories, they provide ample justification for concluding that the 'Most Famous History' not only uses the EFB as a model but borrows heavily in both motif and detail.[224] What remains as novel in 'Friar Bacon' is the use of three magicians (but cf. Marlowe), and the character of Miles. The latter is so distant from the EFB's Wagner as to be scarcely recognizable. Yet Wagner is his starting point, as must have been clear to the author of 'Miles Wagner'.[225] (Miles is a close relative of Robin in *Doctor Faustus*). Of the three magicians of 'Friar Bacon', none of them is truly Faustus, and only Bacon is adequately drawn. His chief characteristic is his sense of rectitude, though the morality of his deception of the usurer is questionable and his motivation for walling England with brass is to acquire everlasting fame. Neither Faustus nor Bacon can brook a rival magician to best him (cf. EFB, c. 47). This professional jealousy is seen at its most intense in Vandermaster, the much vaunted German magician, who repeatedly seeks to be revenged on Bacon for besting him before the king and ambassador. The unholiness of his magic (and, of course, Faustus') is demonstrated by the fearful tumult that is unleashed in the magic duel with Bungy (episode 17) and, like Faustus, both Vandermaster and Bungy are killed: 'the spirits growing too strong for these conjurers and their charms, broke into their circles, and tore them in a thousand pieces, scattering their limbs about the fields' (M: sig. C4v) cf. Faustus' end [2925–32]. Clearly Vandermaster[226] is representative of Faustus as the German magician, set up as an Aunt Sally for Bacon, the superior English magician, to overthrow. The nationalism is apparent in the king's comment in M (episode 9): '"Now Sir, you plainly see my Englishman has outdone your German of whom you boasted so much"' (M: sig. B4v). The motive is only intelligible in terms of an already popular and well-read English Faust book: the besting of Vandermaster is the besting of the Faust book by 'Friar Bacon'. English (or rather, British, since much of it is Merlinic) magic, although a vanity, is not as wicked as German magic and it is put to virtuous purposes such as the righting of wrongs and the defence of the realm (Bacon aids his king as Merlin aids Arthur, by advising him in battle). But even English magic results in evil and the virtuous Bacon abjures it to spend the rest of his life in penance, an ending that commended itself to Prospero, Bacon's literary heir: 'Now I want / Spirits to enforce, art to enchant; / And my ending is despair, / Unless I be relieved by prayer,...' (*The Tempest*, epilogue 13–16. Close parallels between M and *The Tempest* are collated in Appendix 4b.)

To sum up, the clear dependence of 'Friar Bacon' on the EFB shows that it was written in direct imitation of the latter with the intention of exploiting an assured demand. This implies that the EFB was well known and eagerly read before March 1590 so that the limiting dates for publication of the EFB are September 1587 to March 1590, or, to be realistic, 1588–9. This finding, coupled with the bibliographic evidence, enhances Kocher's view, supported by the early English Faust notices, and leaves no occasion for their cavalier dismissal. The following chronology of publication and performance dates, in which speculative items are prefaced by a query, is consistent with all the evidence (all dates are 'old style' but with year beginning 1 January):

1587 Sept	publication of GFB
1588 June	Paul Fairfax practising in London

1588 Oct	Marprelate's 'Epistle' in circulation
?1588 (late)	publication of EFB
1589 Feb 28	Ballad of Doctor Faustus entered
?1589	'Doctor Faustus' written and produced
1589 Nov 5	Harvey's 'Advertisement for Pap-Hatchet'
1589 Dec 1	Spenser's 'Faerie Queene' entered
1590	'Faerie Queene' published; 'Robin Goodfellow' current
1590 Mar 20	'shoulder of mutton' incident
?1590	'Friar Bacon' written and (?) published.
?1590	Greene's *Hon. Hist.* written, produced
1592 Feb 19	Greene's play performed by Strange's men (not 'ne')
1592	plague year, actors touring
1592 ?May	S or O edition of the EFB
1592 Dec 18	Stationers' Court ruling re Jeffes/Orwin
1593 May 30	death of Marlowe
1594 Sept 30	'doctor Fostose' given at the Rose by the Admiral's men and remained in repertoire until Jan 1597
1601 Jan 7	'plaie of Doctor Faustus' entered to Thos. Busshell
1602 Nov 22	payment to Birde & Rowley for 'adicyones in doctor fostes'
1602	revival of 'Doctor Faustus' at the Fortune
1604	earliest surviving edn of A-text (Tho. Busshell) other editions: 1609, 1611
1611 Oct 31	*The Tempest* performed
1616	earliest surviving edn of B-text (John Wright) other editions: 1619, –20, –24, –28, –31
1624 Jan 12	'legend of Frier Bacon' entered to F. Grove

Notes

The reader is referred to the list of abbreviations on pp. xiiff.

1 British Library: C. 27b. 43; *STC* 10711. A detailed bibliography of EFB early editions is provided in Appendix 1. The Orwin edition is available as a facsimile reprint: The English Experience No. 173, Amsterdam and New York (Da Capo Press, Theatrum Orbis Terrarum Ltd) 1969. First modern reprinting: Logeman (1900). The text is also given in Palmer & More, but neither this nor that of Logeman's edition is error-free. Other reprintings: *The Damnable Life*... Neudruck der Ausgabe London 1592, mit einem Nachwort von Renate Noll-Wiemann, Hildesheim, Zurich (Olms) 1985; and in D'Agostini (1978). A modern spelling edition was edited by William Rose, London (Routledge) [1925] (Broadway Translations). The edition printed in Thoms is based upon the Brown/Hotham edition of 1704–7, deriving ultimately, via intermediate

editions, from the edition of 1610. Extensive extracts from the EFB have also appeared in numerous editions of *Dr F* e.g. *The Complete Works of Christopher Marlowe*, ed. Roma Gill, II. *Doctor Faustus*, Oxford (Clarendon Press) 1990. Appendix A.

2 See below, pp. 29–34.

3 The only rival candidate is the Danish translation (1588), Henning, *Bib.*, No. 1052.

4 *Historia von D. Johañ Fausten dem weitbeschreyten Zauberer vnd Schwartzkünstler... Gedruckt zu Franckfurt am Mayn durch Johann Spies. M. D. LXXXVII.* (ed. princeps) (G). Amongst the numerous reprintings (cf. Henning: *Bib.* Part I), the most useful are Henning: *Historia*, and more recently, the 'Kritische Ausgabe' edited by S. Füssel and H. J. Kreutzer, Stuttgart (Reclam) 1988, which provides extensive extracts from source materials, and supersedes Petsch.

5 I.e. descriptive topography, see Agrippa, p. 38: 'Chorographie, the which severally searching out certain particular places doth depaint them with a more perfect and as it were a full finished similitude.'

6 Certainly the translator thought so, cf. [1180f].

7 A collection (original plus English translation) is published in Palmer & More; see also Alexander Tille: *Die Faustsplitter in der Literatur des sechzehnten bis achtzehnten Jahrhunderts nach den ältesten Quellen*, Weimar 1900. For bibliography of works on the historical Faust, see Henning: *Bib.*, I, pp. 87–105. For comprehensive studies see Hans Henning: 'Faust als historische Gestalt', *Jahrbuch der Goethe-Gesellschaft*, NF 21 (1959), pp. 107–39; Ernst Beutler: 'Georg Faust aus Helmstadt', *Goethe-Kalendar auf das Jahr 1936*, Leipzig 1936, pp. 170–210; and particularly Frank Baron: *Doctor Faustus: From History to Legend*, München (Fink) 1978 (Humanistische Bibliothek, Reihe I: Abhandlungen, Bd. 37,); *Faustus: Geschichte, Sage, Dichtung*, München (Winckler) 1982; but despite new evidence (see F. Baron: 'Who was the historical Faustus?', *Daphnis*, 18 [2] (1989), pp. 297–302), Baron's identification of the historical Faust with Georg Helmstetter, though probably correct, remains insecure.

8 Agrippa, Paracelsus and Trithemius were all blackened but their reputations were rescued by their surviving works. Reliable testimony to any of Faust's writings is confined to his 'calling card', quoted by Trithemius in a letter of 1507 (Città del Vaticano, Cod. Pal. lat. 730, fol. 174^{v}) published in his *Epistolarum familiarum libri duo*, Hagenau 1536, pp. 312–14. cf. Baron 1978 (apud n. 7 above), pp. 23–39. The several books of magic falsely attributed to Faust (e.g. '*Doctoris Johannis Fausti magiae naturalis et innaturalis. Erster Theil. Der Dreyfacher Höllenzwang genannt*, Passau, Anno 1505') are seventeenth-century pseudepigraphic works with spurious dates, see Butler, *Rit.* pp. 154–211.

9 The first main collection to be published was that edited by J. Aurifaber (*Tischreden oder Colloquia Doct. Martin Luther...* Eisleben 1566), expanded in numerous subsequent editions. Other important collections are included in the critical Weimar edition, see abbreviations: *Tisch.*

10 *Tisch.* Vol. 3, No. 3601, cf. Palmer & More, p. 93; the phrase occurs in a conversation recorded by A. Lauterbach in 1537.

11 Cf. Frank Baron: 'Which Faust died in Staufen? History and Legend in the *Zimmerische Chronik*', *German Studies Review*, 6 (1983), pp. 185–94.

12 Johannes Gast: *Tomus secundus convivalium sermonum* (Basel 1548), pp. 280f.

13 The words are reported by J. Manlius, a Wittenberg alumnus, in his *Locorum communium collectanea*, Basel (Oporinus) 1562, pp. 42–4 (cf. Palmer & More, pp. 101–3) and their attribution to Melanchthon is thus somewhat insecure. Nevertheless the ascription is supported by Lercheimer, who also attended Melanchthon's lectures, and it would have been generally accepted.

14 Cf. Henning, *Historia* pp. xxv–xxvii; Petsch, p. 214.

15 E.g. W. Bütner: *Epitome historiarum* (Weimar 1576); Andreas Hondorff: *Promptuarium exemplorum* (1568 etc.). Many of Hondorff's tales related of unnamed magicians were subsequently accreted to Faustus.

16 For *Teufelliteratur* see Keith L. Roos: *The Devil in 16th Century Literature: The Teufelbücher*, Bern & Frankfurt (Lang) 1972. The *Theatrum Diabolorum* was compiled by Sigmund Feyerabend and first published at Frankfurt a.M. in 1569 (2nd edn: 1575; 3rd edn (2 vols.): 1587, 1588). *Theatrum de Veneficis*: Frankfurt a.M., 1586. L. Milichius' *Der Zauberteufel* (Frankfurt a.M., 1563) was later included in the *Theatrum Diabolorum*.

17 Johann Weyer (Wier, Wierus), b. Grave 1515, d. 1588, became personal physician to Duke Wilhelm II of Julich-Cleve-Berg. His principal work, *De praestigiis daemonum... libri V* (1st edn: Basel 1563), had enormous impact; there are six Latin editions to 1583, each revised and expanded. The German translation by Füglin was included in the *Theatrum de Veneficis*, 1586, and is available as a facsimile (Darmstadt 1969). The only complete English translation is modern: Johann Weyer: *Witches, Devils and Doctors in the Renaissance: De praestigiis daemonum*, transl. John Shee. Binghampton, N. Y. (Medieval and Renaissance Texts & Studies) 1992.

18 Augustin Lercheimer von Steinfeld is the pseudonym of Hermann Witekind (Wilken), 1522–1603. Following studies at Frankfurt a. d. Oder and Wittenberg (1548 under Melanchthon) he became professor of Greek and mathematics at Heidelberg, with a period of exile (as a Philippist) at Neustadt-on-the-Hardt (1580–3) when, or soon after, he wrote his most important work against the witch craze: *Christlich bedencken und erinnerung von Zauberey* ('Christian Commentary on Magic') (1st edn: Heidelberg 1585, reprinted in Scheible: *Das Kloster*, Vol. V (Stuttgart 1847), pp. 263ff). The expanded third edition (Speyer 1597), containing his criticism of the GFB, is reprinted in Carl Binz: *Augustin Lercheimer und seine Schrift wider der Hexenwahn...*, Strassburg 1888. see also Frank Baron: 'The Faust Book's indebtedness to Augustin Lercheimer and Wittenberg sources', *Daphnis*, 14 (1985), pp. 517–45, and recently Frank Baron in *Faustus on Trial. The origins of Johann Spies's 'Historia' in an age of witch hunting*, Tübingen (Niemeyer) 1992 (Frühe Neuzeit, Bd. 9).

19 For a concise account of the grimoires, see Butler, *Rit.*, pp. 47–89.

20 For Cyprian and Theophilus, see Butler, *Magus*, pp. 87–94, and Palmer & More, pp. 41–58, 58–77. For the student absolved from his pact by Luther, see Widman, Part II, pp. 6–8, and *Tisch.*, Vol. 3, No. 3739.

21 For a concise account of Spies' career, see Friedrich Zarncke: 'Johann Spieß, der Herausgeber des Faust-buches und sein Verlag', reprinted in Zarncke's *Goetheschriften*, Leipzig 1897, pp. 272–309. A more elaborate consideration is provided by Frank Baron in *Faustus on Trial* (see n. 18 above).

22 G: sig.)?(ii^{a}ff. (Henning, *Historia*, p. 3).

23 Spies' dedication is dated 4 September 1587. For the Faust book at the Frankfurt fair see George Willer: *Collectio... omnium librorum... quid in nundinis Francofurtensibus ab anno 1564 usque ad nundinas Autumnales anni 1592...*, Francofurti, Ex Typographica Nicolai Bassei, MDXCII, part 2, p. 302, listing the Spies Faust book (1587, autumn), a 1591 recension (spring), and the rhymed Faust book (1588, spring) under *Teutsche Historische Bücher*.

24 See abbreviations: W. The earliest printing is edited by Gustav Milchsack who discovered the MS: 'Historia D. Johannis Fausti des Zauberers Nach der Wolfenbüttler Handschrift; nebst dem Nachweis eines Teils ihrer Quellen' in G. Milchsack: *Überlieferungen zur Litteratur, Geschichte und Kunst*. II, Wolfenbüttel 1892; see also D'Agostini.

25 Haile (see abbreviations: W), p. 15, reports on the immaculate condition of the MS, its pages still (1961) thickly dusted with blotting sand, suggesting that it had scarcely been read, probably because it had been superseded by the printed edition.

26 Cf. n. 18.

27 For hermetism & Bruno, see Yates; for Dee, see Dee, French, and Charlotte Fell Smith: *John Dee: 1527–1608*, London 1909; see also Frances A. Yates: *The Occult Philosophy in the Elizabethan Age*, London, Boston & Henley (Routledge & Kegan Paul) 1979.

28 Dee in Leipzig 1586 etc., see French, p. 121.

29 Yates, pp. 306f.

30 See Barbara Könnecker: 'Faust-Konzeption und Teufelspakt im Volksbuch von 1587' in *Festschrift Gottfried Weber*, Bad Homburg v.d.H., 1967, pp. 159–213.

31 As reported in the 'Clementine Recognitions'; these, in the Latin translation by Rufinus of Aquileia (d. 410AD) (published editions at Basel 1526, 1536) were the most popular and available of the (? third century) pseudo-Clementine writings in the sixteenth century. Of the remainder, the 'Clementine Homilies' circulated in MS only, the *Epitome de gestis Sancto Petrae* was published (Latin) at Paris in 1555. Both the 'Recognitions' and the 'Homilies' are available in English translation in the Ante-Nicene Christian Library: Vol. III: 'Recognitions', translated by B. P. Pratten, M. Dodds, T. Smith (1867); Vol. XVII: 'Homilies', translated by T. Smith, P. Peterson, Dr Donaldson (Edinburgh 1870). In the 'Recognitions', Simon's foremost disciple and lover is 'Luna' and he asserts that she 'has been brought down from the higher heavens and that she is Wisdom, the mother of all things, for whom ... the Greeks and barbarians contending, were able in some measure to see an image of her' (Book II, c. xii), but in the 'Homilies' (Book II, c. xxv) she is named Helena.

32 Yates, pp. 311f.

33 For genesis of the GFB, see Petsch, pp. xxiiiff, Milchsack (see n. 24 above), Henning *Historia*, pp. xxviii–xl, and Robert Petsch: 'Die Entstehung des Volksbuchs vom Doktor Faust', *Germanisch-Romanisch Monatsschrift*, 3 (1911), pp. 207–24.

34 G: 25, 226: cf. commentary to E: 285f, 2940f.

35 E: 2714–16; G: 204.

36 See abbreviations: Widman.

37 Widman: part I, pp. 39, 59; Mephostophiles' first entry: part I, p. 77.

38 Widman: part I, p. 78.

39 Widman: part I, pp. 106f.
40 Widman: part III, p. 55.
41 See E: 668–70; G: 58 and commentary thereto. Mephostophiles clearly distinguishes between 'we spirits' and the 'devils in hell'.
42 G: c. 15, cf E: 520ff.
43 G: 46f, E: 552–6, but there is no attempt at justification in *Dr F*, cf. B1986–92, where Mephostophilis rejoices that he has deliberately side-tracked Faustus when he was 'i'the way to heaven'.
44 G: c. 65. For a full translation see Appendix 2; see also intro., p. 17.
45 G: 211f.
46 See Henning, *Historia*, pp. 1f.
47 See Henning, *Bib.* , Nos. 1010–29, 1031.
48 *Ein warhaffte vnd erschröckliche Geschicht: Von D. Johann Fausten...* Anno M.D.LXXXVII. [colophon:] Getruckt zu Tübingen bey Alexander Hock im Jahr M.D.LXXXVIII., available as a facsimile: *Der Tübinger Reim-Faust von 1587/88*, hrsg.... von Günther Mahal, Kircheim/Teck (Schweier) 1977; the notices of punishment are cited in Mahal's 'Nachwort', pp. 14f.
49 G: sig.)?(iij[a].
50 I.e. *Christlich bedencken...*, Speyer 1597 (see n. 18 above); see also Henning, *Historia*, pp. lii. f.
51 *Ander theil D. Johann Fausti Historien...* in Druck verfertiget durch F. S. [Fridericus Schotus Tolet], 1593, reprinted (ed. Josef Fritz) Halle 1910.
52 Reprinted with commentary by Hans Henning in *Studien zur Goethezeit*, Weimar 1968, pp. 143–64.
53 *Das ärgerliche Leben... des... D. J. Fausti... aufs neue übersehen und... vermehret durch J. N. Pfitzerum...* Nürnberg 1674. This work contains the germ for Marguerite in Goethe's *Faust*, Part I.
54 *Das Durch die gantze Welt beruffenen Ertz-Schwartz-Künstlers und Zauberers Doctor Johann Fausts, Mit dem Teufel auffgerichtetes Bündnüß*. Frankfurt & Leipzig, 1725. Cf. facsimile edition (ed. Günther Mahal): *Das Faustbuch des Christlich Meynenden von 1725*, Knittlingen 1983.
55 Cf. Konrad Bittner: *Beiträge zur Geschichte des Volksschauspiels vom Doctor Faust*, Hildesheim 1973 (Präger Deutsche Studien, Bd. 27).
56 For a concise account with ample bibliography, see Roy Pascal: *German Literature in the Sixteenth and Seventeenth Centuries*. (Introduction to German Literature, Vol. II), London (Cresset Press) 1968, pp. 65–8, 164.
57 See Henning, *Bib.*, pp. 127–43.
58 See Appendix 1 for a detailed bibliography.
59 Cf. SCR entry of 9 November 1633: assignment of copyright (Francis Grove to Richard Cotes) of 'the history of Doctor Ffaustus in verse'. The work is extant as the *History of Doctor John Faustus, Compiled in Verse*, London, printed by E. Cotes to be sold by Charles Tyns, 1664.
60 Leba M. Goldstein: 'An account of the Faustus Ballad', *The Library*, 5th ser., 16 (1961), pp. 176–89.
61 *The Second Report of Doctor John Faustus, containing his appearances and the deedes of*

Wagner. . ., printed by Abel Jeffes for C. Burby, 1594. Two distinct editions appeared the same year. see A. E. Richards: *Studies in English Faust Literature. I. The English Wagner Book of 1594*, Berlin 1907 (*Literarhistorische Forschungen*, hrsg. v. J. Schick & D. M. Frh. v. Waldberg, Heft 35, Berlin 1907). See also H. Jantz: 'An Elizabethan Statement on the Origin of the German Faust Book', *JEGP*, 51 (1952), pp. 137–53.

62 See Henning, *Bib*. pp. 114–27.

63 See commentary to E: 85, 162–6, 221f, 269, etc.

64 See commentary to E: 258f.

65 D'Agostini (p. 34, n. 18) lists some thirty instances of the EFB text corresponding more closely with W than with the *Historia*, but none may be unequivocally interpreted as showing dependency.

66 See commentary to E: 465f.

67 Such an edition, if it existed, is likely to have been a MS-based piracy, rather than a Spies printing.

68 Figures in square brackets refer to the line register of the present text.

69 Empson, p. 70: 'one might take the nuts to show the careless gaiety of P. F., but they may also hint at some form of torture'.

70 The question of censorship of the EFB is treated in a stimulating and characteristically controversial study by William Empson (see Empson, pp. 80–97) but regrettably his objectivity was blunted by his desire to sanctify Marlowe and he lacked evidence which I have since accumulated; certainly there is nothing to suggest that any possibly censored material offered the least hint that Faustus could escape damnation, other than by repentance.

71 The doggerel verses are absent from W and, like Spies' asides, may have been absent from PF's source. see intro., p. 12.

72 The material of this chapter clearly derives from a source different from that of the earlier chapters; the GFB author has made no attempt to reconcile these disparate sources by keeping Lucifer as Faustus' prince, but PF does so.

73 Empson (p. 71) is amusing here: 'As P. F. adds to the tortures, one might perhaps argue that he is a sadist, but he contrives to take a healthy tone. Even the muck-forks are a kind of sport; all modes of playing catch require skill, and no doubt this one gives the devils a healthy pleasure. Perhaps they were hoping for a game when they brought their muck-forks to the party, as other characters might have brought their tennis racquets.'

74 Logeman, p. 175.

75 See *The Marprelate Tracts 1588, 1589*, ed. William Pierce, London (Clarke) 1911, and William Pierce: *An Historical Introduction to the Marprelate Tracts*, London (Constable) 1908.

76 Rohde, p. 13; he couples the omission with an earlier exclusion of the devil's scorning Faustus during his first attempted conjuration (see commentary to [85]), but the passage omitted is a Spies interpolation (absent from W) and it may not have been present in PF's source (cf. intro. p. 12).

77 Rohde, pp. 10–12.

78 Rohde may have been influenced by his suspicion that PF was himself a 'speculator', cf. Rohde p. 47.

79 Empson, pp. 81–4.
80 See Butler, *Magus*, p. 132.
81 Butler, *Rit.*, pp. 81ff.
82 A work popular from the late fifteenth century, with many sixteenth-century editions, e.g. *M. Elucidarius Von allerhandt geschöpfen Gottes*..., Augsburg 1540, etc.; Frankfurt edns of 1572, 1575.
83 Perhaps supplying: 'Nor can they raise the winde, or rend the cloudes' *Dr F* A89 (absent from B).
84 The 'Clementine Recognitions' (see n. 31 above), Book II, c. ix.
85 See the diary entry under 1588: 'This yeare I began to practise negromancy and call aungells and spirits' – *A selection from the Papers of Dr Simon Forman*, London (Camden Society) 1843, p. 19.
86 See Johnson 1946, p. 243n for a list of these.
87 See Johnson 1945, p. 43: concerning the *coelum empyreum* 'all writers insist that its derivation from the Greek word for "fire" does not imply that the empyrean is hot and flaming, but merely that it possesses incomparable brightness and splendor'.
88 Empson, pp. 77f. I cannot believe that the confusion in this passage is the result of censorship.
89 Johnson 1946, pp. 242f.
90 Hartmann Schedel: 'Weltchronik', i.e. *[Liber Cronicarum]. Register Des buchs der Croniken vnd geschichten... von [H. Schedel] in latein... versammelt vnnd durch Georgium alten [Georg Alt]... in diss teutsch gebracht*, Nürnberg 1493; lengthy extracts of passages relevant to Faustus' tour are printed in Petsch, pp. 169–85.
91 For a catalogue of geographical works, see E. G. R. Taylor: *Tudor Geography 1485–1583*, London 1933, pp. 163–90; *Late Tudor and Early Stuart Geography 1583–1650*, London 1934, pp. 192–223.
92 *Sortae Virgilianae* were popular even in classical times, but by the Middle Ages the poet had become confused with the legendary magician Virgilius; see J. W. Spergo: *Virgil the Necromancer*, Cambridge, Mass. 1934.
93 However, there are no P. F.s in the census provided by Christina H. Garrett in *The Marian Exiles*, Cambridge University Press 1938.
94 Logeman, p. xiii.
95 Logeman, pp. x. ff, 145ff.
96 See abbreviations: *COT*.
97 *A Briefe Collection and compendious extract of strãge and memorable thinges, gathered out of the Cosmography of Sebastian Munster*..., London 1572; cf. commentary to [1713–15].
98 Rohde, pp. 3–9.
99 See commentary to [1693].
100 Notably Sir Henry Wotton (travelled 1589–92), who disguised himself as a swaggering German (see L. Pearsall Smith: *The Life and Letters of Sir Henry Wotton*, (2 vols). Oxford (Clarendon Press) 1907). Another famous dissembler was Anthony Munday, see Munday: *The English Roman Life [1582]*, ed. Philip J. Ayres, Oxford (Clarendon Press) 1980.
101 See commentary to [1321].
102 See commentary to [1546f] and [1582–5].

103 *Polski Słownik Biograficzny*, XI (1964–5) pp. 284f: under Jordan, Spytek Wawrzynce. I am indebted to Prof. Jan Pirozyński of the Biblioteka Jagiellońska, Krakow, and to Dr Władysław Stępniak of the Archiwum Głowne Akt Dawynych, Warsaw, for this identification.
104 I am grateful to Dr Stepniak (see n. 103 above) for investigating these details.
105 The hypothesis that the GFB was brought to England by actors returning from Europe (A.v.d. Velde: *Marlowes Faust*, Bunzlau 1870, p. 23) is invalidated by the finding that the sole acting company (William Kempe's) then touring in Germany returned home before publication of the GFB: cf. Herz: *Englische Schauspieler und englisches Schauspiel zur Zeit Shakespeares in Deutschland*, Dissertation, Bonn 1901). see Rohde, p. 15 n. 1.
106 Rohde, pp. 14–16.
107 See Dee, p. 21: Dee left Mortlake for Gravesend on 21 September 1583.
108 During this trip he made the acquaintance of the hermetist, Dr Hannibal Roselli; see Yates p. 188, French p. 120.
109 2 December, 1589, see Dee, p. 32.
110 The initials in this edition have been reported as 'P.K.' (Ashton: *Chapbooks of the Eighteenth Century*, 1882, p. 28). This is incorrect: the 'K' is, in fact, a very worn 'R'.
111 Neil Brough ('Doctor Faustus and "P.F."', *Notes & Queries*, NS 32 (1955) pp. 15f) extrapolated from the insecurity of the second initial to suggest that the first might also be incorrect and draws attention to an R. F. Gent who translated Dedekind's *Grobianus* (from Latin), a work reprinted at Frankfurt in 1584 and 1586. But this identification is extremely unlikely. A more relevant consideration, perhaps, is that by 1633 (in *The Purple Island* (*STC* 11082)), the initials P. F. were the title-page cipher of the poet Phineas Fletcher (b. 1582).
112 Logeman, p. ix lists Patrick Forbes (1564–1635), Bishop of Aberdeen; Patrick Fitzmaurice, Lord Kerry (in prison 1587–91); Philip Ferdinand (1555?–98), a converted Polish Jew, resident in England and translator of works from Hebrew. Additionally, *STC* yields: Peter Fairlambe ('Recantation of a Brownist', 1606); Petrus Forestus ('Arraignment of urines'), a Dutch physician; Petrus Fradelius; and Petrus Frarinus, a Catholic writing in Latin. None of these are likely candidates.
113 Cf. n. 111 above. One unsolved pseudonym that deserves note is 'Philip Foulface' (a close opposite for Fairfax), 'author' of *Bacchus Bountie*, London 1593, a satire on drunkenness, reprinted in *Harleian Misc.* (1744), II, pp. 285–95.
114 'As for gentlemen, they be made good cheap in England. For whosoever can live idly and without manual labour and will bear the part, charge and countenance of a gentleman, he shall be called master... and shall be taken for a gentleman... and if need be a king of Heralds shall also give him for money arms newly made and mounted...', cited from Thomas Smith's *De Republica Anglorum* in Conyers Read: *Mr Secretary Walsingham*, Oxford 1925, I, p. 6.
115 London, Public Record Office, E157/1. The list only covers the period 1573–8.
116 The following lists exclude persons matriculating after 1587. The names are followed immediately by matriculation/admission dates (where known) in brackets. *Oxford* (*Register of the University of Oxford*, ed. Andrew Clark, Oxford 1889. Vol. I: 1449–1571; Vol. II: 1571–1622):

Paul French: MA 1544–5, fellow All Souls 1547, canon of Windsor 1560, Rector of Little Whitnam in Berks, d. 1600;
Philip Fairburne (Fayerborne) (1581), BA adm. June 1587, demy of Magd. Coll. 1585–9;
Philip Favour (1581), BA 1584/5, MA 1587;
Philip Firmin (Fyrmin) (1581), BA Nov. 1584, MA 1588; theological lecturer in London;
Paul Fitz-Herbert: sup. BA July 1581;
Paul Fitz-Randall: adm. BA Feb 1581/2, possibly the same person as the above;
Philip Forman: fl. 1558, as appellant in a suit v. the widow Forman
Peter French (from Cheshire) (1582 at age twenty-two);
Peter Frye (Frie) (1568/9), BA 1571/2, MA 1575/6
Philip Frye (from Devon) (1577, age sixteen); either he or another Philip Frye is witness in a suit, November 1581;
Cambridge (*University of Cambridge Book of Matriculations and Degrees 1544–1659*, compiled by John Venn & J. A. Venn, Cambridge University Press 1913):
Peregrine Fairfax: BA 1618/19; (unlikely)
Paul Farrar (1564/5);
Philip Fisher (1587), BA 1590/1, MA 1594; (unlikely)
Philologus Fourth (1559);
Peter Foster (1546), BA 1549/50; MA 1553;
Patrick Freborne (1572);
Peter Frenche (1578), BA 1581/2, MA 1585; cf. Peter French at Oxford University;
Peter Fretchwell (1587); (unlikely)
Peter Fuller (1575);
Philip Funston (1569);
Gray's Inn (J. Foster: *The Register of Admissions to Gray's Inn 1521–1889*... London 1889):
Peter Fabian (1527).
Paul Fleetwood of Rosall, Lancs. (1601) and Peter Frank, Gent. (1605), are unlikely candidates.
Middle Temple:
Paul Foxe, fl. 1580, son of William Foxe of London, deceased; (not listed in the register of admissions but mentioned in the Hustings Rolls 265 (64). Neither Lincoln's Inn nor the Inner Temple offer any likely candidates.

117 RCP Ann: translation II. p. 54 (MS: II. fol. 69a).

118 A recipe for 'aqua coelestis' appears in *Arcana Fairfaxiana / Manuscripta* [*c.* 1590], reproduced in traced facsimile, ed. George Weddell, Newcastle-on-Tyne 1890, p. 13. The 'heavenly water' is essentially a distillate of herbs and spices including cinnamon and cardamom.

119 RCB Ann: transcript II. pp. 55f (MS: II. fol. 70b–71a), spellings modernized.

120 All attempts to discover more about Paul Fairfax have proved fruitless. Records searched include: the City and University archives of Leipzig, the two Frankfurts, Würzburg, Cracow and Prague (I am indebted to those archivists and librarians mentioned in the Preface for conducting these searches); the indices of the Reports of the Historical Manuscripts Commission; the Calendars of State Papers (all series);

Acts of the Privy Council; Patent Rolls; Calendars of Assize Records for Kent, Surrey, Herts, Essex and Sussex; Calendar of Inquisitions post mortem, Eliz., James; Records of Chancery Proceedings. Paul Fairfax is not a known member of the illustrious Yorkshire Fairfax family (cf. L. Huntley: *The Fairfaxes of Denton & Nun Appleton*, 1906; R. E. Tickell: *The Tickell and Connected Families...*, London 1948; H. Aveling: *The Catholic Recusancy of the Yorkshire Fairfaxes*, 1955 in *Biographical Studies 1534–1829*, Vol. 3, No. 2 etc.), nor is he named amongst the Lincolnshire or London Fairfaxes, though the latter were armigerous and well represented in this period (see *The Visitation of London in the Year 1568* in *Publications of the Harleian Society*, Vol. 1, London 1868, p. 23; the genealogy given there includes twelve unnamed sons). The search through London parish registers has covered those published by the Harleian Society (*Registers*, Vols. 1–76), and additionally, as suggested by leads, the registers of: St Giles without Cripplegate; St Christopher le Stocks (publ. London 1882); St Magnus the Martyr; St Mary Colechurch; St Botolph, Bishopsgate; All Hallows, London Wall (priv. printed 1878); St Martin's, Ludgate; St Saviour's, Southwark; St Olave's, Tooley Street. Also searched: International Genealogical Index (Feb. 1988) (all counties in England); Boyd's Lists; *London Marriage Licences 1521–1869*, ed. Joseph Foster, London 1887; Allegations for marriage licences, London (Harleian Soc. Publications, Vols. 24, 25); Records of the Grocers' Company, Merchant Taylors' Company, Haberdashers' Company. A possible explanation for the non-appearance of Paul Fairfax in any of these records (although they are incomplete and the search has not been exhaustive) is that he was born abroad or before local parish records were kept (variously 1537, 1557), did not marry and died abroad.

Regarding the persons he claimed to have cured (see intro. p. 31), 'Mr Spagman' is probably Thomas Spagman, haberdasher, of St Martin's, Ludgate, born *c.* 1530, Freeman of the Haberdashers' by patrimony (6 March 1550/1), married Cicely Fellow, widow, by licence (5 Jan 1575/6); their only registered child is a daughter, Catherine (baptized 30 November 1578/9, buried 18 June 1591/2) (see Parish Registers of St Martin's, Ludgate; Haberdashers' Company, Register of Freedom Admissions, Guildhall Library MS 15,857). If this identification is correct, Catherine was nine years old when cured by Paul Fairfax, and lived another two and a half years.

No probable identification can be made for 'Mr Treen of Southwark' although the Treen family were well represented here in the late sixteenth century, three of them Southwark brewers, the most notable being Thomas Treen, brewer, entered in the registers of St Saviour's, Southwark, as father of six children baptized between Jan 1592/3 and June 1608; he is possibly the son of John Trin (Trene), baptized 19 April 1540.

121 All except 1648 edn from *STC*; 1648 edn, see *STC*(w).

122 According to Mr James Lawson, Librarian of Shrewsbury School, the fragment came to light during rebinding work early in this century and its provenance is unknown; it is not mentioned in an annotated shelf catalogue of the library made in the 1890s.

123 R. B. McKerrow: *Printers' and Publishers' Devices in England and Scotland 1485–1640*, London (Bibliographical Soc.) 1913.

124 Orwin's initial I occurs in at least four publications of 1591/2: *STC* 5590: Anthony Colynet: *The True History of the Ciuill Warres of France* (Thomas Orwin for Thomas Woodcock, 1591): sig. L1v; *STC* 11821: Charles Gibbon: *A Work Worth the Reading* (Thomas Orwin to be sold by Henry Kyrkham, 1591): sig. A2; *STC* 11340: Abraham Fraunce: *The Countess of Pembroke's Yuy church* (Thomas Orwin for William Ponsonby, 1591): sig. A2; *STC* 5457: Thomas Cockaine: *A Short Treatise of Hunting* (Thomas Orwin for Thomas Woodcocke, 1591): sig. A3.

125 The most telling comparison between O and '08 is afforded by the number of obvious typographical errors: thirty-three in the former and (on a minimal count) 143 in the latter (some pages are truly terrible).

126 None of Abel Jeffes' (see pp. 45ff) known extant printing involves the use of astrological symbols, and he is unlikely to have printed almanacs or ephemerides since these were a monopoly of Richard Watkins and James Roberts, granted by Letters Patent (see Bennet, p. 64.).

127 'Chap. 13' is given a whole line to itself, quite unnecessarily, and contrary to the practice adopted throughout the edition of setting the chapter number on the same line as the heading wherever possible.

128 It might be argued that since this was a major error occurring so close to the end of the book, the remaining text was reset, but sig. K2v occurs on the outer forme and would probably have been set while the inner forme (including the carefully set final page, sig. K3v) was being printed, so this supposition is most unlikely.

129 A good test is provided by sig. A3 (O, S, '08/10) which is an unindented page of text; O conforms to all but six of the line-breaks in S, and to '08/10 for about half the page. Again, the O and '08/10 line-breaks are identical at the top of O sig. L2v, following a whole page of unindented text.

130 Logeman, p. xv.

131 The following findings are reported in J. H. Jones: '"Invirond round with ayrie mountain tops": Marlowe's source for *Doctor Faustus*', *Notes & Queries*, 236 (NS 38) (1991), pp. 469f.

132 *COT* II, Pars 3, fol. 48. Latin editions including Pars 3 appeared in 1581 and 1588.

133 *COT* Pars I, fol. 36.

134 *The Diary of Philip Henslowe from 1591–1609*, ed. John Payne Collier, London (Shakespeare Soc.) 1845, pp. 42, 46.

135 Arber, III p. 63.

136 Greg & Boswell, p. 44, contractions expanded.

137 Greg, p. 3.

138 Arber, II p. 456.

139 Ibid. The copyright was assigned to Raffe Blore on 2 April 1599 (Arber, III p. 142).

140 *STC* 3351, no printer stated and no date.

141 See Bennett, p. 68f.

142 *STC* 11638: Gascoigne; *STC* 12403: Grove; *STC* 3182: Philocopo. The other works were Thomas Lupton's *Sivquila. Too Good to be True* (*STC* 16953) and George Turberville's translations from Boccacio: *Tragical Tales* (*STC* 24330).

143 *STC* 839 and 836.

144 H. Smith: *The Benefits of Contentation* (*STC* 22695), and *The Sacke of Roome* (*STC* 24569, 24569. 5), entered 2 November 1590 (Arber, II, p. 567).

145 Leonard Digges' *Pantometria* (*STC* 6859); *The Honorable Actions of ... Edward Glemham* (for William Barley) (*STC* 11921).
146 Arber, II, p. 176.
147 Lodge's *Rosalynd, Euphues golden Legacie* (*STC* 16665, previously printed by Orwin, 1590: *STC* 16664) and *Euphues Shadow, The Battaile of the Sences* (*STC* 16656), Nashe's *Pierce Pennilesse* (post 3 September 1592) (*STC* 18372–4), Henry Roberts' *Our Ladys Retorne to England* (*STC* 21087.3) and *A Defiance to Fortune* (*STC* 21078), Robert Greene's *Disputation betweene a He Coney-Catcher and a She Coney-Catcher* (*STC* 12234), and *The History of Quintus Curtius* (*STC* 6146).
148 See Bennett, p. 73.
149 Greg & Boswell, p. 42, with spellings modernized.
150 Register entry of 22 July 1592 (Arber, I, p. 560).
151 Arber, II, p. 618.
152 Ibid. p. 621: entries to Abel Jeffes on 6 October 1592: 'the first, third and ffourth partes of Gerillion' (cf. *STC* 17203; no Jeffes printings of this work are known), Chaucer's works (to be printed for the Company) and 'the Spanishe tragedie of Don Horatio and Bellmipela [sic]'.
153 W. W. Greg: '*The Spanish Tragedy* – a Leading Case', *The Library*, 4th Series, VI (1925–6), pp. 47–56. see also Kirschbaum.
154 W. W. Greg: 'Was the First Edition of *Pierce Pennilesse* a Piracy?', *The Library*, 5th Series, VII (1952), pp. 122–4. (The first edition of *Pierce Pennilesse* was imprinted by Richard Ihones.).
155 Arber, I, p. 561: 13/14 December 1592.
156 Greg & Boswell, p. 44.
157 *STC* 15089, entered to Jeffes 6 October 1592 (Arber, II, p. 621).
158 *STC* 733, entered to White 3 April 1592 (Arber, II, p. 607).
159 Greg & Boswell, p. 44, the spellings modernized.
160 White paid in May 1593, see Arber, II, p. 864.
161 The accounts for 15 July 1592 to 15 July 1593 include £3.10s received of Edward White and Abel Jeffes for confiscated books. Arber, I, p. 563.
162 Of course, it may not have been either, but any work which infringed Company regulations. On 12 October 1593, the register (Arber, I, p. 566) records that Abel Jeffes pawned 'three reams of Catechisms' to the Company; if he had printed these himself he had done so illicitly since the printing of catechisms was the monopoly of William Seres and John Day (Bennett, p. 65). The printer Roger Ward had been imprisoned in 1582 for precisely this offence, and by persevering in his piracies lost three successive presses by 1596 (Bennett, pp. 71–3). Thus Jeffes' punishment would not be out of the ordinary for such a transgression. (It is interesting that Jeffes was printing for Ward in 1589/90; see Arber, II, p. 525 and *STC* 22695, 24569.)
163 See abbreviations: Kirschbaum.
164 Kirschbaum suggests that White was acting honourably, on the assumption that Jeffes' printing career was at an end, but this is unlikely in view of the Court ruling; White's livelihood depended on popular sales and he would have been eager to have both books on his counter while demand was high.
165 1592–3: loan to Abel Jeffes of 10s on 200 copies of *Londons Complaynte* (*STC* 16756) (Arber, I, p. 562f), this pawn redeemed prior to July 1594 (ibid. p. 568); 12 October

1593: loan to Abel Jeffes of £2.7s (ibid., p. 566).

166 *STC* 5324: Giovanni Cipriano: *A most strange and wonderful prophesie*. . ., translated by Anthony Holloway, 1595. *STC* lists three editions and one other issue, all dated 1595.

167 Greg & Boswell, p. xx; Arber, II, p. 825.

168 Arber, III, p. 146.

169 Kirschbaum (p. 510) lists a number of similar instances where the 'amendments' were trivial. Restricting his discussion to editions of plays he concludes '"corrected and amended" almost always refers to changes made in the printing house at the time of the setting up of the new edition. Sometimes the author himself did the correcting.'

170 Cf. p. 12 and n. 62.

171 Cf. commentary to 1320; Palmer & More, p. 177, n. 70.

172 PF dated Faustus' 2nd pact '25th July' [E: 2523; no GFB equivalent], i.e. St James' Day. This is very probably the date on which he translated this material, so if he is to be identified as Paul Fairfax, he was working on his translation soon after his return to England.

173 Greg, p. 7.

174 Paul H. Kocher: 'The English *Faust Book* and the date of Marlowe's *Faustus*', *Modern Language Notes* 55 (1940), pp. 95–101.

175 Arber, II, p. 516.

176 Eyre, II, p. 496.

177 Greg, p. 6.

178 See Goldstein (see n. 60), p. 180.

179 First printed in *Pierces Supererogation Or a New Prayse of the Old Asse* . . . Gabriell Harvey. London, Imprinted by Iohn Wolfe 1593.

180 Greg, p. 5, n. 1.

181 Mar-Martin [pseudonym of John Lyly]: *Pappe with an Hatchet*. . ., s.l., s.d. [1589], sig. B3: 'And one we will coniure up. . .', etc., referring obliquely to Harvey.

182 Greg, p. 5, n. 1.

183 Paul H. Kocher: 'The Early Date for Marlowe's *Faustus*', *Modern Language Notes*, 58 (1943), pp. 539–62.

184 A. B. Grosart (ed.): *The Works of Gabriel Harvey* (The Huth Library), 1884–5, II. p. 209.

185 Virginia F. Stern: *Gabriel Harvey. His Life, Marginalia & Library*. Oxford (Clarendon Press) 1979, pp. 80–5.

186 As Greg (pp. 5f n. 1) is not slow to assert.

187 Hale Moore: 'Gabriel Harvey's References to Marlowe', *Studies in Philology*, 23 (1926), pp. 337–57.

188 'The Damnable Life' is only 80pp, and Holland's book does not run to p. 156. If the reference is to 'Drunken Dunstan', the latter is scarcely a 'pamphlet' (cf. Kocher, see n. 174).

189 All citations are from Ward.

190 I support the latter, see pp. 65f.

191 Arber, IV, p. 110.

192 *STC* 1183; printed by G. P[urslowe] for F. Grove, London 1627.

193 *STC* 1182. 7; [printed by M. Flesher & A. Mathewes for F. Grove; London].

194 *The History of Friar Bacon*, London (Wm. Pickering) 1828, in Thoms, vol. I. Page numbers for this 1828 edition may be converted to references to the 1858 edition by adding 188. Although Thoms states that his source text (*STC* 1184) was undated, in fact the imprint is trimmed, removing the date (1629).

195 See abbreviations: Ward.

196 Kerstin Assarsson-Rizzi: *Friar Bacon and Friar Bungay: A Structural and Thematic Analysis of Robert Greene's Play*, (Lund Studies in English No. 44) 1972.

197 Ibid., p. 25, quoting from Sir J. E. Sandys' essay, 'Roger Bacon in English Literature' in *Roger Bacon. Essays Contributed by Various Writers on the Occasion of the Commemoration of the Seventh Centenary of his Birth*, ed. A. G. Little, Oxford 1914, p. 365.

198 *The Mirror of Alchimy, Composed by the thrice-famous and learned Fryer, Roger Bachon,*... London, Printed for Richard Olive. 1597. The extract incorporated into 'The Famous History' is on pp. 64–7 (cf. Thoms, Vol. I, pp. 24–6).

199 E.g. 'Friar Bacon': 'The Deuill told him *he had not that power of himself*' (Thoms, Vol. I, p. 18); EFB: 'the Spirits answered and laid his case foorth, that *he had no such power of himselfe* [136f]; 'Friar Bacon': '[the king] requested him now to be *no niggard* of his knowledge (Thoms, Vol. I, p. 6); 'he being *no niggard of his cunning*, let them see his glasse' (ibid. p. 58); *Dr F*: 'to whom I must be *no niggard of my cunning*' (A1225; B1575).

200 Assarsson-Rizzi (see n. 196), p. 25.

201 British Library: 1077. g. 32; catalogued as a 'Shorter Version' and tentatively assigned to 1715. The book is a small quarto of three signatures (24pp.), printed on very poor paper, fine as tissue and crumbling with every touch. Fortunately several other copies (and one other edition) exist: [?1715]: printed by Tho. Norris and sold by M. Deacon, London (location: London University Library); *STC*(w) 2887 : for Thos. Norris, London [?1715] (locations: British Library (1077. G. 32), Bodleian (MAL 689(6), Harvard, etc.); London [?1715] (location: Harvard). Thomas Norris was active in London as a bookseller and bookbinder from 1695 to 1732 (deceased) but retired from business shortly after 1720. His London Bridge premises were previously occupied by Josiah Blare. See H. R. Plomer: *A Dictionary of the Booksellers and Printers who were at work in England, Scotland & Ireland from 1641 to 1667*, London (Bibliographical Society) 1907.

202 This may have been inserted by Norris in the belief that his publication was an abridgment, or it may have been transmitted from earlier lost editions. A true abridgment was issued in the mid-eighteenth century, of which there are two editions in the British Library: a London edition [1750?] and one published at Newcastle [1790?] which appears to be a reprinting of the former. These are in three chapters, being substantially the first three chapters of M.

203 In F the chapters are not numbered.

204 This tale is modelled on story 45 in the *Gesta Romanorum*..., Paris (Jehan Petit) 1506, fol. 38.

205 This chapter is not numbered.

206 'Freirs of Berwick' (attributed to Dunbar) in *Ancient Scotch Poems*, ed. Pinkerton, London 1786, pp. 65–85.

207 Cf. Thoms, Preface to *The History of Friar Bacon*.

208 Spenser: *Faerie Queene*, III.iii.10: 'A little while / Before that Merlin died, he did intend / A brazen Wall in compass to compile / About Cairmardin...'.

209 *The Faerie Queene. Disposed into twelue books, fashioning XII morall vertues.* [Books I–III]. Printed for W. Ponsonbie, 1590 (*STC* 23080, 23081 and 23081a). Spenser and Raleigh did not arrive in England with the MS until late October or early November 1589.

210 Spenser: *Faerie Queene*, III.ii.18: 'The great Magitian Merlin had deuiz'd, / By his deep science, and hell-dreaded might, / A looking glasse, right wondrously aguiz'd, / Whose vertues through the wyde world soon were solemniz'd. / [19] It vertue had, to show in perfect sight, / What ever thing was in the world contaynd, / Betwixt the lowest earth and heauens hight, / So that it to the looker appertayned;' (see also verse 21). Also noted by Otto Ritter: 'De Roberti Greene Fabula: *Friar Bacon & Friar Bungay*'. (Dissertation) 1866. See also Robert Recorde: *The Pathway to Knowledge...* (the dedication is dated January 1551/2): [sig. t. iiiv] 'Great talke there is of a glasse that [fryer Bacon] made in Oxforde, in which men myght see thynges that were doon in other places, and that was indeed to be done by power of euyll spirites. But I knowe the reason of it to bee good and naturall, and to be wrought by geometrie...'. As there is no record of the magic mirror in the older Merlin stories, Spenser presumably borrowed from this source. The mirror is then returned to Bacon in 'The Most Famous History'.

211 In 1589 he is eulogized in print by Thomas Newton in an addition to Leland's *Encomia*: Ad D. Guil. Fletuuodum, Rec. Londinensem.... Aequa iustitiam trutinas qui lance seueram, / Et Londiniginis iura Anglia rite recludis, / Fulminea pollens velut alter voce Pericles... see *Principium, Ac illustrium aliquot & eruditorum in Anglia virorum, Encomia...* a Joanne Lelando antiquario conscripta ... quibus etiam adiuncta sunt ... a Thoma Newtono ... London Apud Thomam Orwinium Typographum. 1589. p. 121.

212 See National Dictionary of Biography.

213 In *A Looking Glass for London*, Adam is taken to be hanged for concealing meat in his slops during the fast at Niniveh. Bishop Cooper of Winchester testifies to the seriousness of the English fasting in *An Admonition to the people of England*, an anti-Marprelate tract of 1588–9: '... what a lamentable thing is this, that even now, when the view of the navy of the Spaniard is scant out of sight; ... when the certain purpose of most cruel and most bloody conquest of this realm is confessed by themselves, and blazed before our eyes; when our sighs and groans, with our fasting and our prayers, in show of our repentance, are fresh in memory ...', quoted in Strype: *Annals of the Reformation*, Oxford (Clarendon) 1824, Vol. 3(ii), p. 157f.

214 Arber, v, p. 153, No. 3581: order of 8 February 1588/9; ibid. p. 157, No. 3664: order of 22 February 1589/90.

215 British Library, Lansdowne MS No 62(24).

216 *Acts of the Privy Council of England, New Series* ed J. R. Dasent, Norwich (HMSO) 1899. Vol. 18, p. 434f.

217 The Star Chamber Decree of 1586. see Cyprian Blagden: *The Stationers' Company. A History 1403–1959*, Stanford, Calif. (Stanford Univ. Press) 1977 (reissue of the 1960 edn), p. 72.

218 *Henslowe's Diary*, ed. R. A. Foakes & R. T. Rickert, Cambridge University Press 1961, p. 16: '[under 1591] Rd at fryer bacune th*e* 19 of febreary... satterdaye... xvij s iij d'. 'ne' does not necessarily mean 'new': ibid, p. xxx; see also W. Frazer: 'Henslowe's "ne"', *Notes & Queries*, NS 38 [1] (March 1991), pp. 34–5.

219 F. G. Fleay: 'On the Date of Friar Bacon & Friar Bungay' in Ward as appendix B, pp. cxxxivf.

220 This poses the problem of a lengthy transmission (well over a century) in which MSS or intervening editions are wholly lost to sight. There are no 'Friar Bacon' entries in SCR which cannot be assigned either to F or to a verse treatment published before 1633 (earliest extant edition *c.* 1680), probably the 'history of Fryer Bacon' entered to Henry Gosson on 23 March 1630/1. On the basis of the documented assignments, at least five editions of the verse treatment have failed to survive, and a similar mortality might be expected for the three-sheet 'Most Famous History', M, printed on bad paper and sold (*c.* 1710) for 3d (it is so listed in an advertisement of 'Books Printed for and sold by B. Deacon, at the Angel in Giltspur street, without Newgate' in B. Deacon's edition of *The Renowned History of the Seven Champions of Christendom* (sig. C4v); the Bodleian library copy of this book is bound together with 'The Most Famous History' (Douce R. 528)). Considering the condition of the extant copies of M, the wonder is that any have survived at all.

221 Bacon: Julius Caesar, Julius the Apostate; Vandermaster: Pompey, Hercules, Perseus, Hector; Bungy: St George, Achilles; Faustus: Alexander the Great and his consort, and Helen of Troy.

222 Although the magic mirror does not figure in the printed German Faust Book (nor in the EFB), it does occur in one episode peculiar to W (c. 62). Spies may have excluded the episode on grounds of obscenity, but it involves Faustus using a magic mirror to locate a friend, presumed dead, in a Cairo prison.

223 I Samuel 28: 10: As the Lord liveth, there shall no punishment happen to thee for this thing.

224 Cellini (*Friar Bacon, John of Bordeaux*, ed. Benvenuto Cellini, Florence 1952) had reached the same conclusion, though as it was in respect of the Grove 1627 *Famous History* (F), this was not seen to be significant for dating the EFB.

225 *The history of Friar Bacon: The Second Part: Miles Wagner*, printed for J. Blare, London [n. d.; *c.* 1690].

226 No earlier mentions of this magician are known to me. The name is presumably a contraction of (Johannes) Van der Maas; it may be significant that Weyer reports a tale of Faustus imprisoned at Batenberg on the Maas (see Palmer & More, p. 105–7, citing from *De praestigiis Daemonum*, 4th edn, 1568).

Note on the present text

The text

The text is based on the Orwin 1592 edition (*STC* 10711). This choice is directed both by the availability of the facsimile printing and the completeness of text relative to all later editions. In terms of its departures from the lost first edition, variant analysis shows that it is no more, and probably less, remote than 1608/10 editions, although in certain specifics the latter exclusively retain first edition readings. The two lacunae on sig. A2, indicated by square brackets, are filled from 1608/10. Page breaks in the basic text are indicated by square brackets, giving signature and original pagination, asterisked where this is erroneous. Catch-words have not been supplied, since in all except three instances, these are identical with the following word; the exceptions are: rea- [C3r]; Kalendar [D4r]; mad [H1v].

Style

The original is set in black letter, with Latin words and some names in roman, and some lines in italic type: the general title and chapter heading on sig. A2 and a section heading (lines 1833–5). The present text ignores these differences in type face, but Latin words are rendered in italic. (For the use of bold type, see below: The translation.) The extensive and somewhat arbitrary capitalization of nouns has also been discarded. All macrons and other typographic abbreviations have been silently expanded, but Saint has been abbreviated to St (S. or Sta. before Italian spellings). Faulty type and character inversions (u for n) are corrected without note unless warranted by ambiguity or significance. Ordinal numbers are rendered in the original by the use of a full stop, e.g. '22. year'; in the present text the endings of the ordinal adjectives have been supplied, e.g. '22nd year'.

Orthography

The spelling has been modernized, for the most part silently, but certain archaisms have been retained: fet (fetched), bad (bade), renowmed, astonied, angerly, rid, writ, flang; but 'murther' has been changed to 'murder'. 'Unpossible' and 'unsatiable' have been modernized but 'unmeasurable' (=beyond due measure) is retained. 'Hence' and 'farther' have frequently been replaced by 'thence' and 'further', usually with authority from 1608 etc. Geographical names are a special problem: I have chosen to replace archaic forms by modern equivalents (e.g. 'Livonia' for 'Lieflandt') where the meaning is not in doubt; all major changes (i.e. other than a vowel spelling or a final e) are included in the textual notes.

Reluctantly I have felt it necessary to amend the punctuation. Orwin's punctuation is both intense and haphazard. The colon is frequently used in the capacity of a period, without implying a strong connection between the antecedent and following phrases. In many cases this usage has been retained to avoid interrupting the flow of the prose. However, a very large number of commas have been removed. All apostrophes and quotation marks are mine, the latter often dispensing with brackets which occur in the original, e.g. '"Well," quoth the spirit,' for 'Well (quoth the spirit)'. Nevertheless, old-style genitives, e.g. 'Faustus his house' have been retained. Exclamation marks have been inserted following commands, and interrogation marks indicating indirect questions have been deleted. In addition, I have introduced more frequent paragraphs in an attempt to break up the wall of the text. The vast majority of these changes have been made silently, but all cases where the change has resolved a possible ambiguity are noted.

Collation of editions; emendations

The textual notes list all substantive variants from the editions of 1592, 1608, 1610 and the Shrewsbury fragment. It is clear from the persistence of variants and omissions, that the later seventeenth-century editions derive linearly from '1610', and none shows any reliance on 1592; a full collation of all these editions has therefore been considered unwarranted, but the notes include variant collation with '1618' and major variants from later editions. The notes also include all present emendations, though few lack any textual authority, and of these, only one (at line 1206) is radical.

The translation

Text printed in bold type indicates material departures of the English translation from the German original. To avoid a mottled text, such passages have generally been restricted to those longer than a line. They include both additions and original replacements, so the reader should not expect continuity of non-bold text. A full listing of P. F.'s departures from his source (including imaginative usages, literal renderings and probable mistranslations) is supplied in the Commentary, where translations of the German passages omitted are given. A translation of GFB c. 65, omitted in EFB, is supplied in Appendix 2. (All such translations are by the editor, unless otherwise stated.)

Critical apparatus (for Textual notes)

O:	1592 Orwin edition
S:	Shrewsbury fragment (sheet A only)
'08, '10, '18, etc.:	editions of 1608, 1610, 1618, etc.
O &c:	variant common to O, '08, '10, (and S where appropriate)
'08/10:	variant common to '08 and '10
'08 &c:	variant common to '08, '10 and '18
'18 &c:	variant found in '18 and later editions
T:	all texts, 1592 to 1618 inclusive (including S where relevant)
G:	German Faust Book; Spies ed. princeps pagination given in square brackets
[& var.]:	with minor variants

THE
HISTORIE
of the damnable
life, and deserued death of
Doctor Iohn Faustus,

Newly imprinted, and in conueni-
ent places imperfect matter amended:
according to the true Copie printed
at Franckfort, *and translated into*
English by P.F. *Gent.*

Seene and allowed.

Imprinted at London by Thomas Orwin, and are to be
solde by Edward White, dwelling at the little North
doore of Paules, at the signe of the Gun. 1592.

6 Facsimile of title page of the Orwin 1592 edition of the EFB

[A1r] THE

HISTORY

of the damnable

life, and deserved death of

Doctor John Faustus, 5

Newly imprinted, and in conveni-

ent places imperfect matter amended:

according to the true copy printed

at Frankfurt, *and translated into*

English by P. F. *Gent.* 10

Seen and allowed.

Imprinted at London by Thomas Orwin, and are to be
sold by Edward White, dwelling at the little North
door of Paul's, at the sign of the Gun. 1592.

[A2r(−)] A Discourse of the Most Famous Doctor John Faustus of Wittenberg in 15
Germany, Conjurer, and Necromancer: wherein is declared many strange things
that he himself hath seen and done in the earth and in the air, with his bringing up,
his travels, studies, and last end.

Of his Parentage and Birth. Chap. 1.

John Faustus, born in the town of Rhode, lying in the province of 20
Weimar in Germ[any,] his father a poor husbandman, and not [able] well

17 hath] O,S; had '08 &c
18 travels] '08/10; trauailes O, S, '18
20 lying] O,S; being '08 &c
21 Weimar] Weimer T

to bring him up: but having an uncle at Wittenberg, a rich man, and without issue, took this Faustus from his father and made him his heir, insomuch that his father was no more troubled with him, for he remained with his uncle at Wittenberg, where he was kept at the university in the same city to study divinity. But Faustus being of a naughty mind and otherwise addicted, applied not his studies, but took himself to other exercises: **the which his uncle oftentimes hearing, rebuked him for it, as Eli ofttimes rebuked his children for sinning against the Lord; even so this good man laboured to have Faustus apply his study of divinity that he might come to the knowledge of God and His laws.** But it is manifest that many virtuous parents have wicked children, as Cain, Reuben, Absolom and suchlike have been to their parents: so this Faustus having godly parents, and seeing him to be of a toward wit, were very desirous to bring him up in those virtuous studies, namely, of divinity; but he gave himself secretly to study necromancy and conjuration, insomuch that few or none could perceive his profession.

But to the purpose: Faustus continued at study in the university, and was by the rectors and sixteen masters afterwards examined how he had profited in his studies; and being found by them, that none for his time were able to argue with him in divinity, or for the excellency of his wisdom to compare with him, with one consent they made him doctor of divinity. But Doctor Faustus within short time after he had obtained his degree, fell into such fantasies and deep cogitations that he was marked of many, and of the most part of the students was called the Speculator; and sometime he would throw the Scriptures [A2v (2)] from him as though he had no care of his former profession: so that he began a very ungodly life, as hereafter more at large may appear; for the old proverb saith, Who can hold that will away? So, who can hold Faustus from the devil, that seeks after him with all his endeavour? For he accompanied himself with divers that were seen in those devilish arts and that had the Chaldean, Persian, Hebrew, Arabian and Greek tongues, using figures, characters, conjurations, incantations, with many other ceremonies belonging to these infernal arts, as necromancy, charms, soothsaying, witchcraft, enchant-

23 this Faustus] s, '08 &c; ~ I. ~ o
28 ofttimes] oft times o; oftentimes s, '08 &c
34 and] o, s; who '08 &c
44 marked] o, s; mocked '08 &c
47 very] o,s; most '08 &c
51 Persian] o, '08 &c; Persia s
52 Arabian] o. '08 &c; Arabia s
54 soothsaying] South-saying o; south[sa]yings s; soothsayings '08 &c
enchantment] '18; inchantment o &c

ment, being delighted with their books, words and names so well, that he studied day and night therein: insomuch that he could not abide to be called doctor of divinity but waxed a worldly man and named himself an astrologian, and a mathematician: and for a shadow, sometimes a physician, and did great cures, namely, with herbs, roots, waters, drinks, receipts and clysters. And without doubt he was passing wise, and excellent perfect in the Holy Scriptures: but he that knoweth his master's will and doth it not, is worthy to be beaten with many stripes. It is written, No man can serve two masters; and, Thou shalt not tempt the Lord thy God; but Faustus threw all this in the wind and made his soul of no estimation, regarding more his worldly pleasure than the joys to come: therefore at the day of judgment there is no hope of his redemption.

How Doctor Faustus began to practise in his devilish art and how he conjured the devil, making him to appear and meet him on the morrow at his own house. Chap. 2.

You have heard before, that all Faustus' mind was set to study the arts of necromancy and conjuration, the which exercise he followed day and night: and taking to him the wings of an eagle, thought to fly over the whole world and to know the secrets of heaven and earth; for his speculation was so wonderful, being expert in using his *vocabula,* figures, characters, conjurations and other ceremonial actions, that in all the haste he put in practice to bring the devil before him. And taking his way to a thick wood near to Wittenberg, called in the German tongue Spisser Waldt: that is in English the Spissers' Wood (as Faustus would oftentimes boast of it among his crew, being in his jollity), he came into the same wood towards evening into a crossway, where he made with a wand a circle in the dust, and within that many more circles and characters: and thus he passed away the time until it was nine or ten of the clock [A3r (3)] in the night. Then began Doctor Faustus to **call on Mephostophiles the spirit and to charge him in the name of Beelzebub to appear there personally without any long stay:** then presently the devil began so great a rumour in the wood as if heaven and earth would have come together with wind, the trees bowing their tops to the ground. Then fell the devil to blare as if the whole wood had been full of lions, and suddenly

65 pleasure] O; pleasures S, '08 &c
joys] O. '08 &c; joy S
83 on] S, '08 &c; for O
84 Beelzebub] O; Belzebub S, '08 &c; [also throughout text]
87 the trees bowing] O,S; that ~ bowed '08 &c; *daß sich die Bäum ... bogen* G [8]
88 blare] bleare O &c; bleate '18

about the circle ran the devil as if a thousand wagons had been running
90 together on paved stones. After this at the four corners of the wood it thundered horribly, with such lightnings as if the whole world, to his seeming, had been on fire. Faustus all this while half amazed at the devil's so long tarrying, **and doubting whether he were best to abide any more such horrible conjurings,** thought to leave his circle and depart;
95 whereupon the devil made him such music of all sorts, as if the nymphs themselves had been in place: whereat Faustus was revived and stood stoutly in his circle aspecting his purpose and began again to conjure the spirit **Mephostophiles in the name of the prince of devils to appear in his likeness:** whereat suddenly over his head hanged hovering in the air
100 a mighty dragon. Then calls Faustus again after his devilish manner, at which there was a monstrous cry **in the wood as if hell had been open and all the tormented souls crying to God for mercy.** Presently not three fathom above his head fell a flame in manner of a lightning and changed itself into a globe: yet Faustus feared it not, but did persuade
105 himself that the devil should give him his request before he would leave. Oftentimes after to his companions he would boast that he had the stoutest head (under the cope of heaven) at commandment: whereat they answered, they knew none stouter than the pope or emperor, but Doctor Faustus said: 'The head that is my servant is above all on earth,' and
110 repeated certain words out of St Paul to the Ephesians to make his argument good: The prince of this world is upon earth and under heaven. **Well, let us come again to his conjuration where we left him at his fiery globe: Faustus, vexed at the spirit's so long tarrying, used his charms with full purpose not to depart before he had his intent,** and
115 crying on Mephostophiles the spirit, suddenly the globe opened and sprang up in height of a man: so burning a time, in the end it converted to the shape of a fiery man. This pleasant beast ran about the circle a great while, and lastly appeared in the manner of a grey friar, asking Faustus what was his request. Faustus commanded that the next morning at
120 twelve of the clock he should appear to him at his house; but the devil would in no wise grant. [A3v (5*)] Faustus began again to conjure him in the name of Beelzebub that he should fulfil his request: whereupon the spirit agreed, and so they departed each one his way.

99 hanged] O; hung S, '08 &c
103 fathom] fadome O &c; fathame '18
107 (under] O; ∧ ~ S, '08 &c
heaven)] O; ~ ∧ S, '08 &c
115 spirit,] '08 &c; ~; O; ~: S
118 in the manner] '08 &c; ~ ∧ ~ O, S; *in Gestalt* G [10]

The conference of Doctor Faustus with the spirit **Mephostophiles the morning following at his own house.** *Chap. 3.* 125

Doctor Faustus having commanded the spirit to be with him, at his hour appointed he came and appeared in his chamber, demanding of Faustus what his desire was. Then began Doctor Faustus anew with him to conjure him that he should be obedient unto him, and to answer him certain articles, and to fulfil them in all points. 130

1 That the spirit should serve him and be obedient unto him in all things that he asked of him from that hour until the hour of his death.

2 Further, any thing that he desired of him he should bring it to him.

3 Also, that in all Faustus his demands or interrogations the spirit should tell him nothing but that which is true. 135

Hereupon the spirit answered and laid his case forth, that he had no such power of himself until he had first given his prince (that was ruler over him) to understand thereof, and to know if he could obtain so much of his lord: 'Therefore speak further that I may do thy whole desire to my prince; for it is not in my power to fulfil without his leave.' 'Show me the cause why,' said Faustus. The spirit answered: 'Faustus, thou shalt understand that with us it is even as well a kingdom as with you on earth: yea, we have our rulers and servants, as I myself am one, and we name our whole number the Legion: for although that Lucifer is thrust and fallen out of heaven through his pride and high mind, yet he hath notwithstanding a legion of devils at his commandment that we call the Oriental Princes; for his power is great and infinite. Also there is an host in *Meridie,* in *Septentrio,* in *Occidente*: and for that Lucifer hath his kingdom under heaven, we must change and give ourselves unto men to serve them at their pleasure. It is also certain, we have never as yet opened unto any man the truth of our dwelling, neither of our ruling, neither what our power is, neither have we given any man any gift or learned him any thing, except he promise to be ours.' 140 145 150

Doctor Faustus upon this arose where he sat and said: 'I will have my request and yet I will not be damned.' The spirit answered: 'Then shalt thou want thy desire and yet art thou mine notwithstanding: if any man would detain thee it is in vain, for thine infidelity hath confounded thee.' 155

[A4r (4*)] Hereupon spake Faustus: 'Get thee hence from me, and take St Valentine's farewell and chrism with thee! Yet I conjure thee that thou

133 Further] '08 &c; Farther o, s
139 further] '08, '18; farther o, s, '10
159 chrism] Crisam o &c; Crisman '18

160 be here at evening, and bethink thyself on that I have asked thee and ask thy prince's counsel therein.' Mephostophiles the spirit, thus answered, vanished away, **leaving Faustus in his study, where he sat pondering with himself how he might obtain his request of the devil without loss of his soul: yet fully he was resolved in himself, rather than to**
165 **want his pleasure, to do whatsoever the spirit and his lord should condition upon.**

The second time of the spirit's appearing to Faustus in his house, and of their parley. Chap. 4.

Faustus continuing in his devilish cogitations, never moving out of
170 **the place where the spirit left him (such was his fervent love to the devil),** the night approaching, this swift flying spirit appeared to Faustus, offering himself with all submission to his service, with full authority from his prince to do whatsoever he would request if so be Faustus would promise to be his: 'This answer I bring thee and an answer must thou
175 make by me again, yet will I hear what is thy desire, because thou hast sworn me to be here at this time.' Doctor Faustus gave him this answer, though faintly (for his soul's sake) that his request was none other but to become a devil, or at the least a limb of him, and that the spirit should agree unto these articles as followeth:

180 1 That he might be a spirit in shape and quality.

2 That Mephostophiles should be his servant and at his commandment.

3 That Mephostophiles should bring him any thing, and do for him whatsoever.

185 4 That at all times he should be in his house, invisible to all men, except only to himself, and at his commandment to show himself.

5 Lastly, that Mephostophiles should at all times appear at his command, in what form or shape soever he would.

Upon these points the spirit answered Doctor Faustus, that all this
190 should be granted him and fulfilled, and more, if he would agree unto him upon certain articles as followeth:

First, that Doctor Faustus should give himself to his lord Lucifer, body and soul.

Secondly, for confirmation of the same, he should make him a
195 wri=[A4v (6)]=ting, written with his own blood.

164 fully he was] O; ~ ∧ ~ S, '08 &c
169 continuing] O; continued S, '08 &c
192 his] O; the S, '08 &c

Thirdly, that he would be an enemy to all Christian people.

Fourthly, that he would deny his Christian belief.

Fifthly, that he let not any man change his opinion, if so be any man should go about to dissuade or withdraw him from it.

Further, the spirit promised Faustus to give him certain years to live in health and pleasure, and when such years were expired, that then Faustus should be fetched away, and if he should hold these articles and conditions, that then he should have all whatsoever his heart would wish or desire; and that Faustus should quickly perceive himself to be a spirit in all manner of actions whatsoever. Hereupon Doctor Faustus his mind was so inflamed that he forgot his soul and promised Mephostophiles to hold all things as he had mentioned them: he thought the devil was not so black as they use to paint him, nor hell so hot as the people say, etc. 200 205

The third parley between Doctor Faustus and Mephostophiles about a conclusion. Chap. 5. 210

After Doctor Faustus had made his promise to the devil, in the morning betimes he called the spirit before him and commanded him that he should always come to him like a friar, after the order of St Francis, with a bell in his hand like St Anthony, and to ring it once or twice before he appeared, that he might know of his certain coming. Then Faustus demanded the spirit, what was his name? The spirit answered: 'My name is as thou sayest, Mephostophiles, **and I am a prince but servant to Lucifer: and all the circuit from *septentrio* to the meridian, I rule under him.'** Even at these words was this wicked wretch Faustus **inflamed to hear himself to have gotten so great a potentate to be his servant,** forgot the Lord his maker, and Christ his redeemer, became an enemy unto all mankind, yea, worse than the giants whom the poets feign to climb the hills to make war with the Gods: not unlike that enemy of God and His Christ, that for his pride was cast into hell: so likewise Faustus forgot that the high climbers catch the greatest falls, and that the sweetest meat requires the sourest sauce. 215 220 225

After a while, Faustus promised Mephostophiles to write and make his obligation, **with full assurance of the articles in the chapter before**

197 his] O; the '08 &c; *den* G [17] [S lacks text]
215f demanded the spirit] O; ~ of his ~ S, '08 &c
220 be his servant, forgot] O; ~ ~ ~, forgetting S; serve him, forgetting '08 &c
221 unto] O; to S, '08 &c
223 that enemy] O; the ~ S, '08 &c; *dem bösen Engel* G [19]
224f that the high] O, S; ~ ∧ ~ '08 &c
225f sweetest meat requires] O, S; sweet meats have oft '08 &c

rehearsed. A pitiful case, (Christian Reader,) for certainly this letter or
230 obligation was found in his house after his most lamen = [B1r (7)] = table
end, **with all the rest of his damnable practices used in his whole life.**
Therefore I wish all Christians to take example by this wicked Faustus
**and to be comforted in Christ, contenting themselves with that
vocation whereunto it hath pleased God to call them, and not to
235 esteem the vain delights of this life as did this unhappy Faustus in
giving his soul to the devil**: and to confirm it the more assuredly, he
took a small penknife and pricked a vein in his left hand, and for certainty
thereupon were seen on his hand these words written, as if they had been
written with blood: *O homo fuge*; **whereat the spirit vanished, but
240 Faustus continued in his damnable mind and made his writing as
followeth.**

How Doctor Faustus set his blood in a saucer on warm ashes and writ as followeth. Chap. 6.

I Johannes Faustus, Doctor, do openly acknowledge with mine own
245 hand, to the greater force and strengthening of this letter, that sithence I
began to study and speculate the course and order of the elements, I have
not found through the gift that is given me from above, any such learning
and wisdom that can bring me to my desires: and for that I find that men
are unable to instruct me any further in the matter, now have I Doctor
250 John Faustus, unto the hellish prince of Orient and his messenger
Mephostophiles, given both body and soul, upon such condition that
they shall learn me and fulfil my desire in all things, as they have promised
and vowed unto me, with due obedience unto me, according unto the
articles mentioned between us.

255 Further, I covenant and grant with them by these presents, that at the
end of 24 years next ensuing the date of this present letter, they being
expired, and I in the mean time, during the said years, be served of them at
my will, they accomplishing my desires to the full in all points as we are
agreed, that then I give them full power to do with me at their pleasure, to
260 rule, to send, fetch or carry me or mine, be it either body, soul, flesh, blood
or goods, into their habitation, be it wheresoever: and hereupon, I defy
God and His Christ, all the host of heaven, and all living creatures that

232 take example] '08 &c; ~ an ~ o
Faustus] o; Doctor '08 &c
235 delights] o; delight '08 &c
249 further] '08 &c; farther o

bear the shape of God, yea all that lives; and again I say it, and it shall be so. And to the more strengthening of this writing, I have written it with mine own hand and blood, being in perfect memory, and hereupon I subscribe to it with my name and title, **calling all the infernal, middle and supreme powers to witness of this my letter and** subscription. 265

John Faustus, approved in the elements,
and the spiritual doctor.

[B1V (8)]

How Mephostophiles came for his writing, and in what manner he appeared, and his sights he showed him: and how he caused him to keep a copy of his own writing. Chap. 7. 270

Doctor Faustus sitting pensive, **having but one only boy with him,** suddenly there appeared his spirit Mephostophiles in likeness of a fiery man, from whom issued most horrible fiery flames, **insomuch that the boy was afraid, but being hardened by his master, he bad him stand still and he should have no harm:** the spirit began to blare as in a singing manner. This pretty sport pleased Doctor Faustus well, but he would not call his spirit into his counting house until he had seen more. Anon was heard a rushing of armed men and trampling of horses; this ceasing, came a kennel of hounds and they chased a great hart in the hall and there the hart was slain. **Faustus took heart, came forth and looked upon the hart,** but presently before him there was a lion and a dragon together fighting, so fiercely that Faustus thought they would have brought down the house, but the dragon overcame the lion and so they vanished. 275 280 285

After this came in a peacock with a peahen, the cock brustling of his tail, and turning to the female, beat her, and so vanished. Afterward followed a furious bull that with a full fierceness ran upon Faustus, but coming near him, vanished away. Afterward followed a great old ape, this ape offered Faustus the hand but he refused: so the ape ran out of the hall again. Hereupon fell a mist in the hall, that Faustus saw no light, but it lasted not and so soon as it was gone, there lay before Faustus two great sacks, one full of gold, the other full of silver. 290

Lastly, was heard by Faustus all manner instruments of music, as 295

278 pleased] O, '10, '18; pleases '08
281 came a] O; ~ in ~ '08 &c
287 brustling] brusling T

organs, clarigolds, lutes, viols, citterns, waits, hornpipes, flutes, anomes, harps and all manner of other instruments, the which so ravished his mind that he thought he had been in another world, forgot both body and soul, insomuch that he was minded never to change his opinion concerning
300 that which he had done. Hereat came Mephostophiles into the hall to Faustus, in apparel like unto a friar, to whom Faustus spake: 'Thou hast done me a wonderful pleasure in showing me this pastime. If thou continue as thou hast begun thou shalt win my heart and soul, yea and have it.' Mephostophiles answered: 'This is nothing, I will please thee
305 better: yet that thou mayest know my power and all, ask what thou wilt request of me, that shalt thou have, conditionally hold thy promise, and give me thy hand-writing.' At [B2r (9)] which words the wretch thrust forth his hand, saying: 'Hold thee, there hast thou my promise.' Mephostophiles took the writing and willed Faustus to take a copy of it;
310 with that the perverse Faustus, being resolute in his damnation, wrote a copy thereof and gave the devil the one and kept in store the other. **Thus the spirit and Faustus were agreed and dwelt together: no doubt there was a virtuous housekeeping.**

The manner how Faustus proceeded with his damnable life and of the diligent
315 *service that Mephostophiles used towards him. Chap. 8.*

Doctor Faustus having given his soul to the devil, renouncing all the powers of heaven, confirming this lamentable action with his own blood, and having already delivered his writing now into the devil's hand, the which so puffed up his heart that he had forgot the mind of a man and
320 thought rather himself to be a spirit. This Faustus dwelt in his uncle's house at Wittenberg, who died and bequeathed it in his testament to his cousin Faustus. Faustus kept a boy with him that was his scholar, an unhappy wag, called Christopher Wagner, to whom this sport and life that he saw his master follow seemed pleasant. Faustus loved the boy well,
325 hoping to make him as good or better seen in his devilish exercise than himself; **and he was fellow with Mephostophiles:** otherwise Faustus had no more company in his house but himself, his boy and his spirit, that ever was diligent at Faustus' command, going about the house, clothed

298 forgot] '08 &c; forgat O
309 willed] '08 &c; willing O; *unnd wolte* G [27]
314 with] O; in '08 &c
318 now] '08 &c; not O
321 Wittenberg] [& var.] '08 &c; Wirtenberg O

like a friar, with a little bell in his hand, seen of none but Faustus. For his victual and other necessaries, Mephostophiles brought him at his pleasure from the duke of Saxony, the duke of Bavaria and the bishop of Salzburg: for they had many times their best wine stolen out of their cellars by Mephostophiles. Likewise their provision for their own table, such meat as Faustus wished for, his spirit brought him in; besides that, Faustus himself was become so cunning that when he opened his window, what fowl soever he wished for, it came presently flying into his house, were it never so dainty. Moreover, Faustus and his boy went in sumptuous apparel, the which Mephostophiles stole from the mercers at Nuremberg, Augsburg, Frankfurt and Leipzig: for it was hard for them to find a lock to keep out such a thief. All their maintenance was but stolen and borrowed ware: and thus they lived an odious life in the sight of God, **though as yet the world were unacquainted with their wickedness. It must be so, for their fruits be none other:** as Christ saith through John, where he calls the devil a thief [B2V (10)] and a murderer: **and that found Faustus, for he stole him away both body and soul.** 330 335 340 345

How Doctor Faustus would have married and how the devil had almost killed him for it. Chap. 9.

Doctor Faustus continued thus in his epicurish life day and night, and believed not that there was a God, hell or devil: he thought that body and soul died together **and had quite forgotten divinity or the immortality of his soul** but stood in his damnable heresy day and night. And bethinking himself of a wife, called Mephostophiles to counsel; which would in no wise agree, demanding of him if he would break the covenant made with him, or if he had forgot it. 'Hast not thou,' quoth Mephostophiles, 'sworn thyself an enemy to God and all creatures? To this I answer thee, thou canst not marry; thou canst not serve two masters, God and my prince: for wedlock is a chief institution ordained of God, and that hast thou promised to defy, as we do all, and that hast thou also 350 355

331 Saxony] Saxon T
338 Nuremberg] Norenberg T
339 Augsburg] Auspurg T
Frankfurt] Franckeford [& var.] T
Leipzig] Liptzig [& var.] T
343 through] O; in '08 &c; *durch* G [30]
353 wise] O; case '08 &c
358 hast thou promised] O; thou hast ~ '08 &c
also] O; only [& var] '08 &c

done: and moreover thou hast confirmed it with thy blood. Persuade
360 thyself that what thou doest in contempt of wedlock, it is all to thine own delight. Therefore Faustus, look well about thee and bethink thyself better, and I wish thee to change thy mind: for if thou keep not what thou hast promised in thy writing, we will tear thee in pieces like the dust under thy feet. Therefore sweet Faustus, think with what unquiet life, anger,
365 strife and debate thou shalt live in when thou takest a wife: therefore change thy mind.'

Doctor Faustus was with these speeches in despair: and as all that have forsaken the Lord can build upon no good foundation, so this wretched Faustus, having forsook the rock, fell in despair with himself, **fearing if**
370 **he should motion matrimony any more, that the devil would tear him in pieces. 'For this time,' quoth he to Mephostophiles, 'I am not minded to marry.' 'Then you do well,' answered his spirit. But shortly, and that within two hours after,** Faustus called again his spirit, which came in his old manner like a friar. Then Faustus said unto him: 'I
375 am not able to resist nor bridle my fantasy, I must and will have a wife and I pray thee give thy consent to it.' Suddenly upon these words came such a whirlwind about the place that Faustus thought the whole house would come down. All the doors in the house flew off the hooks; after all this, his house was full of smoke and the floor covered over with ashes: which
380 when Doctor Faustus perceived, he would have gone up the stairs: and flying up, he was taken and thrown into the hall [B3r (11)] that he was not able to stir hand nor foot. Then round about him ran a monstrous circle of fire, never standing still, that Faustus fried as he lay and thought there to have been burned. Then cried he out to his spirit Mephostophiles for
385 help, promising him he would live in all things as he had vowed in his hand-writing. Hereupon appeared unto him an ugly devil, so fearful and monstrous to behold that Faustus durst not look on him. The devil said: **'What wouldst thou have Faustus? How likest thou thy wedding?** What mind art thou in now?' Faustus answered, he had forgot his
390 promise, desiring him of pardon, and he would talk no more of such things. The devil answered: 'Thou were best so to do,' and so vanished.

After appeared unto him his friar Mephostophiles with a bell in his

371 him] O, '10, '18; them '08
372 you do] O; dost thou '08 &c
372f But shortly, and that within] O; ~ ∧ ∧ ∧ ~ '08 &c [O has 'wihtin']
373 called again his] '08 &c; ~ ∧ ~ O
375 nor] O; or '08 &c
377f would come] O; ~ have ~ '08 &c; *als wolte es alles zu Grunde gehen* G [33]
388 wouldst thou have] O, '18; ~ ∧ ~ '08/10
391 The devil answered] O; ∧ ∧ ∧ '08 &c; *Der Satan sagt zu ihm* G [34]

hand, and spake to Faustus: 'It is no jesting with us. Hold thou that which thou hast vowed and we will perform as we have promised: and more than that, thou shalt have thy heart's desire of what woman soever thou wilt, 395 be she alive or dead, and so long as thou wilt, thou shalt keep her by thee.'

These words pleased Faustus wonderful well and he repented himself that he was so foolish to wish himself married, that might have any woman in the whole city brought to him at his command; the which he practised and persevered in a long time. 400

Questions put forth by Doctor Faustus unto his spirit Mephostophiles. Chap. 10.

Doctor Faustus living in all manner of pleasure that his heart could desire, continuing in his amorous drifts, his delicate fare and costly apparel, called on a time his Mephostophiles to him: which being come, brought 405 with him a book in his hand of all manner of devilish and enchanted arts, the which he gave Faustus, saying: 'Hold my Faustus, work now thy heart's desire.' The copy of this enchanting book was afterward found by his servant Christopher Wagner. 'Well,' quoth Faustus to his spirit, 'I have called thee to know what thou canst do if I have need of thy help.' 410 Then answered Mephostophiles and said: 'My Lord Faustus, I am a flying spirit: **yea, so swift as thought can think, to do whatsoever.'** Here Faustus said: 'But how came thy lord and master Lucifer to have so great a fall from heaven?' Mephostophiles answered: 'My lord Lucifer was a fair angel, created of God as immortal, **and being placed in the seraphim,** 415 **which are above the cherubim, he would have presumed unto the throne of God with intent to have** [B3v (12)] **thrust God out of His seat. Upon this presumption the Lord cast him down headlong, and where before he was an angel of light, now dwells he in darkness, not able to come near his first place without God send for him to** 420 **appear before him as Raphael: but unto the lower degree of angels that have their conversation with men he may come, but not unto the second degree of heavens that is kept by the archangels, namely, Michael and Gabriel, for these are called angels of God's wonders; yet are these far inferior places to that from whence my lord and** 425 **master Lucifer fell. And thus far Faustus, because thou art one of the**

397 and he repented] ~ ∧ ~ T
415 seraphim] seraphins T
416 cherubim] cherubins T
419 where before] O, '10, '18; wherefore '08
422 may] '08 &c; was O

beloved children of my lord Lucifer, following and feeding thy mind in manner as he did his, I have shortly resolved thy request, and more I will do for thee at thy pleasure.' 'I thank thee
430 **Mephostophiles,' quoth Faustus, 'Come, let us now go rest, for it is night.' Upon this they left their communication.**

How Doctor Faustus dreamed that he had seen hell in his sleep and how he questioned with his spirit of matters as concerning hell, with the spirit's answer. Chap. 11.

435 **The night following, after Faustus his communication had with Mephostophiles as concerning the fall of Lucifer,** Doctor Faustus dreamed that he had seen a part of hell, **but in what manner it was, or in what place he knew not: whereupon he was greatly troubled in mind** and called unto him Mephostophiles his spirit, saying to him: 'My
440 Mephostophiles, I pray thee resolve me in this doubt: what is hell, what substance is it of, in what place stands it, and when was it made?' Mephostophiles answered: 'My Faustus, thou shalt know that before the fall of my lord Lucifer there was no hell, but even then was hell ordained. **It is of no substance, but a confused thing: for I tell thee, that before**
445 **all elements were made and the earth seen, the spirit of God moved on the waters, and darkness was over all; but when God said, Let it be light, it was so at His word, and the light was on God's right hand and God praised the light. Judge thou further: God stood in the middle,** the darkness was on His left hand, in the which my lord was
450 bound in chains until the day of judgment. In this confused hell is nought to find but a filthy, sulphurish, fiery, stinking mist or fog. Further, we devils know not what substance it is of, **but a confused thing. For as a bubble of water flieth before the wind, so doth hell before the breath of God.** Further, we devils know not how God hath [B4r (13)] laid the
455 foundation of our hell, nor whereof it is: but to be short with thee Faustus, we know that hell hath neither bottom nor end.'

The second question put forth by Doctor Faustus to his spirit, what kingdoms there were in hell, how many, and what were their rulers' names. Chap. 12.

Faustus spake again to Mephostophiles, saying: 'Thou speakest of
460 wonderful things; I pray thee now tell me what kingdoms is there in your

451 filthy] 0; ∧ '08 &c
sulphurish, fiery, stinking] 0, '08; ~ ∧ fire, or ~ '10; ~ ∧ fire, and ~ '18

hell, how many are there, what are they called, and who rules them.' The spirit answered him: 'My Faustus, know that hell is as thou wouldst think with thyself another world, in the which we have our being, under the earth and above the earth, even to the heavens; within the circumference whereof are contained ten kingdoms, namely: 465

1 Lacus mortis.	6 Gehenna.
2 Stagnum ignis.	7 Erebus.
3 Terra tenebrosa.	8 Barathrum.
4 Tartarus.	9 Styx.
5 Terra oblivionis.	10 Acheron.

470

the which kingdoms are governed by five kings, that is, Lucifer in the orient, Beelzebub in *septentrio,* Belial in *meridie,* Astaroth in *occidente* and Phlegeton in the middest of them all: whose rule and dominions have no end until the day of doom. And thus far Faustus, hast thou heard of our rule and kingdoms.' 475

Another question put forth by Doctor Faustus to his spirit concerning his lord Lucifer, with the sorrow that Faustus fell afterwards into. Chap. 13.

Doctor Faustus began again to reason with Mephostophiles, requiring him to tell him in what form and shape, and in what estimation his lord Lucifer was when he was in favour with God. Whereupon his spirit 480 required him of three days respite, which Faustus granted. The 3 days being expired, Mephostophiles gave him this answer: 'Faustus, my lord Lucifer (so called now, for that he was banished out of the clear light of heaven) was at the first an angel of God, he sat on the cherubim and saw all the wonderful works of God, yea he was so of God ordained, for shape, 485 pomp, authority, worthiness and dwelling that he far exceeded all other the creatures of God, [B4v (14)] yea, our gold and precious stones: and so illuminated that he far surpassed the brightness of the sun and all other stars: wherefore God placed him on the cherubim, where he had a kingly office and was always before God's seat, to the end he might be the more 490 perfect in all his beings: but when he began to be high-minded, proud and so presumptuous that he would usurp the seat of His majesty, then was he

467 Erebus] Herebus T
473 no] none T
484f God, he . . . God, yea] O; God, ∧ . . . ∧, yea '08 &c [haplographic line omission]
cherubim] cherubins O [also at 489 (T)]
486f other the] O; the other '08 &c
489 wherefore] O; where '08 &c
492 His] O; Gods '08 &c

banished out from amongst the heavenly powers, separated from their abiding into the manner of a fiery stone that no water is able to quench but continually burneth until the end of the world.'

Doctor Faustus, when he had heard the words of his spirit, began to consider with himself, having divers and sundry opinions in his head: and very pensively (saying nothing unto his spirit), he went into his chamber and laid him on his bed, recording the words of Mephostophiles; which so pierced his heart that he fell into sighing and great lamentation, crying out: 'Alas, ah, woe is me! What have I done? Even so shall it come to pass with me. Am not I also a creature of God's making, **bearing His own image and similitude, into whom He hath breathed the spirit of life and immortality, unto whom He hath made all things living subject?** But woe is me, mine haughty mind, proud aspiring stomach and filthy flesh hath brought my soul into perpetual damnation; yea, pride hath abused my understanding, insomuch that I have forgot my maker, the spirit of God is departed from me, I have promised the devil my soul: and therefore it is but a folly for me to hope for grace but it must be even with me as with Lucifer, thrown into perpetual burning fire. Ah, woe is me that ever I was born.' In this perplexity lay this miserable Doctor Faustus, having quite forgot his faith in Christ, never falling to repentance truly, thereby to attain the grace and Holy Spirit of God again, the which would have been able to have resisted the strong assaults of Satan. For although he had made him a promise, yet he might have remembered through true repentance sinners come again into the favour of God; which faith the faithful firmly hold, knowing they that kill the body are not able to hurt the soul: but he was in all his opinions doubtful, without faith or hope, and so he continued.

Another disputation betwixt Doctor Faustus and his spirit, of the power of the devil and of his envy to mankind. Chap. 14.

After Doctor Faustus had a while pondered and sorrowed with himself of his wretched estate, he called again Mephostophiles [C1r (15)] unto him, commanding him to tell him the judgment, rule, power, attempts, tyranny and temptation of the devil, and why he was moved to such kind of living: whereupon the spirit answered: 'This question that thou

497 divers] '08 &c; diuerse O
498 nothing unto] '18; ~) ~ O &c
spirit)] ~ ∧ T
516 through] '08 &c; throught O
517 they that] O, '10, '18; that they '08

demandest of me, will turn thee to no small discontentment: therefore thou shouldst not have desired me of such matters, for it toucheth the secrets of our kingdom, although I cannot deny to resolve thy request. Therefore know thou Faustus, that so soon as my lord Lucifer fell from heaven he became a mortal enemy both to God and man, and hath used (as now he doth) all manner of tyranny to the destruction of man, as is manifest by divers examples, one falling suddenly dead, another hangs himself, another drowns himself, others stab themselves, others unfaithfully despair and so come to utter confusion. The first man Adam that was made perfect to the similitude of God, was by my lord his policy, the whole decay of man: yea, Faustus, in him was the beginning and first tyranny of my lord Lucifer used to man. The like did he with Cain, the same with the children of Israel when they worshipped strange gods and fell to whoredom with strange women: the like with Saul. So did he by the seven husbands of her that after was the wife of Tobias: likewise Dagon our fellow brought to destruction 30,000 men, whereupon the ark of God was stolen: and Belial made David to number his men, whereupon were slain 60,000, also he deceived king Solomon that worshipped the gods of the heathen. And there are such spirits innumerable that can come by men and tempt them, drive them to sin, weaken their belief: for we rule the hearts of kings and princes, stirring them up to war and bloodshed; and to this intent do we spread ourselves throughout all the world as the utter enemies of God and His son Christ, yea and all those that worship them: and that thou knowest by thyself Faustus, how we have dealt with thee.' To this answered Faustus: 'Why then, thou didst also beguile me.' 'Yea,' quoth Mephostophiles, 'why should we not help thee forwards? For so soon as we saw thy heart, **how thou didst despise thy degree taken in divinity and didst study to search and know the secrets of our kingdom,** even then did we enter into thee, giving thee divers foul and filthy cogitations, pricking thee forward in thine intent and persuading thee that thou couldst never attain to thy desire until thou hadst the help of some devil: and when thou wast delighted with this, then took we root in thee, and so firmly that thou gavest thyself unto us, both body and soul,

530

535

540

545

550

555

534f others unfaithfully] O; other unlawfully '08 &c
538 used] O; ∧ '08 &c
542 30,000] O, G [45], I Sam. 4. 10; 50,000 '08 &c
544 Solomon] Salomon T
551f Yea ... thee forwards] O &c; I did what I could to help thee ~ '18 &c
552 Mephostophiles] O; the spirit '08/10; *der Geist* G [46]
we not] '08/10; not we O
557 hadst] '08 &c; hast O
558 with] O; in '08 &c

560 the which thou (Faustus) canst not deny.' Hereat answered Faustus: 'Thou sayest true Mephostophiles, [C1v (18*)] I cannot deny it. Ah, woe is me, miserable Faustus; how have I been deceived? **Had not I desired to know so much I had not been in this case: for having studied the lives of the holy saints and prophets, and thereby thought myself to 565 understand sufficient in heavenly matters, I thought myself not worthy to be called Doctor Faustus if I should not also know the secrets of hell and be associated with the furious fiend thereof; now therefore must I be rewarded accordingly.'** Which speeches being uttered, Faustus went very sorrowfully away from Mephostophiles.

570 *How Doctor Faustus desired again of his spirit to know the secrets and pains of hell; and whether those damned devils and their company might ever come into the favour of God again or not? Chap. 15.*

Doctor Faustus was ever pondering with himself how he might get loose from so damnable an end as he had given himself unto, both of body and 575 soul: but his repentance was like to that of Cain and Judas, he thought his sins greater than God could forgive: hereupon rested his mind. He looked up to heaven, but saw nothing therein; for his heart was so possessed with the devil that he could think of nought else but of hell and the pains thereof. Wherefore in all the haste he calleth unto him his spirit 580 Mephostophiles, desiring him to tell him some more of the secrets of hell, what pains the damned were in, and how they were tormented, and whether the damned souls might get again the favour of God and so be released out of their torments or not. Whereupon the spirit answered: 'My Faustus, thou mayst well leave to question any more of such matters for 585 they will but disquiet thy mind. I pray thee what meanest thou? Thinkest thou through these thy fantasies to escape us? No, for if thou shouldst climb up to heaven, there to hide thyself, yet would I thrust thee down again; for thou art mine and thou belongest unto our society. Therefore sweet Faustus, thou wilt repent this thy foolish demand, except thou be 590 content that I shall tell thee nothing.' Quoth Faustus ragingly: 'I will know or I will not live, wherefore dispatch and tell me.' To whom Mephostophiles answered: 'Faustus, it is no trouble unto me at all to tell

576 forgive;] ~, O &c; ~: '18
mind.] ~: O, '08; ~, '10, '18
583 their] O, '18; these '08/10
587 yet] O, '10, '18; ∧ '08; *doch* G [50]

thee, **and therefore, sith thou forcest me thereto, I will tell thee things to the terror of thy soul if thou wilt abide the hearing.**

'Thou wilt have me tell thee of the secrets of hell and of the pains thereof. Know Faustus, that hell hath many figures, semblances and names, **but it cannot be named nor figured in such sort unto the living that are damned, as it is unto those that are dead and do both see and feel the** [C2r (19*)] **torments thereof;** for hell is said to be deadly, **out of the which came never any to life again but one, but he is as nothing for thee to reckon upon.** Hell is bloodthirsty and is never satisfied; hell is a valley, into the which the damned souls fall: for so soon as the soul is out of man's body, it would gladly go to the place from whence it came, and climbeth up above the highest hills, even to the heavens, where being by the angels of the first *mobile* denied entertainment (in consideration of their evil life spent on the earth) they fall into the deepest pit or valley which hath no bottom, into a perpetual fire which shall never be quenched. **For like as the flint thrown into the water, loseth not his virtue, neither is his fire extinguished, even so the hellish fire is unquenchable:** and even as the flint-stone in the fire being burned is red hot, and yet consumeth not, so likewise the damned souls in our hellish fire are ever burning but their pains never diminishing. Therefore is hell called the everlasting pain, in which is neither hope nor mercy; so is it called utter darkness, in which we see neither the light of sun, moon, nor star: and were our darkness like the darkness of the night, yet were there hope of mercy, **but ours is perpetual darkness, clean exempt from the face of God.** Hell hath also a place within it called Chasma, out of the which issueth all manner of thunders, lightnings, with such horrible shriekings and wailings that ofttimes the very devils themselves stand in fear thereof: for one while it sendeth forth winds with exceeding snow, hail and rain, congealing the water into ice, with the which the damned are frozen, gnash their teeth, howl and cry and yet cannot die. Otherwhiles it sendeth forth most horrible hot mists or fogs, with flashing flames of fire and brimstone, wherein the sorrowful souls of the damned lie broiling in their reiterated torments. Yea Faustus, hell is called a prison wherein the damned lie continually bound; it is also called *Pernicies* and *Exitium*, death, destruction, hurtfulness, mischief, a

598 unto] O; to '08 &c
601 as] O; ∧ '08 &c
610f fire being . . . red] O; ~ ~ burned as red '08/10; ~ ∧ burned red '18;
611 yet] O, '08, '18; it '10
614 is it] O; it is '08 &c; *Sie heißt auch* G [52]

mischance, a pitiful and an evil thing, world without end. **We have also with us in hell a ladder, reaching of an exceeding height as though it**
630 **would touch the heavens, on which the damned ascend to seek the blessing of God; but through their infidelity, when they are at the very highest degree, they fall down again into their former miseries, complaining of the heat of that unquenchable fire.** Yea sweet Faustus, so must thou understand of hell, the while thou art so desirous to know
635 the secrets of our kingdom. And mark Faustus, hell is the nurse of death, the heat of all fire, the shadow of heaven and earth, the oblivion of all goodness, the pains unspeakable, the griefs unremovable, the dwelling of [C2v (18)] devils, dragons, serpents, adders, toads, crocodiles and all manner of venomous creatures; the puddle of sin, the stinking fog
640 ascending from the Stygian lake, brimstone, pitch and all manner of unclean metals, the perpetual and unquenchable fire, the end of whose miseries was never purposed by God. Yea, yea Faustus, thou sayest I shall, I must, nay, I will tell thee the secrets of our kingdom, for thou buyest it dearly and thou must and shalt be partaker of our torments, that
645 (as the Lord God said) never shall cease: for hell, the woman's belly and the earth are never satisfied. There shalt thou abide horrible torments, trembling, gnashing of teeth, howling, crying, burning, freezing, melting, swimming in a labyrinth of miseries, scalding, burning, smoking in thine eyes, stinking in thy nose, hoarseness of thy speech, deafness of
650 thine ears, trembling of thy hands, biting thine own tongue with pain, **thy heart crushed as in a press, thy bones broken, the devils tossing firebrands upon thee, yea, thy whole carcass tossed upon muckforks from one devil to another,** yea Faustus, then wilt thou wish for death and he will fly from thee, thine unspeakable torments shall be every day
655 augmented more and more, for the greater the sin, the greater is the punishment. How likest thou this, my Faustus, a resolution answerable to thy request?

'Lastly, thou wilt have me tell thee that which belongeth only to God, which is, if it be possible for the damned to come again into the favour of
660 God or not. Why Faustus, thou knowest that this is against thy promise. **For what shouldst thou desire to know that, having already given thy soul to the devil to have the pleasure of this world and to know the secrets of hell? Therefore art thou damned, and how canst thou then come again to the favour of God?** Wherefore I directly answer, no.

629 it] O; the top of the same '08 &c
639 venomous creatures] O; ~ and noisome ~ '08 &c

For whomsoever God hath forsaken and thrown into hell, must there abide His wrath and indignation in that unquenchable fire where is no hope nor mercy to be looked for, but abiding in perpetual pains world without end. For even as much it availeth thee Faustus, to hope for the favour of God again, as Lucifer himself, who indeed although he and we all have a hope, yet is it to small avail and taketh none effect, for out of that place God will neither hear crying nor sighing; **if He do, thou shalt have as little remorse as Dives, Cain, or Judas had.** What helpeth the emperor, king, prince, duke, earl, baron, lord, knight, squire or gentleman, to cry for mercy being there? Nothing: for if on the earth they would not be tyrants and self-willed, rich with covetousness, proud with pomp, gluttons, drunkards, whoremongers, backbiters, robbers, [C3r (19)] murderers, blasphemers and suchlike, then were there some hope to be looked for. **Therefore my Faustus, as thou comest to hell with these qualities, thou must say with Cain,** My sins are greater than can be forgiven; **go hang thyself with Judas; and lastly, be content to suffer torments with Dives.**

'Therefore know Faustus, that the damned have neither end nor time appointed in the which they may hope to be released, for if there were any such hope, that they but by throwing one drop of water out of the sea in a day until it were all dry; or if there were an heap of sand as high as from the earth to the heavens, that a bird carrying away but one corn in a day, at the end of this so long labour, that yet they might hope at the last, God would have mercy on them, they would be comforted: but now there is no hope that God once thinks upon them or that their howlings shall ever be heard. Yea, so impossible as it is for thee to hide thyself from God, or impossible for thee to remove the mountains or to empty the sea, or to tell the number of the drops of rain that have fallen from heaven until this day, or to tell what there is most of in the world, yea and for a camel to go through the eye of a needle: even so impossible it is for thee Faustus, and the rest of the damned, to come again into the favour of God. And thus Faustus hast thou heard my last sentence, and I pray thee, how dost thou like it? But know this, that I counsel thee to let me be unmolested hereafter with such disputations, **or else I will vex thee every limb to thy small contentment.'**

Doctor Faustus departed from his spirit very pensive and sorrowful,

670 is it] O; it is '08 &c
679 must] O; maiest [& var.] '08 &c
689 ever] '08 &c; never O
692 the number of the] O; ∧ ∧ ∧ the '08 &c; *alle Tropffen deß Regens gezehlt* G [61]

laid him on his bed altogether doubtful of the grace and favour of God, wherefore he fell into fantastical cogitations: fain he would have had his soul at liberty again, but the devil had so blinded him and taken such deep root in his heart that he could never think to crave God's mercy, or if by
705 chance he had any good motion, straightways the devil would thrust him a fair lady into his chamber, which fell to kissing and dalliance with him, through which means he threw his godly motions in the wind, going forward still in his wicked practices to the utter ruin both of his body and soul.

710 *Another question put forth by Doctor Faustus to his spirit Mephostophiles of his own estate. Chap. 16.*

Doctor Faustus, being yet desirous to hear more strange things, called his spirit unto him, saying: 'My Mephostophiles, I have yet another suit unto thee, which I pray thee deny not to resolve me of.' 'Faustus,' quoth the
715 spirit, 'I am loth to [C3v (22*)] reason with thee any further, for thou art never satisfied in thy mind but always bringest me a new.' **'Yet I pray thee this once,' quoth Faustus, 'do me so much favour as to tell me the truth in this matter and hereafter I will be no more so earnest with thee.'** The spirit was altogether against it, but yet once more he would
720 abide him: 'Well,' said the spirit to Faustus, 'what demandest thou of me?' Faustus said: 'I would gladly know of thee, if thou wert a man in manner and form as I am, what wouldst thou do to please both God and man?' Whereat the spirit smiled saying: 'My Faustus, if I were a man as thou art, **and that God had adorned me with those gifts of nature as thou once**
725 **hadst,** even so long as the breath of God were by and within me, would I humble myself unto His Majesty, endeavouring in all that I could to keep His commandments, praise Him, glorify Him, that I might continue in His favour, so were I sure to enjoy the eternal joy and felicity of His kingdom.' Faustus said: 'But that have not I done.' 'No, thou sayest true,'
730 quoth Mephostophiles, 'thou hast not done it, but thou hast denied thy Lord and maker, which gave thee the breath of life, speech, hearing, sight and all other thy reasonable senses that thou mightest understand His will and pleasure, to live to the glory and honour of His name and to the advancement of thy body and soul. Him I say, being thy maker, hast thou
735 denied and defied, yea wickedly thou hast applied that excellent gift of thine understanding and given thy soul to the devil: therefore give none

707 motions] o; motion '08 &c

the blame but thine own self-will, thy proud and aspiring mind, which hath brought thee into the wrath of God and utter damnation.' 'This is most true,' quoth Faustus, 'but tell me Mephostophiles, wouldst thou be in my case as I am now?' 'Yea,' saith the spirit (and with that fetched a great sigh), 'for yet would I so humble myself that I would win the favour of God.' 'Then,' said Doctor Faustus, 'it were time enough for me if I amended.' 'True,' said Mephostophiles, 'if it were not for thy great sins, which are so odious and detestable in the sight of God that it is too late for thee, for the wrath of God resteth upon thee.' 'Leave off,' quoth Faustus, 'and tell me my question to my greater comfort.' 740 745

Here followeth the second part of Doctor Faustus his life and practices until his end. Chap. 17

Doctor Faustus having received denial of his spirit to be resolved any more in suchlike questions propounded, forgot all good works and fell to be a calendar-maker by help of his [C4r (23*)] spirit; and also in short time to be a good astronomer or astrologian. He had learned so perfectly of his spirit the course of the sun, moon and stars, that he had the most famous name of all the mathematics that lived in his time, as may well appear by his works dedicated unto sundry dukes and lords: for he did nothing without the advice of his spirit, which learned him to presage of matters to come which have come to pass since his death. The like praise won he with his calendars and almanacks making, for when he presaged upon any change, operation or alteration of the weather or elements, as wind, rain, fogs, snow, hail, moist, dry, warm, cold, thunder, lightning, it fell so duly out as if an angel of heaven had forewarned it. He did not like the unskilful astronomers of our time, that set in winter cold, moist, airy, frosty; and in the dog-days hot, dry, thunder, fire and suchlike; but he set in all his works day and hour, when, where and how it should happen. If any thing wonderful were at hand, as death, famine, plague or wars, he would set the time and place in true and just order, when it should come to pass. 750 755 760 765

A question put forth by Doctor Faustus to his spirit concerning astronomy. Chap. 18.

Doctor Faustus falling to practice and making his prognostications, he was doubtful in many points: wherefore he called unto him Mephosto- 770

758f presaged upon any change, operation] o, '08; ~ of any thing ~ '10,'18 &c

philes his spirit, saying: 'I find the ground of this science very difficult to attain unto: for that when I confer *astronomia* and *astrologia,* as the mathematicians and ancient writers have left in memory, **I find them to vary and very much to disagree**; wherefore I pray thee to teach me the
775 truth in this matter.' To whom his spirit answered: 'Faustus, thou shalt know that the practitioners or speculators, or at least the first inventors of these arts, have done nothing of themselves certain whereupon thou mayst attain to the true prognosticating or presaging of things **concerning the heavens or of the influence of the planets: for if by**
780 **chance some one mathematician or astronomer hath left behind him any thing worthy of memory, they have so blinded it with enigmatical words, blind characters and such obscure figures that it is impossible for an earthly man to attain unto the knowledge thereof without the aid of some spirit or else the special gift of God,**
785 for such are the hidden works of God from men: yet do we spirits that fly and fleet in all elements, know such, and there is nothing to be done, or by the heavens pretended, but we [C4v (22)] know it, except only the day of doom.

'Wherefore Faustus, learn of me: I will teach thee the course and
790 recourse of ♄, ♃, ♂, ○, ♀, ☿ and ☾, the cause of winter and summer, **the exaltation and declination of the sun, the eclipse of the moon, the distance and height of the poles and every fixed star, the nature and operation of the elements fire, air, water, and earth, and all that is contained in them: yea, herein there is nothing hidden from me but**
795 **only the fifth essence, which once thou hadst Faustus, at liberty, but now Faustus, thou hast lost it past recovery: wherefore leaving that which will not be again had, learn now of me to make thunder, lightning, hail, snow and rain: the clouds to rent, the earth and craggy rocks to shake and split in sunder, the seas to swell and roar**
800 **and overrun their marks. Knowest not thou that** the deeper the sun shines, the hotter he pierces? **So, the more thy art is famous whilst thou art here, the greater shall be thy name when thou art gone. Knowest not thou that the earth is frozen, cold and dry; the water running, cold and moist; the air flying, hot and moist; the fire consuming, hot**
805 **and dry? Yea Faustus, so must thy heart be inflamed like the fire to**

790 ♄ . ♃ . ♂ . ○ . ♀ . ☿] O; ♃ ♃ ☿ ~ ∧ ~ '08/10; ♄ . ♃ . ♀ . ☉ . ☿ [& var.] '18 &c
791 the eclipse] O; and ~ '08 &c

mount on high. Learn, Faustus, to fly like myself, as swift as thought
from one kingdom to another, to sit at princes' tables, to eat their
daintiest fare, to have thy pleasure of their fair ladies, wives and
concubines, to use their jewels, and costly robes as things belonging
to thee and not unto them. Learn of me, Faustus, to run through 810
walls, doors and gates of stone and iron, to creep into the earth like a
worm, to swim in the water like a fish, to fly in the air like a bird and
to live and nourish thyself in the fire like a salamander; so shalt thou
be famous, renowmed, far-spoken of and extolled for thy skill:
going on knives, not hurting thy feet; carrying fire in thy bosom and 815
not burning thy shirt; seeing through the heavens as through a crystal,
wherein is placed the planets, **with all the rest of the presaging comets,**
the whole circuit of the world from the East to the West, North and
South: there shalt thou know, Faustus, wherefore the fiery sphere above
♄ and the signs of the zodiac doth not burn and consume the whole face 820
of the earth, being hindered by placing the two moist elements between
them, the airy clouds and the wavering waves of water. **Yea, Faustus, I**
will learn thee the secrets of nature, what the causes that the sun in
summer, being at the highest, giveth all his heat downwards on the
earth; and being in winter at the lowest, giveth all his heat upward 825
into the heavens: that the snow should be of so great virtue as the
honey; and the Lady Saturnia ♓ in *occulto,* more hotter than the sun
in *manifesto.* Come [DIr (23)] **on, my Faustus; I will make thee as**
perfect in these things as myself, I will learn thee to go invisible, to
find out the mines of gold and silver, the fodines of precious stones, 830
as the carbuncle, the diamond, sapphire, emerald, ruby, topaz,
jacinth, garnet, jasper, amethyst, use all these at thy pleasure, take
thy heart's desire. Thy time Faustus, weareth away; then why wilt
thou not take thy pleasure of the world? Come up, we will go visit
kings at their own courts and at their most sumptuous banquets be 835
their guests; if willingly they invite us not, then perforce we will
serve our own turn with their best meat and daintiest wine.'
'Agreed,' quoth Faustus, 'but let me pause a while upon this thou
hast even now declared unto me.'

809 use their] O; ~ all ~ '08 &c
810 to thee] O; unto ~ '08 &c
819f above ♄] O; ~ ∧ '08 &c
827 Saturnia ♓ in] O; ~ ∧ ~ '08 &c
832 garnet] Granat T
jasper] Iaspis T

840 *How Doctor Faustus fell into despair with himself: for having put forth a question unto his spirit, they fell at variance, whereupon the whole rout of devils appeared unto him, threatening him sharply. Chap. 19.*

Doctor Faustus revolving with himself the speeches of his spirit, he became so woeful and sorrowful in his cogitations that he thought himself
845 already frying in the hottest flames of hell; and lying in his muse, suddenly there appeared unto him his spirit, demanding what thing so grieved and troubled his conscience, whereat Doctor Faustus gave no answer: yet the spirit very earnestly lay upon him to know the cause, and if it were possible, he would find remedy for his grief and ease him of his sorrows.
850 To whom Faustus answered: 'I have taken thee unto me as a servant to do me service and thy service will be very dear unto me, yet I cannot have any diligence of thee further than thou list thyself, neither doest thou in any thing as it becometh thee.' The spirit replied: 'My Faustus, thou knowest that I was never against thy commandments as yet, but ready to serve and
855 resolve thy questions. Although I am not bound unto thee in such respects as concern the hurt of our kingdom, yet was I always willing to answer thee and so I am still: therefore my Faustus, say on boldly, what is thy will and pleasure?' At which words, the spirit stole away the heart of Faustus, who spake in this sort: 'Mephostophiles, tell me how and after
860 what sort God made the world and all the creatures in them, and why man was made after the image of God.' **The spirit hearing this, answered: 'Faustus thou knowest that all this is in vain for thee to ask. I know that thou art sorry for that thou hast done, but it availeth thee not, for I will tear thee in thousands of pie** = [DIV (24)] = **ces if thou change**
865 **not thine opinions,' and hereat he vanished away. Whereat Faustus all sorrowful for that he had put forth such a question, fell to weeping and to howling bitterly, not for his sins towards God, but for that the devil was departed from him so suddenly and in such a rage.** And being in this perplexity, he was suddenly taken in such an
870 extreme cold as if he should have frozen in the place where he sat, in which the greatest devil in hell appeared unto him with certain of his hideous and infernal company in the most ugliest shapes that it was possible to think

852 further] '18; farther O &c
855 questions.] ∼, T
857 so I am] O; ∼ ∧ ∼ '08 &c; *bin ich dir doch* G [75]
864 will tear thee in thousands of pieces] O; ∼ [cW: teare sig. D1r] thousand pieces '08 &c
872 in the most] O; ∼ ∧ ∼ '08 &c
possible] O; unpossible '08 &c

upon, **and traversing the chamber round about where Faustus sat. Faustus thought to himself, Now are they come for me though my time be not come, and that because I have asked such questions of my servant Mephostophiles. At whose cogitations,** the chiefest devil which was his lord, unto whom he gave his soul, that was Lucifer, spake in this sort: 'Faustus, I have seen thy thoughts, **which are not as thou hast vowed unto me by virtue of this letter,' and showed him the obligation that he had written with his own blood,** 'wherefore I am come to visit thee **and to show thee some of our hellish pastimes, in hope that will draw and confirm thy mind a little more steadfast unto us.'** 'Content,' quoth Faustus, **'Go to, let me see what pastime you can make.' At which words, the great devil in his likeness sat him down by Faustus,** commanding the rest of the devils to appear in their form as if they were in hell. First entered Belial in form of a bear, with curled black hair to the ground, his ears standing upright: within the ear was as red as blood, out of which issued flames of fire, his teeth were a foot at least long, as white as snow, with a tail three ells long (at the least), having two wings, one behind each arm. And thus one after another they appeared to Faustus in form as they were in hell. Lucifer himself sat in manner of a man, all hairy, but of a brown colour like a squirrel, curled, and his tail turning upwards on his back as the squirrels use; **I think he could crack nuts too like a squirrel.** After him came Beelzebub in curled hair of horseflesh colour, his head like the head of a bull, with a mighty pair of horns and two long ears down to the ground and two wings on his back, with pricking stings like thorns: out of his wings issued flames of fire, his tail was like a cow's. Then came Astaroth in form of a worm, going upright on his tail; he had no feet, but a tail like a slow-worm: under his chaps grew two short hands and his back was coal black, his belly thick in the middle and yellow like gold, having many bristles on his back like a hedgehog. After him came Chamagosta, being white and gray mixed, ex=[D2r (25)]=ceeding curled and hairy: he had a head like the head of an ass, the tail like a cat and claws like an ox, lacking nothing of an ell broad. Then came Anubis: this devil had a head like a dog, white and

880 that] O; which '08 &c
890 one] O, '18; on '08/10
895 of horseflesh] O; ~ a ~ '08 &c
898 cow's] '08 &c; cow O
899 he] O; and '08 &c; *hineyn, hatte keinen Füß* G [79]
902 Chamagosta] O, '08; Chaniagosta [& var.] '10, '18 &c
904 ass, the tail] O; ~ and a ~ '08 &c; *und doch der schwantz* G [79]
905 Anubis] Anobis T

black hair, **in shape of a hog, saving that he had but two feet, one under his throat, the other at his tail:** he was four ells long, with hanging ears like a bloodhound. After him came Dythycan: he was a short thief in form of a pheasant, with shining feathers and four feet: his neck
910 was green, his body red and his feet black. The last was called Drachus, with four short feet like an hedgehog, yellow and green: the upper side of his body was brown and the belly like blue flames of fire, the tail red, like the tail of a monkey. The rest of the devils were in form of unsensible beasts, as swine, harts, bears, wolves, apes, buffs, goats, **antelopes,**
915 **elephants, dragons, horses,** asses, **lions, cats, snakes, toads** and all manner of ugly odious serpents and worms: **yet came in such sort that every one at his entry into the hall made their reverence unto Lucifer and so took their places, standing in order as they came, until they had filled the whole hall: wherewith suddenly fell a most horrible**
920 **thunderclap, that the house shook as though it would have fallen to the ground, upon which every monster had a muckfork in his hand, holding them towards Faustus as though they would have run a tilt at him: which when Faustus perceived, he thought upon the words of Mephostophiles when he told him how the souls in hell were**
925 **tormented, being cast from devil to devil upon muckforks; he thought verily to have been tormented there of them in like sort. But Lucifer perceiving his thought, spake to him: 'My Faustus, how likest thou this crew of mine?'** Quoth Faustus: 'Why came you not in another manner of shape?' Lucifer replied: 'We cannot change our hellish
930 form, we have showed ourselves here as we are there; yet can we blind men's eyes in such sort that when we will we repair unto them as if we were men **or angels of light, although our dwelling be in darkness.'** Then said Faustus: 'I like not so many of you together,' whereupon Lucifer commanded them to depart, except seven of the principal.
935 Forthwith they presently vanished, which Faustus perceiving, he was somewhat better comforted, **and spake to Lucifer: 'Where is my servant Mephostophiles? Let me see if he can do the like,' whereupon came a fierce dragon, flying and spitting fire round about the house, and coming towards Lucifer, made reverence and**
940 **then changed himself to the form of a friar, saying: 'Faustus, what wilt thou?'** Saith Faustus: 'I will that thou teach me to transform myself

910 Drachus] G [80]; Brachus T
928 you not] O; not you '08 &c
941 Saith Faustus] O; Faustus said '08 &c

in like [D2V (26)] sort as thou and the rest have done.' Then Lucifer put forth his paw and gave Faustus a book, saying: 'Hold, do what thou wilt,' which he looking upon, straightways changed himself **into a hog, then into a worm, then into a dragon, and finding this for his purpose, it liked him well.** Quoth he to Lucifer: 'And how cometh it that all these filthy forms are in the world?' Lucifer answered: 'They are ordained of God as plagues unto men, and so shalt thou be plagued,' quoth he, whereupon came scorpions, wasps, emmets, bees and gnats, which fell to stinging and biting him, **and all the whole house was filled with a most horrible stinking fog, insomuch that Faustus saw nothing,** but still was tormented; **wherefore he cried for help saying: 'Mephostophiles my faithful servant, where art thou? Help, help I pray thee.' Hereat his spirit answered nothing, but Lucifer himself said: 'Ho ho ho Faustus, how likest thou the creation of the world?' and incontinent it was clear again,** and the devils and all the filthy cattle were vanished, **only Faustus was left alone, seeing nothing, but hearing the sweetest music that ever he heard before, at which he was so ravished with delight that he forgot the fears he was in before and it repented him that he had seen no more of their pastime.** 945 950 955 960

How Doctor Faustus desired to see hell, and of the manner how he was used therein. Chap. 20.

Doctor Faustus bethinking how his time went away, and how he had spent eight years thereof, he meant to spend the rest to his better contentment, **intending quite to forget any such motions as might offend the devil any more:** wherefore on a time he called his spirit Mephostophiles, and said unto him: 'Bring thou hither unto me thy lord Lucifer, or Belial.' He brought him (notwithstanding) one that was called Beelzebub, the which asked Faustus his pleasure. Quoth Faustus: 'I would know of thee if I may see hell and take a view thereof?' 'That thou shalt,' said the devil, 'and at midnight I will fetch thee.' Well, night being come, **Doctor Faustus awaited very diligently for the coming of the devil to fetch him, and thinking that he tarried all too long, he went to the window where he pulled open a casement, and looking into the element, he saw a cloud in the North more black, dark and** 965 970 975

949 emmets] Emits T
954 his] O; the '08 &c
answered] O &c; answering '18
959 the] O; his '08 &c

obscure than all the rest of the sky, from whence the wind blew most horrible right into Faustus his chamber and filled the whole house with smoke, that Faustus was almost smothered: hereat fell an exceeding thunderclap and withal came a great rugged black [D3r (27)]
980 bear, all curled, and upon his back a chair of beaten gold, **and spake to Faustus, saying: 'Sit up and away with me!' and Doctor Faustus that had so long abode the smoke, wished rather to be in hell than there,** got on the devil, and so they went together. But mark how the devil blinded him and made him believe that he carried him into hell, for he
985 carried him into the air, where Faustus fell into a sound sleep, as if he had sat in a warm water or bath.

At last they came to a place which burneth continually with flashing flames of fire and brimstone, whereout issued an exceeding mighty clap of thunder, with so horrible a noise that Faustus awaked, but the devil went
990 forth on his way and carried Faustus thereinto, yet notwithstanding, howsoever it burnt, Doctor Faustus felt no more heat than as it were the glimpse of the sun in May: there heard he all manner of music to welcome him, but saw none playing on them; it pleased him well, but he durst not ask, for he was forbidden it before. To meet the devil and the guest that
995 came with him, came three other ugly devils, the which ran back again before the bear to make them way, against whom there came running an exceeding great hart which would have thrust Faustus out of his chair, but being defended by the other three devils, the hart was put to the repulse. Thence going on their way Faustus looked, and behold there was nothing
1000 but snakes and all manner of venomous beasts about him, which were exceeding great, unto the which snakes came many storks and swallowed up all the whole multitude of snakes, that they left not one: which when Faustus saw, he marvelled greatly: but proceeding further on their hellish voyage, there came forth of a hollow cliff an exceeding great flying bull,
1005 the which with such a force hit Faustus his chair with his head and horns that he turned Faustus and his bear over and over, so that the bear vanished away, whereat Faustus began to cry: 'Oh, woe is me that ever I came here,' for he thought there to have been beguiled of the devil, and to make his end before his time appointed or conditioned of the devil: but
1010 shortly came unto him a monstrous ape, bidding Faustus be of good cheer, and said: 'Get upon me!' All the fire in hell seemed to Faustus to

977 chamber and] '08 &c; ~ , ∧ 0
996 them] 0; the '08 &c
1010 shortly came] 0; ~ after ~ '08 &c
Faustus be] 0; ~ to ~ '08 &c

have been put out, whereupon followed a monstrous thick fog, that he saw nothing, but shortly it seemed to him to wax clear, where he saw two great dragons fastened to a waggon, into the which the ape ascended and set Faustus therein. Forth flew the dragons into an exceeding dark cloud where Faustus saw neither dragon nor chariot wherein he sat, and such were the cries of tormented souls, with mighty thunderclaps and flashing light = [D3v (28)] = nings about his ears, that poor Faustus shook for fear. Upon this came they to a water, stinking and filthy, thick like mud, into the which ran the dragons, sinking under with waggon and all; but Faustus felt no water but as it were a small mist, saving that the waves beat so sore upon him that he saw nothing under and over him but only water, in the which he lost his dragons, ape and waggon; and sinking yet deeper and deeper, he came at last as it were upon an high rock where the waters parted and left him thereon: **but when the water was gone, it seemed to him he should there have ended his life, for he saw no way but death. The rock was as high from the bottom as heaven is from the earth:** there sat he, seeing nor hearing any man, and looked ever upon the rock; at length he saw a little hole, out of the which issued fire; thought he, How shall I now do? I am forsaken of the devils, and they that brought me hither; here must I either fall to the bottom or burn in the fire or sit still in despair. With that, in his madness he gave a leap into the fiery hole, saying: 'Hold, you infernal hags, take here this sacrifice as my last end, the which I justly have deserved.' Upon this he was entered, **and finding himself as yet unburned or touched of the fire, he was the better appaid, but** there was so great a noise as he never heard the like before, it passed all the thunder that ever he had heard; and coming down further to the bottom of the rock, he saw a fire wherein were many worthy and noble personages, as emperors, kings, dukes and lords and many thousands more of tormented souls, at the edge of which fire ran a most pleasant, clear and cool water to behold, into the which many tormented souls sprang out of the fire to cool themselves; but being so freezing cold, they were constrained to return again into the fire **and thus wearied themselves and spent their endless torments out of one labyrinth into another, one while in heat, another while in cold:** but Faustus standing thus all this while gazing on them that were thus tormented, he saw one leaping out of the fire and screeching horribly, whom he thought

1014 to a] O; unto ~ '08 &c
1020 dragons] O; dragon '08 &c; *sencken sich die Drachen* G [87]
1032 leap] O; scope '08; skip '10, '18 &c; *unnd sprang* G [88]

to have known, wherefore he would fain have spoken unto him, but remembering that he was forbidden, he refrained speaking. Then this
1050 devil that brought him in, came to him again in likeness of a bear, with the chair on his back, and bad him sit up, for it was time to depart: so Faustus got up and the devil carried him out into the air, **where he had so sweet music that he fell asleep by the way.** His boy Christopher being all this while at home and missing his master so long, thought his master would
1055 have tarried and dwelt with the devil for ever: but whilst his boy was in these co=[D4r(29)]=gitations his master came home, for the devil brought him home fast asleep as he sat in his chair, and so he threw him on his bed, where (being thus left of the devil) he lay until day. When he awaked he was amazed, like a man that had been in a dark dungeon,
1060 musing with himself if it were true or false that he had seen hell, or whether he was blinded or not: **but he rather persuaded himself that he had been there than otherwise, because he had seen such wonderful things:** wherefore he most carefully took pen and ink, and wrote those things in order as he had seen: the which writing was afterwards found by
1065 his boy in his study; **which afterwards was published to the whole city of Wittenberg in open print, for example to all Christians.**

How Doctor Faustus was carried through the air up to the heavens to see the world, and how the sky and planets ruled: after the which he wrote one letter to his friend of the same to Leipzig, how he went about the world in eight days.
1070 *Chap. 21.*

This letter was found by a freeman and citizen of Wittenberg, written with his own hand and sent to his friend at Leipzig, a physician named Jonas Victor, the contents of which were as followeth:

Amongst other things (my loving friend and brother) I remember yet
1075 the former friendship had together when we were schoolfellows and students in the university at Wittenberg. Whereas you first studied physic, astronomy, astrology, geometry and cosmography, I, to the contrary

1051 was] O; is '08 &c
1057 his] O; the '08 &c; *auff dem Sessel* G [89]
1067 heavens] O; heaven '08 &c; *das Gestirn* G [91]
1067f the world] O; ~ whole ~ '08 &c
1069 Leipzig] Liptzig T [also at 1072]
1070 21] O; 19 '08 &c
1073 Jonas Victor] Ioue Victori O [Latin dative with inverted n]; Ioue Victory '08 &c; Loue Victory '48

(you know), studied divinity: notwithstanding now in any of your own studies I am seen (I am persuaded) further than yourself: for sithence I began I have never erred, for (might I speak it without affecting my own praise) my calendars and other practices have not only the commendations of the common sort, but also of the chiefest lords and nobles of this our Dutch nation: because (which is chiefly to be noted) I writ and presaged of matters to come, which all accord and fall out so right as if they had been already seen before. And for that (my beloved Victor) you write to know my voyage which I made into the heavens, the which (as you certify me) you have had some suspicion of, although you partly persuaded yourself that it is a thing impossible, no matter for that, it is as it is, and let it be as it will, once it was done, in such manner as now according unto your request I give you here to understand. 1080 1085 1090

I being once laid on my bed, and could not sleep for thinking on [D4v (30)] my calendar and practice, I marvelled with myself how it were possible that the firmament should be known and so largely written of men, or whether they write true or false, by their own opinions, or supposition, or by due observations and true course of the heavens. Behold, being in these my muses, suddenly I heard a great noise, insomuch that I thought my house would have been blown down, so that all my doors and chests flew open, whereat I was not a little astonied, for withal I heard a groaning voice which said: 'Get up! The desire of thy heart, mind and thought shalt thou see.' At the which I answered: 'What my heart desireth, that would I fain see, and to make proof if I shall see I will away with thee.' 'Why then,' quoth he, 'look out at thy window, there cometh a messenger for thee.' That did I, and behold, there stood a waggon with two dragons before it to draw the same, and all the waggon was of a light burning fire, and for that the moon shone I was the willinger at that time to depart: but the voice spake again: 'Sit up and let us away!' 'I will,' said I, 'go with thee, but upon this condition, that I may ask after all things that I see, hear or think on.' The voice answered: 'I am content for this time.' Hereupon I got me into the waggon, so that the dragons carried me upright into the air. The waggon had also four wheels, the 1095 1100 1105 1110

1078 your] O, '10, '18; our '08
1083 writ] '08; write O, '10, '18
1085 Victor] Victori O; Victory [& var.] '08 &c
1087 me)] me ∧ T
1088 impossible,] ~ ∧) T
1096f Behold, being ... that I] O; ~ ∧... ∧ ~ '08 &c [haplographic line omission; parallel text supplied in G]

which rattled so and made such a noise as if we had been all this while running on the stones: and round about us flew out flames of fire, and the higher that I came, the more the earth seemed to be darkened, so that methought I came out of a dungeon; and looking down from heaven,
1115 behold, Mephostophiles my spirit and servant was behind me, and when he perceived that I saw him, he came and sat by me, to whom I said: 'I pray thee Mephostophiles, whither shall I go now?' 'Let not that trouble thy mind,' said he, and yet they carried us higher up.

And now will I tell thee, good friend and schoolfellow, what things I
1120 have seen and proved; for on the Tuesday went I out and on Tuesday seven nights following I came home again, that is, eight days, in which time I slept not, no not one wink came in mine eyes, and we went invisible of any man: and as the day began to appear after our first night's journey, I said to my spirit Mephostophiles: 'I pray thee how far have we now
1125 ridden? I am sure thou knowest: for methinks that we are ridden exceeding far, the world seemeth so little.' Mephostophiles answered me: 'My Faustus, believe me, that from the place from whence thou camest, unto this place where we are now, is already 47 leagues right in height.' And as the day increased, I looked down upon the world: [E1r (31)] there I
1130 saw many kingdoms and provinces, likewise the whole world, Asia, Europe and Africa, I had a sight of: and being so high, quoth I to my spirit: 'Tell me now how these kingdoms lie and what they are called,' the which he denied not, saying: 'See this on our left hand is Hungary, this is also Prussia on our left hand, and Poland, Muscovy, Tartascelesia,
1135 Bohemia, Saxony: and here on our right hand, Spain, Portugal, France, England, and Scotland: then right out before us lie the kingdoms of Persia, India, Arabia, the King of Alchar and the great Cham: now are we come to Wittenberg and are right over the town of Vienna in Austria, and ere long will we be at Constantinople, Tripoli and Jerusalem, and after
1140 will we pierce the frozen zone and shortly touch the horizon and the zenith of Wittenberg.' There looked I on the Ocean Sea and beheld a great many of ships and galleys ready to the battle, one against another: and thus I spent my journey, now cast I my eyes here, now there, toward

1117 whither] '08; whether O, '10, '18
1123 our] O; my '08 &c
1129f world ... world, Asia] O &c; ~ ∧ ... ∧ ~ '18 &c
I saw] '08/10; saw I O; *sahe ich* G [95]
1133 Hungary] Hungaria T
1134 Muscovy] Muscovia T
1137 Alchar] O; Althar '08 &c [MS misread]
1138 Vienna] Weim T

South, North, East and West. I have been in one place where it rained and hailed, and in another where the sun shone excellent fair, and so I think 1145 that I saw the most things in and about the world, **with great admiration that in one place it rained and in another hail and snow, on this side the sun shone bright, some hills covered with snow never consuming, other were so hot that grass and trees were burned and consumed therewith.** Then looked I up to the heavens, and behold, they 1150 went so swift that I thought they would have sprung in thousands. Likewise it was so clear and so hot that I could not long gaze into it, it so dimmed my sight: and had not my spirit Mephostophiles covered me as it were with a shadowing cloud I had been burnt with the extreme heat thereof, for the sky the which we behold here when we look up from the 1155 earth, is so fast and thick as a wall, clear and shining bright as a crystal, **in the which is placed the sun, which casteth forth his rays or beams over the universal world to the uttermost confines of the earth.** But we think that the sun is very little: no, it is altogether as big as the world. **Indeed the body substantial is but little in compass but the rays or** 1160 **stream that it casteth forth, by reason of the thing wherein it is placed, maketh him to extend and show himself over the whole world: and we think that the sun runneth his course and that the heavens stand still; no, it is the heavens that move his course and the sun abideth perpetually in his place; he is permanent and fixed in** 1165 **his place, and although we see him beginning to ascend in the orient or East, at the highest in the meridian or South, setting in the occident or West, yet is he at** [E1v (32)] **the lowest in septentrio or North, and yet he moveth not. It is the axle of the heavens that moveth the whole firmament, being a chaos or confused thing, and** 1170 **for that proof, I will show thee this example, like as thou seest a bubble made of water and soap blown forth of a quill is in form of a confused mass or chaos, and being in this form, is moved at pleasure of the wind, which runneth round about that chaos and moveth him also round: even so is the whole firmament or chaos, wherein are** 1175 **placed the sun and the rest of the planets, turned and carried at the pleasure of the spirit of God, which is wind. Yea Christian Reader, to the glory of God and for the profit of thy soul, I will open unto thee the divine opinion touching the ruling of this confused chaos, far**

1157 or] O; and '08 &c
1176 sun] ~, T
planets,] ~ ∧ T
1179 ruling] O; rule '08 &c

1180 **more than any rude German author, being possessed with the devil, was able to utter; and to prove some of my sentence before to be true, look into Genesis unto the works of God, at the creation of the world: there shalt thou find that the spirit of God moved upon the waters before heaven and earth were made. Mark how He made it and how**
1185 **by His word every element took his place: these were not His works but His words; for all the words He used before, He concluded afterwards in one work, which was in making man: mark reader, with patience for thy soul's health, see into all that was done by the word and work of God: light and darkness was, the firmament stood,**
1190 **and there great ⊙ and little light ☽ in it: the moist waters were in one place, the earth was dry and every element brought forth according to the word of God. Now followeth His works: He made man like His own image. How? Out of the earth? The earth will shape no image without water: there was one of the elements. But all**
1195 **this while where was wind? All elements were at the word of God, man was made and in a form by the work of God, yet moved not that work before God breathed the spirit of life into his nostrils and made him a living soul: here was the first wind and spirit of God out of His own mouth, which we have likewise from the same seed which was**
1200 **only planted by God in Adam, which wind, breath or spirit, when he had received, he was living and moving on earth, for it was ordained of God for his habitation, but the heavens are the habitation of the Lord: and like as I showed before of the bubble or confused chaos made of water and soap, through the wind and breath of man is**
1205 **turned round and carried with every wind, even so the firmament wherein the sun and the rest of the planets are fixed, is moved, turned, and carried with the wind, breath or spirit of God, for the heavens and firmament are movable as the chaos but the sun is fixed in the firmament.** And further, my good [E2r (33)] schoolfellow, I was
1210 thus nigh the heavens, where methought every planet was but as half the earth, and under the firmament ruled the spirits in the air; and as I came down I looked upon the world and the heavens, and methought that the earth was enclosed in comparison within the firmament, as the yolk of an

1190 there] '08 &c; their O
⊙] O; ☿ '08 &c
1193 like] O; after '08 &c
1206 fixed, is moved] ~ ∧ ~ T
1209 firmament] O; firmaments '08 &c
further] '18; farther O &c

egg within the white, and methought that the whole length of the earth was not a span long and the water was as if it had been twice as broad and long as the earth. Even thus at the eight days' end came I home again and fell asleep, and so I continued sleeping three days and three nights together: and the first hour that I waked, I fell fresh again to my calendar and have made them in right ample manner as you know; and to satisfy your request, for that you writ unto me, I have in **consideration of our old friendship had at the University of Wittenberg,** declared unto you my heavenly voyage, wishing no worse unto you than unto myself, that is, that your mind were as mine in all respects. *Dixi.*

Doctor Faustus the Astrologian.

How Doctor Faustus made his journey through the principal and most famous lands in the world. Chap. 22.

Doctor Faustus having overrun fifteen years of his appointed time, he took upon him a journey with full pretence to see the whole world: and calling his spirit Mephostophiles unto him, he said: 'Thou knowest that thou art bound unto me upon conditions, to perform and fulfil my desire in all things, wherefore my pretence is to visit the whole face of the earth, visible and invisible when it pleaseth me; wherefore I enjoin and command thee to the same.' Whereupon Mephostophiles answered: 'I am ready my Lord at thy command,' and forthwith the spirit changed himself into the likeness of a flying horse, **saying: 'Faustus sit up, I am ready.' Doctor Faustus loftily sat upon him and forward they went.**

Faustus came through many a land and province; as Pannonia, Austria, Germany, Bohemia, Silesia, Saxony, Meissen, Thuringia, Franconia, Swabia, Bavaria, **Styria, Carinthia,** Poland, Lithuania, Livonia, Prussia,

1215f and long] O; ~ as ~ '08 &c
1218 waked] O; awaked '08 &c
1220 writ] O, '18; write '08 &c
1226 Chap. 22.] O; ∧ ∧ '08 &c
1230 bound unto] O; ~ to '08 &c
1236 forward] O; forwards '08 &c
1238 Germany] Germania T
Silesia] Slesia T
Meissen] Missene T
Thuringia] During T
Franconia] Francklandt [& var.] T
1239 Swabia] Shawblandt T
Bavaria] Beyerlandt [& var.] T
Lithuania] Litaw T
Livonia] Liefland [& var.] T

1240 **Denmark,** Muscovy, **Tartary, Turkey, Persia, Cathay, Alexandria, Barbary, Guinea, Peru, the Straits of Magellan, India, all about the frozen zone and Terra Incognita, Nova Hispaniola, the isles of Terzera, Madeira, St Michael's, the Canaries and the Tenerife,** into Spain, the Mainland, Portugal, Italy, **Campania, the Kingdom of**
1245 **Naples, the isles of Sicily, Malta, Majorca, Minorca, to the Knights of the Rhodes, Candy or** [E2V (34)] **Crete, Cyprus, Corinth, Switzerland,** France, Friesland, Westphalia, Zeeland, Holland, Brabant **and all the 17 provinces in Netherland, England, Scotland, Ireland, all America and Iceland, the out isles of Scotland, the Orkneys,**
1250 **Norway, the Bishopric of Bremen** and so home again. All these kingdoms, provinces and countries he passed in 25 days, in which time he saw very little that delighted his mind: **wherefore he took a little rest at home, and burning in desire to see more at large and to behold the secrets of each kingdom,** he set forward again on his journey upon his
1255 swift horse Mephostophiles and came to Trier, for that he chiefly desired to see this town and the monuments thereof; but there he saw not many wonders, except one fair palace **that belonged unto the bishop, and also a mighty large castle** that was built of brick, **with three walls and three great trenches,** so strong that it was impossible for any prince's
1260 power to win it; then he saw a church, wherein was buried Simeon and the Bishop Popo: their tombs are of most sumptuous, large marble stone, closed and joined together with great bars of iron: from whence he departed to Paris where he liked well the academy; and what place or kingdom soever fell in his mind, the same he visited.

1265 He came from Paris to Mainz where the river of Main falls into the

1240 Muscovy] Muscovia T
Tartary] Tartaria T
1241 Barbary] Barbaria T
Straits of] O; ~ ∧ '08 &c
Magellan] Magelanes O, '08; Magenelanes '10, '18
1243 Madeira] Mederi T
Tenerife] Tenorrifocie [& var.] T
1244 Mainland] Mayne Land O; main land '08 &c
1245 Sicily] Sicilia T
Majorca] Maioria T
Minorca] Minoria T
1249 Iceland] Island T
Orkneys] Orchades T
1250 Bremen] Breame T
1255 Trier] G [100]; Treir O; Trent '08 &c
1261 large] O; ∧ '08 &c; *unglaubichen grossen steinen* G [100]
1265 Mainz] Mentz [& var.] T

Rhine; notwithstanding he tarried not long there but went to Campania in the kingdom of Neapolis, in which he saw an innumerable sort of cloisters, nunneries and churches, great and high houses of stone, **the streets fair and large and straight forth from one end of the town to the other as a line, and all the pavement of the city was of brick and** 1270 **the more it rained in the town, the fairer the streets were; there saw he the tomb of Virgil and the highway that he cut through that mighty hill of stone in one night, the whole length of an English mile: then he saw the number of gallies and argosies that lay there at the city head, the windmill that stood in the water, the castle in the** 1275 **water and the houses above the water, whereunder the gallies might ride most safely from rain or wind;** then he saw the castle on the hill over the town and many monuments within: also the hill called Vesuvius, whereon groweth all the Greekish wine and most pleasant sweet olives.

From thence he came to Venice, whereat he wondered not a little to see 1280 a city so famously built standing in the sea: **where through every street the water ran in such largeness that great ships and barques might pass from one street to another, having yet a way on both sides the water whereon men and horse might pass;** he marvelled also how it was possible for so much victual to be found in the town and so good 1285 cheap, considering [E3r (35)] that for a whole league off nothing grew near the same. **He wondered not a little at the fairness of St Mark's place and the sumptuous church standing therein called St Mark's; how all the pavement was set with coloured stones and all the rood or loft of the church double gilded over.** 1290

Leaving this, he came to Padua, beholding the manner of their academy, **which is called the mother or nurse of Christendom; there he heard the doctors and saw the most monuments in the town, entered his name into the university of the German nation and wrote himself Doctor Faustus the insatiable speculator:** then saw he the 1295 worthiest monument in the world for a church, named St Anthony's Cloister, which for the pinnacles thereof and the contriving of the church,

1266 to] o; in '08; into '10, '18; *kam in Campanien* G [101]
1270 as a line] o, '10, '18; ~ ∧ ~ '08
1276 the gallies] o; ∧ ~ '08 &c
1278 within] o; therein '08 &c
1282 ran in] o; came into '08 &c
1285 for so] o; ∧ ~ '08 &c
1286 league off] o; ~ ∧ '08 &c
1291 Padua] '18; Padoa o &c; [also at 1300]
1297 contriving] o; contrivement '08 &c

hath not the like in Christendom. This town is fenced about with three mighty walls of stone and earth, betwixt the which runneth goodly 1300 ditches of water: **twice every 24 hours passeth boats betwixt Padua and Venice with passengers as they do here betwixt London and Gravesend, and even so far they differ in distance:** Faustus beheld likewise the Council House and the castle with no small wonder.

Well, forward he went to Rome, which lay, and doth yet lie, on the river 1305 Tiber, the which divideth the city in two parts: **over the river are four great stone bridges and upon the one bridge called Ponte S. Angelo is the castle of S. Angelo, wherein are so many great cast pieces as there are days in a year and such pieces that will shoot seven bullets off with one fire; to this castle cometh a privy vault from the church 1310 and palace of St Peter, through the which the Pope (if any danger be) passeth from his palace to the castle for safeguard.** The city hath eleven gates, and a hill called Vaticinium, whereon St Peter's church is built: **in that church the holy fathers will hear no confession without the penitent bring money in his hand. Adjoining to this church is 1315 the Campo Santo, the which Carolus Magnus built, where every day thirteen pilgrims have their dinners served of the best: that is to say, Christ and his twelve apostles. Hard by this he visited the churchyard of St Peter's where he saw the pyramid that Julius Caesar brought out of Africa; it stood in Faustus his time leaning 1320 against the church wall of St Peter's, but now Papa Sixtus hath erected it in the middle of St Peter's churchyard; it is 24 fathom long and at the lower end six fathom four square, and so forth smaller upwards; on the top is a crucifix of beaten gold, the stone standeth on four lions of brass. Then he visited the seven churches of Rome, that 1325 were: St Peter's, St Paul's, St Sebastian's, St John Lateran, St Laurence, St Mary Magdalene, and Sta. Maria Maggiore: then went he** [E3v (36)] **without the town, where he saw the conduits of water that run level through hill and dale, bringing water into the town fifteen Italian miles off:** other monuments he saw, too many to recite, 1330 but amongst the rest he was desirous to see the Pope's palace and his manner of service at his table, wherefore he and his spirit made themselves

1305 Tiber] Tybris [& var.] T
1308 in a] O; ~ the '08 &c
that] O; as '08 &c
1319 out] O; forth '08 &c
1320 Papa] O; Pope '08 &c
1326 Maria Maggiore] Marie maiora T

invisible and came into the Pope's court and privy chamber, where he was. There saw he many servants attendant on His Holiness, with many a flattering sycophant carrying of his meat, and there he marked the Pope and the manner of his service, which he seeing to be so unmeasurable and 1335 sumptuous, 'Fie,' quoth Faustus, 'why had not the devil made a pope of me?' Faustus saw notwithstanding in that place those that were like to himself, proud, stout, wilful, gluttons, drunkards, whoremongers, breakers of wedlock and followers of all manner of ungodly exercises: wherefore he said to his spirit: 'I thought that I had been alone a hog or 1340 pork of the devil's, but he must bear with me yet a little longer, for these hogs of Rome are already fatted and fitted to make his roast meat; **the devil might do well now to spit them all and have them to the fire, and let him summon the nuns to turn the spits: for as none must confess the nun but the friar, so none should turn the roasting friar** 1345 **but the nun.'**

Thus continued Faustus three days in the Pope's palace, and yet had no lust to his meat, but stood still in the Pope's chamber **and saw every thing whatsoever it was. On a time the Pope would have a feast prepared for the cardinal of Pavia, and for his first welcome the** 1350 **cardinal was bidden to dinner:** and as he sat at meat, the Pope would ever be blessing and crossing over his mouth. Faustus could suffer it no longer **but up with his fist and smote the Pope on the face,** and withal he laughed that the whole house might hear him, yet none of them saw him nor knew where he was: the Pope persuaded his company that it was a 1355 damned soul, commanding a mass presently to be said for his delivery out of purgatory, which was done. The Pope sat still at meat, but when the latter mess came in to the Pope's board, Doctor Faustus laid hands thereon saying: 'This is mine.' And so he took both dish and meat and fled unto the Capitol or Campadolia, calling his spirit unto him and said: 1360 'Come let us be merry, for thou must fetch me some wine and the cup that the Pope drinks of, and here upon Monte Caval will we make good cheer in spite of the Pope and all his fat abbey lubbers.' His spirit hearing this, departed towards the Pope's chamber, where he found them yet sitting

1334 sycophant] O, '18; sycophants '08/10
1337 saw notwithstanding in that place] O; ~ there ~ ∧ ∧ ∧ '08 &c; *sahe auch darinnen* G [103]
those that] O; such as '08 &c
1342 fatted] '08 &c; fatned O
1356 commanding a mass] O; ~ ∧ ~ '08 &c
1359 fled] O; flew '08 &c; *flogen* G [105]
1362 will we] O; we will '08 &c

1365 and quaffing: wherefore he took from before the Pope the fairest piece of plate or drinking goblet, and a flagon of wine, and brought [E4r (37)] it to Faustus; but when the Pope and the rest of his crew perceived they were robbed **and knew not after what sort, they persuaded themselves that it was the damned soul that before had vexed the Pope so and that**
1370 **smote him on the face,** wherefore he sent commandment through all the whole city of Rome, that they should say mass in every church and ring all the bells for to lay the walking spirit, **and to curse him with bell, book and candle, that so invisibly had misused the Pope's Holiness, with the cardinal of Pavia and the rest of their company:** but Faustus
1375 notwithstanding made good cheer with that which he had beguiled the Pope of, **and in the midst of the order of St Bernard's barefooted friars, as they were going on procession through the market place called Campa de fiore, he let fall his plate, dishes and cup, and withal for a farewell he made such a thunderclap and a storm of rain,**
1380 **as though heaven and earth should have met together.**

And so he left Rome and came to Milan in Italy, near the Alps or borders of Switzerland, where he praised much to his spirit the pleasantness of the place, the city being founded in so brave a plain, by the which ran most pleasant rivers on every side of the same, having besides
1385 within the compass or circuit of seven miles, seven small seas: he saw also therein many fair palaces and goodly buildings, the duke's palace and the mighty strong castle which is in manner half the bigness of the town. Moreover, it liked him well to see the hospital of St Mary's, with divers other things. **He did nothing there worthy of memory but he**
1390 **departed back again towards Bologna, and** from thence to Florence, where he was well pleased to see the pleasant walk of merchants, the goodly vaults of the city, **for that almost the whole city is vaulted and the houses themselves are built outwardly, in such sort that the people may go under them as under a vault:** then he perused the
1395 sumptuous church in the duke's castle called Nostra Donna, Our Lady's church, in which he saw many monuments, as a marble door most huge to look upon; the gate of the castle was bell-metal, wherein are graven the holy patriarchs, with Christ and his twelve apostles, and divers other

1370 all] O; ∧ '08 &c
1376 Bernard's] Barnards T
1379 and a storm] O; ~ ∧ ~ '08 &c
1381 Milan] Millain [& var.] T
1390 Bologna] Bolognia T
1394 may] O; ∧ '08 &c
1395 Nostra] O, '18; Vostra '08/10

histories out of the Old and New Testament. **Then went he to Sienna, where he highly praised the church and hospital of Sta. Maria Formosa, with the goodly buildings, and especially the fairness and greatness of the city, and beautiful women.** Then came he to Lyons in France, where he marked the situation of the city, which lay between two hills, environed with two waters: one worthy monument in the city pleased him well, that was the great church **with the image therein; he commended the** [E4v (38)] **city highly for the great resort that it had unto it of strangers.** 1400 1405

From thence he went to Cologne, which lieth upon the river of Rhine, wherein he saw one of the ancientest monuments of the world, the which was the tomb of the three kings that came by the angel of God and their knowledge they had in the star, to worship Christ: which when Faustus saw, he spake in this manner: 'Ah, alas good men how have you erred and lost your way, you should have gone to Palestine and Bethlehem in Judea, how came you hither? Or belike after your death you were thrown into **Mare Mediterraneum about Tripolis in Syria; and so you fleeted out of the Straits of Gibraltar into the Ocean Sea, and so into the bay of Portugal; and not finding any rest you were driven alongst the coast of Galicia, Biscay and France and into the Narrow Seas, then from thence into Mare Germanicum, and so I think taken up about the town of Dort in Holland,** you were brought to Cologne to be buried: **or else I think you came more easily with a whirlwind over the Alps, and being thrown into the river of Rhine, it conveyed you to this place where you are kept as a monument.'** There saw he the church of St Ursula, where remains a monument of the 1000 virgins: it pleased him also to see the beauty of the women. Not far from Cologne lieth the town of Aachen where he saw the gorgeous temple that the emperor Carolus Quartus built of marble stone for a remembrance of him, to the end that all his successors should there be crowned. From Cologne and Aachen he went to Geneva, a city in Savoy, lying near Switzerland: it is a town of 1410 1415 1420 1425

1399 Sienna] Sena T
1408 Cologne] Cullin T; [also at 1420, 1425, 1428]
1410 of the three] O; ~ ∧ ~ '08 &c; *die 3.König* G [107]
1413 Palestine] Palestina T
Bethlehem] Bethelem [& var.] T
1414 hither] O, '10, '18; thither '08; *hieher* G [107]
1416 Gibraltar] Gibalterra [& var.] T
1423 kept as a] O; ~ ∧ ~ '08 &c
monument.] '08 &c; ~? O
1426 Aachen] Ach T; [also at 1428]
1427f end that all] O, '18; ~ ∧ ~ '08/10
1429 Geneva] '18; Genf [& var.] O &c

1430 great traffic, the lord thereof is a bishop, **whose wine-cellar Faustus and his spirit visited for the love of his good wine.**

From thence he went to Strasbourg, **where he beheld the fairest steeple that ever he had seen in his life before, for on each side thereof he might see through it, even from the covering of the minster to the**
1435 **top of the pinnacle, and it is named one of the wonders of the world:** wherefore he demanded why it was called Strasbourg: his spirit answered: 'Because it hath so many highways coming to it on every side, for Stras in Dutch is a highway, and hereof came the name. **Yea,' said Mephostophiles, 'the church which thou so wonderest at, hath more revenues**
1440 **belonging to it than the twelve dukes of Silesia are worth, for there pertain unto this church 55 towns and 463 villages besides many houses in the town.'** From thence went Faustus to Basel in Switzerland, whereas the river of Rhine runneth through the town, **parting the same as the river of Thames doth London: in this town of Basel he saw**
1445 **many rich monuments,** the town walled with brick, and round about without it goeth a great trench: [F1r (39)] no church pleased him but the Jesuits' church, **which was so sumptuously builded and beset full of alabaster pillars.** Faustus demanded of his spirit how it took the name of Basel: his spirit made answer and said, that **before this city was founded,**
1450 **there used a basiliscus, a kind of serpent, this serpent killed as many men, women and children as it took a sight of: but there was a knight that made himself a cover of crystal to come over his head and so down to the ground, and being first covered with a black cloth, over that he put the crystal, and so boldly went to see the basiliscus, and**
1455 **finding the place where she haunted, he expected her coming, even before the mouth of her cave: where, standing a while, the basilisk came forth, who, when she saw her own venomous shadow in the crystal, she split in a thousand pieces; wherefore the knight was**

1433 thereof] O; thereat '08 &c
1434 minster] '08 &c; minister O
1437 Stras] O; Stros [& var.] '08 &c; *Strassen* G [108]
1440 Silesia] Slesia T
1442 thence] '08 &c; hence O
Basel] Basile T [also at 1444]
1445f about without] O; ~ it ~ '08 &c
1447 beset] O; set '08 &c
1449 Basel] Basile [& var.] T; [also at 1461f]
founded] O; found '08 &c
1451 it] O; he '08 &c
1455 she haunted] '08 &c; he ~ O
her coming] '08 &c; his ~ O
1456 basilisk] Basylike O; Basilaske '08; Basiliscus '10, '18

richly rewarded of the emperor: after the which the knight founded this town upon the place where he had slain the serpent, and gave it the name of Basel in remembrance of his deed. 1460

From Basel Faustus went to Constance in Switzerland, at the head of the Rhine, where is a most sumptuous bridge that goeth over the Rhine, even from the gates of the town unto the other side of the stream: at the head of the river of Rhine is a small sea, called of the Switzers the Black Sea, twenty thousand paces long and fifty hundred paces broad. The town Constance took the name of this: **the emperor gave it to a clown for expounding of his riddle, wherefore the clown named the town Costnitz, that is in English, cost nothing.** From Constance he came to Ulm, where he saw the sumptuous townhouse built by two-and-fifty of the ancient senators of the city. It took the name of Ulma, for that the whole land thereabout are full of elms: but Faustus minding to depart from thence, his spirit said unto him: 'Faustus think on the town as thou wilt, it hath three dukedoms belonging to it, the which they have bought with ready money.' From Ulm, he came to Würzburg, the chiefest town in Franconia, wherein the bishop altogether keepeth his court, through the which town passeth the river of Main that runs into the Rhine: thereabout groweth strong and pleasant wine, the which Faustus well proved. **The castle standeth on a hill on the North side of the town, at the foot whereof runneth the river:** this town is full of beggarly friars, nuns, priests and Jesuits: for there are five sorts of begging friars, besides three cloisters of nuns. **At the foot of the castle stands a church, in the which there is an altar where are engraven all the four elements and all the orders and degrees in heaven, that any** [F1V (40)] **man of understanding whosoever that hath a sight thereof, will say that it is the artificiallest thing that ever he beheld.** 1465 1470 1475 1480 1485

From thence he went to Nuremberg, whither as he went by the way, his spirit informed him that the town was named of Claudius Tiberius the son of Nero the tyrant. In the town are two famous cathedral churches, the one called St Sabolt, the other St Laurence; in which church hangeth all the relics of Carolus Magnus, that is his cloak, his hose and doublet, his 1490

1462 Constance] Costuitz T; [also at 1467, 1469]
Switzerland] Sweitz T
1469 Costnitz] Costuitz T
cost nothing] T; ~ me ~ '22
1472 minding] O, '18; minded '08/10
1475 Würzburg] Wartzburg T
1476 Franconia] Frankelandt [& var.] T
1487 Nuremberg] Norenberg T; [also at 1495]

sword and crown, his sceptre and his apple. It hath a very gorgeous gilden conduit in the market of St Laurence, in which conduit is the spear that thrust our Saviour into the side and a piece of the Holy Cross; the wall is
1495 called the fair wall of Nuremberg, and hath 528 streets, 160 wells, four great, and two small clocks, six great gates and two small doors, eleven stone bridges, twelve small hills, ten appointed market places, thirteen common hothouses, ten churches. Within the town are thirty wheels of water-mills; it hath 132 tall ships, two mighty town walls of hewn stone
1500 and earth, with very deep trenches. The walls have 180 towers about them and four fair platforms, ten apothecaries, ten doctors of the common law, fourteen doctors of physic.

From Nuremberg he went to Augsburg, where at the break of the day, he demanded of his spirit whereupon the town took his name. 'This
1505 town,' saith he, 'hath had many names. When it was first built, it was called Vindelica: secondly, it was called Zizaria, the iron bridge: lastly by the emperor Octavius Augustus, it was called Augusta, **and by corruption of language the Germans have named it Augsburg.'** Now for because that Faustus had been there before, he departed without
1510 visiting their monuments to Ravensburg, where his spirit certified him that the city had had seven names, the first Tiberia, the second Quadratis, the third Hyaspolis, the fourth Reginopolis, the fifth Imbripolis, the sixth Ratisbon, lastly Ravensburg. The situation of the city pleased Faustus well, also the strong and sumptuous buildings: by the walls thereof
1515 runneth the River of Danube, in Dutch called Donau, into the which, not far from the compass of the city, falleth nearhand threescore other small rivers and fresh waters. Faustus also liked the sumptuous stone bridge over the same water, with the church standing thereon, the which was founded 1115, the name whereof is called St Remedian: in this town
1520 Faustus went into the cellar of an innholder and let out all the wine and

1492 gorgeous] O; glorious '08 &c; *schönen* G [111]
1497 appointed] O &c; fair '18 &c
1503 Nuremberg] Norenberg [& var.] T
Augsburg] Auspurg T; [also at 1508]
1505 saith] O; quoth '08 &c; *sprach* G [112]
1507f by corruption] O; ~ the ~ '08 &c
1510 Ravensburg] Rauenspurg T; *Regenspurg* G [112] [also at 1513]
1512 Hyaspolis] G [112]; Hyaspalis O; Heaspalis '08 &c
1513 Ratisbon] Ratisbona T
lastly] O; the last '08 &c
the city] O; this ~ '08 &c; *Dise Statt* G [113]
1515 Danube] Danubia T; [also at 1532]
Donau] Donow T
1519 Remedian] O; Remadian '08 &c; *Remigien* G [113]

beer that was in his cellar, after the which feat, he returned unto Munich in Bavaria, a right prince=[F2r (41)]=ly town. The town appeared as if it were new, with great streets therein, both of breadth and length: from Munich to Salzburg, where the bishop is always resident: **here saw he all the commodities that were possible to be seen, for at the hill he saw** 1525 **the form of a bell made in crystal, an huge thing to look upon, that every year groweth bigger and bigger by reason of the freezing cold.** From thence he went to Vienna, in Austria: this town is of so great antiquity that it is not possible to find the like. 'In this town,' said the spirit, 'is more wine than water, for all under the town are wells, the which 1530 are filled every year with wine, and all the water that they have, runneth by the town, that is the river Danube.'

From thence he went unto Prague, the chief city in Bohemia. This is divided into three parts, that is, Old Prague, New Prague and Little Prague. Little Prague is the place where the emperor's court is placed 1535 upon an exceeding high mountain: **there is a castle wherein are two fair churches. In the one he found a monument which might well have been a mirror to himself, and that was the sepulchre of a notable conjurer, which by his magic had so enchanted his sepulchre that whosoever set foot thereon should be sure never to die in their beds.** 1540 **From the castle he came down and went over the bridge.** This bridge hath twenty-and-four arches. **In the middle of this bridge stands a very fair monument, being a cross builded of stone and most artificially carved.** From thence he came into the Old Prague, the which is separated from the New Prague with an exceeding deep ditch, and round about 1545 enclosed with a wall of brick. **Unto this is adjoining the Jews' town, wherein are thirteen thousand men, women and children, all Jews.** There he viewed the college **and the garden where all manner of savage beasts are kept; and from thence he fet a compass round about the three towns, whereat he wondered greatly to see so mighty** 1550 **a city to stand all within the walls.**

From Prague, he flew into the air and bethought himself what he might do, or which way to take, so he looked round about, and behold, he had espied a passing fair city which lay not far from Prague, about some four-and-twenty miles, and that was Breslau in 1555

1521 his cellar] O; the ~ '08 &c
Munich] Mentz T; *München* G [113]; [also at 1524]
1526 a bell] '08 &c; Abel O;
1528 thence] '08 &c; hence O; [also at 1533]
1542 of this bridge] O; ~ the ~ '08 &c

Silesia; in the which, when he was entered, it seemed to him that he had been in paradise, so neat and clean was the streets and so sumptuous was their buildings. In this city he saw not many wonders except the brazen virgin that standeth on a bridge over the
1560 **water, and under the which standeth a mill like a powder-mill, which virgin is made to do execution upon those disobedient town-born children that be so wild that their parents cannot** [F2V (42)] **bridle them; which when any such are found with some heinous offence, turning to the shame of their parents and kindred, they are**
1565 **brought to kiss this virgin, which openeth her arms, the person then to be executed kisseth her, then doth she close her arms together with such violence that she crusheth out the breath of the person, breaketh his bulk, and so dieth: but being dead, she openeth her arms again and letteth the party fall into the mill where he is**
1570 **stamped in small morsels which the water carrieth away, so that no part of him is found again.**

From Breslau he went toward Cracow in the kingdom of Poland, where he beheld the academy, the which pleased him wonderful well. In this city the king most commonly holdeth his court **at a castle, in which**
1575 **castle are many famous monuments. There is a most sumptuous church in the same, in which standeth a silver altar, gilded and set with rich stones, and over it is a conveyance full of all manner silver ornaments belonging to the mass. In the church hangeth the jaw bones of an huge dragon that kept the rock before the castle was**
1580 **edified thereon. It is full of all manner of munition and hath always victual for three year to serve 2,000 men. Through the town runneth a river called the Vistula or Wissel, whereover is a fair wooden bridge. This water divideth the town and Casmere; in this Casmere dwelleth the Jews, being a small walled town by themselves, to the**
1585 **number of 25,000 men, women and children. Within one mile of the town there is a salt-mine where they find stones of pure salt of a 1,000 pound, or 2,000 pound or more in weight, and that in great quantity.**

1556 Silesia] Sclesia T
in the which] '08 &c; into which O
1567 person] O; partie '08 &c
1570 no] '08 &c; not any O
1572 Cracow] Cracovia [& var.] T
Poland] Polonia T
1580 manner of munition] '08 &c; ∼ ∧ ∼ O
1582 Vistula] O; Vestual '08 &c
1587 2000] '08 &c; 900 O

This salt is as black as the Newcastle coals when it comes out of the mines, but being beaten to powder, it is as white as snow. The like they have four mile from thence at a town called Buchnia. From 1590 **thence, Faustus went to Sandetz; the captain thereof was called Don Spiket Jordan. In this town are many monuments, as the tomb or sepulchre of Christ, in as ample manner as that is at Jerusalem, at the proper costs of a gentleman that went thrice to Jerusalem from that place and returned again. Not far from that town is a new town,** 1595 **wherein is a nunnery of the order of St Dioclesian, into which order may none come except they be gentlewomen and well formed and fair to look upon, the which pleased Faustus well: but having a desire to travel further and to see more wonders,** mounting up towards the East, over many lands and provinces, as into Hungary, 1600 Transilvania, Shede, Ingratz, Sardinia, and so into Constantinople, where the Turkish emperor kept his court.

This city was surnamed by Constantine the founder thereof, being builded of very fair stone. In the same [F3r (43)] the Great Turk hath three fair palaces, the walls are strong, the pinnacles are very huge and the 1605 streets large: **but this liked not Faustus, that one man might have so many wives as he would.** The sea runneth hard by the city, the wall hath eleven gates. Faustus abode there a certain time to see **the manner of the Turkish emperor's service at his table, where he saw his royal service to be such that he thought if all the Christian princes should** 1610 **banquet together and every one adorn the feast to the uttermost, they were not able to compare with the Turk for his table and the rest of his country service, wherefore it so spited Faustus that he vowed to be revenged of him, for his pomp he thought was more fit for himself:** wherefore as the Turk sat and ate, Faustus showed him a little 1615 apish play: for round about the privy chamber, he sent forth flashing flames of fire, insomuch that the whole company forsook their meat and fled, except only the Great Turk himself: him Faustus had charmed in such sort that he could neither rise nor fall, neither could any man pull him up. With this was the hall so light, as if the sun had shined in the house. 1620 Then came Faustus in form of a pope to the Great Turk, saying: 'All hail Emperor, now art thou honoured that I so worthily appear unto thee as

1599 further] '08 &c; farther O
1600 Hungary] Hungaria T
1601 Ingratz] O; Ingatz '08 &C
Sardinia] O; Sardinie '08/10; Sardenie '18
1615 and ate] O; at meat '08 &c; *und asse* G [116]

thy Mahomet was wont to do.' Hereupon he vanished, and forthwith it so thundered that the whole palace shook: **the Turk greatly marvelled**
1625 **what this should be that so vexed him, and was persuaded by his chiefest counsellors that it was Mahomet, his prophet, the which had so appeared unto them,** whereupon the Turk commanded them to fall down on their knees and to give him thanks for doing them so great honour as to show himself unto them; but the next day Faustus went into
1630 the castle where he kept his wives and concubines, in the which castle might no man upon pain of death come, except those that were appointed by the Great Turk to do them service, and they were all gelded, **which, when Faustus perceived, he said to his spirit Mephostophiles: 'How likest thou this sport? Are not these fair ladies greatly to be pitied,**
1635 **that thus consume their youth at the pleasure of one only man?' 'Why,' quoth the spirit, 'mayest not thou instead of the emperor, embrace his fairest ladies? Do what thy heart desireth herein, and I will aid thee, and what thou wishest, thou shalt have it performed.'** Wherefore Faustus **(being before this counsel apt enough to put such**
1640 **matters in practice)** caused a great fog to be round about the castle, both within and without, and he himself appeared amongst the ladies in all things as they use to paint their Mahomet, **at which sight, the ladies fell on their knees and** [F3v (44)] **worshipped him. Then Faustus took the fairest by the hand and led her into a chamber, where after his**
1645 **manner he fell to dalliance, and thus he continued a whole day and night: and when he had delighted himself sufficiently with her, he put her away and made his spirit bring him another, so likewise he kept with her 24 hours play, causing his spirit to fetch him most dainty fare.** And so he passed away six days, having each day his pleasure
1650 of a sundry lady, and that of the fairest, all which time the fog was so thick, **and so stinking, that they within the house thought they had been in hell for the time, and they without wondered thereat, in such sort that they went to their prayers calling on their god Mahomet and worshipping of his image.** Wherefore the sixth day Faustus exalted
1655 himself in the air, like to a pope, in the sight of the Great Turk and his people, and he had no sooner departed the castle but the fog vanished away, whence presently the Turk sent for his wives and concubines, demanding of them if they knew the cause why the castle was beset with a mist so long? They said, that it was the god Mahomet himself that caused

1623 Mahomet] '08 &c, G [117]; Mahumet O; [also passim to 1668]
1626 the which] O; ∧ ~ '08 &c
1642 things] O; points '08 &c

it, and how he was in the castle personally full six days, and for more certainty, 'He hath lain with six of us these six nights one after another.' Wherefore the Turk hearing this fell on his knees and gave Mahomet thanks, **desiring him to forgive him for being offended with his visiting his castle and wives those six days: but the Turk commanded that those whom Mahomet had lain by, should be most carefully looked unto, persuading himself (and so did the whole people that knew of it)** that out of their Mahomet should be raised a mighty generation; but first he demanded of the six ladies if Mahomet had had actual copulation with them, according as earthly men have. 'Yea my Lord,' quoth one, **'as if you had been there yourself, you could not have mended it,** for he lay with us stark naked, kissed and colled us, and so delighted me that for my part, I would he came two or three times a week to serve me in such sort again.' 1660 1665 1670

From whence, Faustus went to Alkar, the which beforetime was called Chairam or Memphis; in this city the Egyptian sultan holdeth his court. From thence the river Nile hath his first head and spring: it is the greatest freshwater river that is in the whole world, and always when the sun is in Cancer, it overfloweth the whole land of Egypt: then he returned again towards the North-east and to the town of Ofen and Sabatz in Hungary. This Ofen is the chiefest city in Hungary and standeth in a fertile soil, wherein groweth most excellent wine, and not far from the town there is a well, called Zipzar, the water whereof changeth iron [F4r (45)] into copper: here are mines of gold and silver and all manner of metal; we Germans call this town Ofen, but in the Hungarian speech it is Start. In the town standeth a very fair castle, and very well fortified. From thence he went to Austria and through Silesia into Saxony, unto the towns of 1675 1680 1685

1661 lain] lien O; line '08 &c
us these six] O; ~ ∧ ~ '08 &c
another. Wherefore the] O; ~ ∧ The '08 &c
1662 fell on] O; ~ down upon '08 &c
1665 lain] O; line '08 &c
1666 did the] O; ~ al ~ '08 &c
1668f had had] O; ~ not '08 &c
1674 whence] '08 &c; hence O
Alkar] O; Althar '08 &c
beforetime] O; beforetimes '08 &c
1675 sultan] Souldane [& var.] T
1676 thence] '18; hence O &c
Nile] Nilus T
1679 Sabatz] O, G [120]; Sebatz '08; Sebata [and var.] '10, '18 &c
1679f Hungary] Hungaria T
1685 thence] '08 &c; hence O; *Von dannen* G [120]
1686 Silesia] Slesia T

Magdeburg and Leipzig and Lübeck. Magdeburg is a bishopric: in this city is one of the pitchers wherein Christ changed the water into wine at Cana in Galilee. **At Leipzig nothing pleased Faustus so well as the**
1690 **great vessel in the castle, made of wood, the which is bound about with 24 iron hoops and every hoop weigheth 200 pound weight; they must go upon a ladder of 30 steps high before they can look into it. He saw also the new churchyard, where it is walled, and standeth upon a fair plain: the yard is 200 paces long, and round about in the**
1695 **inside of the wall are goodly places separated one from each other to see sepulchres in, which in the middle of the yard standeth very sumptuous: therein standeth a pulpit of white work and gold.** From thence he came to Lübeck and **Hamburg, where he made no abode, but away again to** Erfurt in Thuringia, where he visited the Freskold,
1700 and from Erfurt he went home to Wittenberg, when he had seen and visited many a strange place, being from home one year and a half, in which time he wrought more wonders than are here declared.

How Faustus had a sight of Paradise. Chap. 23.

After this, Doctor Faustus set forth again, visited these countries of
1705 Spain, Portugal, France, England, Scotland, Denmark, Sweden, Poland, Muscovy, India, Cathay, Africa, Persia and lastly, Barbary amongst the blackamoors, and in all his wandering he was desirous to visit the ancient monuments and mighty hills, **amongst the rest beholding the high hill called Tenerife, was desirous to rest upon it: from thence** he went into
1710 the isle of Britain, wherein he was greatly delighted to see the fair water and warm baths, the divers sorts of metal, with many precious stones and divers other commodities the which Faustus brought thence with him.

1687 Leipzig] Liptzig [& var.] T; [also at 1689]
1689 Galilee] Galile [& var.] T
1691 they] O; you '08 &c
1694f in the inside] O; ~ ~ side '08; ∧ ~ side '10, '18 &c
1698 thence] hence T
1699 Erfurt] Erford [& var.] T
Thuringia] Duringen T
1703 23] O, '22 &c; 34 '08 &c
1706 Cathay] Cataia T
Barbary] Barbaria T
1707 blackamoors] '08 &c; Blacke mores O
1709 Tenerife] Treno Riefe [& var.] T
1710 Britain] Brittany [& var.] T; *Britannia* G [121]

He was also at the Orkneys behind Scotland, **where he saw the tree that bringeth forth fruit that when it is ripe, openeth and falleth into the water, whereof engendreth a certain kind of fowl or bird;** these islands 1715 are in number 23 but 10 of them are not habitable, the other 13 are inhabited.

From thence, he went to the hill of Caucasus, which is the highest in all that tropic: it lieth near the borders [F4v (46)] of Scythia; hereon Faustus stood and beheld many lands and kingdoms. Faustus being on such an 1720 high hill, thought to look over all the world and beyond, for he meant to see Paradise, but he durst not commune with his spirit thereof: and being on the hill of Caucasus, he saw the whole land of India and Scythia, and towards the East as he looked he saw a mighty clear strike of fire coming from heaven upon the earth, even as it had been one of the beams of the 1725 sun; he saw in the valley four mighty waters springing: one had his course towards India, the second towards Egypt, the third and fourth towards Armenia. When he saw these, he would needs know of his spirit what waters they were, and from whence they came. His spirit gave him gently an answer, saying: 'It is Paradise that lieth so far in the East, the garden 1730 that God Himself hath planted with all manner of pleasure, and the fiery stream that thou seest, is the walls or defence of the garden, but that clear light that thou seest so far off, is the angel that hath the custody thereof with a fiery sword: and although that thou thinkest thyself to be hard by, thou hast yet farther thither from hence than thou hast ever been. The 1735 water that thou seest divided in four parts, is the water that issueth out of the well in the middle of Paradise. The first is called Ganges or Phison, the second, Gihon or Nilus, the third Tigris, and the fourth Euphrates, also thou seest that he standeth under Libra and Aries right up towards the zenith, and upon this fiery wall standeth the angel Michael with his 1740 flaming sword to keep the tree of life the which he hath in charge. But,' the spirit said unto Faustus, 'neither thou, nor I, nor any after us, yea all men whosoever are denied to visit it, or to come any nearer than we be.'

1713 Orkneys] Orchades T
1718 thence] hence T
1721 meant] O; went '08 &c; *vermeynet* G [122]
1732 defence] O; fence '08 &c
but that clear] O, '22; ~ is ~ '08, '10; ~ the ~ '18
1733 light that thou] O, '08; ~ ∧ ~ '10, '18
off, is the] O, '22; ~ that ~ '08,10; ~, that ~ ~ '18
1735 farther] O; further '08 &c
1738 Nilus, the third Tigris, and] O, '18 &c; ~ ∧ ∧ ∧ ~ '08/10; *Nilus, Tigris und* G [124]
1739 right up] O; ~ ∧ '08 &c; *reicht biß an Himmel* G [124]

Of a certain comet that appeared in Germany, and how Doctor Faustus was
1745 *desired by certain friends of his to know the meaning thereof. Chap. 24*

In Germany over the town of St Eisleben was seen a mighty great comet, whereat the people wondered; but Doctor Faustus, being there, was asked of certain of his friends his judgment or opinion in the matter. Whereupon he answered: 'It falleth out often by the course and change of
1750 the sun and moon, that the sun is under the earth and the moon above; but when the moon draweth near the change, then is the sun so strong that he taketh away all the light of the moon, in such sort that he is as red as blood: [G1r (47)] **and to the contrary, after they have been together, the moon taketh her light again from him,** and so increasing in light to the full,
1755 **she will be as red as the sun was before, and** changeth herself into divers and sundry colours, of the which springeth a prodigious monster, or as you call it, a comet, which is a figure or token appointed of God as a forewarning of his displeasure: as at one time he sendeth hunger, plague, sword or suchlike: being all tokens of his judgment; the which comet
1760 cometh through the conjunction of the sun and moon begetting a monster, whose father is the sun and whose mother is the moon, ☉ and ☽.'

A question put forth to Doctor Faustus concerning the stars. Chap. 25.

There was a learned man of the town of Halberstadt, named N. V. W.,
1765 invited Doctor Faustus to his table, but falling into communication before supper was ready, they looked out of the window, and seeing many stars in the firmament, this man being a doctor of physic and a good astrologian, said: 'Doctor Faustus, I have invited you as my guest, hoping that you will take it in good part with me, and withall I request you to
1770 impart unto me some of your experience in the stars and planets.' And seeing a star fall, he said: 'I pray you Faustus, what is the condition, quality or greatness of the stars in the firmament?' Faustus answered him: 'My friend and brother, you see that the stars that fall from heaven when they come on the earth they be very small to our thinking as candles, but

1746 Eisleben] Eizleben T
1751 he] O; it '08 &c
1764 Halberstadt] O; Holberstat '08 &c
1764f N. V. W., invited] O; N. ∧ W. who ~ '08 &c; *N. V. W.,* G [126]
1772 greatness] O; greatest '08 &c
1774 on] O; to '08 &c; *fallen auff die Erden* G [129]

being fixed in the firmament there are many as great as this city, some as great as a province or dukedom, other as great as the whole earth, other some far greater than the earth: for the length and breadth of the heavens is greater than the earth twelve times, and from the height of the heavens there is scarce any earth to be seen, yea the planets in the heavens are some so great as this land, some so great as the whole empire of Rome, some as Turkey, yea one so great as the whole world.' 1775 1780

[G1v (48)]

How Faustus was asked a question concerning the spirits that vex men. Chap. 26.

'That is most true,' saith he to Faustus, 'concerning the stars and planets: but I pray you in what kind or manner do the spirits use or vex men so little by day and so greatly by night?' Doctor Faustus answered: 'Because the spirits are by God forbidden the light, their dwelling is in darkness, and the clearer the sun shineth, the further the spirits have their abiding from it; but in the night when it is dark, they have their familiarity and abiding near unto us men. For although in the night we see not the sun, yet the brightness thereof so lighteneth the first moving of the firmament as it doth that on earth in the day, by which reason we are able to see the stars and planets in the night; even so the rays of the sun piercing upwards into the firmament, the spirits abandon the place and so come near us on earth in the darkness, filling our heads with heavy dreams and fond fantasies, with shrieking and crying in many deformed shapes: as sometimes when men go forth without light, there falleth to them a fear, that their hair standeth on end; so many start in their sleep thinking there is a spirit by him, gropeth or feeleth for him, going round about the house in his sleep, and many suchlike fantasies: and all this is for because that in the night the spirits are more familiarly by us than we are desirous of their company, and so they carry us, blinding us and plaguing us more than we are able to perceive.' 1785 1790 1795 1800

1777 for] O; as '08 &c
1778 than the] O; then ∧ '08 &c
1792 that] O; thee '08/10; here '18 &c
1795 earth in the darkness, filling] O; ~ on ~ ~ ~ '08/10; ~, ∧ ~ ~ ∧ ~ '18 &c
1796 fantasies] O; fancies '08 &c
shrieking] schriching O, '08; schriking '10. '18
1798 on] '08 &c; an O
1800 fantasies] O; fancies '08 &c; *phantaseyen* G [128]
because that in] O; ~ ∧ ~ '08 &c

How Doctor Faustus was asked a question concerning the stars that fall from
1805 *heaven. Chap. 27.*

Doctor Faustus being demanded the cause why the stars fell from heaven, he answered: 'That is but our opinion; for if one star fall, it is the great judgment of God upon us, as aforewarning of some great thing to come: for when we think that a star falleth, it is but as a spark that issueth
1810 from a candle or a flame of fire, **for if it were a substantial thing we should not so soon lose the sight of them as we do.** And likewise, if so be that we see as it were a stream of fire fall from the firmament, as oft it happeneth, yet are they no stars, but as it were a flame of fire vanishing; **but the stars are substantial, therefore are they firm and not falling.** If
1815 [G2r (49)] there fall any, it is a sign of some great matter to come, as a scourge to a people or country, and then such star falling, the gates of heaven are opened, and the clouds send forth floods, or other plagues, to the damage of the whole land and people.'

How Faustus was asked a question as concerning thunder. Chap. 28.

1820 In the month of August, there was over Wittenberg a mighty great lightning and thunder, and as Doctor Faustus was jesting merrily in the market-place with certain of his friends and companions being physicians, they desired him to tell them the cause of that weather. Faustus answered: 'It hath been commonly seen heretofore, that before a thunderclap fell a
1825 shower of rain or a gale of wind, for commonly after a wind followeth a rain, and after a rain, a thunderclap: such things come to pass when the four winds meet together in the heavens, the airy clouds are by force beaten **against the fixed crystalline firmament, but when the airy clouds meet with the firmament they are congealed and so strike**
1830 **and rush against the firmament as great pieces of ice when they meet on the water, the echo thereof soundeth in our ears,** and that we call thunder, which indeed is none other than you have heard.'

The third and last part of Doctor Faustus his merry conceits, showing after what sort he practised nigromancy in the courts of great princes, and lastly of his fearful
1835 and pitiful end.

1831 echo thereof] O, '08; each other '10, '18 &c
1834 nigromancy] nicromancie O, '10, '18; necromancie '08; *Nigromantia* G [132]

How the emperor Carolus Quintus requested of Faustus to see some of his cunning, whereunto he agreed. Chap. 29.

The emperor Carolus the fifth of that name was personally with the rest of his nobles and gentlemen at the town of Innsbruck where he kept his court, unto the which also Doctor Faustus resorted, and being there well 1840 known of divers nobles and gentlemen, he was invited into the court to meat, even in the presence of the emperor: whom when the emperor saw, he looked earnestly on him, thinking him by his looks to be some wonderful fellow, wherefore he asked one of his nobles whom he should be: who answered that he was called Doctor Faustus. Whereupon the 1845 emperor held his peace [G2v (50)] until he had taken his repast, after which he called unto him Faustus into the privy chamber, whither being come, he said unto him: 'Faustus, I have heard much of thee, that thou art excellent in the black art, and none like thee in mine empire, for men say that thou hast a familiar spirit with thee and that thou canst do what thou 1850 list. It is therefore,' saith the emperor, 'my request of thee that thou let me see a proof of thine experience, and I vow unto thee by the honour of mine imperial crown, none evil shall happen unto thee for so doing.' Hereupon Doctor Faustus answered His Majesty that upon those conditions he was ready in anything that he could, to do His Highness' commandment in 1855 what service he would appoint him. 'Well, then hear what I say,' quoth the emperor. 'Being once solitary in my house, I called to mind mine elders and ancestors, how it was possible for them to attain unto so great a degree of authority, yea so high, that we, the successors of that line, are never able to come near. As for example, the great and mighty monarch of 1860 the world Alexander Magnus, was such a lantern and spectacle to all his successors, as the chronicles make mention of so great riches, conquering and subduing so many kingdoms, the which I and those that follow me (I fear) shall never be able to attain unto: wherefore, Faustus, my hearty desire is that thou wouldst vouchsafe to let me see that Alexander and his 1865 paramour, the which was praised to be so fair, and I pray thee show me them in such sort that I may see their personages, shape, gesture and apparel as they used in their lifetime, and that here before my face; to the end that I may say I have my long desire fulfilled, and to praise thee to be a famous man in thine art and experience.' 1870

1851 saith] O; said '08 &c
1852 mine] O; my '08 &c
1862 make] '08/10; makes O, '18

Doctor Faustus answered: 'My most excellent lord, I am ready to accomplish your request in all things, so far forth as I and my spirit are able to perform: yet Your Majesty shall know that their dead bodies are not able substantially to be brought before you, but such spirits as have
1875 seen Alexander and his paramour alive, shall appear unto you in manner and form as they both lived in their most flourishing time: and herewith I hope to please Your Imperial Majesty.' Then Faustus went a little aside to speak to his spirit, but he returned again presently, saying: 'Now if it please Your Majesty you shall see them, yet upon this condition: that you
1880 demand no question of them, nor speak unto them,' which the emperor agreed unto. Wherewith Doctor Faustus opened the privy-chamber door, where presently entered the great and mighty emperor Alexander Magnus, in all things to look upon as if he had been a = [G3r (51)] = live, in proportion a strong thickset man, of a middle stature, black hair, and that
1885 both thick and curled, head and beard, red cheeks and a broad face, with eyes like a basilisk. He had on a complete harness **burnished and graven, exceeding rich to look upon;** and so passing towards the emperor Carolus, he made low and reverent courtesy: whereat the emperor Carolus would have stood up to receive and greet him with the like
1890 reverence, but Faustus took hold of him and would not permit him to do it. Shortly after, Alexander made humble reverence and went out again, and coming to the door his paramour met him: she coming in, she made the emperor likewise reverence. She was clothed in blue velvet, wrought and embroidered with pearls and gold, she was also excellent fair like milk
1895 and blood mixed, tall and slender, with a face round as an apple; **and thus she passed certain times up and down the house,** which the emperor marking, said to himself: 'Now have I seen two persons which my heart hath long wished for to behold, and sure it cannot otherwise be,' said he to himself, 'but that the spirits have changed themselves into these forms
1900 and have not deceived me,' calling to his mind the woman that raised the prophet Samuel: and for that the emperor would be the more satisfied in the matter, he thought, I have heard say that behind her neck she had a great wart or wen; wherefore he **took Faustus by the hand without any words and** went to see if it were also to be seen on her or not, but she
1905 perceiving that he came to her, bowed down her neck, where he saw a great wart, and hereupon she vanished, leaving the emperor and the rest well contented.

1894 pearls] '08 &c; pearl O; *Perlen* G [136]

How Doctor Faustus in the sight of the emperor conjured a pair of hart's horns upon a knight's head that slept out of a casement. Chap. 30.

When Doctor Faustus had accomplished the emperor's desire in all things as he was requested, he went forth into a gallery, and leaning over a rail to look into the privy garden, he saw many of the emperor's courtiers walking and talking together, and casting his eyes now this way, now that way, he espied a knight leaning out at a window of the great hall; who was fast asleep (for in those days it was hot) but the person shall be nameless that slept, for that he was a knight, although it was done to [G3v (52)] a little disgrace of the gentleman. It pleased Doctor Faustus, through the help of his spirit Mephostophiles, to firm upon his head as he slept, an huge pair of hart's horns, and as the knight awaked thinking to pull in his head, he hit his horns against the glass that the panes thereof flew about his ears. Think here how this good gentleman was vexed, for he could neither get backward nor forward; which when the emperor heard **all the courtiers laugh, and came forth to see what was happened, the emperor also when he beheld the knight with so fair a head,** laughed heartily thereat, and was therewithal well pleased: at last Faustus made him quit of his horns again, but the knight perceived how they came, etc. 1910 1915 1920 1925

How the above-mentioned knight went about to be revenged of Doctor Faustus. Chap. 31.

Doctor Faustus took his leave of the emperor and the rest of the courtiers, at whose departure they were sorry, giving him many rewards and gifts: but being a league and a half from the city he came into a wood, where he beheld the knight that he had jested with at the court, with others in harness, mounted on fair palfreys and running with full charge towards Faustus; but he seeing their intent, ran towards the bushes, and before he came amongst the bushes he returned again, running as it were to meet them that chased him. Whereupon suddenly all the bushes were turned into horsemen, which also ran to encounter with the knight and his 1930 1935

1916 although] o; though '08 &c
was done] o; ~ all ~ '08 &c
1922 heard] o; ~, '08 &c
1923 laugh] o; laught '08 &c
happened, the] o; ~. The '08 &c
1932 court,] '08 &c; ~ ∧ o
others] '08 &c; other o

company, and coming to them, they enclosed the knight and the rest, **and told them that they must pay their ransom before they departed.**
1940 Whereupon the knight seeing himself in such distress, besought Faustus to be good to them, which he denied not, but let them loose, yet he so charmed them that everyone, knight and other, for the space of a whole month did wear a pair of goat's horns on their brows, and every palfrey a pair of ox-horns on their head: and this was their penance appointed by
1945 Faustus, etc.

How three young dukes being together at Wittenberg to behold the university, requested Faustus to help them at a wish to the town of Munich in Bavaria, there to see the duke of Bavaria his son's wedding. Chap. 32.

Three worthy young dukes, the which are not here to be named, but being
1950 students altogether at the University of Wittenberg, [G4r (53)] met on a time all together, where they fell to reasoning concerning the pomp and bravery that would be at the city of Munich in Bavaria at the wedding of the duke's son, wishing themselves there but one half hour to see the manner of their jollity: to whom one replied, saying to the other two
1955 gentlemen: 'If it please you to give me the hearing, I will give you good counsel that we may see the wedding and be here again tonight, and this is my meaning: let us send to Doctor Faustus, make him a present of some rare thing and so open our minds unto him, desiring him to assist us in our enterprise, and assure ye he will not deny to fulfil our request.' Hereupon
1960 they all concluded, sent for Faustus, told him their mind and gave him a gift and invited him to a sumptuous banquet, wherewith Faustus was well contented and promised to further their journey to the uttermost. And when the time was come that the duke his son should be married, Doctor Faustus called unto him the three young gentlemen into his house,
1965 commanding them that they should put on their best apparel and adorn themselves as richly as they could. He took off his own great large cloak, went into a garden that was adjoining unto his house and set the three young dukes on his cloak, and he himself sat in the midst, but he gave them in charge that in any wise they should not once open their mouths to
1970 speak or make answer to any man so soon as they were out, no, not so much as if the duke of Bavaria or his son should speak to them or offer

1938 enclosed] '18; closed O; inclosed '08/10; *umbringet* G [140]
1947 Munich] Menchen T; [also at 1952, 1975]
1969 should] O, '18; would '08/10

them courtesy, they should give no word or answer again, to the which they all agreed. These conditions being made, Doctor Faustus began to conjure, and on a sudden arose a mighty wind, heaving up the cloak, and so carried them away in the air, and in due time they came unto Munich to 1975 the duke's court, where being entered into the outmost court, the marshal had espied them, who presently went to the duke, showing His Grace that all the lords and gentlemen were already set at the table, notwithstanding, there were newly come three goodly gentlemen with one servant, the which stood without in the court. Wherefore the good old duke came out 1980 unto them, welcoming them, requiring what they were, and whence: but they made no answer at all, **whereat the duke wondered, thinking they were all four dumb; notwithstanding for his honour's sake he took them into his court and feasted them.** Faustus notwithstanding spake to them: 'If any thing happen otherwise than well, when I say, Sit up, then 1985 fall you all on the cloak, and good enough.' Well, the water being brought, and that they must wash, one of the three had so much manners as to desire [G4v (54)] his friend to wash first, which when Faustus heard, he said: 'Sit up!' and all at once they got on the cloak, but he that spake fell off again; the other two with Doctor Faustus, were again presently at 1990 Wittenberg, but he that remained was taken and laid in prison: wherefore the other two gentlemen were very sorrowful for their friend, but Faustus comforted them, promising that on the morrow he should also be at Wittenberg.

Now all this while was this duke taken in a great fear and stricken into 1995 an exceeding dump, wondering with himself that his hap was so hard to be left behind, and not the rest, and now being locked and watched with so many keepers, there was also certain of the guests that fell to reasoning with him to know what he was, and also what the other were that were vanished away, but the poor prisoner thought with himself, 'If I open 2000 what they are, then it will be evil also with me.' Wherefore all this while he gave no man any answer, so that he was there a whole day and gave no man a word. Wherefore the old duke gave in charge, that the next morning they should rack him until he had confessed: which when the young duke heard, he began to sorrow and to say with himself: 'It may be 2005 that tomorow, if Doctor Faustus come not to aid me, then shall I be racked and grievously tormented, insomuch that I shall be constrained by force to tell more than willingly I would do.' But he comforted himself

1983 honour's] honor T
1995 in a great] o; ~ ∧ ~ '08 &c

with hope that his friends would entreat Doctor Faustus about his
2010 deliverance, as also it came to pass, for before it was day, Doctor Faustus was by him, and he conjured them that watched him into such a heavy sleep that he with his charms made open all the locks in the prison and therewithal brought the young duke again in safety to the rest of his fellows and friends, where they presented Faustus with a sumptuous gift,
2015 and so they departed the one from the other, etc.

How Doctor Faustus borrowed money of a Jew and laid his own leg to pawn for it. Chap. 33.

It is a common proverb in Germany, that although a conjurer have all things at commandment, the day will come that he shall not be worth a
2020 penny: so is it like to fall out with Doctor Faustus in promising the devil so largely: and as the devil is the author of lies, even so he led Faustus his mind in practising of things to deceive the people and blinding them, wherein he took his whole delight, thereby to bring himself to riches, yet notwithstanding, in the end he [HIr (55)] was never the richer. And
2025 although that during four-and-twenty years of his time that the devil set him, he wanted nothing, yet was he best pleased when he might deceive anybody: for out of the mightiest potentates' courts in all those countries, he would send his spirit to steal away their best cheer.

And on a time being in his merriment where he was banqueting with
2030 other students in an inn whereunto resorted many Jews, which when Doctor Faustus perceived, he was minded to play some merry jest to deceive a Jew, desiring one of them to lend him some money for a time. The Jew was content and lent Faustus threescore dollars for a month, which time being expired, the Jew came for his money and interest, but
2035 Doctor Faustus was never minded to pay the Jew again: at length the Jew coming home to his house and calling importunately for his money, Doctor Faustus made him this answer: 'Jew, I have no money, nor know I how to pay thee, but notwithstanding, to the end that thou mayest be contented, I will cut off a limb of my body, be it arm or leg, and the same
2040 shalt thou have in pawn for thy money, yet with this condition, that when I shall pay thee thy money again, then thou also give me my limb.' The Jew that was never friend to a Christian, thought with himself, this is a

2025 although that] 0; ~ ∧ '08 &c
2040 for] 0; of '08 &c
2041 also] 0; shalt '08 &c

fellow right for my purpose, that will lay his limbs to pawn for money: he
was therewith very well content; wherefore Doctor Faustus took a saw
and therewith seemed to cut off his foot (being notwithstanding nothing 2045
so). Well, he gave it to the Jew, yet upon this condition, that when he got
money to pay, the Jew should deliver him his leg, to the end he might set it
on again. The Jew was with this matter very well pleased, took his leg and
departed: and having far home, he was somewhat weary, and by the way
he thus bethought him, What helpeth me a knave's leg if I should carry it 2050
home? It would stink and so infect my house, besides it is too hard a piece
of work to set it on again, wherefore what an ass was Faustus to lay so dear
a pawn for so small a sum of money. 'And for my part,' quoth the Jew to
himself, 'this will never profit me anything,' and with these words he cast
the leg away from him into a ditch. All this Doctor Faustus knew right 2055
well; therefore, within three days after, he sent for the Jew to make him
payment of his 60 dollars. The Jew came and Doctor Faustus demanded
his pawn, there was his money ready for him: the Jew answered, the pawn
was not profitable or necessary for anything and he had cast it away; but
Faustus threateningly replied: 'I will have my [H1v (56)] leg again or else 2060
one of thine for it.' **The Jew fell to entreating, promising him to give
him what money he would ask, if he would not deal straitly with
him,** wherefore the Jew was constrained to give him 60 dollars more to be
rid of him, and yet Faustus had his leg on, for he had but blinded the Jew.

How Doctor Faustus deceived an horse-courser. Chap. 34. 2065

In like manner he served an horse-courser at a fair called Pheiffring, for
Doctor Faustus through his cunning had gotten an excellent fair horse,
whereupon he rid to the fair, where he had many chapmen that offered
him money: lastly, he sold him for 40 dollars, willing him that bought
him, that in any wise he should not ride him over any water, but the horse- 2070
courser marvelled with himself that Faustus bad him ride him over no
water. 'But,' quoth he, 'I will prove,' and forthwith he rid him into the
river. Presently the horse vanished from under him and he sat on a bundle
of straw, insomuch that the man was almost drowned. The horse-courser
knew well where he lay that had sold him his horse, wherefore he went 2075

2045 foot] o; leg '08 &c; *Fuß* G [149]
2051 home?] '08/10; ~, o; ~ ∧ '18
2061 entreating] o; intreat '08 &c
2066 an] o, '10; a '08, '18
2072 But] '18; (but o &c

angerly to his inn, where he found Doctor Faustus fast asleep and snorting on a bed, but the horse-courser could no longer forbear him, took him by the leg and began to pull him off the bed, but he pulled him so, that he pulled his leg from his body, insomuch that the horse-courser
2080 fell down backwards in the place. Then began Doctor Faustus to cry with an open throat: 'He hath murdered me.' Hereat the horse-courser was afraid and gave the flight, thinking none other with himself, but that he had pulled his leg from his body; by this means Doctor Faustus kept his money.

2085 *How Doctor Faustus ate a load of hay. Chap. 35.*

Doctor Faustus being in a town of Germany called Zwickau, where he was accompanied with many doctors and masters, and going forth to walk after supper, they met with a clown that drove a load of hay. 'Good even, good fellow,' said Faustus to the clown, 'What shall I give thee to let
2090 me eat my bellyful of hay?' The clown thought with himself, What a [H2r (57)] madman is this to eat hay! Thought he with himself, Thou wilt not eat much. They agreed for three farthings he should eat as much as he could: wherefore Doctor Faustus began to eat, and that so ravenously that all the rest of his company fell a-laughing, blinding so the poor clown that
2095 he was sorry at his heart, for he seemed to have eaten more than the half of his hay, wherefore the clown began to speak him fair, for fear he should have eaten the other half also. **Faustus made as though he had had pity on the clown and went his way.** When the clown came in place where he would be, he had his hay again as he had before, a full load.

2100 *How Doctor Faustus served the twelve students. Chap. 36.*

At Wittenberg before Faustus his house, there was a quarrel between seven students and five **that came to part the rest, one part being stronger than the other.** Wherefore Faustus seeing them to be overmatched, conjured them all blind, insomuch that the one could not
2105 see the other, and yet he so dealt with them that they fought and smote at one another still, whereat all the beholders fell a-laughing: and thus they continued blind, beating one another, until the people parted them and

2076 to] 0, '10, '18; unto '08
2080 fell down] 0; ~ ∧ '08 &c

led each one to his own home: where being entered into their houses, they received their sight perfectly again.

How Faustus served the drunken clowns. Chap. 37. 2110

Doctor Faustus went into an inn, wherein were many tables full of clowns, the which were tippling can after can of excellent wine, and to be short, they were all drunk, and as they sat, they so sang and hallooed that one could not hear a man speak for them. This angered Doctor Faustus; wherefore he said to those that had called him in: 'Mark, my masters, I will 2115 show you a merry jest.' The clowns continuing still hallooing and singing, he so conjured them that their mouths stood as wide open as it was possible for them to hold them, and never a one of them was able to close his mouth again: by and by the noise was gone. The clowns notwithstanding looked earnestly one upon another and wist not what 2120 [H2v (58)] was happened; wherefore one by one they went out, and so soon as they came without, they were as well as ever they were: but none of them desired to go in any more.

How Doctor Faustus sold five swine for six dollars apiece. Chap. 38.

Doctor Faustus began another jest: he made him ready five fat swine, the 2125 which he sold to one for six dollars apiece upon this condition, that the swine-driver should not drive them into the water. Doctor Faustus went home again, and as the swine had filed themselves in the mud, the swine-driver drove them into a water, where presently they were changed into so many bundles of straw swimming upright in the water. The buyer 2130 looked wishly about him and was sorry in his heart, but he knew not where to find Faustus, **so he was content to let all go and to lose both money and hogs.**

How Doctor Fautus played a merry jest with the duke of Anholt in his court. Chap. 39. 2135

Doctor Faustus on a time came to the duke of Anholt, the which welcomed him very courteously; this was in the month of January, where

2108 home] o; house '08 &c; *alle zu Hauß führen* G [154]
2110 How Faustus] o; ~ Doctor ~ '08 &c
drunken] '08 &c; dronken o
2113 drunk] dronken o; drunken '08 &c
2121 wherefore] o; ∧ '08 &c
2137 was in the] o; ~ ∧ ~ '08 &c

sitting at the table, he perceived the duchess to be with child, and
forbearing himself until the meat was taken from the table, and that they
2140 brought in the banqueting dishes, said Doctor Faustus to the duchess:
'Gracious Lady, I have always heard that the great bellied women do
always long for some dainties. I beseech therefore Your Grace hide not
your mind from me, but tell me what you desire to eat.' She answered him:
'Doctor Faustus, now truly I will not hide from you what my heart doth
2145 most desire, namely, that if it were now harvest, I would eat my bellyful of
ripe grapes and other dainty fruit.' Doctor Faustus answered hereupon:
'Gracious Lady, this is a small thing for me to do, for I can do more than
this.' Wherefore he took a plate and made open one of the casements of
the window, holding it forth, where incontinent he had his dish full of all
2150 manner of fruits, as red and white grapes, pears and apples, the which
came from out of strange countries. All these he presented the duchess,
saying: 'Madame, I [H3r (59)] pray you vouchsafe to taste of this dainty
fruit, the which came from a far country, for there the summer is not yet
ended.' The duchess thanked Faustus highly and she fell to her fruit with
2155 full appetite. The duke of Anholt notwithstanding could not withhold to
ask Faustus with what reason there were such young fruit to be had at that
time of the year? Doctor Faustus told him: 'May it please Your Grace to
understand that the year is divided into two circles over the whole world,
that when with us it is winter, in the contrary circle it is notwithstanding
2160 summer, for in India and Saba there falleth or setteth the sun, so that it is
so warm that they have twice a year fruit: and, gracious Lord, I have a
swift spirit, the which can in the twinkling of an eye fulfil my desire in
anything, wherefore I sent him into those countries, who hath brought
this fruit as you see,' whereat the duke was in great admiration.

2165 *How Doctor Faustus through his charms made a great castle in presence of the duke of Anholt. Chap. 40.*

Doctor Faustus desired the duke of Anholt to walk a little forth of the
court with him, wherefore they went both together into the field, where
Doctor Faustus through his skill had placed a mighty castle: which when
2170 the duke saw, he wondered thereat, so did the duchess and all the
beholders, that on that hill which was called the Rohumbuel, should on

2140 said Doctor Faustus] O; Doctor Faustus said '08 &c; *Sagt D. Faustus* G [156]
2145f of ripe grapes] O; ~ ∧ ~ '08 &c; *frische Trauben* G [156]
2156 that] O, '10, '18; the '08
2171 was] O; is '08 &c; *Rohmbühel genannt* G [159]

the sudden be so fair a castle. At last Doctor Faustus desired the duke and
the duchess to walk with him into the castle, which they denied not. This
castle was so wonderful strong, having about it a great and deep trench of
water, the which was full of fish and all manner of waterfowl, as swans, 2175
ducks, geese, bitterns and suchlike. About the wall was five stone doors
and two other doors: also within was a great open court, wherein were
enchanted all manner of wild beasts, especially such as were not to be
found in Germany, as apes, bears, buffs, antelopes and suchlike strange
beasts. Furthermore, there were other manner of beasts, as hart, hind and 2180
wild swine, roe and all manner of landfowl that any man could think on,
the which flew from one tree to another. After all this, he set his guests to
the table, being the duke and the duchess with their train, for he had
provided them a most sumptuous feast, both of meat and all manner of
drinks, for he set nine mess of meat upon the board at once, and all this 2185
[H3v (60)] must his Wagner do, place all things on the board, the which
was brought unto him by the spirit invisibly, of all things that their hearts
could desire, as wildfowl and venison, with all manner of dainty fish that
could be thought on, of wine also great plenty and of divers sorts, as
French wine, Cologne wine, Crabatsher wine, Rhenish wine, Spanish 2190
wine, Hungarian wine, Würzburg wine, malmsey and sack: in the whole,
there were an hundred cans standing round about the house. This
sumptuous banquet the duke took thankfully and afterwards he departed
homewards, and to their thinking they had neither eaten nor drunk, so
were they blinded the whilst that they were in the castle: but as they were 2195
in their palace they looked towards the castle and behold, it was all in a
flame of fire, and all those that beheld it wondered to hear so great a noise
as if it were great ordinance should have been shot off; and thus the castle
burned and consumed away clean. Which done, Doctor Faustus returned
to the duke, who gave him great thanks for showing them of so great 2200
courtesy, giving him an hundred dollars and liberty to depart or use his
own discretion therein.

2176 bitterns] Bitters T
2179ff and suchlike ... wild swine] O &c; [paraphrased in '18 &c]
2187 hearts] '08 &c; heart O
2188 wildfowl and venison] O; ~ ∧ ~ '08 &c
with] O; and '08 &c
2190 Cologne] Cullin T
2191 Würzburg] Watzburg O &c; Warzburg '18
2194 nor] O; or '08 &c
2196 behold, it was all] O; beheld ∧ ~ ~ ~ '08/10; beheld ∧ ~ ∧ ~ '18; *das sie alles wol sehen kundten* G [162]
in] O; on '08 &c

How Doctor Faustus with his company visited the bishop of Salzburg his wine-cellar. Chap. 41.

2205 Doctor Faustus having taken his leave of the duke, he went to Wittenberg, near about Shrovetide, and being in company with certain students, Doctor Faustus was himself the god Bacchus, who having well feasted the students before with dainty fare **after the manner of Germany, where it is counted no feast except all the bidden guests**
2210 **be drunk,** which Doctor Faustus intending, said: 'Gentlemen and my guests, will it please you to take a cup of wine with me in a place or cellar whereunto I will bring you?' and they all said willingly: 'We will.' Which when Doctor Faustus heard, he took them forth, set either of them upon an holly wand, and so were conjured into the bishop of Salzburg his cellar,
2215 for there about grew excellent pleasant wine: there fell Faustus and his company to drinking and swilling, not of the worst but of the best, and as they were merry in the cellar, came down to draw drink the bishop's butler: which when he perceived so many persons there he cried with a loud voice: 'Thieves, thieves!' This spited Doctor Faustus wonderfully,
2220 wherefore he made every [H4r (61)] one of his company to sit on their holly wand and so vanished away, and in parting Doctor Faustus took the butler by the hair of the head and carried him away with them, until they came unto a mighty high lopped tree, and on the top of that huge tree he set the butler, where he remained in a most fearful perplexity, and Doctor
2225 Faustus departed to his house where they took their *valete* one of another, drinking the wine the which they had stolen in great bottles of glass out of the bishop's cellar. The butler that had held himself by the hand upon the lopped tree all the night, was almost frozen with cold, espying the day, and seeing the tree of so huge great highness, thought with himself, 'It is
2230 impossible to come off this tree without peril of death.' At length he had espied certain clowns which were passing by: he cried: 'For the love of God, help me down.' The clowns seeing him so high, wondered what madman would climb to so huge a tree, wherefore as a thing most miraculous, they carried tidings unto the bishop of Salzburg; then was
2235 there great running on every side to see a man in a huge tree, and many

2205 taken his leave] O; ~ ∧ ~ '08 &c
2214 were] O; was '08 &c
2223 unto] O; to '08 &c
2224 perplexity, and] O; perplexitie: ∧ '08 &c; *und* G [164]
2234 unto] O; to '08 &c
2235 a man] O; him '08 &c
a huge] O; the '08 &c

devices they practised to get him down with ropes, **and being demanded by the bishop how he came there, he said that he was brought thither by the hair of the head of certain thieves that were robbing of the wine-cellar, but what they were he knew not, 'For,' said he, 'they had faces like men, but they wrought like devils.'** 2240

How Doctor Faustus kept his Shrovetide. Chap. 42.

There were seven students and masters that studied divinity, *juris prudentia,* and *medicina;* all these having consented were agreed to visit Doctor Faustus and so to celebrate Shrovetide with him: who being come to his house, he gave them their welcome, for they were his dear friends, 2245 desiring them to sit down, where he served them with a very good supper of hens, fish and other roast, yet were they but slightly cheered: wherefore Doctor Faustus comforted his guests, excusing himself that they stole upon him so suddenly that he had not leisure to provide for them so well as they were worthy. 'But my good friends,' quoth he, 'according to the 2250 use of our country we must drink all this night, and so a draught of the best wine to bedward is commendable. For you know that in great potentates' courts they use as this night great feasting, the like will I [H4v (62)] do for you: for I have three great flagons of wine, the first is full of Hungarian wine, containing eight gallons, the second of Italian wine, 2255 containing seven gallons, the third containing six gallons of Spanish wine, **all the which we will tipple out before it be day.** Besides, we have fifteen dishes of meat, **the which my spirit Mephostophiles hath fet so far that it was cold before he brought it,** and they are all full of the daintiest things that one's heart can devise. But,' saith Faustus, 'I must 2260 make them hot again: and you may believe me, gentlemen, that this is no blinding of you, whereas you think that it is no natural food; **verily, it is as good and as pleasant as ever you ate.'** And having ended his tale, he commanded his boy to lay the cloth, which done, he served them with fifteen mess of meat, having three dishes to a mess, the which were of all 2265 manner of venison and other dainty wildfowl, and for wine there was no lack, as Italian wine, Hungarian wine and Spanish wine: and when they were all made drunk, and that they had almost eaten all their good cheer,

2240 they wrought] '08 &c; the ~ o;
2241 42] o, '10, '18; 47 '08
2248 stole] '08 &c; stale o
2256 gallons, the third containing] o, '18; ~; ~ ~ containeth '08/10
2265 were of all] o; ~ ∧ ~ '08 &c; *von allerley* G [166]

they began to sing and to dance until it was day and then they departed
2270 each one to his own habitation: at whose parting, Doctor Faustus desired
them to be his guests again the next day following.

How Doctor Faustus feasted his guests on the Ash Wednesday. Chap. 43.

Upon Ash Wednesday came unto Doctor Faustus his bidden guests the
students, whom he feasted very royally, insomuch that they were all full
2275 and lusty, singing and dancing as the night before: and when the high
glasses and goblets were caroused one to another, Doctor Faustus began
to play them some pretty jests, insomuch that round about the hall was
heard most pleasant music, and that in sundry places, in this corner a lute,
in another a cornet, in another a cittern, gittern, clarigolds, harp,
2280 hornpipe: in fine, all manner of music was heard there at that instant,
whereat all the glasses and goblets, **cups and pots, dishes and all that
stood on the board,** began to dance: then Doctor Faustus took ten stone
pots and set them down on the floor, where presently they began to dance
and to smite one against the other that the shivers flew round about the
2285 whole house, whereat the whole company fell a-laughing. Then he began
another jest; he set an instrument on the table and caused a monstrous
great ape to come in amongst them, which ape began to [11r (63)] dance
and to skip, showing them many merry conceits. In this and suchlike
pastime they passed away the whole day, where, night being come,
2290 Doctor Faustus bade them all to supper, which they lightly agreed unto,
for students in these cases are easily entreated: wherefore he promised
to feast them with a banquet of fowl and afterwards they would all go
about with a mask. Then Doctor Faustus put forth a long pole out of the
window, whereupon presently there came innumerable of birds and
2295 wildfowl, and so many as came had not any power to fly away again, but
he took them and flang them to the students: who lightly pulled off the
necks of them, and being roasted they made their supper, which being
ended they made themselves ready to the mask. Doctor Faustus
commanded every one to put on a clean shirt over his other clothes, which
2300 being done, they began to look one upon another: it seemed to each one of

2270 each] O; every [& var.] '08 &c
2275 singing and dancing] O; dancing ~ singing '08 &c; *sangen, sprangen* G [167]
2277 jests] O; feats '08 &c; *Gauckelspiel* G [167]
2279 cittern, gittern] O; Cithern, ∧ '08 &c; *Geigen, Cythern, Harpffen* G [167]
2283 and] '08 &c; add O
2292 all go] O; go all '08 &c

them they had no heads, and so they went forth unto certain of their neighbours, at which sight the people were wonderfully afraid. **And as the use of Germany is, that wheresoever a mask entereth, the good man of the house must feast them:** so when these maskers were set to their banquet, they seemed again in their former shape with heads, 2305 insomuch that they were all known what they were: and having sat and well eaten and drunk, Doctor Faustus made that every one had an ass's head on, with great and long ears. So they fell to dancing and to drive away the time until it was midnight and then every man departed home, **and as soon as they were out of the house each one was in his natural** 2310 **shape again,** and so they ended and went to sleep.

How Doctor Faustus the day following was feasted of the students, and of his merry jests with them while he was in their company. Chap. 44.

The last Bacchanalia was held on Thursday, where ensued a great snow, and Doctor Faustus was invited unto the students that were with him the 2315 day before, where they had prepared an excellent banquet for him: which banquet being ended, Doctor Faustus began to play his old pranks, and forthwith were in the place thirteen apes that took hands and danced round in a ring together, then they fell to tumbling and to vaulting one over another, that it was most pleasant to behold, then they leaped out of 2320 the window and vanished away. Then they set before Doctor Faustus a roasted calf's head: which one of [11v (64)] the students cut a piece off, and laid it on Doctor Faustus his trencher, which piece being no sooner laid down but the calf's head began to cry mainly out like a man: 'Murder, murder! Out alas what doest thou to me?' Whereat they were all amazed, 2325 but after a while considering of Faustus his jesting tricks they began to laugh and then they pulled in sunder the calf's head and ate it up. Whereupon Doctor Faustus asked leave to depart, but they would in no wise agree to let him go, except that he would promise to come again. Presently then Faustus, through his cunning, made a sledge, the which 2330 was drawn about the house **with four fiery dragons: this was fearful for the students to behold, for they saw Faustus ride up and down as though he should have fired and slain all them in the house.** This sport continued until midnight with such a noise that they could not hear

2307 eaten] eat [& var.] T
2319 tumbling] '08 &c; tumble O
vaulting] vauting T
2324f Murder, murder!] Murther, murther T

2335 one another, and the heads of the students were so light that they thought themselves to be in the air all that time.

How Doctor Faustus showed the fair Helena unto the students upon the Sunday following. Chap. 45.

The Sunday following came these students home to Doctor Faustus his
2340 own house and brought their meat and drink with them: these men were right welcome guests unto Faustus, wherefore they all fell to drinking of wine smoothly: and being merry, they began some of them to talk of the beauty of women, **and every one gave forth his verdict what he had seen and what he had heard.** So one among the rest said: 'I never was so
2345 desirous of anything in this world as to have a sight (if it were possible) of fair Helena of Greece, for whom the worthy town of Troy was destroyed and razed down to the ground.' Therefore, saith he, that in all men's judgment she was more than commonly fair, because that when she was stolen away from her husband, there was for her recovery so great
2350 bloodshed.

Doctor Faustus answered: 'For that you are all my friends and are so desirous to see that famous pearl of Greece, fair Helena, the wife of King Menelaus and daughter of Tyndareus and Leda, sister to Castor and Pollux, who was the fairest lady in all Greece: I will therefore bring her
2355 into your presence personally, and in the same form of attire as she used to go when she was in her chiefest flower and pleasantest prime of youth. The like have I done for the emperor Carolus Quintus: at his desire I showed him Alexander the Great and his pa=[12r(65)]=ramour. But,' said Doctor Faustus, 'I charge you all that upon your perils you speak not
2360 a word, nor rise up from the table so long as she is in your presence.' And so he went out of the hall, returning presently again, after whom immediately followed the fair and beautiful Helena, whose beauty was such that the students were all amazed to see her, esteeming her rather to be a heavenly than an earthly creature. This lady appeared before them in a
2365 most sumptuous gown of purple velvet, richly imbrodered. Her hair hanged down loose as fair as the beaten gold, and of such length that it reached down to her hams; with amorous coal-black eyes, a sweet and

2343 verdict] verdit T
2353 Tyndareus] Tindalus [& var.] T
2356 flower] flowers [& var.] T
2357 Quintus] O; Magnus '08 &c; *Carolo Quinto* G [172]
2367 with amorous] O; ~ her ~ '08/10; having most ~ '18 &c; *mit schönen* G [173]

pleasant round face, her lips red as a cherry, her cheeks of roseal colour, her mouth small, her neck as white as the swan, tall and slender of personage, and in sum, there was not one imperfect part in her. She 2370 looked round about her with a rolling hawk's eye, a smiling and wanton countenance, which near-hand inflamed the hearts of the students but that they persuaded themselves she was a spirit, wherefore such fantasies passed away lightly with them: and thus fair Helena and Doctor Faustus went out again one with another. But the students at Doctor Faustus his 2375 entering again into the hall, requested of him to let them see her again the next day, for that they would bring with them a painter and so take her counterfeit, which he denied, affirming that he could not always raise up her spirit, but only at certain times. 'Yet,' said he, 'I will give you her counterfeit, which shall be always as good to you as if yourselves should 2380 see the drawing thereof,' which they received according to his promise, but soon lost it again. The students departed from Faustus home every one to his house, but they were not able to sleep the whole night for thinking on the beauty of fair Helena. Wherefore a man may see that the devil blindeth and inflameth the heart with lust oftentimes, that men fall in 2385 love with harlots, **nay, even with furies,** which afterward cannot lightly be removed.

How Doctor Faustus conjured away the four wheels from a clown's waggon. Chap. 46.

Doctor Faustus was sent for to a marshall of Brunswick who was greatly 2390 troubled with the falling sickness. Now Faustus had this use, never to ride but walk forth on foot, **for he could** [12v (66)] **ease himself when he list,** and as he came near unto the town of Brunswick, there overtook him a clown with four horses and an empty waggon, to whom Doctor Faustus jestingly to try him, said: 'I pray thee, good fellow, let me ride a little to 2395 ease my weary legs,' which the buzzardly ass denied, saying that his horses were also weary, and he would not let him get up. Doctor Faustus did this

2370 part] o; place '08 &c; *untädlin* G [173]
2373f wherefore... them] o &c; [paraphrased in '18 &c]
fantasies] phantasies o; fancies '08 &c
2375f at ... hall] o &c; [paraphrased in '18 &c]
2376 entering again] o; ~ in ~ '08/10
2383 the whole] o; that ~ '08 &c
2386f harlots ... removed] o &c; whereby their minds can afterwards be hardly ~ '18 &c
2390 a marshall] '08/10; the ~ o, '18; *einem Marschalk* G [175]
2391f use, ... ease] o &c; [paraphrased in '18 &c]
2392f he list] '18; his ~ o &c 2397 also] o; all '08 &c

but to prove the buzzard, if there were any courtesy to be found in him if need were.

2400 But such churlishness as is commonly found among clowns, was by Doctor Faustus well requited, even with the like payment: for he said unto him: 'Thou doltish clown, void of all humanity, seeing thou art of so currish a disposition, I will pay thee as thou hast deserved, for the four wheels of thy waggon thou shalt have taken from thee. Let me see then 2405 how canst thou shift.' Hereupon his wheels were gone, his horses also fell down to the ground as though they had been dead: whereat the clown was sore afright, measuring it as a just scourge of God for his sins and churlishness: wherefore all troubled, and wailing, he humbly besought Doctor Fautus to be good unto him, confessing he was worthy of it, 2410 notwithstanding if it pleased him to forgive him, he would hereafter do better. Which humility made Faustus his heart to relent, answering him on this manner: 'Well, do so no more, but when a poor weary man desireth thee, see that thou let him ride. But yet thou shalt not go altogether clear, for although thou have again thy four wheels, yet shalt 2415 thou fetch them at the four gates of the city.' So he threw dust on the horses and revived them again, and the clown for his churlishness was fain to fetch his wheels, spending his time with weariness, **whereas before he might have done a good deed, and gone about his business quietly.**

How four jugglers cut one another's head off and set them on again; and how 2420 *Doctor Faustus deceived them. Chap. 47.*

Doctor Faustus came in the Lent unto Frankfurt fair, where his spirit Mephostophiles gave him to understand that in an inn were four jugglers that cut one another's head off, and after their cutting off, sent them to the barber to be trimmed, which many people saw. This angered Faustus (for 2425 he meant to have himself the only cock in the devil's basket) and he went to the place where they [13r (67)] were, to behold them. And as these jugglers were together, ready one to cut off the other's head, there stood

2398 the buzzard] O &c; this clowne '18 &c
2400 as is] O &c; ∧ ∼ '18 &c
2402 humanity] O, '22; humility [& var.] '08 &c
2407 afright] O; afrighted '08 &c
2408 troubled] O; trembling '08 &c; *bekümmert* G [176f]
2411 relent] O; repent '08 &c; *Faustum die Demuth erbarmete* G [177]
2417f weariness ... quietly] T; [paraphrased in '22]
2421 Frankfurt] Franckfort [& var.] T
2427 the other's] O; anothers '08 &c

also the barbers ready to trim them, and by them upon the table stood likewise a glass full of distilled water, and he that was the chiefest among them stood by it. Thus they began: they smote off the head of the first, and presently there was a lily in the glass of distilled water, where Faustus perceived this lily as it were springing, and the chief juggler named it the tree of life. Thus dealt he with the first, making the barber wash and comb his head, and then he set it on again; presently the lily vanished away out of the water, hereat the man had his head whole and sound again. The like did they with the other two: and as the turn and lot came to the chief juggler that he also should be beheaded, and that his lily was most pleasant, fair and flourishing green, they smote his head off, and when it came to be barbed it troubled Faustus his conscience, **insomuch that he could not abide to see another do anything, for he thought himself to be the principal conjurer in the world,** wherefore Doctor Faustus went to the table whereas the other jugglers kept that lily, and so he took a small knife and cut off the stalk of the lily, **saying to himself, none of them should blind Faustus:** yet no man saw Faustus to cut the lily, but when the rest of the jugglers thought to have set on their master's head, they could not, wherefore they looked on the lily and found it a-bleeding: by this means the juggler was beguiled and so died in his wickedness, yet not one thought that Doctor Faustus had done it.

How an old man the neighbour of Faustus, sought to persuade him to amend his evil life and to fall unto repentance. Chap. 48.

A good Christian, an honest and virtuous old man, a lover of the Holy Scriptures, who was neighbour unto Doctor Faustus: when he perceived that many students had their recourse in and out unto Doctor Faustus, he suspected his evil life, wherefore like a friend he invited Doctor Faustus to supper unto his house, unto the which he agreed; and having ended their banquet, the old man began with these words: 'My loving friend and neighbour Doctor Faustus, I have to desire of you a friendly and Christian request, beseeching you that you will vouchsafe not to be angry with me, but friendly resolve me in my doubt, and take my poor inviting in good

2429 among] O; amongst '08 &c
2432 perceived] O; perceiving '08 &c
were springing] O; was ~ '08 &c
2437 his lily] O; this ~ '08 &c; *seine Lilien* G [179]
2446 a-bleeding] O; bleeding '08 &c
2449 an] O, '18; the '08/10; *einem* G [181]
2457 have] O; am '08 &c; *ich habe zu euch ein . . . Bitt* G [181]

2460 part.' To whom Doctor Faustus answered: 'My loving neighbour, I pray you say your mind.'

Then began the old patron to say: 'My good neighbour, you know in the [13v (68)] beginning how that you have defied God and all the host of heaven, and given your soul to the devil, wherewith you have incurred 2465 God's high displeasure and are become from a Christian far worse than a heathen person. Oh consider what you have done! It is not only the pleasure of the body but the safety of the soul that you must have respect unto: of which if you be careless, then you are cast away and shall remain in the anger of almighty God. But yet is it time enough, Doctor Faustus, if 2470 you repent and call unto the Lord for mercy, as we have example in the Acts of the Apostles, the eighth chapter, of Simon in Samaria, who was led out of the way, affirming that he was *Simon homo sanctus*. This man was notwithstanding in the end converted, after that he had heard the sermon of Philip, for he was baptized and saw his sins and repented. Likewise I 2475 beseech you, good brother Doctor Faustus, let my rude sermon be unto you a conversion; and forget the filthy life that you have led, repent, ask mercy and live: for Christ saith, Come unto me all ye that are weary and heavy laden, and I will refresh you. And in Ezekiel: I desire not the death of a sinner, but rather that he convert and live. Let my words, good 2480 brother Faustus, pierce into your adamant heart, and desire God for His son Christ His sake, to forgive you. Wherefore have you so long lived in your devilish practices, knowing that in the Old and New Testament you are forbidden, and that men should not suffer any such to live, neither have any conversation with them, for it is an abomination unto the Lord; 2485 and that such persons have no part in the Kingdom of God?'

All this while Doctor Faustus heard him very attentively, and replied: 'Father, your persuasions like me wondrous well and I thank you with all my heart for your good will and counsel, promising you so far as I may to follow your discipline,' whereupon he took his leave. And being come 2490 home, **he laid him very pensive on his bed,** bethinking himself of the words of the good old man, and in a manner began to repent that he had

2463f host of heaven] '08 &c; ~ ∧ ~ O
2469 is it] O; it is '08 &c
2471 eighth chapter] eight Chap. O; 8. chap '08 &c
2477 all ye that] O, '18 &c; ~ ∧ ~ '08/10
2478 laden] '08 &c; loden O; *beladen* G [183]
2479 he convert] O; ~ will ~ '08 &c; *das er sich bekehr* G [183]
2488 so far] O; as ~ '08 &c; *so viel* G [184]
2489 follow] O; allow '08 &c; *nachzukommen* G [184]
2491 the good old] O; ~ ∧ ~ '08 &c

given his soul to the devil, intending to deny all that he had promised unto Lucifer. Continuing in these cogitations, suddenly his spirit appeared unto him clapping him upon the head, and wrung it as though he would have pulled his head from his shoulders, saying unto him: 'Thou knowest, Faustus, that thou hast given thyself body and soul unto my lord Lucifer and hast vowed thyself an enemy unto God and unto all men; and now thou beginnest to harken to an old doting fool which persuadeth thee as it were unto God, when indeed it is too late, for that thou art the devil's, and he hath good power presently to fetch [14r (69)] thee: wherefore he hath sent me unto thee, to tell thee, **that seeing thou hast sorrowed for that thou hast done,** begin again and write another writing with thine own blood, if not, then will I tear thee all to pieces.' Hereat Doctor Faustus was sore afraid and said: 'My Mephostophiles, I will write again what thou wilt;' wherefore he sat him down, and with his own blood he wrote as followeth, which writing was **afterward sent to a dear friend of the said Doctor Faustus being his kinsman.** 2495 2500 2505

How Doctor Faustus wrote the second time with his own blood and gave it to the devil. Chap. 49.

I Doctor John Faustus, acknowledge by this my deed and handwriting, that sith my first writing, which is seventeen years, that I have right willingly held, and have been an utter enemy unto God and all men, the which I once again confirm, and give fully and wholly myself unto the devil both body and soul, even unto the great Lucifer: and that at the end of seven years ensuing after the date of this letter, he shall have to do with me according as it pleaseth him, either to lengthen or shorten my life as liketh him: and hereupon I renounce all persuaders that seek to withdraw me from my purpose by the word of God, either ghostly or bodily. And further, I will never give ear unto any man, be he spiritual or temporal, **that moveth any matter for the salvation of my soul.** Of all this writing and that therein contained, be witness, my own blood, the which with mine own hand I have begun, and ended. 2510 2515 2520

Dated at Wittenberg, **the 25th of July.**

2492 unto] O; to '08 &c
2495 his head] '08 &c; the ~ O; *den Kopff* G [185]
his shoulders] '08 &c; the ~ O
2496 unto my lord] O; to ~ ~ '08 &c
2498 to an] O; unto ~ '08 &c
2522 hand] hands T

And presently upon the making of this letter, he became so great an
2525 enemy unto the poor old man that he sought his life by all means possible; but this godly man was strong in the Holy Ghost, that he could not be vanquished by any means: for about two days after that he had exhorted Faustus, as the poor man lay in his bed, suddenly there was a mighty rumbling in the chamber, the which he was never wont to hear, and he
2530 heard as it had been the groaning of a sow, which lasted long: whereupon the good old man began to jest and mock, and said: 'Oh what barbarian cry is this? Oh fair bird, what foul music is this of a fair angel, that could not tarry two days in his place? [I4v (70)] Beginnest thou now to run into a poor man's house where thou hast no power, and wert not able to keep
2535 thine own two days?' With these and suchlike words the spirit departed. And when he came home Faustus asked him how he had sped with the old man: to whom the spirit answered, the old man was harnessed and that he could not once lay hold upon him: but he would not tell how the old man had mocked him, for the devils can never abide to hear of their fall. Thus
2540 doth God defend the hearts of all honest Christians that betake themselves under his tuition.

How Doctor Faustus made a marriage between two lovers. Chap. 50.

In the city of Wittenberg was a student, a gallant gentleman, named N. N. This gentleman was far in love with a gentlewoman, fair and proper of
2545 personage. This gentlewoman had a knight that was a suitor unto her, and many other gentlemen, the which desired her in marriage, but none could obtain her. So it was that this N. N. was very well acquainted with Faustus **and by that means became a suitor unto him to assist him in the matter,** for he fell so far in despair with himself that he pined away to the
2550 skin and bones. But when he had opened the matter unto Doctor Faustus, he asked counsel of his spirit Mephostophiles, the which told him what to do. Hereupon Doctor Faustus went home to the gentleman and bade him be of good cheer, for he should have his desire, for he would help him to that he wished for, and that this gentlewoman should love none other but
2555 him only: wherefore Doctor Faustus so changed the mind of the damsel by a practice he wrought, that **she would do no other thing but think on him whom before she had hated, neither** cared she for any man but

2539 abide to hear of] o, '18; ~ ^ ^ ~ '08/10
2542 Chap.] Cap. o, '18; Cha. '08; Ch. '10

him alone. The device was thus: Faustus commanded this gentleman that he should clothe himself in all the best apparel that he had and that he should go unto this gentlewoman, and there to show himself, giving him also a ring, commanding him in any wise that he should dance with her before he departed. Wherefore he followed Faustus his counsel, went to her, **and when they began to dance they that were suitors began to take every one his lady in his hand, and this good gentleman took her whom before had so disdained him,** and in the dance he thrust the ring into her hand that Doctor Faustus had given him, the which she no sooner touched but she fell immediately in love with him, **beginning in the dance to** [K1r (71)] **smile and many times to give him winks, rolling her eyes, and in the end** she asked him if he could love her and make her his wife. He gladly answered, he was content: and hereupon they concluded, and were married by the means and help of Doctor Faustus, for which he received a good reward of the gentleman.

How Doctor Faustus led his friends into his garden at Christmas and showed them many strange sights in his 19th year. Chap. 51.

In December, about Christmas, in the city of Wittenberg, were many young gentlewomen, the which were come out of the country to make merry with their friends and acquaintance: amongst whom there were certain that were well acquainted with Doctor Faustus, wherefore they were often invited as his guests unto him, and being with him on a certain time after dinner, he led them into his garden where he showed them all manner of flowers and fresh herbs, trees bearing fruit and blossoms of all sorts, insomuch that they wondered to see that in his garden should be so pleasant a time as in the midst of summer: and without in the streets and all over the country, it lay full of snow and ice. Wherefore this was noted of them as a thing miraculous, **each one gathering and carrying away all such things as they best liked, and so departed delighted with their sweet smelling flowers.**

2559 the best] '08 &c; his ∼ o
2572 for which] o; ∼ there '08/10; ∼ the which '18; *darvon* G [191]
he received ... gentleman] o &c; [paraphrased in '18 &c]
2573 his garden] o, '18; the ∼ '08/10; *seinem* G [191]
2576 gentlewomen] o; gentlemen '08 &c; *Frauenzimmers* G [191]
2582 that in his] o; ∼ ∧ ∼ '08 &c;
2582f should be so pleasant] o &c; ∼ ∧ ∼ flourish '18 &c
2583 a time] o; that ∼ '08/10; at that ∼ '18 &c
midst] o, '18; middle '08/10

How Doctor Faustus gathered together a great army of men in his extremity against a knight that would have injured him on his journey. Chap. 52.

2590 Doctor Faustus travelled towards Eisleben, and when he was nigh half the way, he espied seven horsemen, and the chief of them he knew to be the knight to whom he had played a jest in the emperor's court, for he had set a huge pair of hart's horns upon his head: and when the knight now saw that he had fit opportunity to be revenged of Faustus he ran upon
2595 him, himself and those that were with him, to mischief him, intending privily to shoot at him: which, when Doctor Faustus espied, he vanished away into the wood which was hard by them. But when the knight perceived that he was vanished away, he caused [K1v (72)] his men to stand still, where as they remained they heard all manner of warlike
2600 instruments of music, as drums, flutes, trumpets and suchlike, and a certain troop of horsemen running towards them. Then they turned another way and there also were assaulted on the same side: then another way and yet they were freshly assaulted, so that which way soever they turned themselves he was encountered: insomuch that when the knight
2605 perceived that he could escape no way, but that they his enemies laid on him which way soever he offered to fly, he took a good heart and ran amongst the thickest, **and thought with himself better to die than to live with so great an infamy.** Therefore, being at handy-blows with them, he demanded the cause why they should so use them: but none of
2610 them would give him answer until Doctor Faustus showed himself unto the knight, where withal they enclosed him round and Doctor Faustus said unto him: 'Sir, yield your weapon and yourself, otherwise it will go hardly with you.' The knight that knew none other but that he was environed with an host of men (where indeed they were none other than
2615 devils), yielded. Then Faustus took away his sword, his piece and horse, with all the rest of his companions'. And further he said unto him: 'Sir, the chief general of our army hath commanded to deal with you according to the law of arms. You shall depart in peace whither you please.' And then he gave the knight an horse after the manner, and set him thereon; so he
2620 rode, the rest went on foot until they came to their inn, where being

2590 Eisleben] Eyszleben [& var.] T
2594f upon him, himself] O; ~ ∧ ~ '08/10; ~ ~ ∧ '18 [with 'and those... with him' in parentheses]
2596 shoot at him] O; ~ ∧ ~ '08/10; slay him '18; *uff in zu schiessen* G [193]
2613 hardly] O; hard '08 &c
knight that knew] O; ~ ∧ ~ '08 &c; *Der Freyherr vermeynte nit anders* G [196]
2616 companions'] ~ ∧ T

alighted, his page rode on his horse to the water, and presently the horse vanished away, the page being almost sunk and drowned, but he escaped: and coming home, the knight perceived his page so bemired and on foot, asked where his horse was become? Who answered that he was vanished away: which when the knight heard, he said: 'Of a truth, this is Faustus his doing, for he serveth me now as he did before at the court, only to make me a scorn and a laughing-stock.' 2625

How Doctor Faustus caused Mephostophiles to bring him seven of the fairest women that he could find in all those countries he had travelled in, in the 20th year. Chap. 53. 2630

When Doctor Faustus called to mind that his time from day to day drew nigh, he began to live a swinish and epicurish life, wherefore he commanded his spirit Mephostophiles to bring him [K2r (73)] seven of the fairest women that he had seen in all the time of his travel: which being brought, first one, and then another, he lay with them all, insomuch that he liked them so well that he continued with them in all manner of love and made them to travel with him in all his journeys. These women were two Netherlanders, one Hungarian, one English, two Walloons, one Franconian: and with these sweet personages he continued long, yea even to his last end. 2635 2640

How Doctor Faustus found a mass of money when he had consumed 22 of his years. Chap. 54.

To the end that the devil would make Faustus his only heir, he showed unto him where he should go and find a mighty huge mass of money, and that he should have it in an old chapel that was fallen down, half a mile distant from Wittenberg; there he bade him to dig and he should find it, the which he did, and having digged reasonable deep he saw a mighty huge serpent, the which lay on the treasure itself. The treasure itself lay like an huge light burning: but Doctor Faustus charmed the serpent that he crept into a hole, and when he digged deeper to get up the treasure, he found nothing but coals of fire: there also he heard and saw many that 2645 2650

2638 Netherlanders] O, '08; Netherlands '10, '18
English] T; Scotish '22
Walloons] Wallons T
2639 Franconian] Francklander T
2649 Doctor] '08 &c; D. O

were tormented, yet notwithstanding he brought away the coals, and when he was come home it was all turned into silver and gold, as after his death was found by his servant, the which was almost about estimation, a
2655 thousand guilders.

How Doctor Faustus made the spirit of fair Helena of Greece his own paramour and bedfellow in his 23rd year. Chap. 55.

To the end that this miserable Faustus might fill the lust of his flesh and live in all manner of voluptuous pleasures, it came in his mind after he had
2660 slept his first sleep, and in the 23rd year past of his time, that he had a great desire to lie with fair Helena of Greece, especially her whom he had seen and showed unto the students of Wittenberg, wherefore he called unto him his spirit Mephostophiles, commanding him to bring him the fair Helena, which he also did. Whereupon he fell in love with her and made
2665 her his common concubine and bedfellow, for she was so beautiful and delightful a piece that he could not be one [K2V (74)] hour from her **if he should therefore have suffered death, she had so stolen away his heart: and to his seeming,** in time she was with child, and in the end brought him a man child, whom Faustus named Justus Faustus: this child
2670 told Doctor Faustus many things that were to come and what strange matters were done in foreign countries: but in the end when Faustus lost his life, the mother and the child vanished away both together.

How Doctor Faustus made his will, in the which he named his servant Wagner to be his heir. Chap. 56.

2675 Doctor Faustus was now in his 24th and last year and he had a pretty stripling to his servant, the which had studied also at the University of Wittenberg. This youth was very well acquainted with his knaveries and sorceries, so that he was hated as well for his own knaveries as also for his master's: for no man would give him entertainment into his service
2680 because of his unhappiness but Faustus. This Wagner was so well beloved with Faustus that he used him as his son: for do what he would his master was always therewith well content. And when the time drew nigh that Faustus should end, he called unto him a notary and certain masters, the

2657 55] O, '18; 34 '08; 35 '10
2671 matters] O; things '08 &c; *ding* G [199]
2675 his] O; this '08 &c; *diss* G [200]
2682 content] O; contented '08 &c

which were his friends and often conversant with him, in whose presence he gave this Wagner his house and garden. Item, he gave him in ready money 1,600 guilders. Item, a farm. Item, a gold chain, much plate and other household stuff. This gave he all to his servant, and the rest of his time he meant to spend in inns and students' company, drinking and eating, with other jollity: and thus he finished his will for that time. 2685

How Doctor Faustus fell in talk with his servant touching his testament, and the covenants thereof. Chap. 57. 2690

Now when this will was made, Doctor Faustus called unto him his servant, saying: 'I have thought upon thee in my testament, for that thou hast been a trusty servant unto me and a faithful, and hast not opened my secrets: and yet further,' said he, 'ask of me before I die what thou wilt and I will give it unto thee.' His [K3r (75)] servant rashly answered: 'I pray you let me have your cunning.' To which Doctor Faustus answered: 'I have given thee all my books, upon this condition, that thou wouldst not let them be common but use them for thine own pleasure and study carefully in them. And dost thou also desire my cunning? That mayest thou peradventure have if thou love and peruse my books well. **Further,' said Doctor Faustus, 'seeing that thou desirest of me this request, I will resolve thee:** my spirit Mephostophiles his time is out with me and I have nought to command him as touching thee, yet will I help thee to another if thou like well thereof.' And within three days after he called his servant unto him, saying: 'Art thou resolved? Wouldst thou verily have a spirit? Then tell me in what manner or form thou wouldst have him?' To whom his servant answered that he would have him in the form of an ape: whereupon presently appeared a spirit unto him in manner and form of an ape, the which leaped about the house. Then said Faustus: 'See, there hast thou thy request, but yet he will not obey thee until I be dead, for when my spirit Mephostophiles shall fetch me away, then shall thy spirit be bound unto thee if thou agree: and thy spirit shalt thou name Akercock, for so is he called: but all this is upon condition that thou publish my cunning and my merry conceits, with all that I have done (when I am dead) in an history: and if thou canst not remember all, thy spirit Akercock will help thee: so shall the great acts that I have done be manifested unto the world.' 2695 2700 2705 2710 2715

2687 This] o; That '08 &c
2687f his time] o, '18; the ~ '08/10
2692 this] o; his '08 &c; *das* G [202]
2713 Akercock] Akercocke o &c; Abercocke [& var.] '18 &c; [also at 2716]

How Doctor Faustus having but one month of his appointed time to come, fell to mourning and sorrow with himself for his devilish exercise. Chap. 58.

2720 Time ran away with Faustus as the hour-glass, for he had but one month to come of his 24 years, at the end whereof he had given himself to the devil body and soul, as is before specified. Here was the first token, for he was like a taken murderer or a thief, the which findeth himself guilty in conscience before the judge have given sentence, fearing every hour to
2725 die: for he was grieved, and wailing spent the time, went talking to himself, wringing of his hands, sobbing and sighing, he fell away from flesh and was very lean and kept himself close: neither could he abide to see or hear of his Mephostophiles any more.
[K3v (76)]

How Doctor Faustus complained that he should in his lusty time and youthful
2730 *years die so miserably. Chap. 59.*

This sorrowful time drawing near so troubled Doctor Faustus that he began to write his mind, to the end he might peruse it often and not forget it, and is in manner as followeth.

'Ah Faustus, thou sorrowful and woeful man, now must thou go to the
2735 damned company in unquenchable fire, whereas thou mightest have had the joyful immortality of the soul, the which thou now hast lost. Ah gross understanding and wilful will, what seizeth on my limbs other than a robbing of my life? Bewail with me, my sound and healthful body, wit and soul, bewail with me, my senses, for you have had your part and pleasure
2740 as well as I. Oh Envy and Disdain, how have you crept both at once into me, and now for your sakes I must suffer all these torments. Ah whither is pity and mercy fled? Upon what occasion hath heaven repaid me with this reward by sufferance to suffer me to perish? Wherefore was I created a man? The punishment that I see prepared for me of myself now must I
2745 suffer. Ah miserable wretch, there is nothing in the world to show me comfort: then woe is me, what helpeth my wailing?'

2722 as is] O; ~ it ~ '08 &c
2723 murderer] murtherer T
2727 kept] '08 &c; kpt O
2738 body, wit] O; ~ and ~ '08 &c; *Leib, Vernunfft* G [206]
2741 now] O; howe '08 &c
torments.] ~? O; ~, '08/10; ~ ∧ '18

Another complaint of Doctor Faustus. Chap. 60.

'Oh poor, woeful and weary wretch: oh sorrowful soul of Faustus, now art thou in the number of the damned, for now must I wait for unmeasurable pains of death, yea far more lamentable than ever yet any creature hath suffered. Ah senseless, wilful and desperate forgetfulness! O cursed and unstable life! O blind and careless wretch, that so hast abused thy body, sense and soul! O foolish pleasure, into what a weary labyrinth hast thou brought me, blinding mine eyes in the clearest day? Ah weak heart! O troubled soul, where is become thy knowledge to comfort thee? O pitiful weariness! Oh desperate hope, now shall I never more be thought upon! Oh, care upon carefulness, and sorrows on heaps! Ah grievous pains **that pierce my panting heart,** whom is there now that can deliver me? Would to God that I knew where to hide me, or into what place to creep or fly. Ah, woe, woe is me, be where I will, yet am I taken.' Herewith poor [K4r (77)] Faustus was so sorrowfully troubled that he could not speak or utter his mind any further. 2750 2755 2760

How Doctor Faustus bewailed to think on hell and of the miserable pains therein provided for him. Chap. 61.

'Now thou Faustus, damned wretch, how happy wert thou if as an unreasonable beast thou mightest die without soul, so shouldst thou not feel any more doubts. But now the devil will take thee away both body and soul, and set thee in an unspeakable place of darkness: for although others' souls have rest and peace, yet I poor damned wretch must suffer all manner of filthy stench, pains, cold, hunger, thirst, heat, freezing, burning, hissing, gnashing and all the wrath and curse of God, yea all the creatures that God hath created are enemies to me. And now too late I remember that my spirit Mephostophiles did once tell me there was a great difference amongst the damned; for the greater the sin, the greater the torment: for as the twigs of the tree make greater flame than the trunk thereof, and yet the trunk continueth longer in burning; even so the more that a man is rooted in sin, the greater is his punishment. Ah thou 2765 2770 2775

2755f thee? o pitiful weariness! Oh] o; ~ ∧ ∧ ∧ ~ '08 &c; *O erbärmliche Müheseligkeit* G [208]
2759 Would to God] '08 &c; ~ ∧ ~ o
2764 Chap. 61] '10, '18; ∧ ∧ o; Chap. 6 ∧ '08
2775 the tree] o; a ~ '08 &c

perpetual damned wretch, now art thou thrown into the everlasting fiery lake that never shall be quenched: there must I dwell in all manner of
2780 wailing, sorrow, misery, pain, **torment, grief, howling, sighing, sobbing, blubbering,** running of eyes, stinking at nose, gnashing of teeth, fear to the ears, horror to the conscience and shaking both of hand and foot. Ah that I could carry the heavens on my shoulders, so that there were time at last to quit me of this everlasting damnation! Oh who can
2785 deliver me out of these fearful tormenting flames, the which I see prepared for me? Oh there is no help, nor any man that can deliver me, nor any wailing of sins can help me, neither is there rest to be found for me day nor night. Ah woe is me, for there is no help for me, no shield, no defence, no comfort. Where is my hold? **Knowledge dare I not trust: and for a soul**
2790 **to god-wards, that have I not,** for I shame to speak unto Him: if I do, no answer shall be made me, but He will hide His face from me, to the end that I should not behold the joys of the chosen. What mean I then to complain where no help is? No, I know no hope resteth in my groanings. I have desired it should be so and God hath said Amen to my misdoings: for
2795 now I must have shame to comfort me in my calamities.'
[K4v (78)]

Here followeth the miserable and lamentable end of Doctor Faustus, by the which all Christians may take an example and warning. Chap. 62.

In the 24th year Doctor Faustus his time being come, his spirit appeared unto him, giving him his writing again and commanding him to make
2800 preparation, for that the devil would fetch him against a certain time appointed. Doctor Faustus mourned and sighed wonderfully and never went to bed, nor slept wink for sorrow. Wherefore his spirit appeared again, comforting him and saying: 'My Faustus, be not thou so cowardly minded; for although that thou losest thy body, it is not long unto the day
2805 of judgment, and thou must die at the last, although thou live many thousand years. The Turks, the Jews and many an unchristian emperor, are in the same condemnation: therefore (my Faustus) be of good courage and be not discomforted, for the devil hath promised that thou shalt not

2781 sobbing, blubbering, running] O; ~ ∧ ~ '08 &c; *mit weinen der Augen* G [214f]
2783 on my] O; upon ~ '08 &c
2787f nor night] O; or ~ '08 &c; *weder Tag noch Nacht* G [215]
2798 In the 24th ... time being] O; The full time of doctor Faustus his 24. yeares being '08 &c; *Die 24. Jar deß Doctor Fausti waren erschienen* G [216]
2801 Doctor] '08 &c; D. O

be in pains as the rest of the damned are.' This and suchlike comfort he gave him, but he told him false and against the saying of the Holy Scriptures. Yet Doctor Faustus, that had none other expectation but to pay his debts with his own skin, went on the same day that his spirit said the devil would fetch him, unto his trusty and dearest beloved brethren and companions, as masters, and bachelors of arts and other students more, the which had often visited him at his house in merriment: these he entreated that they would walk into the village called Rimlich, half a mile from Wittenberg, and that they would there take with him for their repast part of a small banquet, the which they all agreed unto: so they went together and there held their dinner in a most sumptuous manner. Doctor Faustus with them (dissemblingly) was merry, but not from the heart: wherefore he requested them that they would also take part of his rude supper: the which they agreed unto: 'For,' quoth he, 'I must tell you what is the victualler's due.' And when they slept (for drink was in their heads) then Doctor Faustus paid and discharged the shot and bound the students and the masters to go with him into another room, for he had many wonderful matters to tell them: **and when they were entered the room as he requested,** Doctor Faustus said unto them as hereafter followeth. [L1r (81*)]

2810

2815

2820

2825

An oration of Faustus to the students. Chap. 63.

'My trusty and well-beloved friends, the cause why I have invited you into this place is this: Forasmuch as you have known me this many years, in what manner of life I have lived, practising all manner of conjurations and wicked exercises, the which I have obtained through the help of the devil, into whose devilish fellowship they have brought me, the which use the like art and practice, urged by the detestable provocation of my flesh, my stiff-necked and rebellious will, with my filthy infernal thoughts, the which were ever before me, pricking me forward so earnestly that **I must perforce have the consent of the devil to aid me in my devices. And to the end I might the better bring my purpose to pass, to have the devil's aid and furtherance, which I never have wanted in mine actions,** I have promised unto him at the end and accomplishing of 24 years, both body and soul, to do therewith at his pleasure: and this day, this dismal day, those 24 years are fully expired, for night beginning, my

2830

2835

2840

2814 of arts] of Art T
2832 I have obtained] O; ~ ∧ ~ '08 &c
2834 flesh, my] O; ~, & ~ '08 &c; *Fleisch und Blut, mein* G [219]

hour-glass is at an end, the direful finishing whereof I carefully expect: for out of all doubt this night he will fetch me, to whom I have given myself in
2845 recompense of his service, both body and soul, and twice confirmed writings with my proper blood. Now have I called you, my well-beloved lords, friends, brethren and fellows, before that fatal hour, to take my friendly farewell, to the end that my departing may not hereafter be hidden from you, beseeching you herewith, courteous and loving lords
2850 and brethren, not to take in evil part anything done by me, but with friendly commendations to salute all my friends and companions wheresoever: desiring both you and them, if ever I have trespassed against your minds in anything, that you would all heartily forgive me: and as for those lewd practices the which this full 24 years I have followed,
2855 you shall hereafter find them in writing: and I beseech you let this my lamentable end to the residue of your lives be a sufficient warning, that you have God always before your eyes, praying unto Him that He would ever defend you from the temptation of the devil and all his false deceits, not falling altogether from God as I, wretched and ungodly damned
2860 creature, have done, having denied and defied baptism, the sacraments of Christ's body, God Himself, all heavenly powers and earthly men, yea, I have denied such a God that desireth not to have one lost. Neither let the [LIV (80)] evil fellowship of wicked companions mislead you as it hath done me. Visit earnestly and oft the church, war and strive continually
2865 against the devil with a good and steadfast belief on God and Jesus Christ, and use your vocation in holiness. Lastly, to knit up my troubled oration, this is my friendly request, that you would to rest and let nothing trouble you: also if you chance to hear any noise or rumbling about the house, be not therewith afraid, for there shall no evil happen unto you: also I pray
2870 you arise not out of your beds. But above all things I entreat you, if you hereafter find my dead carcass, convey it unto the earth, for I die both a good and bad Christian; a good Christian, for that I am heartily sorry, and in my heart always pray for mercy, that my soul may be delivered: a bad Christian, for that I know the devil will have my body, and that would I
2875 willingly give him so that he would leave my soul in quiet: wherefore I pray you that you would depart to bed, and so I wish you a quiet night, which unto me notwithstanding will be horrible and fearful.'

This oration or declaration was made by Doctor Faustus, and that with

2849 courteous and loving] O; ~ ∧ ~ '08 &c
2871 unto the] O; into ~ '08; in ~ '10, '18
2872ff bad Christian; a good … delivered: a bad Christian for] O; ~ ~ ∧ … ∧ for '08 &c; [haplographic 2 line omission; parallel text supplied in G]

a hearty and resolute mind, to the end he might not discomfort them: but the students wondered greatly thereat, that he was so blinded, for knavery, conjuration and suchlike foolish things, to give his body and soul unto the devil: for they loved him entirely **and never suspected any such thing before he had opened his mind to them:** wherefore one of them said unto him: 'Ah, friend Faustus, what have you done to conceal this matter so long from us? We would by the help of good divines and the grace of God, have brought you out of this net and have torn you out of the bondage and chains of Satan, whereas now we fear it is too late, to the utter ruin of your body and soul.' Doctor Faustus answered: 'I durst never do it, although I often minded to settle myself unto godly people, to desire counsel and help, as once mine old neighbour counselled me, that I should follow his learning and leave all my conjurations. Yet when I was minded to amend and to follow that good man's counsel, then came the devil and would have had me away, as this night he is like to do, and said, so soon as I turned again to God he would dispatch me altogether. **Thus, even thus, (good gentlemen, and my dear friends) was I enthralled in that satanical band, all good desires drowned, all piety banished, all purpose of amendment utterly exiled, by the tyrannous threatenings of my deadly enemy.'** But when the students heard his words, they gave him counsel to do naught else but call upon God, desiring [L2r (81)] Him, for the love of His sweet son Jesus Christ's sake, to have mercy upon him, teaching him this form of prayer: O God be merciful unto me, poor and miserable sinner, and enter not into judgment with me, for no flesh is able to stand before thee. Although, O Lord, I must leave my sinful body unto the devil, being by him deluded, yet thou in mercy mayest preserve my soul.

2880 2885 2890 2895 2900 2905

This they repeated unto him, yet it could take no hold, but even as Cain he also said his sins were greater than God was able to forgive; for all his thought was on his writing: he meant he had made it too filthy in writing it with his own blood. The students and the other that were there, when they had prayed for him, they wept, and so went forth, but Faustus tarried in the hall: and when the gentlemen were laid in bed, none of them could sleep, for that they attended to hear if they might be privy of his end. It happened between twelve and one o'clock at midnight, there blew a

2910

2887 of the bondage] O, '18; ~ ∧ ~ '08/10; *auß dem netz* G [222]
2888 soul.] '08 &c; ~? O
2896 piety] O; pitty [& var.] '08 &c
2912 might] O, '18; may '08; ['10 imperfect, lacking text]
2913 o'clock] a clock O, '08, '18; ['10 imperfect, lacking text]

mighty storm of wind against the house as though it would have blown
2915 the foundation thereof out of his place. Hereupon the students began to fear and got out of their beds, comforting one another, but they would not stir out of the chamber: and the host of the house ran out of doors, thinking the house would fall. The students lay near unto that hall wherein Doctor Faustus lay, and they heard a mighty noise and hissing as
2920 if the hall had been full of snakes and adders: with that the hall door flew open wherein Doctor Faustus was, then he began to cry for help, saying: 'Murder, murder!' but it came forth with half a voice hollowly: shortly after they heard him no more. But when it was day the students, that had taken no rest that night, arose and went into the hall in the which they left
2925 Doctor Faustus, where notwithstanding they found no Faustus, but all the hall lay besprinkled with blood, his brains cleaving to the wall: for the devil had beaten him from one wall against another, in one corner lay his eyes, in another his teeth, a pitiful and fearful sight to behold. Then began the students to bewail and weep for him, and sought for his body in many
2930 places: lastly they came into the yard where they found his body lying on the horse dung, most monstrously torn and fearful to behold, for his head and all his joints were dashed in pieces.

The forenamed students and masters that were at his death, have obtained so much that they buried him in the village where he was so
2935 grievously tormented. After the which, they returned to Wittenberg, and coming into the house of Faustus, they found the servant of Faustus very [L2v (80*)] sad, unto whom they opened all the matter, who took it exceeding heavily. There found they also this history of Doctor Faustus, noted and of him written, as is before declared, all save only his end, the
2940 which was after by the students thereto annexed: further, what his servant had noted thereof, was made in another book. **And you have heard that he held by him in his life the spirit of fair Helena, the which had by him one son, the which he named Justus Faustus:** even the same day of his death they vanished away, both mother and son. The house before
2945 was so dark that scarce anybody could abide therein. The same night Doctor Faustus appeared unto his servant lively, and showed unto him many secret things the which he had done and hidden in his lifetime.

2921 then] o; that '08 &c
2922 Murder, murder!] murther, murther, T
2925 found no] o; ~ not '08 &c; *keinen* G [225]
2928 pitiful and fearful sight] o, '10, '18; ~ ∧ ∧ ~ '08; *ein greulich vnd erschrecklich Spectackel* G [225]
2929 bewail] o; wail '08 &c; *jn zubeklagen* G [225]

Likewise there were certain which saw Doctor Faustus look out of the window by night as they passed by the house.

And thus ended the whole history of Doctor Faustus his conjuration and other acts that he did in his life; out of the which example every Christian may learn, but chiefly the stiff-necked and high-minded may thereby learn to fear God and to be careful of their vocation and to be at defiance with all devilish works, as God hath most precisely forbidden, to the end we should not invite the devil as a guest, nor give him place as that wicked Faustus hath done: for here we have a fearful example of his writing, promise and end, that we may remember him: that we go not astray, but take God always before our eyes, to call alone upon Him, and to honour Him all the days of our life, with heart and hearty prayer, and with all our strength and soul to glorify His holy name, defying the devil and all his works, to the end we may remain with Christ in all endless joy: Amen, amen, that wish I unto every Christian heart, and God's name to be glorified. Amen. 2950 2955 2960

FINIS

[L3r (-)]

Here followeth the contents of this book. 2965

2966 page] Pag. 0; [the register of chapters is exclusive to 0]

3016 Leipzig] Lyptzig o

3065 FINIS

Commentary Notes

Key to the Commentary Notes

As the notes supply many different needs and a particular catchword may require several heterogeneous pieces of commentary, to avoid confusion a regular ordering of the information has been adopted, each category of commentary being preceded by a distinguishing symbol.

The ordering is as follows:

(i) (immediately following the bracket (])) translation notes. These supply an exact translation of passages from GFB omitted or modified by PF. Where commentary is necessary, this is separated from the translated passage by a bullet (●).

(ii) ¶: elucidation of obsolete or archaic usages

(iii) †: commentary on textual variants

(iv) ◇: concordance with Marlowe's *Doctor Faustus*

(v) ‡: biblical references

(vi) §: commentary on topographical sources, etc. (This is largely restricted to the material exclusive to EFB; for sources of GFB, see e.g. Petsch)

Abbreviations

In addition to the abbreviations listed on p. xiiff and the critical apparatus (p. 89), the following have been employed:

A, B: in Marlowe concordance, Marlowe's *Doctor Faustus*, 1604 and 1616 texts respectively, with line numbers from Greg

E: material exclusive to EFB

dir. sp.: PF converts reported speech in G to direct speech

rep. sp.: PF converts direct speech in G to reported speech

lit.: literal translation

loose: loosely translated, often with abbreviation

mistrans.: probable mistranslation by PF

transp.: transposed
TW: Text word

Standard abbreviations for biblical references.

Notes

1 **G:** (see Plate 1, p. 2) The life of Dr Johann Faustus, the renowned sorcerer and black magician; how he sold himself to the devil for a specified term, what curious exploits he devised and practised during that time, until he finally received his well-deserved reward.

For the most part gathered from his own posthumous papers and published as a terrible and horrific example and a sincere warning to all the overweening, inquisitive and ungodly.

James 4
Submit yourselves to God: resist the devil, and he will flee from you.

CUM GRATIA ET PRIVILEGIO
Printed at Frankfurt am-Main by Johann Spies. MD.LXXXVII

6f **Newly imprinted... amended]** † Since this statement (or variant) occurs in all extant editions, including S, there is no reason to assume that it originated with Orwin (cf. intro. pp. 44, 52)

8 **true copy]** ¶ authentic edition

11 **seen and allowed]** § Such an assurance that the book had been passed by the licensing authorities (the Bishop of London) is fairly rare and suggests sensitive material

15–18 **A Discourse... end]:** an abbreviated translation of the GFB titlepage (see above). PF omits Spies' Dedicatory Preface and 'Foreword to the Christian Reader'

16 **necromancer]** ¶ not restricted to the narrower sense of raising the dead, but becoming synonymous with the earlier 'nigromancer', i.e. black magician, as used in Scot, e.g. p. 382f

19 **Of his... Chap. 1]** G [1]: A Discourse of Dr Johann Faustus the renowned sorcerer. Of his birth and education. [Chap. 1]

20 **Rhode]** G [1]: *Rod* ◇ A13, B13: Rhodes § either Roda near Altenburg or Rödingen near Weimar. This supposed birthplace is unique to the Faust Book; other traditions favour Kundling (i.e. Knittlingen) near Bretten (Manlius/Melanchthon), and the Mark Sondwedel (i.e. Salzwedel) (Widman, Part 1, p. 1). Beutler (1936) and Baron (1972) (cf. intro., n. 7) argue in favour of Helmstedt near Heidelberg

21 **husbandman]** ¶ a tenant farmer, as opposed to a yeoman

22–6 **but having... divinity]** ◇ A14–16; B14–16

22 **Wittenberg]** G [1] adds: a pious Christian like his parents

23 **from... father]** E
24 **insomuch... him]** E
26f **being... addicted]** E
28 **exercises]** G [2] adds: and abused the word of God ◇ A24, B23
28–31 **the which... laws]** E, omitting an exoneration of Faustus' parents from blame for his wickedness [G: 3]
29 **Eli... Lord]** ‡ 1 Sam. 2: 22–5
33 **Cain]** ‡ Gen. 4 passim
Reuben] ‡ Gen. 35: 22; 49: 4
Absolom] ‡ 2 Sam. 15–18;
34 **toward wit]** ¶ a promising intellect, PF's translation for G [2]: signs of a powerful *ingenium* and *memoriam*
36 **secretly]** E, replacing G [3]: it was common knowledge that he was dabbling in magic
37 **insomuch... profession]** E
38 **Faustus... study]** G [3]: Faustus had a quick, scholarly head and a propensity for study
38–42 **and was... with him]** G [4]: the rectors examined him for his Master's degree and 16 others with him, but such was his skill in rhetoric and disputation that he surpassed them all ◇ A19f, B18f
43f **within... degree]** E
44 **fell... cogitations]** G [4]: was so bent on folly, so unmindful of his vocation and so opinionated [*hat er auch einen thummen, unsinnigen unnd hoffertigen Kopff gehabt*] ¶ fantasies: vain suppositions, speculations (*OED* sb. 5), cf. also at 586 ◇ A136
44f **was marked... students]** E; † the var. 'mocked' is probably a MS misread
45 **Speculator]** G [4] adds: he fell into bad company ¶ speculator: natural philosopher, or one who studied the heavens, but cf. 776
46 **from him]** G [4]: [lit.] behind the door and under the bench
48f **Who... away?]** G [4]: he who is hell-bent cannot be stayed § cf. Tilley (H515), citing the present usage
51 **that... and]** E; ◇ A24, B23
54 **arts]** G [5] adds: these scrips were naught but Dardanian arts
necromancy] G [5]: *Nigromantiae* ◇ A26f, B25f
57 **himself]** G [5] adds: a Doctor of Medicine and became
58 **for a shadow]** ¶ for the sake of appearance, as a cover (usage not listed in *OED*)
58f **sometimes... cures]** ◇ A44–52, B42–49 ¶ waters: distillates and infusions, cf. intro. p. 31, n. 118
61 **Scriptures]** G [5] adds: He knew the rule of Christ full well
61f **but he... many stripes]** ‡ Luke 12: 47
62f **It is... masters]** as G [6], absent from W ‡ Matt. 6: 24
63f **Thou shalt... God]** ‡ Matt. 4: 7
65 **regarding... come]** E; † the S var. 'joy' is probably an edit, cf. intro., p. 42 ◇ A28, B27
66 **therefore... redemption]** G [6]: so there is no excusing him

67f **How... house]** G [6]: Dr Faustus a physician
70f **study... conjuration]** G [6]: to love that which was not to be loved
71 **necromancy... exercise]** ¶ exercise: magical practice (also at 325, 2719, 2832) ◇ A24, B23
72 **wings]** ◇ A22, B21
72f **to fly... world]** E
73f **for... wonderful]** G [6]: His vain and insolent curiosity [*Fürwitz, Freiheit und Leichtfertigkeit*] so provoked him ¶ speculation: observation of the heavens (*OED* 2b) ◇ A358, B338
74 ***vocabula*]** ¶ (L.) names, i.e. of God, e.g. Jehovah, Eloi, Agla, Tetragrammaton, etc., used in conjurations, cf. Butler, *Rit.*, pp. 73ff
76 **And]** G [6] adds: as others have also reported
77 **in the... tongue]** E
77f **Spisser Waldt]** G [7]: *Spesser Wald*
78 **that is... Wood]** E ● 'Sparrow's Wood' is a better translation
78f **would... jollity]** G [7]: himself attested afterwards ¶ jollity: either 'revelry' (*OED* 2) or 'insolent presumption' (*OED* 4)
81 **within... characters]** G [7]: above it two others so that these intersected with the larger circle ◇ A251–5, B234–8
82 **and thus... until]** E
83–5 **call... stay]** G [7]: conjure the devil ● PF's dramatic remodelling of his source (the direct call on Mephostophiles in the name of Beelzebub) is paralleled in *Dr F*, cf. intro., pp. 19ff ◇ A260–3, B244f
85 **stay]** G [7] adds: Surely the devil must have laughed to himself and turned his backside, thinking: Come now, I shall cool your ardour and make such a monkey of you that I'll gain your soul as well as your body, and you'll still think it fair dealing; but I'll not come myself – I'll send you my messenger. And so it transpired: the devil made a complete ass of Faustus and lured him to the halter. When Dr Faustus began to conjure, the devil pretended to be none too keen to join the dance ● 'Surely... halter' absent from W ● PF does well to omit this passage with its farcical overtones
presently] ¶ at once
86f **as if... wind]** G [8]: [and such a wind[W]] as if everything would have come down
87 **the trees bowing]** † '08 &c probably transmit the original, edited in O
88 **blare]** G [8]: make ¶ roar (*OED* v. 1)
lions] G [8]: devils ◇ A157, B146
89 **a thousand]** E
90 **on paved stones]** E
91f **as if... fire]** G [8]: then suddenly a great sound of gunfire, then a brightness
92 **fire]** G [8] adds: then singing and music as from many a tuneful instrument was heard in the wood, then some dances followed by jousting with lance and sword
amazed] ¶ perplexed (*OED* 2)
93 **so long tarrying]** ◇ A262, B246 (cf. also at 113)
93f **and doubting... conjurings]** E

95f **as if... revived]** E; § 'the nymphs' are probably the Muses, renowned for their song and musicianship, cf. Peele's *The Arraignment of Paris* (1584) which uses a chorus of Muses as Diana's nymphs. PF may have in mind the musical contest between Marsyas and Apollo, judged by the Muses; Apollo won because, unlike the flautist Marsyas, he could play his instrument upside-down and both play and sing at the same time. Apollo then flayed Marsyas alive and nailed his skin to a tree (cf. Graves *The Greek Myths*, Harmondsworth, 1957 edn I. 77). Marlowe may have picked up on this veiled reference for A658f, B598f

96f **and stood... purpose]** G [8]: he recovered his former resolve, determined upon his rash and wicked enterprise regardless of the outcome ¶ stoutly: resolutely, bravely, possibly even stubbornly (*OED* adv. 4); aspecting his purpose: expecting to achieve his aims (*OED* aspect, v. 1)

98 **spirit]** G [8f]: devil, just as before, whereupon the devil provided the following spectacle

98f **Mephostophiles... likeness]** E; ◇ A260, B244

99 **his head]** G [9]: the circle

hovering] G [9] adds: and fluttering

100 **dragon]** G [9] adds: or griffon

after... manner] E

101 **there... cry]** G [9]: the creature wailed piteously

101f **in... mercy]** E

103 **flame... lightning]** G [9]: fiery star

104f **yet... leave]** G [9]: even the bold Dr Faustus was unnerved yet he clung to his purpose, exulting that the devil should be subservient to him

106 **Oftentimes]** E

107 **stoutest head]** ¶ chief ruler, but 'stoutest' may bear the sense of 'most rebellious' (*OED* adj. 4b)

whereat they] G [9]: whereat the students

111 **The prince... heaven]** ‡ Eph. 2: 2; 6: 12, but neither is as specific as John 14: 20

112–14 **Well... intent]** E; ¶ with full purpose: fully determined

114f **and... spirit]** G [9]: He conjured this star once, twice and thrice

116 **up]** G [10] adds: a flame

so burning a time] G [10]: then it subsided into six little lights: one sprang on high, a second beneath it

117 **pleasant beast]** E; ¶ pleasant: merry, amusing (*OED* a. 4), but more likely, the usage is ironic, cf. 2639 below

118 **grey friar]** ◇ A269, B253

119 **the next morning]** G [10]: on the morrow

120 **clock]** G [10] adds: at night

122 **Beelzebub]** G [10]: his master

123 **and so... way]** E

124f **Mephostophiles... house]** E

126f **Doctor... appointed]** G [11]: The next day, after he had come home, Doctor Faustus summoned the spirit to his chamber

128 **was.]** G [11] adds: It is astonishing that a spirit which has forfeited the aid of God can beguile a man so. But, as the saying goes, such fellows are bound to meet up with the devil eventually, either here or there.

129 **that he... him]** E

130 **and to fulfil... points]** E

131–5 **That the... true]** ◇ A281f, B262f; A338–40, B318–20

133 **Further]** † the earlier preferred form, 'farther', is generally changed to 'further' in '08, and always in '18; cf. 139, 249, 852, 1209, 1599, 1735

any thing... him] G [12]: that he should not withhold any information demanded of him

136 **Hereupon... forth]** G [12]: The spirit rejected the proposals and refused on the grounds

136–9 **that he... lord]** ◇ A285–7, B266–8

139f **Therefore... prince]** E

140 **leave.]** G [12] adds: 'How am I to understand that,' asked Faustus, 'Are you not powerful enough to have this authority?' The spirit answered: 'No.'

144 **the Legion]** ‡ e.g. Mark 5: 9

146f **that... infinite]** mistrans. for G [13]: We call him the Prince of Orient since he has his dominion in the East ● cf. intro., pp. 19f ◇ A260, B243f; A307f, B288f

147f ***Meridie, Septentrio, Occidente*]** ¶ (L.): South, North, West

148f **under heaven]** ¶ beneath the sphere of the Moon; the argument is that since Lucifer has assumed sovereignty over the whole of the sublunary sphere, the spirits who dwell there must be obedient to him and transform themselves at his command

150 **pleasure.]** G [13] adds: For no human being, however skilled and powerful, could ever bring Lucifer into subjection. And so he sends a spirit, and such am I.

152f **neither... ours]** G [13]: For after the death of the damned, they will learn of it from direct experience ◇ A295f, B276f

154 **arose... sat]** mistrans. for G [13]: was much alarmed [*entsetzt sich*]

154f **I... request]** E

155–7 **Then shalt... thee]** expressed in G [14] by five lines of doggerel. The following translation is from Butler, *Rit.*, p. 165: And wilt thou not, yet tis thy lot; / Since tis thy lot, thou'lt fly me not; / Should one hold thee, thou'lt know it not; / Thou'lt fly me not, prayers help no jot. / Thy heart's despair has brought thee there. ¶ want: lack

158f **take St Valentine's... with thee]** ¶ chrism: oil mixed with balm, for sacramental anointing; the phrase is equivalent to 'a pox on thee';

159 **thee!]** G [14] adds: But as the spirit was about to vanish, Dr Faustus, irresolute from then on, was of a different mind

159–61 **Yet I... therein]** dir. sp., the first of many passages which PF intensifies in this way ◇ A344f, B324f

160 **and bethink... thee]** G [14]: to hear his further proposals

160f **and ask... therein]** E

161 **Mephostophiles]** E

162–6 **leaving... upon]** E, omitting G [14]: Here we may see the heart and mind of this ungodly Faustus. For even after the devil had, as they say, sung him 'O poor Judas' [a German mocking song] and told him that he would have to go to hell, he still persisted in his stubbornness [absent from w] ● PF focusses on Faustus' predicament, introducing the possibility that he might outwit the spirit, perhaps by the introduction of an escape clause ◇ A438–43, B390–5

167f **The second. . parley]** G [15]: The second disputation between Dr Faustus and the spirit whose name is Mephostophiles. ● This is the first time the name is introduced in G § For possible derivations of the name cf. Butler *Magus* p. 132

169–71 **Faustus... devil]** E; † 'continuing' is an O edit

171 **the night approaching]** G [15]: around vesper time, that is between three and four o'clock

swift] E

173 **prince]** G [15]: commander

173f **if so... his]** E

177f **though... him]** absent from w ● cf. 180; in G, spirit and devil are virtually synonymous terms, but this is not the case in Widman (cf. intro., p. 7). PF acknowledges the existence of 'middle powers' at 266 ¶ limb: member (*OED* sb[1]. 3), also at 2737; cf. 'members of Christ' in 1 Cor. 6: 15; faintly: possibly 'feignedly' (*OED* adv. 1), but more probably 'hesitantly' (*OED* adv. 3b)

180–8 **That he... would]** ◇ A541–9, B487–95

180 **That he... spirit]** § For the thesis that this is Faustus' escape plan, cf. Empson, pp. 121ff

181–4 PF transposes articles 2 and 3

181 **Mephostophiles]** G [16]: the spirit ● also at 183 and 187

185 PF's 4th article combines articles 4 and 5 in G [16]

187 **5]** corresponds to 6th article in G [16]

191 **articles]** G [17] adds: If he would do this there would be no further difficulties

192f **give... soul]** G [17]: swear on oath to become the sole property of the spirit † 'his' is probably an O edit ◇ A472, B420

194f **make him... blood]** ◇ A475, B423

196 **an enemy... people]** In Widman (Part I, pp. 42f), the sociable Faustus rejects this clause, agreeing only to be an enemy to those who are hostile to him

197 **his]** † '08 &c transmit the literal transl., edited in O

198f **that he let... it]** § Faustus contravenes this clause in chapter 48, (2449 etc) and is forced to make a new pact

200f **in health and pleasure]** E § Christopher Ricks ('*Doctor Faustus* and Hell on Earth', *Essays in Criticism*, 35, (1985) pp. 101–20) sees the guaranteed life-span as an important motivation when plague was so rife

204 **perceive... spirit]** § No immediate change is apparent, but later Faustus is able to fly through the air [1654f], change his shape [944] and render himself invisible [1331f]

205f **his mind... inflamed]** G [18]: was so reckless in his pride and arrogance

206 **that]** G [18] adds: although it had just troubled him

Mephostophiles] G [18]: the wicked spirit [also 'spirit' at 209]

207f **the devil... him]** § Tilley (D255) cites this as the earliest usage

209f **about... conclusion]** G [18]: concerning his contract

212 **betimes]** ¶ early

214 **like St Anthony]** E; § The bell was the identifying attribute of St Anthony of Padua (1195–1231) who became a Franciscan in 1220. As patron of the lower animals he is often depicted accompanied by an ass. PF is fond of parading the bell (cf. 329, 392), so perhaps he is inviting his readers to think of Faustus as an ass

216f **as thou sayest]** E ● PF's remodelling has rendered Faustus' question redundant, so this interpolation becomes necessary

217f **and I... him']** E ● By making Mephostophiles a prince, PF raises the status of both protagonists; Faustus is now too puffed up in his conceit to withdraw. § Scot (p. 499), drawing on Psellus' *de operatione daemonum*, says that spirits 'of that sort or company called *Principatus* [are] of all other the most easy to be conjured'

218 **meridian]** ¶ the South (*OED*[2] sb. 3)

219 **at... was]** G [19]: in this hour

219f **inflamed... servant]** E

221 **and Christ... redeemer]** E

221f **an enemy... than]** G [19]: a member of the vexatious devil. The cause of his defection was naught but his proud conceit, presumption, arrogance and despair in God, like to [mostly absent from w] † 'unto' is preferred to 'to' 5 times in O, 3 times in '08, and twice in '10 &c. cf. 598, 810, 1014, 1230, 2076, 2223, 2234, 2492

222f **climb the hills]** G [19]: raise mountain on mountain § cf. Robert Graves: *The Greek Myths*, Harmondsworth 1957, I, pp. 136f. The giants' revolt, in which they piled Mt Pelion on Mt Ossa to besiege the gods on Olympus, supplies a classical parallel for Lucifer's rebellion

223 **that enemy]** † an O, S edit

225 **the high... falls]** § Tilley (C414), citing this usage

225f **and that... sauce]** E; ◇ B1911 § Tilley (M839): Sweet Meat must have sour sauce.

227 **Faustus]** G [19] adds: with gross impudence

promised... make] G [19]: formulated

228 **obligation]** ¶ contract

228f **with... Reader)]** E

231 **with... life]** E; § i.e. Faustus' account of his deeds, cf. 2938–40

232–6 **by this... devil]** G [20]: lest they should give place to the devil and jeopardize their body and soul, as happened with Faustus' poor house-boy whom his master soon seduced with this diabolic work ● PF's emphasis on the sanctity of vocation displays a Calvinist tendency (cf. 2953). † The '08 &c var. 'Doctor' may be a veiled topical allusion, directed at Dr Dee, or (post 1594) Dr Lopez

236 **and... assuredly]** G [20]: When the two parties were mutually agreed

237 **small]** G [20]: sharp pointed

pricked a vein] ◇ A497, B444

238f **seen on... vanished]** ◇ A517–24, B464–70

239 ***O homo fuge*]** ‡ 1 Tim. 6: 11 (Vulgate): Tu autem, O homo Dei, haec fuge

239–41 **whereat... followeth]** E, replacing G [20]: i.e. O man, flee from him and do what is right, etc. ● In EFB, the warning is sufficient to drive Mephostophiles away yet Faustus persists, demonstrating his wilfulness

242 **ashes]** G [21]: coals ◇ A503, B450

244–61 **I... wheresoever]** ◇ A550–7, B496–502

246 **speculate]** ¶ observe and theorize upon, cf. 74

the course... order of] E

247 **above]** G [21] adds: and so graciously imparted

249f **Doctor... Faustus]** E

250f **the hellish... Mephostophiles]** G [21]: the present emissary spirit called Mephostophiles, a servant of the hellish prince of Orient

251 **both body and soul]** G [21]: myself ◇ A507, B454

252 **learn]** ¶ teach (*OED* v. 4)

253f **according... us]** E

255 **Further]** G [22]: In return, however

258f **they... agreed]** W [absent from G]: provided I am sufficiently satisfied in my demands of him ● This is a mild escape clause, excluded from W by Spies but reintroduced, possibly independently, by PF.

261 **into... wheresoever]** G [22]: and shall be his for evermore

262 **God and His Christ]** E

262f **creatures... God]** G [22]: persons

266f **calling... and]** E, recognizing the legal need for a witness, and supplying an epic touch to this microcosmic deal, well-suited to Faustus' character. The 'middle powers' are neither angels nor devils, but nature spirits, e.g. nymphs, goblins, salamanders, etc.; cf. Empson, pp. 98–106.

268 **approved]** ¶ experienced (*OED*. 1)

269 **spiritual]** ¶ here with double meaning, 'ghostly' (i.e. theological) and 'having the nature of a spirit'

doctor.] G [23] adds here, as chapter 7, a set of three moralistic doggerel verses, absent from W.

270–2 **How... Chap. 7]** G [24]: In what form the devil appeared to Faustus. [chap. 8] [heading supplied from register of contents]

273 **Doctor Faustus... him]** G [24]: At the third parley Faustus' spirit and *famulus* appeared in a merry mood and provided the following show. ● PF misinterprets *famulus* (here meaning 'familiar spirit') as 'house-boy', probably because of 285f, see below

275–7 **insomuch... harm]** E; ● Having introduced the boy, PF applies his intensely visual imagination

277f **as... manner]** G [24]: like the singing of monks, and nobody knew what kind of singing it was ¶ blare: howl (*OED* v. 1: to roar with a prolonged sound in weeping, as a child)

279 **counting house]** ¶ privy chamber

more] G [24]: the outcome

280 **Anon was heard]** ● the beginning of another set of diabolic manifestations (cf. 85–104; 987–1011); the pattern is much the same in all: hart, bull, ape, etc.

282f **Faustus... hart]** E

284f **so fiercely... house]** G [25]: the lion defended itself bravely

285f **and... vanished]** E; G [25] adds: Doctor Faustus' house-boy says he saw a winged serpent which filled the entire room; its belly was dappled white and yellow, its wings and upper parts were black, and half the tail was coiled like a snail's shell. ● The German text ('house-boy says') implicitly refers to the lost 'Wagner's life of Faustus', cf. intro., p. 7

287f **brustling... vanished]** G [25]: they began to quarrel but were soon reconciled ¶ brustling: raising the feathers (*OED* vbl. sb[2]; earliest listing: 1622)

289 **Faustus]** G [25] adds: who was greatly perturbed

291 **the hand]** lit. G [25]: *die Handt*

but he refused] G [25]: sprang upon him and embraced him ● PF's 'refused' probably stresses the fact that Faustus has not yet delivered his pact (cf. 308) and remains uncertain until he is 'ravished' by music (297)

292 **saw no light]** G [25f]: was unable to see

296f **organs... harps]** G [26]: an organ, a positive organ, harps, lutes, fiddles, trombones, pipes, krummhorns, transverse flutes and the like (one with four voices) ● A similar list occurs at 2278–80, and entrancing music at 958f and 992, so even in G secular music is beguiling – a Calvinist tendency intensified by PF (cf. 297f)

clarigolds] ¶ According to Frances Palmer of the Horniman Museum, London, a variant for clavichords, probably unfamiliar by the late sixteenth century and rare earlier

citterns] ¶ a small instrument of the lute family. cf, Michael Praetorius' *Syntagma musicum* Bd. II. *De Organographia*, Wolfenbüttel 1619, Plate XVI No. 7 ('klein englische Zitterlein') (I thank Frances Palmer for this reference)

waits] wind instruments, e.g. hautboys, shawms or flutes (*OED*[2] wait sb. 10, citing EFB)

anomes] ¶ apparently a unique usage, meaning unknown. Logeman assumes an incomprehensible misprint or misread, but it is invariant in all extant editions

297 **the which... mind]** E; ◇ A143, B132; A658f, B598f

298 **another world]** G [26]: heaven, but in fact he was with the devil. This lasted a full hour ['but... devil' absent from W]

300 **done]** G [26]: for he supposed he would never regret it. Here we may see how the devil sang sweetly so that Dr Faustus would not retract but would be all the keener to complete the deed, and would think: I have seen nothing unpleasant or evil, no, nothing but delight ● omitted by PF as unnecessary

303f **thou shalt... have it]** G [27]: You will please me very well

304–6 **This is... have]** ◇ A528–31, B476–79

307 **the wretch]** G [27] Faustus

307f **the wretch... promise']** ◇ A533f, B480

309 **willed]** † the O var. is an edit

310f **with that... other]** G [27]: which the wicked Faustus did. § The copy of the pact is a logistical requirement for its appearance in the book

311–13 **Thus... housekeeping]** E, displaying customary irony
314 **The manner... and]** E
315 **Chap. 8]** G [28]: [Chap. 9]
316f **renouncing... heaven]** G [28]: it is safe to assume he was deserted by God and all the heavenly host
318 **now]** † the O var. must be a misprint; Logeman suggested 'written note', but he had not seen '08 etc.
318–20 **the which... spirit]** G [28]: In so doing he had behaved not as a just and pious husbandman, but rather as the devil. As Christ our Lord sayth, there is in each of us a lodging reserved for the devil. He had moved in and made himself at home. Dr Faustus had invited the devil to be his guest, as the saying goes. [absent from W]
322 **cousin]** ¶ kinsman, especially nephew (*OED* sb. 1)
boy] G [28]: young schoolboy
scholar] G [29]: *famulus*
323 **unhappy wag]** ¶ wickedly mischievous lad, cf. 2680
sport] ¶ a diverting occupation
325 **seen]** ¶ versed (*OED* ppl. a. 2)
326 **and he... Mephostophiles]** PF, replacing G [29]: and like all youngsters, he was more prone to wickedness than piety ¶ fellow: associated, probably in the bad sense of accomplice
328 **was diligent... command]** E
329 **with... Faustus]** E, replacing G [29]: whenever he was summoned in the study which was always kept locked
331 **Salzburg]** G [29] adds: as Faustus himself admitted
334 **him in]** G [30]: from all the neighbouring gentry, sumptuous fare from the courts of counts and princes
335 **cunning]** ¶ skilled in magic (*OED* a. 3)
335f **what fowl... for]** § cf. 2293–7 for the application of this trick
336f **were... dainty]** E
338 **stole]** G [30] adds: by night
339 **and Leipzig]** E
339f **for it... thief]** G [30]: for the merchants do not tend their shops at night. The tanners and cobblers were similarly abused
341 **ware]** G [30] adds: a most profitable housekeeping
342f **though as... other]** E
343 **through]** † O transmits the literal transl., edited in '08 &c ‡ John 8: 44; 10: 10;
344f **and that... soul]** E, replacing G [30]: which he is. In addition, the devil promised [31] to give Faustus 25 crowns a week, making 1300 a year. This was his annual allowance ● PF probably found this notion of a pension too farcical
346f **and how. . it]** E
347 **Chap 9]** G [31]: [chap. 10]
348 **epicurish]** ¶ devoted to sensual pleasures, cf. also at 2632
349 **believed... devil]** ◇ A573, B519; A580–2, B525–8
350f **and had... soul]** E
351 **but stood... heresy]** G [31]: he was pricked by sexual desire ¶ stood in:

obstinately persisted in (*OED* stand, v. B. 72b)

351–66 **And bethinking... mind]** loose, dir. sp.

351f **And... wife]** ◇ A587, B532

353 **wise]** † the var. 'case' is an alternative MS reading

356 **thou canst... masters]** ‡ Matt. 6: 24

357 **ordained of God]** ◇ A599, B540 ‡ Gen. 2: 24

358 **also]** † 'only' (*OED* adv. 3: specially) is probably original, edited in O

361f **look well... mind]** ◇ A590

363 **tear... pieces]** ◇ A387, B361

368 **foundation]** G [32] adds: and are led and seduced by the devil ‡ 1 Cor. 3: 11

369 **forsook the rock]** ‡ Luke 6: 48

369–73 **fearing... after]** E

370 **motion]** ¶ suggest, propose

372 **his spirit]** G [32]: his monk, whose urgings against matrimony were akin to those of all monks and nuns who practise celibacy and exhort others to do likewise

374–6 **'I am ... to it']** G [33]: 'I am determined to marry, come what may.' ¶ fantasy: amorous inclinations (*OED* fancy, 8b.) cf. 2373 ◇ A588, B533 § Faustus is following the injunctions of St Paul: 1 Cor. 7: 2,9

375 **will... wife]** ◇ A591f

379 **smoke... ashes]** G [33]: fire as if it would be charred to cinders

383 **fried as... and]** E

385f **as he... handwriting]** G [33]: according to his wishes and counsel ¶ handwriting: written contract

386 **an ugly devil]** G [33]: the devil incarnate

388 **'What wouldst... wedding?]** E; † the O var. is independently recovered by '18

389f **forgot his promise]** G [33]: not fully kept his promise, he had not [34] worked out all the implications of the contract

390f **and he... such things]** E

391 **the devil]** G [34]: Satan † the '08 &c var. is probably a careless omission
'Thou... do'] G [34]: 'So, keep to it! I warn you, keep to it!'

392f **with a... hand]** E

393 **It is... with us]** E

394f **and we... than that]** G [34]: and I shall satisfy your desires in another manner which you will not wish to change for the rest of your life. Since you cannot be chaste

395f **thou shalt... thee]** ◇ A601–3, B542–4

396 **be she... wilt]** G [34]: from this city or wherever else you may have seen her; and in that shape she shall live with you and serve your lust ● cf. intro., p. 19

397 **well]** G [34] adds: so that his heart trembled for joy

398ff **that might... time]** E, replacing G [34]: He was inflamed with such passion and lust that he spent night and day looking out for beautiful women. [35] He was so libidinous that he would fornicate with one devil one day and have another in mind on the morrow. ● Once again PF avoids the implication of succubae (cf. 396 above) ¶ persevered: continued

401f **Chap. 10]** G [35]: [chap. 11]

403f **living... apparel]** G [35]: indulged in vile and shameful lechery with the devil ¶ drifts: schemes (*OED* sb. 5), referring to 399

405 **called... him]** E

405–8 **brought... desire]** ◇ A607, B548

406 **devilish... arts]** G [35]: sorcery and *nigromantia*

407f **saying... desire']** E, replacing G [35]: so that he and his devilish mistress might entertain themselves ● Further suppression of succubae by PF (cf. 396 above)

408 **enchanting book]** G [35]: Dardanian art

409 **Wagner.]** G [35] adds: Shortly thereafter, pricked on by his vain curiosity, Faustus summoned Mephostophiles for a conversation

409f **'I have... help']** G [35]: 'Tell me, my servant, what kind of a spirit are you?'

412 **yea... whatsoever]** E, replacing G [36]: ruling beneath the heavens

413 **have... great a]** E

414–18 **Lucifer... headlong]** ◇ A309–13, B290–4

415 **as immortal]** G [36]: a creature of bliss

415–31 **and being... communication]** E, replacing G [36]: Such angels are called *Hierarchiae*, and they were three: the seraph, the cherub and the throne angel. The first prince ruled the office of the angels; the duty of the second is to govern, preserve and protect mankind; those of the third rank keep our devilish power in check. These are therefore called princes and powers. They are also called the angel of great works of wonder, the angel of the annunciation and the angel who cares for human expectations. So, Lucifer was one of these beautiful archangels and was called Raphael, the other two, Gabriel and Michael. § The source for G is Schedel, fol. 6a, based on pseudo-Dionysus with additions (Lucifer as Raphael) from unknown sources

416–18 **he would... headlong]** § cf. Scot, p. 501: 'Lucifer is cited as the name of an angel, who on a time being desirous to be checkmate with God himself, would needs (when God was gone a little aside) be sitting down, or rather pirking up in God's own principal and cathedral chair; and that therefore God cast him and all his confederates out of heaven.' (In terms of their dry humour, Scot and PF are kindred spirits.)

432–4 **How... Chap. 11]** G [37]: A disputation on hell and its caverns [chap. 12]

435f **The night... Lucifer]** E

437 **that... part]** G [37]: as one might say ● PF interprets 'dreamed' literally, hence the addition of 'night' at 435

437–9 **but in... mind]** E

439–41 **'My... made?']** dir. sp. ◇ A562, B508

444–9 **It is... middle]** E ¶ seen: furnished ‡ Gen. 1: 2–4 § The placing of God between the light on His right and the darkness on His left probably reflects the universal tradition of Judgment pictures, etc.

449 **the darkness... hand]** G [37]: there is there a darkness

450 **until... judgment]** G [37]: cast out from God and remanded that he might be brought to judgment ‡ Jude 5: 6; 2 Peter 2: 4

451 **filthy]** ¶ murky, thick (*OED* a. 1b) † the omission from '08 &c is probably a careless oversight

452 **what... is of]** G [38]: in what form and manner hell is made

452–4 **but a... God]** E; § The soap bubble simile (source not found) recurs at 1172 and 1203f

458 **Chap. 12]** G [38]: [Chap. 13]

459–61 **Faustus... them']** G [38]: The spirit had also to report to Faustus on the habitation, government and power of the devils

462f **hell is... world]** G [38]: our habitation encompasses as much as the whole world above hell

464 **even... heavens]** ◇ A563, B509

465 **ten kingdoms]** G [38], with W, adds: [domains or principalities of the devils, besides four W] governments and kingdoms which are the foremost amongst us and mightiest [39] of all. The [ten W] kingdoms are: ● Here is a strong indication that PF did not have recourse to W

466–70 **Lacus mortis... Acheron]** § The source is Elucidarius (cf. Petsch, p. 162)

471 **the which... five kings]** G [39]: in which rule the devils called Phlegeton. There are four monarchies among them.

472f **and Phlegeton... all]** transp., mistrans.

476f **Another... Chap. 13]** G [40]: A question on the former state of the fallen angel. [Chap. 14]

480 **in favour... God]** G [40]: in heaven

481 **which... granted]** E

483–93 **Lucifer... powers]** ◇ A309–13, B290–4

484 **sat... cherubim]** G [40]: was a cherub

487–9 **and so... stars]** ◇ A606, B547

489 **wherefore]** G [41] adds: as soon as God created him

cherubim] G [41]: His hill

kingly] G [41]: princely

490 **and was... seat]** E

492 **usurp... majesty]** G [41]: rise up over the Orient

494 **no water... quench]** G [41]: never cools

495 **world']** G [41] adds: He had been adorned with the crown of heavenly splendour but because he acted in conscious and wilful defiance of his Creator, God set Himself in the judgment seat and condemned him straight to hell, damned to remain there for eternity. ● PF's Mephostophiles is less explicit in stressing the comparison with Faustus

499 **Mephostophiles]** G [42] adds: how the devil, the fallen angel, had been so splendidly adorned by God, and how, if only he had not been so arrogant and defiant, he might have dwelt in heaven for ever, but was now cast out by God eternally

501 **What... done?]** E

502–5 **bearing... subject?]** E

505 **aspiring stomach]** ¶ ambitious disposition

506 **filthy]** ¶ contemptible (*OED* a. 4)

507 **abused my understanding]** G [42]: provoked my mind ¶ abused: misapplied

508 **the spirit... from me]** E
have promised... my] G [42]: allowed the devil to persuade me to give him my body and
510 **burning fire]** G [42]: damnation and misery. What am I laying up for myself?
512 **having... Christ]** G [43]: but he would not take hope nor affirm his faith,
513 **again]** G [43] adds: If only he had thought: The devil has painted me in such colours that I must be seen from heaven. Now will I turn again to God and beg for His grace and pardon, and do the greatest penance which is to sin no more. He ought to have gone to church, kept Christian fellowship and followed the rule of the Holy Scriptures.
515 **Satan]** G [43]: the devil
515–18 **although he... soul]** G [43]: even if he had had to yield him his body, he might yet have saved his soul
518 **doubtful]** ¶ uncertain
521 **and... mankind. Chap. 14]** G [44]: [Chap. 15]
522f **After... estate]** G [44]: When Doctor Faustus had somewhat recovered from his despondency
524 **attempts]** ¶ either 'assaults' (*OED* sb. 3), or synonymous with 'temptation'
527 **therefore]** G [44]: besides which
533–5 **another hangs... despair]** ◇ A650f, B591 ¶ unfaithfully: lacking in faith (cf. *OED* unfaith); the var. 'unlawfully' means 'contrary to (spiritual) principles' (*OED* unlawful a. 2)
535 **and so... confusion]** G [45]: and so forth
Adam] ‡ Gen. 3
536 **his policy]** G [45]: who begrudged him his perfection
538 **my lord Lucifer]** G [45]: Satan ● Gen. 3 does not name the serpent
Cain] ‡ Gen. 4
539 **children of Israel]** ‡ Num. 25: 1,2
540 **the like... Saul]** G [45]: One of our number provoked Saul to madness and suicide ‡ 1 Sam. 19: 9; 31: 4
540f **So did... Tobias]** G [45]: The spirit Asmodeus killed seven men as they gratified their lust ‡ Tobit 3: 8
541 **Dagon]** ‡ 1 Sam. 4: 10,11; 5: 2
543 **David]** ‡ 2 Sam. 24: 1,15; 1 Chron. 21: 1,14 (giving 70,000 slain)
544 **Solomon]** ‡ 1 Kings 11: 4–8
546–50 **for we... thee]** omitting G [46]: we use every sort of sly trick and subtlety to undermine men's faith and pervert them, strengthening our ranks as best we may
551 **beguile me.]** G [46] adds: Tell me the truth, I pray thee
551f **Yea... forwards]** † the '18 var. censors this sensitive question, cf. intro., p. 18
551–6 **Yea... intent]** ◇ B1988–92
552–8 **For so... some devil]** loose
553–5 **didst despise... kingdom]** E
558 **devil:]** G [47] adds: We made you so eager that, day nor night, you could find no peace, but all your thoughts were centred on how you might accomplish magic. And when you summoned us we made you bold and reckless so that

you would rather be led to the devil than be dissuaded from your purpose

558f **root in thee]** G [47] adds: so that you were utterly determined to procure yourself a spirit

559 **thou gavest... soul]** ◇ A577f, B523f

562–8 **Had not... accordingly]** E, replacing G [48]: 'If only I had been pious, kept God's commandments, and not allowed the devil to take so firm a root I should not have placed my body and soul in such a plight. Oh, what have I done?' 'There you have it,' replied the spirit. ● PF makes Faustus' desire to know the 'secrets of hell' his motivation for the pact ◇ A1515–7, B2119–21

571 **hell]** G [48] adds: called Gehenna

571f **and whether... Chap 15]** G [48]: [Chap 16]

573–5 **ever... soul]** G [48]: was stricken with remorse and thoughts of what little he had gained by forfeiting future bliss and selling himself to the devil for temporal pleasures

575 **Judas]** G [49] adds: his remorse was sincere but he despaired of God's grace and thought it impossible that he might ever be restored to His favour. Just as Cain ‡ cf. Gen. 4: 13

578f **and the... thereof]** G [49]: that is, he considered what he had done and thought that by frequent and prolonged discussion with his spirit he would bring himself to a state in which he might be counselled to reform through penitence and renunciation of his evil ways. But it was all in vain; the devil had bound him too fast

580 **some... of hell]** G [49]: what hell was, and how it was [50] constructed

583 **Whereupon... answered]** G [50]: The spirit answered none of these questions but said

584f **for they... mind]** transp.

585f **Thinkest... us?]** ◇ B1908–10

586–8 **if thou... again]** ◇ A1462, B2048

588–90 **Therefore... nothing]** loose

591 **dispatch]** ¶ make haste (*OED* v. 9)

593f **and therefore... hearing]** E

595–657 **Thou wilt... request]** numerous transpositions

596 **figures]** ¶ representations (*OED* sb. 9)

597–9 **but it... thereof]** E ¶ in such sort: in the like manner

600f **out of... upon]** E § Jesus Christ 'descended into hell and on the third day he rose again'

601 **bloodthirsty]** G [51]: a thirsty place for there is no refreshment to be had

602 **valley]** G [51] adds: not far from Jerusalem (that is, the throne of heaven) ‡ 2 Kings 23: 10; Jer. 19: 6

602–7 **into the... bottom]** G [51]: This vale of hell is so wide and deep that the damned are eternally confined in its wilderness and can never climb to those heights where the citizens of the heavenly Jerusalem dwell. Others speak of hell as a place so extensive that the damned who must dwell there can see no end to it.

608–10 **For like... unquenchable]** E

616f **but... God]** E

618–22 **out of… frozen]** G [52]: like the bottomless rift produced by an earthquake when the bedrock is cleaved and shaken apart; the depths of the chasms are very windy. The passages of hell are regular, now broad, [53] now narrow, then broad again and so forth. Hell is also called Petra, a rock or cliff, for indeed, there are rocks of several kinds, as *saxum, scopulus, rupes* and *cautes*. There are no loose stones or earth among the fells of hell, for God laid the foundations like the firmament of heaven, quite hard, pointed and rough, like a mountain top

626 **bound]** G [53] adds: another name is *Damnatio*, for the souls in hell are convicted and damned to eternal captivity; their sentence is pronounced to them as it is in the courts.

627 ***Pernicies, Exitium***] ¶ Latin synonyms for destruction, ruin

627f **death… evil thing]** G [53]: *Confutatio, Damnatio, Condemnatio* and the like

628–33 **We have… fire]** E, replacing G [54]: The souls cast themselves into these depths, just as climbers upon a high peak, looking down into the valley, lose their balance and fall. But he who is in despair does not climb up there to look at the view: the higher he climbs, the further he has to fall. So it is with the damned souls: the greater the sin, the deeper the level to which the sinner must fall. Finally, hell is constructed in such a fashion that it cannot be fathomed, for God vented His anger in creating this place for the damned, and it has many names, such as the house of shame, a maw, a deep, and the nadir of hell. For the damned souls have not merely to sit lamenting in the eternal fires: they must utter obscenities, mock and rail against [55] God and His holy ones, and for this purpose they dwell in the maw and throat of hell. This maw is insatiable, craving fresh souls, eager for their seduction and damnation. § PF's allegory of the ladder may be an attack on neoplatonic magic, cf. Giordano Bruno, *Lo Spaccio della bestia trionfante* (printed in London, 1584), p. 236: 'wise men… with magic and divine rites rose to the height of Divinity by means of that same ladder of Nature by which Divinity descends to the lowest of things in order to communicate herself', quoted in translation by Roy T. Eriksen: *The Forme of Faustus' Fortune*, (1987), p. 64

629 **it]** † self-evidently an O edit.

638 **adders… crocodiles]** E

639f **the puddle… lake]** G [55]: a stench of water

643 **nay, I will]** E

643–5 **the secrets… cease]** G [55]: what miseries the damned [56] suffer, or are to suffer, in hell. My dear Faustus, perhaps you should consult the scriptures, for it is concealed from me. However, I shall tell just the same tale of the woes and conditions of hell and of its unbearable torments. The damned are faced with the dreadful conditions I have just described ◇ A566, B512

645f **for hell… satisfied]** ‡ Prov. 30: 15,16

646 **thou]** G [56]: they ● Throughout the following, PF involves Faustus directly, whereas the German text refers always to 'the damned', 'they', etc.

thou] G [56] adds: lament their sins and evil lives, bewailing the abominable stench, their confinement and debility and the clamour of shrieks and lamentations. They cry out to God in their anguish

647 **crying]** G [56] adds: Why shouldn't they tremble and howl? Why shouldn't they lament? For they are shunned by all God's creation [57] and held in everlasting disgrace while the holy are accorded eternal joy and honour... [We spirits shall be freed, for we too have hopes of bliss W] but the damned will bewail the insufferable cold...

648 **swimming... miseries]** G [57]: the unbearable darkness and stench, the remorseless lash and the hideous faces of the devils

650–3 **thy heart... another]** E; ◇ B2020f § The image of the muckforks recurs at 921–5; cf. intro., pp. 16f

655f **for the... punishment]** transp., omitting antecedent G [57]: some suffer much more severely than others § For the notion that the torments are progressively increased, cf. Robert Persons: *The Christian Exercise* (Rouen, 1582), p. 53: '... evil men when they die do not commonly carry with them all their demerit and evil, for that they leave behind them either their evil example, or their children and familiars corrupted by them, or else books and means which may in time corrupt other. All which being not yet done but coming to pass after their death, they cannot so conveniently receive their judgment for the same presently, but as the evil falleth out, so their pains are to be increased... the pains of the wicked... are daily augmented.' This appears to set limits to God's omniscience

658 **God,]** G [58] adds: Be that as it may, I will answer your question, first treating of the nature of hell and how it was created in God's anger, to see if we can formulate some principles

661–4 **For what... God]** E

668–70 **For even... effect]** G [58]: For if the damned could share our hopes of salvation [59] (we spirits expect it constantly) they would rejoice and sigh longingly for the time to come. But they have as little hope of receiving grace as the devils in hell following their fall and repudiation. ● PF ignores the distinction made here in G between 'we spirits' and the 'devils in hell' ◇ A644, B585

671f **if He do... had]** E, omitting G [59]: their consciences will be awakened and will prick them incessantly ● cf. 678–81 for the continuation of the simili; ‡ Dives: Luke 16: 19–31; Cain: Gen. 4: 13; Judas: Matt. 27: 5

673f **duke... gentleman]** G [59]: counts and other rulers

674–8 **for if... looked for]** loose

678f **Therefore... Cain]** E

680f **go hang... Dives]** E; ◇ B2027

690 **heard]** G [61] adds: No, they will lie in hell like the bones of the dead, nagged by death and their consciences and their initial confidence and trust in God will be of no avail; He will not even think of them

690f **so impossible... mountains]** G [61]: even if you could hide yourself in hell until all the mountains had fallen together in a heap and were moved from one place to another...

693 **or to... world]** E

a camel] G [61]: an elephant or camel ‡ cf. Mark 10: 25

696f **and I... like it?]** E

698f **or else... contentment]** E, replacing G [62]: for I am not obliged to answer such questions
701 **laid... bed]** E
702 **cogitations]** G [62] adds: debating them day and night ¶ fantastical cogitations: vain speculations
702f **fain... but]** G [62]: but it could have no lasting or beneficial effect, for
702–4 **fain... mercy]** ◇ A647, B589
705f **would... him a]** G [62]: would come to him in the guise of ● Once again the woman is real in EFB
708f **to the... soul]** E
710f **of his... Chap. 16]** G [63]: [Chap. 17]
712 **being... things]** E
713–16 **'My Mephostophiles... new']** dir. sp.
716–19 **'Yet I... thee']** E
724f **and that... hadst]** E § Mephostophiles implies that by becoming a spirit, Faustus has renounced his humanity, lost the grace of God and the freedom of the will, and his understanding is perverted; cf. 731–6
726 **Majesty]** G [64] adds: that I might not provoke His anger against me
732 **reasonable]** ¶ rational
736 **and given... devil]** E
737f **which hath... damnation]** G [64]: whereby you have lost your most precious jewel, the sanctuary of God
741 **for yet... that]** G [65]: and small question of it. For even if I had already sinned against God
743f **if it... God that]** G [65]: if you could have attained the grace of God before you committed your heinous sin, but
744 **too late]** ◇ A707, B648; B1993
745f **'Leave off... comfort']** G [65]: 'Leave me in peace,' said Dr Faustus. 'Then give me some peace from your questioning,' retorted the spirit
748 **Chap. 17]** G [66]: [Chap. 18]
750 **forgot... works]** G [66]: had to make the best of it
751 **calendar-maker]** ¶ author of predictive almanacs
753 **the course... stars]** G [66]: star-lore
753f **that he... time]** G [66]: and it is well known that all his writings were greatly admired amongst mathematicians ¶ mathematics: mathematicians
758f **upon... elements, as]** E
759f **wind,... cold]** PF inserts: rain, dry, cold
761 **as if... forewarned it]** E
762 **of our time]** E
762f **cold... fire]** PF inserts: moist, airy, dry, fire
765 **plague]** E
768 **Chap. 18]** a conflation of G: [chaps. 19–21]
769f **he was... wherefore]** G [68]: having done so for two years
771–5 **saying... matter]** G [68]: asking his opinion on *astronomia* or *astrologia* as practised by the mathematicians ◇ A662f, B602f
772–84 **when I... gift of God]** § This echoes passages in Agrippa, p. 45: 'very skilfull

mathematicians... confess that it is impossible to find out any certain thing concerning the knowledge of judgments...'; p. 46: 'they... write so divers and contrary opinions upon one thing, that it is impossible for an Astrologian to pronounce any certain thing upon so variable and disagreeing opinions, except there be in him some inward perceiving of things to come and hidden, and inspiration of foreknowledge, or rather a secret and privy inspiration of the devil...'

776 **speculators]** ¶ prognosticators (*OED* 3; earliest listing: 1652) § see Agrippa, p. 52b: 'Speculatorie, which doth interpret thunder, lightning and other impressions of the elements, moreover monstrous and strange sights seldom seen, yet with no other way than by conjecture and similitude... it doth very much err, because all these be natural works, and not prognostical.' This possibly explains the Faust-book inclusion of chapters on thunder and comets

776f **or at... arts]** E

779–84 **concerning... of God]** E; ¶ blinded: obscured; blind: having secret meaning (*OED* a. III. 8)

786 **fleet]** ¶ float, swim

in all elements] G [68]: beneath the heavens

787 **pretended]** ¶ intended

787f **except... doom]** E, omitting G [68]: for we are ancient spirits experienced in the celestial motions. Yes, my dear Faustus, I could make you practica, calendars [69] and nativities for all time, year after year, and as you know, I have never misinformed you. But it is probably true that in olden times those who lived for five or six hundred years may have attained an understanding of the principles of this art. For such long life-spans allowed them to observe the completion of a great year so that they might interpret it and record the passage of the comets. But all recent, inexperienced astrologers base their predictions on likelihood and supposition. ¶ day of doom: Judgment Day

789–839 **'Wherefore... unto me]** largely E with occasional fragments from G chapters 20 and 21, where the cosmology is so confused and outmoded that PF chose to replace it. In the following translations of these chapters, passages used by PF are presented in bold type:

G [69]: Concerning winter and summer. [chap. 20]

Faustus thought it very strange that God should have created winter and summer upon earth, so he asked his spirit [70] the origin of the seasons. The spirit replied very briefly: 'My lord Faustus, surely you, as a physicist, can deduce this for yourself from the movement of the sun! Know then, that from the moon to the fixed stars is the region of fire, **but the earth is cold and frigid. For the deeper the sun shines the hotter it is**, and that is the cause of summer. When the sun stands high, then it is cold, resulting in winter.

Concerning the course of the heavens, its lights and origin. [chap. 21]

As mentioned before, Doctor Faustus had been forbidden to ask any more questions on divine or celestial matters. This troubled him sorely; day and night he plotted how he might camouflage his interest in the divine [71] creation. So he no longer asked about the joys of the blessed, or about the angels or the pains of hell, for he knew his spirit would not entertain such questions. Instead he had to feign an interest where he might receive an answer, so he decided to frame his questions under the pretext that the information was serviceable and necessary to the philosopher for the study of astronomy or astrology. Accordingly he asked his spirit to expound the course of the heavens, its lights and origins.

'My Lord Faustus,' said the spirit, 'it was God, your Maker, who created the world and all the elements beneath the heavens, for in the beginning, God created the heavens out of the midst of the waters and separated the waters from the waters and called the firmament heaven. [72] It is a mobile, spherical disc created from water congealed and solidified like a crystal, **and up in the sky it looks like a crystal, wherein are fixed the stars.** Through the revolution of the heavens **the world is divided in four parts: East, West, North and South.** The heavens rotate so fast that the world would break in pieces were it not prevented by the [contrary W] motion of the planets. **Heaven is also furnished with fire so hot, that were it not for the clouds with their cooling waters the elements beneath it would ignite.** Within the firmament of the fixed stars are **the seven planets: Saturn, Jupiter, Mars, Sol, Venus, Mercury and Luna** and all the heavens move except the fiery heaven. The world is divided in four parts, namely **fire, [73]** air, earth and water and so are the spheres and their creatures, each taking their matter and characteristics from one of these. Thus the uppermost heaven is fiery and shining, the middle and lower are clear and airy. The uppermost is heated and illuminated directly owing to the nearness of the sun, but the lowest is lit by reflection of earth-shine and is cold and dark in those places which the reflected rays cannot reach. Here in this gloomy air we spirits dwell, cast out into the darkness, amidst violent storms, thunder, hail, snow and the like, so that we may tell the seasons of the year and what the weather should be. Heaven has also twelve spheres encompassing the earth and the water, if they may all be called heavens.' [74] The spirit also told him the ruling of the planets and the grade of each with respect to the rest. § cf. intro., p. 22

789f **course... ☾]** ◇ A671, B612

790 **♄ , ... ☾]** † cf. intro., p. 39; see also below, at 819f, 827

795 **fifth essence]** ¶ according to ancient and medieval philosophy, the substance, latent in all things, of which the heavenly bodies were composed, but here Mephostophiles refers to the soul

796f **thou hast... learn]** ◇ A330f, B310f

797f **to make... rain]** ◇ A610, B551

798 **the clouds... rent]** ◇ A89

800f **the deeper... shines]** § i.e. the higher the sun in the sky; the words seem to relate to the shadow of a gnomon on a vertical wall, cf. G: 70: When the sun stands high, then it is cold. (cf. at 789–839 above)

803–5 **the earth... dry?]** § cf. e.g. Agrippa: *De occulto philosophia libri tres*, [cologne] 1533, p. 4: 'Est enim ignis calidus et siccus, terra sicca et frigida, aqua frigida et humida, aer humidus et calidus...'

810–16 **Learn... shirt]** ‡ Prov. 6: 27,28: Can a man take fire in his bosom, and his clothes not be burned, etc. § cf. the magical powers claimed by Simon of

Samaria (see intro., p. 22); also Scot, p. 100: 'it is absolutely against the ordinance of God (that made me a man) that I should fly like a bird, or swim like a fish or creep like a worm.'

817 **presaging comets]** § cf. 1757–9

818 **the whole... West]** ◇ A675, B615

819f **above ♄]** † cf. 790, above § The 'fiery sphere above ♄' is the *coeleum empyreum*, see intro., p. 23.

826–8 **the snow...** *manifesto*] § this is probably PF's mumbo-jumbo, cf. intro., pp. 21, 34

827 ♓ **]** astrological sign for Pisces; † see 790 above; § as for 826–8 above

830 **fodines]** ¶ mines, cf. L. *fodio*, to dig or delve; *salis fodinae*: Daniel Cellarius: *Speculum orbis terrarum*, 1578; not listed *OED*

833 **Thy time... away]** ◇ A1134–6

840–2 **How Doctor... Chap. 19]** conflates material from G chapters 22 and 23: G [74]: Doctor Faustus asked how God created the world and of the birth of mankind; his spirit, true to his type, gave him a totally false answer. [chap. 22] G [77]: All the devils of hell are presented to Dr Faustus in their infernal shapes and the seven principal spirits are named. [chap. 23] ¶ rout: assembly

843–5 **Doctor... suddenly]** G [74]: While Dr Faustus was still sorrowing and downcast,

846 **spirit]** G [74] adds: to console him

852 **diligence]** ¶ service

further... thyself] E

855f **I am... kingdom]** ◇ A698f, B640f

such respects... kingdom] G [75]: many respects

859–61 **who spake... God]** dir. sp. ◇ A694, B634

860f **and all... God']** G [75]: and of the birth of mankind

861–9 **The spirit... rage]** E, replacing the residue of G, chapter 22: [75] The spirit answered with an unholy lie, saying, 'The world, my Faustus, was never born and neither will it die. Likewise, the human race has existed for ever and had no first beginning. The earth had to nourish itself and the sea separated itself from the earth; [76] they made an amicable agreement, as if they could talk. The earth claimed as its own the fields, meadows, woods and herbage, while the sea claimed the fish and all else that it contains. But the remainder of creation, namely of mankind and the heavens, they conceded to God, so that ultimately they became subservient to him. From this organisation arose the four principles of air, fire, water and earth. I cannot report otherwise or more briefly.' On consideration, Dr Faustus refused to entertain these notions but held to what he had read in the first chapter of Genesis where Moses gives a different account: there Faustus found little to contradict. ● cf. intro., pp. 15ff

864 **will... pieces]** † the omission of 'tear thee in a' in '08 &c shows that these editions were page for page copies of a precursor ed. ◇ A709, B650

865 **and hereat... away]** ◇ A702, B644

869–73 **And being... upon]** G [77]: Doctor Faustus' prince and rightful master came to pay him a visit. He was so horrible that Dr Faustus was quite unnerved, for although it was summer, such coldness emanated from the devil that Dr Faustus thought he would freeze to death. ◇ A713, B654; A716, B657

873–6 **and traversing... cogitations]** E

874f **Now... come]** ◇ A719, B659

877 **Lucifer]** G [77]: Belial ● The confusion in G concerning the name of Faustus' 'prince and rightful master' must arise from a conflation of different sources, cf. intro., p. 7

878 **Faustus]** G [77] adds: when you awoke at midnight

878–80 **which are... blood]** E, replacing G [77]: and saw that you would gladly see the seven principal spirits ◇ A720–2, B660–2

881–3 **and to... us]** E, replacing G [77]: together with my principal counsellors and servants, that you might see them. ◇ A730, B669f

883–5 **Go to... Faustus]** E, replacing G [78]: 'Where are they then?' 'Outside,' said Belial

885f **commanding... hell]** transp.; G [78]: Each spirit came to Faustus in his hall, one after another, so that there was not place for them all to sit

886 **First entered]** E

887 **to... ground]** E

888 **as red... fire]** G [78]: a brightly glowing red

888f **were a... long]** E

890 **two]** G [78]: three

one... arm] G [78]: at the neck

890f **they appeared... hell]** G [78]: Belial presented them to Dr Faustus, giving their names and saying what they were. The first to enter were the seven principal spirits, the first being Lucifer, Doctor Faustus' rightful lord, to whom he had sold himself

892 **like a]** G [78] adds: red

893f **I think... squirrel]** E; § cf. intro., n. 69, but this may also be a reference to Luther's experience in the Wartburg of a strange nocturnal intruder (presumed to be a devil) which took hazel nuts, one by one, from a sack on the table and cracked them on the roof beam, see *Tisch* Vol. 6, No. 6816

895f **a mighty... horns]** E

896 **long ears... ground]** G [79]: frightful ears

897 **on his back]** G [79]: half green, half yellow

899 **like]** G [79]: of the colour of

900 **under... chaps]** G [79]: above

short] G [79] adds: bright yellow

901 **thick... middle]** G [79]: whitish

many] G [79] adds: finger-length

902 **his]** G [79] adds: chestnut-brown

Chamagosta] G [79]: Satan [*Satanas*] ● Perhaps PF is reluctant to mock Satan, a servant of God (Job 1); the name Chamagosta appears to be a unique occurrence, presumably PF's invention. Cham (i.e. Ham, son of Noah) was traditionally credited with the origin of sorcery and the invocation of wicked spirits (cf. Scot, p. 386) and Holinshed's *Chronicle* (1587 ed.: p. 21 col. b) states that nations other than the Egyptians 'abhorred him for his wickedness, calling him Chemesencia, that is, the impudent, infamous and wicked Cham'. There may also be confusion with Chamos, worshipped by the Moabites (Numbers 21: 29; Bishops' Bible, 1588 and earlier). Chamagosta presumably means 'seducer of Cham'.

904 **like an ox]** E

906 **hair]** G [79] adds: with the black parts flecked with white, the white with black

906f **in shape... tail]** E

907 **with]** G [79] adds: feet and

908f **a short thief]** G [80]: an ell in length

909 **pheasant]** G [80]: partridge

910 **his body... black]** E

911 **like... hedgehog]** E

912f **like... monkey]** E. G [80] adds: These seven together with Belial, their leader, were in the colours described

913 **unsensible]** ¶ irrational

914f **antelopes... horses]** E, omitting G [80]: beavers, boars

915 **lions... toads]** E

915f **and all... worms]** G [80]: etc., and the like

916–28 **yet came... mine?]** E, replacing G [80]: In such forms and colours they appeared to him, and so many that several had to go out of the hall. Dr Faustus marvelled greatly and asked the seven around him: ● PF's 'thunderclap', etc. foreshadow Faustus' end, cf. 2913–18 ● for the muckforks, cf. commentary to 650–3

929 **Lucifer]** G [80]: They

929–32 **We... darkness]** dir. sp.

930 **there]** G [80] adds: although we are even more hideous and frightful [81] there
blind] ¶ deceive (*OED* v. 2), cf. also at 1061, 1802, 2262

932 **or angels... darkness]** E

933–5 **I like... vanished]** G [81]: that seven were sufficient and begged the others might take their leave, which they did

935 **vanished]** G [81] adds: Then Faustus begged that they would give him a demonstration; they consented and each in turn as before, they changed themselves into all kinds of animal including great birds, serpents and reptiles, bipeds and quadrupeds

936–41 **and spake... thou?]** E

942f **Then Lucifer... paw]** G [81]: They said yes

943 **gave... book]** ◇ A802f, B736f

943f **saying... himself]** G [81]: suggesting he try it, which he did

944–6 **into a... well]** E; ¶ worm: serpent, snake (*OED* sb. 1)

946f **Quoth... world?]** G [81]: Before they took their leave Dr Faustus could not forbear to ask who had created vermin (*Unziffer*) ¶ filthy forms: here, insects, literally 'disgusting creatures', possibly 'creatures delighting in filth', such as flies

947 **Luficer]** G [81]: They

948 **men,]** G [81] adds: since Adam's fall

and so... plagued] G [81]: We can as readily change into different kinds of vermin as into other animals. [82] Dr Faustus laughed and begged to see it. They complied and immediately disappeared from sight. ● PF treats the plaguing as a minor punishment for Faustus' question on the creation of the world, cf. 955

949 **came]** G [82] adds: all manner of insect into Dr Faustus' hall

scorpions... gnats] G [82] includes: ants, leeches, gad-flies, crickets, grasshoppers, bees, gnats, fleas, lice, spiders, wasps

949f **which... biting him]** E abbreviates the tormenting

950f **and all... nothing]** E

952–6 **wherefore he... again]** E, replacing G [82]: In all he was sorely troubled by the insects and rightly said, 'I think you're all young devils.' He could no longer remain indoors because of them, but as soon as he went outside his torment was over and he was free of them

955 **how... world?]** ◇ A735, B675

956 **filthy cattle]** G [82]: vermin ¶ 'cattle' included bees, etc., so here 'stinging insects' (*OED* sb. 4b, first listing of usage: 1589)

957–60 **only Faustus... pastime]** E; § cf. 295–8, where Faustus is also 'ravished' by music

961f **desired... Chap. 20]** G [83]: travelled to hell [Chap. 24]

964f **he meant... contentment]** G [83]: he extended his aims from day to day, but most of his time was spent on study and research, questions and disputations, being much troubled with thoughts of hell

965f **intending... any more]** E, a logical continuation of PF's remodelling of chapter 19

967f **'Bring... Belial']** dir. sp.

969 **Beelzebub]** G [83] adds: beneath the heavens

969f **I would... thereof]** dir. sp.; ◇ A799–801, B733–5

970 **if I... hell]** G [83]: if a spirit would take me to hell and back ● By omitting 'and back', PF makes Faustus' request ambiguous, and Beelzebub's reply 'at midnight I will fetch thee' (971) is a two-fold promise, foreshadowing the end.

take a view thereof] G [83]: examine its basis, attributes and substance

971f **night being come]** G [84]: when it was pitch dark

972–9 **Doctor... thunderclap]** E ● Besides intensifying the prelude to departure, PF carefully arranges the mechanics of leaving the house through the open casement.

979f **a great... curled]** G [84]: Beelzebub

980 **chair... gold]** G [84]: cage-like seat made of bones ● It is uncharacteristic of PF to delete the curious, but here he applies moral allegory: the road to hell is paved with gold, etc.

980–2 **and spake... there]** E

987 **At last]** G [84]: soon

a place] G [84]: a mountain as high as a great peak

993 **them]** G [84f] adds: for the brightness of the fire

994 **devil]** G [85]: Beelzebub

996 **bear]** G [85]: Beelzebub
997 **hart]** G [85] adds: with great antlers
chair] G [85] adds: so that he feared greatly
999 **on their way]** G [85]: deeper into the cavern
1001 **storks]** G [85]: flying bears ● The 'flying bears' image is overworked and PF's 'storks' are appropriate combatants for the snakes.
1001–3 **swallowed... greatly]** G [85]: fought with the snakes and overcame them so that he passed through with greater safety
1004 **bull]** G [86] adds: which charged at Dr Faustus, bellowing with rage
1006 **bear]** G [86]: devil [lit.: worm]
1006f **so that... away]** E, replacing G [86]: Doctor Faustus fell out of the chair deeper and deeper into the abyss ● It is surprising that PF should ignore this arresting image
1008 **there... devil]** G [86]:, Now am I done for, because he could no longer see his spirit
1010f **bidding... upon me']** G [86]: who caught him and saved him
1013 **but shortly... he saw]** G [86]: the fog gathered to form a cloud, out of which came
1015 **Forth... cloud]** G [86]: An impenetrable darkness lasted for a quarter of an hour ● This is preceded in W by an extra sentence of which PF shows no knowledge
1016 **sat]** G [86] adds: Deeper and deeper they drove. [87] Then, suddenly, this stinking, thick fog dispersed and he beheld his steed and cart again
1017 **cries of... souls, with]** E
1018 **poor... fear]** G [87]: even the bravest of men would have trembled, let alone Dr Faustus
1019 **water... mud]** G [87]: large expanse of rough water
1021 **as it... mist]** G [87]: great heat
1023 **dragons... waggon]** G [87]: horse and cart
1024 **rock]** G [87]: peaked crater
1025–7 **but when... earth]** E
1028 **sat he]** G [87] adds: like one half-dead
1028f **upon the... fire]** G [87]: into the crater, from which issued a draught, and all around was nothing but water
1031 **fall... fire]** G [88]: throw myself into the crater or the water
1031f **or... despair]** G [88]: or perish up here
1032 **leap]** † the '08 var. 'scope' (*OED* sb[1]: a leap or skip; verbal usages from 1572 apply only to horses) probably derives from the original, edited in O and '10.
1033 **infernal hags]** G [88]: spirits
1033f **take here... deserved]** ◇ A1318, B1833
1034 **Upon... entered]** G [88]: Just as he pitched himself headlong into the abyss
1034f **and finding... but]** E; ¶ appaid: contented (*OED* apay v. 1)
1036f **it passed... heard]** G [88]: the mountain and peaks reverberated so much that he thought it was nothing less than a salvo of cannon
1040 **tormented souls]** G [88]: soldiers in armour

1042 **to cool]** G [88]: to drink, bathe and refresh
1042f **but... again]** G [88]: others, being cold, ran
1043 **fire]** G [88] adds: to warm themselves
1043–5 **and thus... cold]** E
1045–9 **but Faustus... speaking]** G [88]: Doctor Faustus stepped into the flames and tried to grasp one of the damned souls but when he supposed he had him in his hands he disappeared. However, he could not stay there [89] longer on account of the heat
1049f **this devil]** G [89]: his dragon or Beelzebub
1050 **in likeness... bear]** E
1052 **air]** G [89] adds: for Dr Faustus could no longer endure the thunder and tumult, fog, sulphur, smoke and fire, frost and heat, especially since he had seen the weeping and wailing and gnashing of teeth etc.
1052f **where... way]** E
1054f **would have tarried]** G [89]: having desired to see hell, had been shown more than he had wished
1057 **his]** † '08 &c transmit the literal transl., edited in O
1059 **awaked]** G [89] adds: and saw the daylight
dungeon] G [89f] adds: for in hell he had seen nothing but the flames and what they had illuminated
1061 **or not]** G [90]: which was indeed the case for had he really seen hell he would never have wished to go there
1061–3 **but he... things]** E
1064f **by his... study]** G [90]: in a sheaf of papers in his own hand inserted between the pages of a book
1065f **which... Christians]** E ● It is possible that PF had learned of such a publication while at Leipzig (cf. intro., pp. 27, 29). None has survived. Mephostophiles is absent from the main part of the story and the use of Beelzebub suggests a separate source.
1067–70 **How... Chap. 21]** G [91]: How Doctor Faustus journeyed up into the heavens. [Chap. 25] ◇ A810–2, B558–60; B778f
1070 **21]** † for the possible significance of variant chapter nos., cf intro. p. 51
1071 **letter]** G [91]: history [*Geschicht*]
by a... Wittenberg] E ● The meticulousness of this inclusion suggests further local hearsay (cf. 1065f); the 'found' letter is supposed to be Faustus' copy of the one sent to Leipzig.
1074 **brother]** ¶ a common form of address amongst alumni, etc., no consanguinity implied.
1079 **I... yourself]** G [91]: I have become your equal in this art [92] and you have sought my advice on various matters. As is apparent from your letters of thanks, I have never withheld anything or declined to answer, and I am still always ready to oblige you if you should visit me.
1080f **(might... praise)]** E, omitting G [92]: I am equally gratified by the renown and praise you have accorded me.
1081–5 **my calendars... before]** not in W; ¶ calendars, practices: predictive

almanacs; • 'practices' is PF's translation for *practica*, rather than contemporary usage (cf. 1092)

1082f **of... nation]** E ¶ Dutch: German (*deutsch*); perhaps PF is explicit to avoid any suggestion that members of the English nobility might have praised the works.

1083 **(which... noted)]** E

1084f **as if... before]** E

1085 **(my beloved Victor)]** E

1088f **it is]** G [92] adds: You also state that it would have to have been with the devil's aid, or accomplished by magic. Really, now! [*Ja wett, Fritz*]

1091 **laid... bed]** E

for thinking] G [93]: and thought

1094f **or whether... heavens]** G [93]: although they cannot investigate it by direct observation but only by speculation and from books and opinions

1096 **being... muses]** E; ¶ muses: musings, reflections; † '08 &c suffer from a haplographic line omission, cf. intro. pp. 39f

1098 **astonied]** G [93]: terrified

1100–02 **What... with thee]** G [93]: If I may see what is just now in my mind and is presently my chief desire

1102f **there... thee]** G [93]: and you will see your transport

1103 **there stood]** G [93]: flying down towards me I saw

1103–5 **a waggon... fire]** ◇ A814f, B781f; B562f

1104 **before... same]** E

1105f **I was... depart]** E, omitting G [94]: I inspected my horse and carriage. The wings of the dragons were brown and black, flecked with white, the back the same, but the belly, head and neck of a greenish hue, speckled with yellow and white

1109 **got me into]** G [94]: climbed on to the casement and jumped into my carriage

1111f **we... stones]** G [94]: I were travelling on land ¶ stones: cobblestones

us] G [94]: the wheels

1113 **earth]** G [94] world [*die Welt*]

1114 **I... dungeon]** G [94]: as if I were driving from bright daylight into a dark hole • PF inverts the sense of the German, where the higher regions are increasingly darker

1115f **was behind... by me]** G [94]: rushed up and sat beside me in the carriage

1119 **good... schoolfellow]** E

1121 **seven... following]** E ◇ B790, 870

1123 **after... journey]** E

1126 **the world... little]** G [95]: I can tell from the world. And as long as I was away from home I was neither thirsty nor hungry • Evidently there is a displacement in the German text, recognized by PF

1128 **leagues]** G: *Meilen* • The German mile was variously 3 or 4 English miles, the 'great league of Germany' 5 English miles. (*OED* league sb[1]: Blundevil *Exercises*, 1594)

height] ◇ B786f

1129f **world... world Asia]** † '18 &c suffer from a haplographic line omission
1130 **and provinces]** G [95] principalities and waters
1130f **Asia, Europe]** ◇ B789: 'East to West'
1132 **lie... they are]** E
1133–43 **this is... journey]** G [96]: item, this is Prussia, back there is Sicily, Poland, Denmark, Italy, Germany. But tomorrow you will see Asia and Africa. Item, Persia and Tartary, India, Arabia. And because we are driving with the wind we now see Pomerania, Russia and Prussia, likewise Poland, Germany, Hungary and Austria. On the third day I saw greater and lesser Turkey, Persia, India and Africa. Before me I saw Constantinople and in the Persian Sea and the sea around Constantinople I beheld many ships and armadas sailing hither and thither. Constantinople appeared scarcely big enough to accommodate three houses, the people but a span in height. I travelled in July and it was very hot.
1134 **Tartascelesia]** ¶ Thoms: Tartary and Silesia
1137 **Alchar]** ¶ Cairo; † The '08 &c var. is a MS misread
1140 **zone]** ◇ B784 ● The globe was divided in five zones: the torrid zone between the tropics, two temperate zones and two frozen zones, i.e. the polar regions (An. 1551); cf. also at 1242
1141 **Ocean Sea]** ¶ the ocean, not the Mediterranean
1144 **South... West]** ◇ B784: 'quarters of the skye'
rained] G [97] adds: and in another thundered
1146–50 **with great... therewith]** E
1150 **Then... behold, they]** G [97]: Having now been 8 days in the sky, I saw from afar that the heavens
1151 **swift]** ◇ B789: 'his Dragons swiftly glide'
thousands]: G [97] adds: or would have broken the world to pieces
1153f **covered... cloud]** G [97]: made a breeze
1155 **sky]** G [97]: firmament [lit: clouds: *das Gewülcke*]
1156 **wall]** G [97] adds: and rocks
bright] ◇ B785: 'bright circle'
1156–8 **in the... earth]** E, omitting G [97]: and the rain which comes from thence until it falls on the earth, is so clear as to be transparent. The movement of the firmament [*das Gewülcke*] in the heavens is so forceful that it always moves from East to West, carrying the stars, sun and moon along with it, causing them to move, as we see, [98] from their rising to their setting.
1159 **little]** G [98] scarcely as big as the base of a barrel
as big... world] G [98]: greater than the whole world, for I could see no end to it.
1160–209 **Indeed... firmament]** E, omitting G [98]: Thus must the moon receive its light from it at night when the sun goes down, and this is why it shines so brightly by night and also why the sky is so bright, it being day there while it is night and dark on the earth. Thus I saw more than I had desired.
1163–70 **and we think... firmament]** § cf. intro. pp. 22–4. *Pace* Rohde, it is ludicrous to think that Dr Dee could have written this.

1177 **Yea, Christian reader]** ● PF's open interjection as author, cf. intro., p. 24

1180 **German author]** i.e. Faustus. PF chooses to accept the letter as valid

1190 ⊙] cf. commentary to 790

1197f **breathed... soul]** ‡ Gen. 2: 7

1206 **is]** † without this emendation the sentence appears confusing, but clearly it is the firmament which is 'moved' etc, while the planets are 'fixed'. cf. 1163–70, above.

1209f **And further... methought]** E, omitting G [98]: one star was more than half as big as the earth

1210 **every]** G [98]: one
but as half] G [98]: as big as

1212 **looked... heavens]** ◇ B783f

1213 **was enclosed... firmament]** E

1216 **eight... again]** ◇ B790, 870

1218 **the first... waked]** E

1219 **and have... know]** E, parallel with transp. G [99]: check in your books whether my account does not accord with them

1220 **for that... me]** E

1220f **in consideration... Wittenberg]** E

1222f **my heavenly... Dixi]** E, omitting G [99]: with friendly greetings

1225f **How... Chap. 22]** G [99]: Doctor Faustus' third journey, to various kingdoms and principalities and the principal countries and nations. [Chap. 26]

1227 **having... time]** G [99]: in his sixteenth year

1228 **with full... world]** E ¶ pretence: intention

1228–34 **and calling... command]** G [99]: and commanded his spirit Mephostophiles to convey him wheresoever he desired ◇ B876

1235 **flying horse]** G [99]: horse, but winged like a dromedary

1235f **saying... went]** E; ¶ loftily: proudly, in a lofty manner

1237 **Pannonia]** ¶ a region of Hungary

1238 **Meissen]** ¶ the town in upper Saxony

1239–50 **Styria... home again]** G [100]: Lithuania, Livonia, Prussia, Muscovy, Friesland, Holland, Westphalia, Zeeland, Brabant, Flanders, France, Spain, Portugal, Italy, Poland, Hungary, and back again to Thuringia. ● PF is keenly interested in topography (cf. 1253: 'burning with desire') and his additions demonstrate his knowledge

1240 **Cathay]** ¶ China

1242 **frozen zone]** ¶ cf. 1140, above
Nova Hispaniola] ¶ Mexico

1243 **Terzera, ... St Michaels]** ¶ two of the Azores

1244 **Mainland]** ¶ possibly the Spanish main; P & M (p. 175) suggest the province of Maine, France

1252–4 **wherefore... kingdom]** E

1255 **Trier]** † the '08 &c var., 'Trent', is a highly significant MS misread, cf. intro., p. 43f

1256 **town]** G [100] adds: because it looked so Gothic [*altfränckisch*]

1257f	**that... castle]** E
1258f	**with three... trenches]** E; ◇ A825, B806 ● Not in *COT*, cf. intro., p. 44
1259f	**it was... win it]** G [100]: they need fear no enemy ◇ A826, B807
1260	**Simeon]** § a Greek hermit who occupied (AD 1028–35) the E. tower of the Porta Negra.
1261	**Bishop Popo]** § Archbishop Poppo (1016–47) restored and expanded the proto-cathedral after its devastation by the Normans.
	large] † O transmits the original
1265–7	**Paris... Neapolis]** ◇ A827–30, B808–11
1266	**to]** † an O edit
1268–77	**the streets... wind]** E, omitting G [101]: so splendidly decorated that he marvelled thereat ◇ A831–6, B812–6; § cf. *COT* I, f. 47: Viae... perelegantes, directaeque; cf. Hoby, p. 28: the streets... are for the most part narrower than in any other city, notwithstanding they are of a good length and very straight
1272	**tomb of Virgil]** § a Roman columbarium on the hill of Posilipo, West of Naples, traditionally the tomb of Virgil; cf. Turler, p. 163: near unto the first chapel or church ... is seen the grave of Virgil Maro.
	high way] § the Grotta di Posilipo, the tunnel road linking Naples with Puteoli, engineered by L. Cocceius Auctus for Agrippa under Augustus (cf. Strabo: *Rerum Geographicarum* 5. 4. 5, 5. 4. 7); cf. Hoby, p. 30: On the West side of Naples is a high way that two carts may easily go together, cut out of the rock by force of hand under the hill Posilipo. It is well 700 paces [*c.* 3,500 ft] in length and more than 12 in breadth... who first made this Grotta is uncertain, for there are diverse opinions; cf. also Turler, p. 161; cf. *COT* V. fol. 65: Sed praeteramus vulgi sermoneum insulsum, magicis poetae Virgilii (cuius anti fauces cryptae sepulchrum fuisse plures tradunt) incantamentis illud attribuentis;
1275	**windmill]** § cf. *COT* I fol. 47, where the plan shows what appears to be a windmill (more probably a windlass) on the *molo grande*; if PF was not at Naples, he may have confused *moles* (piers) and *molae* (mills): *COT*. l. c. : Extra muros australi parte, moles in mari conspicuntur, ad portus tutelam, navibus ex omnibus orbis partibus perpetuo pleni
1277f	**on the hill... within]** G [101]: or fortress, newly built, prized above all other building in Italy on account of its height, thickness and width, the variously decorated towers, walls, palace and bedchambers
1279	**olives]** G [101] adds: and several other kinds of fruit trees
1280	**Venice]** ◇ A837, B817
1281–4	**where... pass]** E
1286f	**considering... same]** E, replacing transp. G [101f]: he saw that all the merchandise and the necessities for civilization were shipped in
1287–90	**He wondered... gilded over]** E, replacing G [102]: He saw also the broad houses and tall towers and pinnacles of the temples and buildings founded and built in the midst of the water. ◇ A838f, B818–21
1289	**rood or loft]** ¶ P & M (p. 176) suggest 'rood-loft': a loft or gallery forming the head of a rood screen
1291	**Padua]** ◇ A837, B817

1292–5 **which... speculator]** E ¶ nation: a community of students of a particular nationality, usually with their own buildings, administration, etc. ; speculator: see 776, above.

1297 **Cloister]** G [102]: church
which... church] E

1298 **Christendom]** G [102]: Italy

1300–2 **twice... distance]** E

1303 **Council House. . castle]** for transp. G [102]: therein is a fortress and keep, their architecture of different styles, there is also a fair cathedral, and a town hall so fine that it has no equal in the world

1304 **lay... lie]** G [102] lies

1305–11 **over... safeguard]** E, replacing corrupt G [102]: and across from the proper side, the city is compassed by seven hills

1305–8 **Tiber... year]** ◇ A853–9; [B836–45: *two* bridges]; § cf. Thomas, fol. 23r: Upon this river of Tiber in Rome be four bridges, the first and fairest is it that passeth from the city unto castle S. Angelo and is commonly called Ponte di Sant' Angelo;

1309–11 **to this... safeguard]** ◇ A854, B839: 'safe passage'; § cf. Fulvius, fol. 20: una strada secreta, che va dal palazzo [del Vaticano] sino à castel santo Angelo, per commodo de' Pontefici, e per loro commodita e sicurezza;

1312 **gates]** ◇ A860, B847
Vaticinium] G [102]: *Vaticanum* ● The text-word (= prediction, soothsaying) is probably intended as an anti-papist pun
church] G [103]: minster or cathedral

1313–29 **in that... off]** E, replacing G [103]: There lies the Pope's palace, beautifully set with a fine pleasure garden, and alongside, the Lateran church containing all manner of relics, and called the apostolic church, certainly one of the most sumptuous and renowned churches in the world. He also saw the ruins of many pagan temples. Item, many columns, triumphal arches, etc.

1315 **Campo Santo]** § cf. Fulvius, fol. 145v: Hoggi è un Cimeterio molto frequentato nel campo Santo, vicino alla Chiesa di Santo Pietro nel Vaticano;

1318f **pyramid... Africa]** ¶ pyramid: obelisk; ◇ A860f, B846; § it was brought from Egypt on the orders of Caligula and erected in the circus of Gaius and Nero (later site of St Peter's 'churchyard'); cf. Thomas, fol. 33v: there is but one [obelisk] standing, which is in the Vatican on the South side of Saint Peter's church, called La Guglia, being 72 foot high of the very stone itself, besides the base and 4 great lions of marble that it is set upon: and hath on the top a great ball of brass gilt, with the ashes of Caesar in it, as some hold opinion.

1320 **Papa Sixtus hath]** § Pope Sixtus V (d. 27 Aug. 1590): the tense 'hath' suggests he was thought to be alive at the time of writing; cf. Fulvius, fol. 128: Questo obelisco ... l'anno passato 1586 fu con grandissima spesa, e artificio fatto da Nostro Signore Sisto V dal suo primo luogo nel mezzo della piazza di S. Pietro, e consecrato all Santissima Croce del Salvator nostro con gran solennità, e vi fu trasferito da Messer Domenico Fontano da Meli Architetto di suo Santità; – a stupendous engineering feat, described in detail with lavish illustration in Domenico Fontana: *Della trasportatione dell'obelisko Vaticano*, Roma 1590. Fulvius, fol. 316f, says the transportation (in an immense wooden cradle infested with pullies) was effected using 40 windlasses and 160 horses (four per windlass), with 800 men to attend the 'cradle', all coordinated by the trumpeters of the Pope's light horse at the direction of the architect.

1321 **24 fathom]** § PF's dimensions are ludicrously and uniquely wrong. 24 yards would be correct, with a base measurement of 8′4″ (calculated from Fulvius). PF is unlikely to have visited Rome.

1324 **seven churches]** § cf. Hoby, p. 25: There be seven famous churches about Rome, as St Peter, St John Lateran, Santa Maria Maggiore, Santa Croce in Jerusalem, these within the walls; and St Paul, St Laurence and St Sebastian without the walls.

1327 **conduits]** § Thomas, fol. 27, lists the lengths of 4 conduits as 8, 22, 35 and 42 miles respectively

1330f **but amongst... table]** G [103]: wherein Doctor Faustus found his pleasure and recreation ◇ A818, B566

1331–3 **wherefore... he was]** G [103]: He went invisible to the pope's palace

1333f **attendant... sycophant]** E

1334f **and there... to be]** E

1342–6 **the devil... nun]** E

1347 **Thus]** PF omits G [104]: And because he had heard much of Rome, by his magic

days] G [104] adds: invisible

1348–51 **and saw... dinner]** E; ◇ A819, B567, B800; A869, B855

1350 **Cardinal of Pavia]** PF's invention; ◇ A878f: 'Cardinal of Lorraine', B910: 'Cardinals of France and Padua'

1351–3 **would... face]** G [104]: was about to eat, he made the sign of the cross before him, and whenever he did this Doctor Faustus blew in his face ◇ A899, A902, A904f

1354f **yet... was]** G [104]: then he wept as one in earnest and the attendants did not know what was happening.

1356f **commanding... done]** G [104] adds: begging for absolution, for which the Pope set him a penance. Doctor Faustus laughed at this, delighted with such deception ◇ A895–8, B1095–1100

1357 **The Pope... meat, but]** E

1358f **laid hands... meat]** G [105]: famished, put out his hand, and at once the meats, together with the dish, flew into it † The '08 var. (1359), 'flew', is an exact translation; ◇ A887, B1080; A892, B1084

1360 **Capitol or Campadolia]** G [105]: a hill at Rome called Capitolium, and ate with relish § cf. Thomas, fol. 25v: The next hill, first called Tarpeius, after Capitolinus, and now Campidoglio

1360–7 **calling his... Faustus]** G [105]: together with his spirit... Also, he sent his spirit back to bring him none but the best wine from the Pope's table, together with the silver goblets and flagons

1361 **fetch... wine]** ◇ B1086, where the words are spoken by the Pope

1362 **Monte Caval]** § cf. Thomas, fol. 26v: the hills Viminalis and Quirinalis stretch down by Monte Cavallo unto Tiber; cf. Hoby, p. 24: Quirinale, otherwise called Monte Cavallo by the reason of two horses of marble that were made by Phidias and Praxiteles, set upon there;

1363 **lubbers]** ¶ abbey-lubber: a derogatory term (post-Reformation) for a monk, associated with idleness, gourmandizing, etc.; ◇ B1090

1368–70 **and knew... face]** E

1372 **walking spirit]** G [105]: dead soul ◇ A898f, B1100

1372–4 **and to curse... company]** G [105]: and condemn him to purgatory ◇ A908–10, B1108–10

1376–80 **and in ... together]** E, omitting G [105f]: Silver vessels such as these were found after his departure. It being now midnight and Faustus well sated, he again took to the skies with his spirit ● PF's dramatic sense requires the scene to end with a bang, but it costs Faustus his plate, etc. (1378), explaining PF's careful omission of these items from his will (cf. 2687f); ◇ A914–29, B1111–25

1378 **Campa de fiore]** ¶ the Campo dei fiori, adjacent to the Palazzo Farnese

1381f **near... Switzerland]** E

1383 **the city... plain]** E, omitting G [106]: for the heat is not intense there ¶ brave: admirable, fair (*OED* adj. 3)

1385 **within... miles]** E
seas] G [106]: lakes [*See*] ¶ seas: lakes (*OED* sb. 3)

1386 **buildings... palace]** G [106]: strong, well built temples... but Gothic

1387 **which is... town]** E

1388 **Saint Mary's]** G [106]: Our Lady

1389f **He did... and]** E, demonstrating that PF knows the route

1391 **the pleasant... merchants]** E

1392–4 **for that... vault]** E

1394–6 **then he... monuments]** G [106]: the finely appointed orchard at Sta. Maria. The church [of St Laurence W] which lies in the castle grounds is furnished with delightful galleries

1395 **in the duke's castle]** § Logeman (p. 154) suggests that this confusion (cf. commentary to 1397) shows that PF was never in Florence, but the argument is weak

1396f **door... upon]** G [106]: absolutely vertical tower

1397 **of the castle]** G [106]: through which one passes § PF's error; in fact, the Baptistry of St John, with its celebrated bronze doors decorated with reliefs by Andreas Pisano and Lorenzo Ghiberti.

1397f **the holy... other]** E

1399–402 **Then... women]** E, replacing G [106]: the region grows good wine and [107] the people there are artistic and good craftsmen.

1403 **where he... city]** E

1405–7 **with... strangers]** E, omitting G [107]: and near it a splendid column with beautifully carved reliefs. § cf. *COT*, I, f. 10: Eo accedit... undique gentium mercatores;

1409 **wherein... world]** G [107]: therein is a chapter called the High Chapter

1415–20 **Mare... Holland]** G [107]: sea, floated into the Rhine ● PF airs his geographical knowledge while quietly deriding the relics, cf. 1420–3

1420–3 **or else... monument.]** E

1421 **over the Alps]** ◇ B1019

1424 **1000]** G [107]: 11000 [correct] § According to legend, St Ursula was an English princess, murdered at Cologne, along with her 11,000 virgin attendants, while returning from a pilgrimage to Rome (Baedeker: *The Rhine*, 4th edn, 1900, p. 50).

1426 **Aachen]** G [107] adds: an imperial seat

1427 **Quartus]** E, in error for 'Magnus', but a difficult misread, so the error is probably PF's, possibly conditioned by knowledge learned at Prague where Charles IV (1316–78) founded St Vitus' cathedral, and later, the Karlštejn castle where the imperial insignia were kept

1428f **he went to]** G [108]: he returned to Italy, to visit the city of

1430f **whose... wine]** G [108]: an abundance of good wine is grown there.

1432–5 **where he... world]** E ¶ minster: church § *COT* I. f. 33: Est quoque in hac urbe, nobile et ingens quoddam opus, cuius simile nec in Germanea, neque in Italia aut Gallia invenitur, nempe sumptuosissima illa turris... Haec ab ipsis fundamentis usque ad supremum culmen, quadris, et pulchre figuratis lapidibus est erecta ubique aeri, et vento pervia, patetque ascensus eius quatuor cochleis. ... supremus nodus, qui inferius vix modi magnitudinem habere videtur, tantus est, ut capacitas eius recipiat v. aut vi. personas homines.

1436–8 **his spirit... name]** dir. sp.

1437f **for Stras... highway]** E

1438–42 **Yea... town]** E, replacing G [108]: There is a cathedral there. ● PF's use of 'the twelve dukes of Silesia' testifies to his interest in Silesia, corroborated by his inclusion of Breslau (cf. 1555 etc.); see Samuel Lewkenor: *A Discourse... of all those cities wherein ... flourish... Universities*, London 1600, sig. P1r: [referring to Cracow] But the people... made choice of twelve Magistrates... which magistrates or earls do unto this day retain their ancient name and dignity.'

1442 **thence]** † O prefers 'hence' to 'thence' here and at 1528, 1533, 1676, 1685, and to 'whence' at 1674. At 1698, 1718, all texts give 'hence' where 'thence' is now preferred

1443–5 **parting... monuments]** E

1446 **trench]** G [108] adds: The country is very fertile and old buildings are yet to be seen there, also a college

1447 **Jesuits' church]** G [108]: Carthusian house

1447f **which was... pillars]** E

1449–61 **before this... deed]** E, replacing G [108]: it derived from a basilisk which used to live there ● This derivation is recorded by Felix Fabri (d. 1502) (*Fratris Felicis Fabri Tractatus De Civitate Ulmensi*, hrsg. v. Gustav Veesenmeyer, *Bibliothek des litterarischen Vereins in Stuttgart*, Bd,186, Tübingen 1889, p. 6: [referring to Basel] 'Vulgus tamen dicit sic eam nominari a basilico ibi latitante olim et plurimos sua inspectione inficiente, post cuius defectum civitati nomen sordidum reliquit.' But in Fabri's account the basilisk is slain by a shepherd magically protected by a floral crown. The EFB story bears obvious similarities to that of Perseus and Medusa.

1450 **basiliscus... killed]** ◇ B951

1451 **it]** † O initially makes the basilisk male (cf. 1455) but does not extend the edit to 1456 etc.

1462 **Constance]** † the text reading, 'Costuitz' (for 'Costnitz') must derive from a misread or (less likely) an inverted n in an early edition, transmitted to all subsequent editions. The error makes nonsense of the pun on *kost' nichts* (cf. 1469)

1462f **at the... of the Rhine]** E

1464f **at the... Rhine]** E

1465f **called... Sea]** E

1466 **fifty hundred]** G [109]: 15,000 § cf. *COT* II. 41: Viginti millia passuum in longitudine patet...: latitudine alibi decem, alibi a quindecim millia passuum extenditur

1467 **of this]** G [109]: from Constantine

1467–9 **the emperor... nothing]** E, either PF's invention, or, more likely, a local commonplace

1470 **town-house]** ¶ (*OED* 1) town hall

1470f **where... city]** G [109]: Ulm is on the Danube, but another river, the Blau, flows through the city. There is a beautiful minster. The magnificent building of this parish church of Sta. Maria was begun in the year 1377. For ornamentation and artistry its like is scarce to be seen; it contains 52 altars and serves 52 benefices and there is a sumptuously wrought tabernacle. • PF seems to have tired of the 'Blue Guide' approach, but he translates the Nuremberg description in full

1474 **dukedoms]** G [109]: counties

1475 **money]** G [109] adds: and paid for all their privileges and liberties.

he came to] G [109]: travelling aloft with his spirit, Faustus saw many countries and cities from afar, amongst them a [110] large town close to a formidable castle. Here he landed and found it to be

1477 **that runs... Rhine]** E

1478 **the which... proved]** transposed, replacing G [110]: besides grain and abundant crops

1478–80 **The castle... river]** E

1480–2 **beggarly... nuns]** G [110]: mendicant orders: Benedictines, Stephanites, Carthusians, Knights Hospitallers of St John, and Teutonic Knights. Apart from the bishop's cathedral there are three Carthusian churches, 4 mendicant orders, 5 convents, [5 parish churches[W]], 2 hospitals, [also a convent or chapel[W]] of Sta. Maria, a superb building at the city gate. Having taken a thorough view of the city, Doctor Faustus entered the bishop's castle during the night, explored it fully and found all manner of provisions. On the neighbouring hillside he found a chapel hewn from the rock

1482–6 **At the... beheld]** E; ¶ artificiallest: most skilfully made or contrived (*OED* a. 6) § 'church' probably refers to the monastery of St Burkard, which stands at the foot of the Marienberg, but the altar remains unidentified
1488f **the son... tyrant]** G [111]: Nero
1489 **famous cathedral]** G [111]: parish
1490 **Sabolt]** G [111] adds: who is buried there
1491 **his hose... doublet]** E
1493 **conduit]** G [111] adds: called the *Schön Brunn*
of St Laurence] E
is] G [111] adds: or is supposed to be
1493f **that thrust]** G [111]: that Longinus thrust
1494f **the wall... Nuremberg, and]** G [111]: this town
1495 **160]** G [111]: 116
1498 **hothouses]** ¶ bath-houses
thirty] G [111]: 68
1499 **tall ships]** G [111]: captaincies (*Hauptmannschafft*) ● a puzzling mistranslation
1500 **The walls have]** E
about them] E
1501 **apothecaries]** G [111] adds: 68 watchmen, 24 policemen or informers, 9 municipal knights
1506 **the iron]** G [112]: then the iron
1507f **and by... Augsburg]** E
1510 **where]** G [112] adds: as Doctor Faustus was inclined to go on,
1513 **Ratisbon]** G [112] adds: that is Tyberius, son of Augustus, secondly the square city, thirdly from the coarse speech of the later inhabitants of the region, fourthly *Germanos*, the Germans, fifthly the royal citadel, sixthly Regensburg, city of rain, and finally, the seventh, from the great traffic of rafts and [113] ships
1515f **not far... city]** E
1517 **waters]** G [113] adds: almost all navigable
Faustus also liked the] G [113]: There is a
1519 **Remedian]** G [113]: *Remigien* † the E text-word is possibly a MS misread § *COT* I (Index: Ratispona): Remensium ecclesia S. Remigii appellata
1520 **Faustus]** G [113] adds: did not remain long but
innholder] G [113] adds: of the Tall Bush
let out all the] G [113]: stole
1521 **Munich]** † 'Mentz' (all texts) (= Mainz) is possibly a misread for 'Menchen' (cf. 1947)
1522 **town]** G [113]: region
1523 **length]** G [113] adds: and well-appointed houses
1524 **where the... resident]** G [113]: an episcopal city in Bavaria, which has also had several previous names. The region is one of ponds, downs, lakes and mountains where they hunt game birds and deer
1524–7 **here saw... cold]** E; † the O var. (1526), 'Abel', could be an attempted reminder of Faustus as Cain, but is possibly a jibe at Abel Jeffes

1528 **Austria:]** G [113] adds: for he saw the town from afar. According to his spirit

1529 **like]** G [113] adds: and took its name from Flavius, [114] the Roman governor. The city is well fortified with a very broad ditch and rampart; the circuit of the walls is 300 paces. The houses are generally painted; a university has been built next to the imperial residence. The municipal government comprises only 18 persons. Item. 1200 horses are required to bring in the vintage

1529–32 **In this... Danube]** G [114]: There is an extensive system of undergound cellars, the lanes are cobbled, the houses have cheerful rooms and parlours, ample stabling, and are furnished with all kinds of decoration

1533 **From thence... unto]** G [114]: From Vienna he took to the skies again and from his high vantage point he saw a city yet far off. It was

1535 **Prague is]** G [114]: Prague comprises the left bank

1536 **mountain]** G [114] adds: and the episcopal cathedral of St Vitus

1536–41 **there is... bridge]** E

1542–4 **In the... carved]** E

1544 **From thence... Prague]** G [114]: Old Prague lies on the plain

1546f **Unto this... Jews]** E ● cf. 1584f § *COT* I. 29: Parte ea, quae magis vertit ad flumen inflexum, versus septentrionem, Iudae suas fixerunt sedes, quae magnitudine iustum oppidum aequare possunt ● 13,000 is a gross overestimate (as is that for Cracow, cf. 1584f below). In 1652 there were only 2000 Jews in the ghetto, probably the largest number since 1541 when all but 15 families were expelled. (*Jewish Encyclopaedia*, 1925, Vol. 10, pp. 156–7)

1548–51 **and the... walls]** E, replacing G [115]: the city is surrounded by a wall § *COT* I (Index: Prague): In hoc horto aluntur leones, intra ligneos cancellos inclusi

1552–72 **From Prague... Breslau]** E

1559–71 **the brazen... found again]** § There is no archival testimony to any such 'virgin' at Breslau, though there is a tale of an 'iron maiden' of Breslau in the Kaiserburg, formerly on the site of the Matthiasstift at the Oderthor; see 'Die eiserne Jungfrau von Breslau' in Hermann Goedsche (ed.): *Schlesischer Sagen-, Historien- und Legendenschatz*, Meissen 1840, pp. 39–42. An engine identical to the EFB 'virgin', but not associated with Breslau, is described by Arkon Daraul (*Secret Societies*, 1961, p. 203) as a mode of execution employed by the Vehm courts, but no source is cited

1559 **brazen]** ¶ made of brass

1572 **he went toward]** G [115]: Doctor Faustus journeyed to the North and saw yet another city which, on coming lower, he found to be

in the kingdom] G [115]: the capital

1573 **the which... well]** E

1574–99 **at a... wonders]** E, replacing G [115]: it takes its name from the Polish duke Craco. The town is surrounded by tall towers and has a rampart and a moat irrigated by a fishing stream. There are 7 gates and many large and beautiful churches. The region is one of mighty peaks and mountains, one so high it might be thought to support the heavens. Doctor Faustus descended amongst them and was able to see into the town; however, he did not enter it, but bypassed it, remaining invisible. [116] He spent several days resting on this hill ¶ conveyance: contrivance (*OED* 11d.: earliest listing: An. 1596); edified: built

1575–8 **sumptuous church... mass]** § The cathedral church of St Wacław, containing the tomb of St Stanisław, with a silver altar, made 1509–12, by Albert Glim in Nuremberg. (Tadeusz Wojciechowski: *Kosciół katedrelny w Krakowie*, Krakow 1900, p. 90)

1579 **dragon... rock]** § *Martini Cromeri de origine et rebus gestis Polonorum libri xxx* in J. Pistorius: *Polonicae historiae corpus...*, tom 2, Basel 1582, p. 421: 'Fertur etiam, immanem beluam, quam Holophagum vocant, in antro montis, cui arx Cracoviensis superimposita est, cubile habentem, et viciniam omnem devorandis pecudibus, iumentis et hominibus vastantem..'. According to Dr Stępniak of the Archiwum Głowne Akt Dawynych, the bones may still be seen outside the cathedral church.

1582–5 **Vistula... children]** § *COT* VI, 43, quoting from Daniel Cellarius, *Speculum orbis terrarum*, 1578: Vistulae flumini ex altera parte ponti iungitur ligneo, qui ad Casimiriam urbem ducit... [not Cellarius:] Ad ortum Casimiriae adiacet opidum Hebraeorum, in unum peculiarem civitatis locum compulsorum, iisdem inclusum moenibus: ubi scholam illi habent seu synagogam. ● Once again, the number of Jews is wildly inaccurate. According to a tax registration of 1578 there were 2060 Jewish souls in the Kazimierz, cf. Majer Balaban: *Dzieje Żydów w Krakowie i na Kazimierzu (1306–1868)*, Tom. 1 (1304–1655), Krakow 1912, pp. 102f.

1582 **Wissel]** § cf. modern Wisła.

1587 **2000]** o's '900' is surely a misread

1588–90 **This salt... Buchnia]** § cf. Martin Cromer in Pistorius (see 1462, above) I. p. 80: Salis apud Bochniam et Veliscam in satrapia Cracoviensi... Color lapidei in massa lividus est fere, ac luto respersus. Candidum et in modum chrystalli pellucidum rarius est. Tritum candet aliud alio magis. Coctum vero despumatis sordibus candidissumum redditur, nivi non dissimile.

1591f **Don Spiket Jordan]** § see intro., p. 28

1600f **as into... Sardinia]** E, replacing G [116]: and for several days journeyed over the sea with nothing to view but sky and water. Eventually he came to Thrace or Greece § Neither 'Shede' nor 'Ingratz (Ingatz)' are known; possibly thc two words combined are a reading for a MS attempt at Szigeth. 'Sardinia' is equally suspect.

1601 **Constantinople]** G [116] adds: which the Turks now call *Teucros* ◇ A1027, B1161

1602 **court.]** G [116] adds: Here Doctor Faustus accomplished many exploits and hoodwinked Sultan Suleiman as related below. ◇ B1180

1603 **surnamed]** ¶ renamed (cf. *OED* surname v,3)

1603f **the founder... stone]** E, replacing G [116]: This city is adorned with so many pinnacles, towers and great buildings that it might well be called New Rome.

1604 **Great Turk]** ◇ B1180

1606f **but this... would]** E ● This is uncharacteristically hypocritical of Faustus, unlike the malicious envy of 1613f; PF is presumably voicing his own sentiments, but he has to be wary since Turkey was virtually an ally of England

1608–15 **the manner... himself]** E, replacing G [116]: the might and authority of the Turkish emperor and the pomp and grandeur of his court ¶ spited: offended, annoyed (*OED* spite v. 3) § The Levant trade took many English merchants to Constantinople, and reports would have been numerous.

1615 **and ate]** † O transmits the literal transl., edited in '08 &c

1616 **apish]** ¶ foolish, trifling (*OED*. a. 2)

1617f **the whole... fled]** G [117]: everyone ran to extinguish the flames

1621 **Faustus]** G [117]: Faustus' spirit

1624–7 **the Turk... them]** E

1627f **commanded... give]** G [117]: fell down on his knees, calling upon his Mahomet, praising and worshipping him

1632–8 **which, when... performed]** E; ¶ sport: jest; ● Faustus' pity of the ladies (1634) seems to recommend female promiscuity, but perhaps PF intends Faustus to pity them for having to share one man and thus receive inadequate attention

1639f **(being... practice)]** E

1642 **paint]** ¶ depict

Mahomet,] G [118] adds: as his spirit had done before

1642–9 **at which... fare]** E

1649f **having each... fairest]** G [118]: ate, drank, made merry and satisfied his desires

1651–4 **and so... image]** E, replacing G [118]: Meanwhile the Turk ordered his people to celebrate with great ceremony ● 'worshipping his image' shows PF's ignorance of Muslim belief

1661 **'He hath... another']** dir. sp.

1663–7 **desiring him... it]** E

1667f **that out... generation]** transp. G [118]: [Faustus] had said that a great people and valiant heroes would be engendered from his seed

1669 **had actual... them]** G [119]: shown good prowess in bed

1669–73 **'Yea... again]** dir. sp.

1670f **as if... it]** E ¶ mended: improved upon (*OED* mend v. 11)

1671 **colled]** ¶ embraced, especially about the neck (*OED* coll v[1]. 1)

1673 **again']** G [119] adds: but they had not been able to understand his speech. The priests advised the Turk not to believe it had been Mahomet, thinking it had been a phantom. But the wives said, phantom or no, he had been very friendly with them and had shown masterly prowess whether it were once or six times a night or even more, and in sum, they were all highly satisfied, etc. This caused the emperor much reflexion and put him in great perplexity.

1676 **first head]** ¶ source

1679 **Ofen]** Buda (*COT* I. 41: Buda, vulgo Ofen)

Sabatz] § P & M (p. 188) suggest Šabac, 39 miles W of Belgrade

1681 **wherein groweth... wine]** E

1682 **called Zipzar]** E

1683 **we]** G [120]: the ● It is unusual for PF to affect German nationality in this way
1686 **Austria... into]** E, again airing PF's knowledge of routes
1687 **and Leipzig]** E
1689–97 **At Leipzig... gold]** E
1691 **they]** † the '08 &c var., 'you', probably transmits the original, suggesting that P. F. personally visited this barrel; cf. intro., pp. 27
1693 **churchyard]** ¶ cemetery (*OED* 2) § 'Der Gottesacker... ist sehr groß und dermaßen mit einer schönen und zierlichen Kirche, auch inwendig um und um mit artigen Schwibbögen und kunstreichen Epitaphis gezirt und aussen mit Mauern wohlverwahrt das seinesgleichen in ganz Europa schwerlick zu finden.' – Ulrich Groß: 'Wahrhaftigen Beschreibung der Stadt Leipzig', Leipzig 1587, quoted in *Quellen zur Geschichte Leipzigs*, hrsg. v. Gustav Wustman, Bd. I., Leipzig 1889, pp. 8ff. 'round about in the inside of the wall' would appear to echo 'auch inwendig um und um...' etc., suggesting that Groß is PF's corroborative source here and indicating PF's presence in Leipzig in 1587.
1698 **Lübeck]** G [120] adds: a bishopric in Saxony
Hamburg... to] E ● cf. intro., p. 29
1699 **he visited... Freskold]** G [120]: there is a university [*hohe Schul*] ¶ Freskold: P & M (p. 189) suggest 'frescade' – a cool walk or shady alley, but I find this doubtful, as unworthy of PF's attention; some variant of 'free school' is a possibility
1700f **he went... half]** ◇ A933f
1702 **wrought... wonders]** G [121]: saw more countries
1703 **How... Chap. 23]** G [121]: Concerning paradise. [Chap. 27]
1704 **After this... again]** G [121]: When Doctor Faustus was in Egypt where he visited the city of Cairo, he flew into the air and journeyed over many a land and kingdom
1705f **Spain... Persia]** PF inserts: Portugal, Scotland, Muscovy and Cathay
1707f **the ancient... and]** E
1708 **hills]** G [121] adds: peaks and islands
1708f **amongst the... thence]** E
1710 **Britain]** † the emendation is based on the German text; 'Brittany' is probably a misread for 'Brittainy' (cf. Marlowe: *Edward II*, II. ii. 42)
1711 **baths]** G [121]: springs
many. . stones] G [121]: the stone of God and many others
1713 **behind Scotland]** G [121]: in the ocean and pertain to Britain
1713–15 **where he... bird]** E, referring to the well-known fable of the barnacle goose, cf. *A Briefe Collection... of strange and memorable thinges, gathered out of the Cosmographie of Sebastian Munster...*, London (Thomas Marsh) 1572, fol. 3r: 'In Scotland there be certain trees which bring forth a fruit folded and wrapped up in the leaves, and that fruit, when in convenient time it falleth into the water running by the tree, it reviveth and taketh life and is transformed into a living fowl which some call a goose of the tree or a barnacle.' This is almost certainly PF's direct source.

1719 **tropic]** ¶ region (usage not listed in *OED*)
near... of] G [121]: between India and

1720f **Faustus... beyond]** E, replacing G [122]: and across the breadth of the ocean. Pepper trees are as common there as our juniper bushes here. Crete, an island in Greece, lies in the middle of the Candy Sea and belongs to the Venetians; malmsey is made there. The island is full of wild goats but there are no deer, nor any dangerous animals, neither snakes, wolves nor foxes, but there are large, poisonous spiders. The spirit Mephostophiles told him of all these islands and many more and directed his journey so that he might spy them out and visit them. But to come to the point: Doctor Faustus' motive for visiting these high places was not simply to gaze upon the ocean and the surrounding lands

1721 **meant]** † O provides the correct reading

1724 **saw a]** G [123] adds: brightness extending to the North meridian
strike] ¶ streak, possibly by analogy with lightning-strike

1724f **coming from... earth]** G [123]: ranging from the earth to heaven and back again to the earth, as high as a small island

1726 **waters]** ‡ Gen. 2: 10

1729 **came]** G [123] adds: So, with a trembling heart, he questioned his spirit
gently] ¶ courteously

1730 **garden]** ‡ Gen. 2: 8

1732f **but... is the]** † the numerous vars. here suggest transmissions of deranged and transposed type in an early edition

1733f **angel... sword]** G [124]: fiery sword with which the angel protects this garden ‡ Gen. 3: 24

1734 **and although... by]** E

1735 **been]** G [124] adds: You could have seen it better when you were aloft but you didn't notice it, etc.

1737f **The first... Euphrates]** ‡ Gen. 2: 11–14

1739 **under... Aries]** i.e. on the equator

1740 **Michael]** G [124]: Cherub

1741 **to keep... charge]** G [124]: ordained as a protection

1743 **visit... be']** G [124]: go there

1744f **Of... Chap. 24]** G [125]: Concerning a comet. [Chap. 28] ◇ for this and the following three chapters, cf. A939–41

1746 **Germany... St]** E ● 'St' here is probably an uncancelled MS error.

1751 **he]** † O attempts to rationalize the genders of 'sun' (masc.) and 'moon' (fem.), but this only adds to the confusion resulting from PF's literal translation of the personal pronouns. In German, *Sonne* is feminine and *Mond* masculine; thus at 1752, 'he' refers to the moon, not the sun, and the text then accurately describes the appearance of the moon during a lunar eclipse. PF's additions at 1753f and 1755 are an attempt to reconcile the visual phenomena with his mistranslation

1753f **and to... him]** E

1754 **and so... full]** G [125]: and when next the moon rises to the zenith, she

1755 **she will... before, and]** E
1757 **figure]** ¶ sign (usage not listed in *OED*)
1759 **sword]** G [125]: unrest and war. Item, floods, cloud-burst, conflagration
1761 **monster,]** G [126] adds: Then the wicked spirits who know God's ordinances have their instruments at the ready. Such comets are like bastards among the true stars
1763 **A question... Chap. 25]** G [126]: Concerning the stars. [Chap. 29]
1764 **N. V. W]** § identified by Helmut Häuser (*Gibt es eine gemeinsame Quelle zum Faustbuch von 1587 und Goethes Faust? Eine Studie über die Schriften des Arztes Dr. Nikolaus Winkler*. 1973) as Dr Nicholas Winkler, city physician of Halberstadt, which the historical Faust may have visited in 1521 (cf. Gerd Wunder, *Nachwort* to facsimile ed. of Widman, 1978)
1767 **firmament]** G [126] adds: it being then autumn
1768–72 **said... firmament']** dir. sp.
1770 **in the... planets]** G [126]: concerning the brightness of the heavens and the number of the stars
1771f **condition... firmament']** G [127]: occasion for such an event ● PF is a careful editor and reframes the question to accord with Faustus' answer; the reason for stars falling from heaven is discussed in chapter 27 (cf. 1806)
1773f **see... earth]** G [127]: know that the smallest stars in the sky, although
1777 **for]** G [127] adds: , as I myself have seen,
1782f **Chap. 26]** G [127]: [Chap. 30]
1785f **so little... night]** G [127]: not only by day but also by night
1787 **in darkness]** G [128]: beneath the clouds ● Here, contrary to 1113, PF adopts the GFB view that during the day the heavens are dark but are illuminated by the sun at night (cf. 1791–4)
1791 **moving... firmament]** G [128]: heaven ¶ first moving: presumably, the primum mobile
1792 **that]** a clumsy translation, signifying 'the things'; '18's 'here' is best
1792f **by which... night]** G [128]: so that even in the deep of the night we are able to discern the heavens even if the stars are not shining
1794 **spirits]** G [128] adds: , which cannot endure the light
1796 **fantasies]** ¶ fond fantasies: foolish imaginings; † in O, consistently preferred to 'fancies', cf. 1800, 2373
crying] G [128]: appearing
1798 **that... end]** E, replacing G [128]: for by night you have many a phantasy which [129] would not trouble you in daytime § Scot, p. 153: 'some never fear the devil but in a dark night,... a churchyard, where a right hard man heretofore scant durst pass by night but his hair would stand upright'
1801f **than we... company]** E
1802 **carry]** ¶ influence, lead astray (*OED* v. 20)
1802f **more... perceive]** E
1805 **Chap. 27]** G [129]: [Chap. 31] [W inserts here an additional chapter: 'A further question on the brightness of the stars', of which PF shows no awareness]
1806f **Doctor... answered]** E, replacing G [129]: As for the stars which flare up and

fall to earth this is nothing new but happens every night

1807–9 **That is... falleth]** transp. ; PF largely remodels this chapter.

1810f **for if... do]** E, replacing G [129]: These snuffs, as we may call them, are tough and greenish black

1814 **but the... falling]** E, replacing G [130]: One snuff is much greater than another because the stars themselves are of different sizes

1816f **the gates... forth]** G [130]: would bring the clouds of the sky down with it, causing ¶ gates: floodgates, cf. Gen. 7: 11

1817 **other plagues]** G [130]: a conflagration

1819 **How... Chap. 28]** G [130]: Concerning thunder. [Chap. 32]

1820 **In]** G [130]: One evening, in

Wittenberg] G [130] adds: a hailstorm with

1821 **jesting merrily]** G [130]: standing ● PF visualizes every scene and provides Faustus with a livelier presence.

1824–6 **fell a... thunderclap]** G [131]: it first becomes windy, but after it has thundered for a while there is a heavy downpour

1828–31 **against... ears]** E, replacing G [131]: one against another, or are gathered together to produce a black rain cloud such as the one we now see above the town. Then, when the storm increases, the spirits join battle at the four corners of heaven so that the skies resound with the clash ● PF provides the more 'scientific' explanation; the simile of colliding ice-bergs suggests personal experience

1832 **heard.]** G [131] adds: Depending on the force of the wind, the thunder may persist or it may be driven away quickly; in that case, note the direction of the wind which drives the storm. It is often from the South but sometimes from the East, the West or the North

1833 **conceits]** ¶ tricks, fanciful actions (*OED* sb. 8b)

1834 **nigromancy]** ¶ black magic, see 16, above

1836f **How... Chap. 29]** G [132]: A tale of Doctor Faustus and the emperor Carolus Quintus. [Chap. 33]

1838 **Carolus... fifth]** ◇ A944

1841f **nobles... emperor]** ◇ A945

1841 **gentlemen]** G [133] adds: for his art and skill, especially those whom he had relieved from serious injuries and sickness with his medicines and treatment

1842 **meat]** ¶ food

even... emperor] E

1843–5 **thinking... be]** G [133]: wondering who he might be

1846 **repast]** G [133] adds: this was in summer after the feast of St Philip and St James

1848–53 **Faustus... doing]** dir. sp. ◇ A1040–9

1849 **and none... empire]** E; ◇ B1192

1850 **familiar]** G [133]: soothsaying [*Warsager*]

1850f **and that... list]** E

1853 **none evil... happen]** ‡ cf. 1 Sam. 28: 10 (Saul's promise to the witch of Endor)

1854 **upon... conditions]** E

1855f **to do... appoint him]** ◇ A1055
1856–77 **Well, ... Majesty]** ◇ B1193–7; A1057–91, B1264–6;
1857 **house]** G [133]: camp
1861f **his successors]** G [134]: emperors
1864 **hearty]** ¶ heartfelt (*OED* a. 4)
1866 **the which... fair]** E
1868 **and that... face]** E
1869 **say... praise]** G [134]: know
1872 **request... things]** G [134] repeats the detailed request
1874 **substantially... you]** G [135]: raised from the dead and brought here, for that is impossible ¶ substantially: materially
spirits] G [135]: ancient spirits
1877 **a little aside]** G [135]: out of the emperor's chamber
1878–80 **'Now... them']** dir. sp. ◇ B1284f
1882f **entered... Magnus]** ◇ A1101, B1292
1884 **of a middle stature]** E
black] G [135]: reddish blond
1885 **broad]** G [135]: stern
1886f **burnished... upon]** E
1888–91 **made low... it]** ◇ B1297–1307; 1748f
1890 **took hold... and]** E
1892 **paramour... coming in]** ◇ A1101, B1295
1893 **reverence]** ¶ obeisance
1894 **fair]** G [136] adds: and rosy-cheeked
1894f **milk and blood]** lit.
1895 **and thus... house]** E
1900f **the woman... Samuel]** ‡ 1 Sam. 28: 7–24
1901–3 **would be... wart]** ◇ A1102–5, B1309–15
1903f **took Faustus... and]** E; PF is visualizing again (cf. 1890, where Faustus allows himself the familiarity of physically restraining the emperor).
1904f **but she... neck]** G [137]: she stood stock still for him
1906f **leaving the... contented]** G [137]: and herewith was the emperor's request fulfilled.
1908 **in the... emperor]** E
1909 **that slept... Chap. 30]** E; G [137]: [Chap. 34]
1910 **had]** G [137] adds: , as reported,
1911 **requested,]** G [137] adds: in the evening, after the horns had been blown summoning the courtiers to dinner
1911f **over a... garden]** E
1914f **a knight... asleep]** ◇ B1202f; B1223f; B1228
1917–19 **It pleased... horns]** ◇ A1111, B1319f
1917f **the help]** G [138]: the loyal, active help
1918 **firm]** G [138]: charm ¶ firm: fix
1920 **head,]** G [138] adds: he discovered the mischief
1920f **glass... ears]** E, replacing G [138]: the partially closed windows
1922–4 **which... head]** G [138]: which the emperor noticed and † The vars. at 1922f

result in alternative sequences of events (in '08 &c, the courtiers laugh when the emperor is informed and then go to see the knight), but they are without significance for the scene in *Doctor Faustus* ◇ A1112–5, B1321–3, B1326

1925f	**at last... again]** ◇ A1130, B1360
1926	**but the... etc.]** E, concluding this and the following two chapters with 'etc.' with no authority from G
1928	**Chap. 31]** G [139]: [Chap. 35] ◇ cf. B IV. iii (B1371 etc.) passim
1932	**beheld]** G [139]: perceived seven horsemen. It was
1934	**Faustus]** G [139] adds: with their weapons at the ready, for the knight had recognized him
1936f	**turned into]** G [139]: full of ◇ cf. A612, B553
1938	**and coming... them]** G [140]: who took to their heels but were caught nonetheless
1938f	**and told... departed]** E
1940	**seeing... distress]** E
1945	**etc.]** G [140]: Thus was the knight defeated by means of the enchanted horsemen.
1946	**being... university]** E
1947	**help... wish]** G [142]: transport them through the air
	Munich] cf. commentary to 1521
1948	**Chap. 32]** G [142]: [Chap. 37] ● PF omits G [Chap. 36]: 'How Doctor Faustus ate a peasant's load of hay, together with wain and horses', probably because of its similarity to G [Chap. 40]
1954	**jollity]** ¶ (*OED* 2) festivity
1955	**If]** G [143]: My cousins, if
1967	**went into]** G [143]: spread it in
1971	**the duke... son]** G [144]: anyone at the duke of Bavaria's palace
1976	**where... court]** G [144]: They travelled invisibly, unseen by anyone, until they arrived at the court. There ● Both here and at 1981f, PF refuses to entertain 'invisibly'; cf. Scot, p. 432: [It is a] most apparent impudency to say that a man is no man, or to be extenuated into such a quantity as thereby may be invisible and yet remain in life and health.' PF objects to the invisibility of the three counts, not of Faustus, cf. scenes at Rome and Constantinople
1980	**good]** E
1981	**welcoming. . whence]** G [144]: and spoke to them
1982–4	**whereat... them]** E, replacing G [144]: This happened in [145] the evening as the company was about to dine. For, by Faustus' art, they had spent the whole day invisible and had seen all the pomp of the wedding without any interference.
1984–6	**Faustus... enough']** dir. sp., loose
1986	**and... enough]** G [145]: they would be whisked away in the twinkling of an eye
	Well] G [145]: While they were being addressed by the duke of Bavaria, they giving no response
1987f	**had... first]** G [145]: was about to disobey Faustus' command ● PF is fairly

contemptuous of German manners, especially their drinking habits, cf. intro., p. 24

1989f **they got... again]** G [145]: two of the counts and Doctor Faustus disappeared

1990 **presently]** G [145]: at midnight

1992 **friend]** G [146]: cousin

1996 **dump]** ¶ melancholy, depression (*OED* sb[1]. 2)

hap] ¶ lot

1997 **and not... rest]** E

1998f **there... know]** G [146]: he was asked

1999 **what he was]** G [146]: what was going on

2000 **open]** ¶ reveal

2003 **the old... charge]** G [146]: it was decided

2013f **the rest... friends]** G [147]: Wittenberg

2015 **and so... etc.]** E

2017 **Chap. 33]** G [147]: which he had sawed off in the Jew's presence. [Chap. 38]

2018–20 **although... penny]** G [147]: a conjurer shall not be three farthings the richer in a year

2020f **in promising... largely]** G [147]: great were the promises made by his spirit but they were false ¶ making such a costly promise (*OED* 'largely' adv. 6)

2023 **wherein... delight]** G [147]: for such were the skills he had taught him

2023–7 **yet... anybody]** G [148]: for his time was not yet up and the promise that he would never lack for money or goods was valid only for four years from the date of the contract ● The German is not only ambiguous and difficult to construe, but seems to imply a breach of contract on the devil's part; PF will have none of it.

2028 **would... spirit]** G [148]: had used his art

cheer] G [148] adds: Doctor Faustus would have to concede that his spirit was in the right and instead of contradicting him, he should think how experienced he had become

2029 **And... time]** G [148]: After this clarification from his spirit

2030–2 **whereunto... Jew]** G [148]: Now, since he had run out of money he was obliged to raise some with the Jews ● In EFB, Faustus is more antisemitic than in G, for his action is gratuitous

2042f **is a... purpose]** G [149]: must be a desperate fellow

2045 **foot]** † O transmits the original, edited in '08 &c to conform with the continuation (2047 etc.)

2052f **wherefore... money]** G [150]: and this is a poor pledge. To think that he could do no better than pledge his own limb!

2054 **words]** G [150] adds: (as the Jew afterwards related)

2057 **of... dollars]** E

2060f **replied: ... it']** dir. sp.

else... thine] G [150f]: recompense him

2061–3 **The Jew... him]** E

2064 **for... Jew]** E

2065 **horse-courser]** ¶ horse dealer
Chap. 34] G [151]: [Chap. 39] ◇ cf. A. xi (A1143 etc.), B IV. V (B1523 etc) passim; B1611–22; B1624–9
2066 **Pheiffring]** G [151]: *Pfeiffering* § Although the German text is ambiguous, this is probably the name of the horse, not the fair
2069 **dollars]** G [151]: florins
2072 **But... prove']** E ¶ prove: test
2077 **could... forbear him,]** E
2079 **body]** G [152]: arse
2082 **gave the flight]** lit.; G [152]: *gab die Flucht* ● The poor quality of the translation here probably reflects PF's lack of interest in this material.
2085 **Chap. 35]** G [152]: [Chap. 40] ◇ cf. B1600–7
2087 **doctors and]** E, boosting the protagonist
2088 **clown]** ¶ peasant, rustic
load of hay] G [152]: large cart full of gleanings
2088–90 **Good... hay?]** dir. sp.
2090–2 **with... much]** G [153]: he was joking with him
2092 **three farthings]** G [153]: a kreuzer or lion-penny
2097f **Faustus... way]** E
2100 **How... Chap. 36]** G [153]: A brawl between 12 students. [Chap. 41]
2102f **that came... other]** E
2110 **Chap. 37]** G [154]: [Chap. 42] ◇ cf. B1758–69
2112f **the which... drunk]** G [154]: who had taken too much wine
2116 **show... jest]** G [154]: soon put a stop to that.
2120 **wist]** ¶ knew
2122f **none... more]** G [155]: they stayed there no longer
2124 **dollars]** G [155]: florins [also at 2126]
Chap. 38] G [155]: [Chap. 43]
2125 **jest]** G [155]: venture
2128 **filed]** ¶ defiled, dirtied
2130 **swimming upright]** G [155]: floating [*schwammen... empor*]
2131 **wishly]** ¶ intently, longingly
2132 **where... Faustus]** G [155]: how this had happened, or who had sold him the swine
2132f **so... hogs]** E
2134 **duke of Anholt]** G [156]: prince of Anhalt
2135 **Chap. 39]** G [156]: [Chap. 44] ◇ cf. A1232–57; B1646–74
2136 **duke of Anholt]** G [156]: count of Anhalt (they are now princes) ● PF uses 'duke', 'duchess' throughout this and the following chapters to translate *Graf, Gräfin* ◇ A1222, B1571
2140 **banqueting dishes]** G [156]: confections ¶ banquet: sweetmeats, fruit, etc., so this is an exact translation
2141 **great bellied]** G [156]: pregnant
2147f **for I... this]** E, replacing G [157]: and in half-an-hour Your Grace's wish shall be satisfied
2148 **a plate]** G [157]: two silver vessels

2148–50 **made open... apples]** G [157]: put them outside the window. When it was time he reached out of the window and retrieved them, one filled with red and white grapes, the other with apples and pears ¶ incontinent: immediately

2151 **strange]** ¶ foreign

2154 **thanked... and]** E

2155 **appetite]** G [157] adds: and great amazement

2158 **circles]** i.e. hemispheres

2159 **the contrary circle]** G [157]: East and West

2160 **for in]** G [158]: for the sky is round and the sun has now risen to its highest here so that we have short, winter days, but in the East and West as in
there... sun] G [158]: the sun does not rise so high

2161 **fruit:]** G [158] adds: Item. It is night here when day is dawning there. For the sun has gone beneath the earth, and here is a similitude: the flowing sea is above the level of the earth and were it not obedient to the Divine Will it could flood the world in an instant. When the sun rises in those lands, it is setting here ● PF does well to omit this passage, which only compounds the confusion

2162f **fulfil... anything]** G [158]: transform himself as he will ◇ A111, B106

2165 **Faustus]** G [159] adds: wrought a second wonder to please this count and

2166 **Chap. 40]** G [159]: [Chap. 44a]

2167 **Doctor Faustus]** G [159]: Before Doctor Faustus took his leave he

2169 **Faustus]** G [159] adds: that night
mighty castle] ◇ B1641

2170f **the beholders]** G [159]: her ladies

2171 **Rohumbuel]** G [159]: Rohmbühel, which lies not far from the town

2173 **the castle]** G [159] adds: and take some lunch there

2174 **so wonderful... having]** G [160]: fashioned by magic as to have

2176 **geese, bitterns]** G [160]: herons

2176f **About... other doors]** G [160]: In this ditch there stood five stone towers [*Thürn*] and two gates [*Thor*]

2179 **buffs]** ¶ wild oxen (*OED* sb² I. 1)
antelopes] G [160]: chamois

2183 **being... train]** E

2188–91 **as wildfowl... sack]** PF rejects the detailed bill of fare given in G [161], a list of 14 animals, 16 fishes and 19 birds culled from Peter Dasypodius: *Dictionarium Latino-Germanicum...*, Argentorati, 1537; he also reduces the wine list by 11 varieties

2194f **so were... castle]** G [162]: they were so famished ● cf. 2261–3, where Faustus provides real food for the students.

2196–8 **they looked... off]** loose

2200f **great thanks... him]** E

2204 **Chap. 41]** G [162]: [Chap. 45]

2207 **Bacchus]** i.e. presiding host of the Bacchanalia, a students' resurrection of the pagan feast, held around shrovetide.

2208–10 **after the... drunk]** E, replacing G [163]: they wished to celebrate Bacchanalia to the full

2210–12 **said... will']** dir. sp.
2211 **cup of wine]** G [163]: all the splendid liquor he would offer them
2213f **them forth... into]** G [163]: a ladder in his garden and seated them each upon a rung and drove off with them, so that the same night they arrived in ● 'holly wand' is an amusing mistranslation of *Sprosse*, which, besides meaning the rung of a ladder, can mean a sprig or sprout, a point or a prong. The students will have had an uncomfortable journey.
2217 **cellar]** G [163] adds: and Doctor Faustus had taken a flint with him that he might see all the barrels
2218f **which when... Thieves]** loose
2220f **wherefore... away]** G [163]: he warned his companions they must be off
2223 **lopped]** G [164]: fir
2228 **lopped]** E, prefiguring G [164]: which had no branches either above or below
2230–2 **At length... down]** loose, using dir. sp.
2232–4 **what... miraculous]** E
2235 **to see... tree]** E
2236–40 **and being... devils]** E, replacing G [164]: But still the butler couldn't tell who it was he had found in the cellar, nor who had put him on the tree ● PF's ending is far superior to the German
2241 **How... Chap. 42]** G [165]: Tuesday, the second day of carnival. [Chap. 46]
2242 **and]** G [165]: of whom four were
2243 **consented]** G [165]: celebrated the first day of carnival at Doctor Faustus' house
2248f **they... that]** rep. sp.
2250–2 **according... commendable]** G [165]: it will get better before we take our nightcap [*Schlaff Trunck*: PF always mistranslates this term, cf. 2823]
2253 **as]** † possibly in error for 'at'
2253f **the like... you]** G [165]: you too shall have your share, and this is why I regaled you with such meagre fare, scarce sufficient to allay your hunger
2254–7 **first... wine]** loose, cf. G [166], where the capacities are 5, 8 and 8 measures
2257 **all... day]** E, attacking German drinking habits – the revellers are each to drink 18 pints of wine at a sitting
2258f **the which... it]** E, replacing G [166]: outside in my garden
2259 **fet]** ¶ fetched
2262f **verily... ate]** E
2264 **boy]** G [166] adds: Wagner
2264–8 **he served... cheer]** ◇ A1272f, B1783f
2267 **Italian wine]** G [166] adds: a presentation wine
2268 **that they... good cheer]** G [166]: yet there was much [167] food remaining ● PF emphasizes the gluttony, cf. 2257
2272 **Chap. 43]** G [167]: [Chap. 47]
2275 **high]** ¶ tall
2278 **and that... places]** G [167]: yet no one could fathom whence it came. For as soon as one instrument stopped another began, here an organ, there a positive organ
2278–80 **lute... hornpipe]** cf. G [167]: lutes, viols, citterns, harps, krummhorns,

trombones, pipes and [168] transverse flutes ● cf. the similar list at 296f ¶ gittern: according to Frances Palmer of the Horniman Museum, London, this is probably the *quinterna*, a guitar-shaped member of the lute family (see Praetorius, at 296f above, Plate XVI, No. 4)

2281f **cups... board]** E

2284f **the shivers... house]** G [168]: they shattered and smashed themselves to pieces

2286 **jest;]** G [168] adds: He had a cock brought in from the yard. When they gave it something to drink it began to whistle most naturally

2288 **showing... conceits]** E

2290 **lightly]** ¶ readily

2291 **for students... entreated]** E

2295 **but]** G [169]: and when he had caught a goodly number

2297 **and being roasted]** G [169]: There were larks, fieldfare and four wild ducks

2299 **clean... clothes]** G [169]: white shirt and allow him to do as he would

2301 **they had no heads]** § Scot (p. 315) says this is supposed to be achieved by burning a candle doctored with a preparation of arsenic and sulphur; he also describes an oil which makes those anointed with it appear to have asses' heads (cf. 2307f)

2302–4 **And as... them]** E; ¶ feast: entertain, not necessarily lavishly

2304f **to their banquet]** G [169]: at table by their hosts to receive their carnival cakes ¶ banquet: see 2140 above

2306f **and... drunk]** G [169]: Shortly after,

2310f **and as... again]** E

2312f **How... Chap. 44]** G [170]: What happened on Thursday, the fourth night of carnival. [Chap. 48]

2315f **that were... before]** E

2326 **considering... tricks]** E

2327 **in sunder]** ¶ asunder

2328f **asked... promise]** G [171]: went home early but promised

2330–3 **the which... house]** E, replacing G [171]: in the shape of a dragon. Doctor Faustus sat on its head and the students in the body and on its tail were four enchanted monkeys, cavorting merrily, one of them playing a shawm. The sledge moved by itself wherever they wished.

2335f **the heads... time]** G [171]: the students thought they had cruised through the air

2337f **the Sunday following]** G [171]: Low Sunday [also at 2339]

2338 **Chap. 45]** G [171]: [Chap. 49] ◇ A1275–1300, B1785–1811

2339 **students]** G [171] adds: unexpectedly

2343f **and every... heard]** E

2344–7 **I was... ground']** dir. sp.

2351 **are all... and]** E

2352 **that famous... Greece]** E

2356 **chiefest... youth]** G [172]: lifetime

2358–60 **But', said... presence]** dir. sp.

2359 **upon your perils]** ¶ lest you be in serious danger (*OED* peril sb. 3b)

2360 **so long... presence]** G [173]: nor attempt to greet her

2362 **the fair... beautiful]** G [173]: queen

2363f **amazed... creature]** G [173]: quite distracted and burning with desire

2371f **rolling... countenance]** G [173]: shameless and mischievous expression

2372 **near-hand]** ¶ almost (*OED*. 2)

2378 **counterfeit]** ¶ portrait, likeness (*OED* sb. 3)

2379–81 **Yet... thereof]** dir. sp.

2380f **which... thereof]** G [174]: from which they might make copies

2382 **but... it again]** E, replacing G [174]: They distributed the paintings far and wide, for it was a superb picture of a beautiful woman, but no one could learn who had painted this for Faustus

2386 **nay,... furies]** E; † '18 prudishly resolves the amusing ambiguity of the continuation, suggestive of PF's personal experience

2388 **away]** G [175]: into the air

2389 **Chap. 46]** G [175]: [Chap. 50]

2390 **a marshall]** '08 &c transmit the original transl., edited in O

2391 **falling sickness]** G [175]: consumption [*Schwindsucht*] ¶ epilepsy

2392f **for he... list]** E; ¶ ease himself: relieve his bowels (*OED* v. 1c)

2393 **near]** G [175] adds: and within sight of

2395f **said... legs']** dir. sp.

2396 **buzzardly ass]** G [175f]: numskull [*Dölpel*] ¶ buzzard: a worthless, stupid or ignorant person (*OED* sb^{1}. 2)

2396f **that his... up]** G [176]: he would have enough bother without that

2402 **void... . humanity]** G [176]: worthless scum [*nichtswerdiger Unflat*] † 'humility' ('08 &c) is probably a misread

2403 **disposition]** G [176] adds: and will behave thus to others and doubtless already have done

2404 **have... thee]** G [176]: find at the four several gates of the city

2405 **were gone]** G [176]: sprang into the air and were to be found each at a different gate, yet no one had observed it

2408 **troubled]** † O retains original transl., '08 &c transmit a misread
wailing] G [177] adds: with outstretched hands and bended knee

2412f **'Well,... ride]** dir. sp.
but... ride] G [177]: for there is nothing so shameful as churlishness and want of charity, which are rooted in pride

2414 **clear]** G [177] adds: for since you thought it such a great inconvenience to let another ride in your empty waggon you shall be repaid in like measure

2417f **whereas... quietly]** E, replacing G [178]: thus churlishness met its true master

2420 **Chap. 47]** G [178]: [Chap. 51] [Recension C of the GFB includes the 8 'Erfurt' chapters at this point]

2422 **inn]** G [178] adds: in the Jewish district

2430 **it.]** G [179] adds: He was the executioner
they smote. . . first] transp. In G [179] the lily is grown before the head is struck off

2431f **where... perceived]** E

2435f **The... two;]** G [179] adds a repetition of the detailed process
2437 **his lily]** † '08 &c transmit an error
2439 **barbed]** ¶ trimmed, shaven (*OED* barb v. 1)
2439–41 **insomuch... world]** E, replacing G [180]: he was annoyed by the arrogance of the chief magician who had been so impudent as to blaspheme and laugh while his head was being cut off • PF avoids the implausible sensibility of the GFB Faustus, providing him with a motivation consistent with e.g. 2424f
2442 **small]** E
2443 **the stalk... lily]** G [180]: flowers and slit the stalk in twain
2443f **saying... blind Faustus]** E, pursuing the psychology of 2439f
2447 **wickedness]** G [180] adds: so the devil rewards all his servants by cutting them off short • The magician has died unshriven.
2447f **not one]** G [180] adds: knew how the stalk had come to be slit, or
2450 **Chap. 48]** G [181]: and what unkindness he received. [Chap. 52] ◇ cf. A1302–41, B1813–56
2451 **man]** G [181]: physician
2453f **he suspected... life]** G [181]: whose house was the abode not of God and His angels but of the devil and his crew, he took it upon himself to dissuade Doctor Faustus from his diabolical life
2454 **suspected]** ¶ paid regard to, took note of (*OED* suspect v. 6; earliest listing: 1590)
like a friend] G [181]: out of Christian zeal
2459 **friendly... doubt, and]** E
2460f **answered: ... mind']** dir. sp.
2463 **defied]** G [182]: denied
2465f **far worse... person]** G [182]: a proper heretic and devil
2466 **Oh... done!]** ◇ A1314, B1830, B1843
2468f **of which... God]** loose
2471 **Acts... Samaria]** ‡ Acts 8: 9,10,13
2471f **was led... was]** G [182f]: led many astray, for they held him to be a god and called him the Power of God or
2474 **saw... sins]** G [183]: believed in the Lord Jesus Christ and afterwards was much in Philip's company, as the Acts of the Apostles specifically report
2475 **rude]** E ¶ unlearned
2476 **filthy]** ¶ wicked, immoral (*OED* 3) ◇ A1307f
2477 **live:]** G [183] adds: for there are many good examples, such as the thief on the cross, St Peter, Matthew and Mary Magdalen
saith] G [183] adds: to all sinners
2477f **Come... heavy laden]** ‡ Matt. 11: 28, (AV) but I have not found 'heavy' in any bible ante-1592, nor in The Book of Common Prayer (gospel for St Matthew's Day: 'Come unto me all ye that labour and are laden') (edns of 1549, 1564, 1580); it may be PF's fortuitous translation (GFB has unqualified *beladen*)
2479 **live]** G [183] adds: for his hand is not cut off lest he should no longer be able to help himself ‡ Ezek. 18: 23; 33: 11
2480 **adamant]** E

2481f	**Wherefore... practices]** G [184]: Refrain from your wicked practices, for sorcery is against God's commandment
2482f	**Old... forbidden]** ‡ Exod. 22: 18; Levit. 20: 6,27; Deut. 18: 12; Acts 13: 10
2484	**Lord:]** G [184] adds: Thus St Paul calls Bar Jehu, or Elimas, the sorcerer, a child of the devil and an enemy to all righteousness
2487–9	**'Father... discipline]** dir. sp.; ¶ persuasions: arguments ◇ A1324–6, B1839f
2490	**he laid... bed]** E • cf. 499
2491f	**and... devil]** ◇ A1330–2, B1844–6
2493	**Lucifer]** G [185]: the devil
2494f	**and wrung... shoulders]** G [185]: as if he would have twisted it round † O transmits the original, edited in '08 &c
2495–505	**Thou knowest... wilt']** dir. sp.
2496	**thou... given]** G [185]: it was his impudent wilfulness which had persuaded him to give
2497	**men]** G [185] adds: and he could not now revoke it
2501f	**that seeing... done]** E
2503	**blood]** G [185] adds: and promise that he would never again allow anyone to admonish or seduce him to repentance. And he had better say at once whether he would do it or no. • The promise required by G is in the written contract (2519), so PF deems it unnecessary here
2503–5	**if not... wrote]** ◇ A1335–9, B1849–54
2506f	**afterward... kinsman]** E, replacing G [186]: found after his death • This provides a fictitious provenance for the text of the contract, but cf. commentary to 1065f
2509	**Chap. 49]** G [186]: [Chap. 53]
2514	**great]** G [186]: mighty god
2516f	**either... him]** G [186]: besides which he promises me [neither] to shorten [n]or lengthen my life, be it in death or hell, nor force me to suffer any pain. • The German text is clearly corrupt here, requiring the inserted emendations, but PF accepts it as it is
2517f	**withdraw... purpose]** G [187]: dissuade, teach, train, instruct or threaten me
2520	**that moveth... soul]** E
2523	**the 25th... July]** E • This is probably the date on which PF translated this passage; if so, the translation was made in the summer of 1588 (cf. intro. p. 52, n. 172)
2524	**letter]** G [187]: damnable and godless contract
2524f	**he became... means]** ◇ A1342–5, B1857–60
2526	**this godly... Ghost]** G [187]: but the man's Christian prayers and conduct gave the foul fiend such a drubbing
2531f	**barbarian cry]** G [187f]: bucolic music [*Bäurisch Musica*]
2532	**Oh fair bird]** E
	foul] G [188]: beautiful • PF discards the sarcasm of G to pun on 'fowl'
2533	**his place]** G [188]: Paradise
2533f	**a poor man's house]** G [188]: other people's houses
	where... power] E

2535 **the... departed]** G [188]: he had driven the spirit away

2536 **And... home]** E

2537 **harnessed]** G [188] adds: , meaning with prayer

2538 **but he... how]** G [188]: besides which,

2539 **hear of]** G [188]: be mocked, particularly concerning ◇ cf. A1384f § Mockery (often crude in the extreme) was Luther's recommended method for banishing poltergeists, cf. *Tisch.*, Vol. 6, No. 6817, quoted in Widman, sig. †3

2542 **Chap. 50]** G [188]: in his seventeenth year. [Chap. 54] ● It is a pity PF cut this heading as it starts the final count-down

2547 **obtain her]** G [189] adds: and as for the above-mentioned gentleman, he especially amongst them was the least regarded by her
Faustus] G [189] adds: and had often wined and dined with him

2548f **and by... matter]** E

2550 **But when... Faustus]** G [189]: and fell sick. When Doctor Faustus learned that this nobleman was so seriously ill

2551 **he]** i.e. Faustus

2551f **told him... do]** G [189]: explained his condition and indicated its cause

2552 **gentleman and]** G [189] adds: revealed to him the cause of his sickness, at which he marvelled; then Faustus

2555 **wherefore]** G [190]: and so it transpired, for

2556f **she would... neither]** E

2558 **alone.]** G [190] adds: although her suitors included rich and distinguished gentry
The device... thus:] E

2560 **go]** G [190] adds: with him

2560–2 **and there... departed]** G [190]: as she was sitting in her garden with her ladies, and when they began to dance he was to dance with her. He gave him a ring for his finger: so soon as he should touch her with this finger during the dance, her heart would turn to him and thenceforth to no other. But he was not to mention marriage, for she herself would broach the subject. Then he took a distillate and sprinkled it over the nobleman who instantly became extremely handsome, and together they went to the garden.

2563–5 **and when... him]** E

2565–7 **thrust... but]** G [191]: touched her and

2567–9 **beginning... end]** E, replacing G [191]: the maid was pierced by Cupid's arrow, for she had no rest that whole night for thinking on him. Early next morning she sent for him

2573f **How... Chap. 51]** G [191]: Of the many different plants growing in Faustus' garden on Christmas Day in his 19th year. [Chap. 55]

2576f **to make... acquaintance]** G [192]: to visit their brothers who were studying there

2579–85 **and being... miraculous]** loose

2581f **trees... all sorts]** G [192]: Also there were lovely vines hanging with all kinds of grapes, and briars with red, white and pink roses

2585–7 **each one... flowers]** E

2588f **extremity... Chap. 52]** G [193]: 19th year, against the knight whom he had charmed with horns at the emperor's court. [Chap. 56] ◇ cf. B IV. iii (B1483 etc.)
2593–9 **and when... still]** loose
2596 **privily]** ¶ secretly
shoot at him] † O transmits the exact transl., edited in '08 &c
2597 **into the... them]** G [194]: for he had made himself invisible ● Once again PF avoids explicit invisibility
2601 **certain troop]** G [194]: some hundred
2601–4 **Then... encountered]** loose
2607f **and thought... infamy]** E
2608 **handy-blows]** ¶ fighting at close-quarters
2612f **'Sir... you']** dir. sp.
2614f **(where... devils)]** G [195]: whereas it was a delusion wrought by Faustus
2616 **him]** G [195]: the knight, who did not recognize Faustus
2618 **in peace... please]** G [195]: because you are assailing one who has requested help from our commander ● It is surprising that PF rejects the German here, with its double meaning
2619 **the knight... manner]** G [195]: them enchanted horses, pieces and swords ¶ after the manner: according to custom
2620 **the rest... foot]** E
2624f **asked... heard]** G [196]: and as soon as he heard the cause
2625–7 **'Of a... laughing-stock]** dir. sp.
2628–30 **How... Chap. 53]** G [196]: Doctor Faustus' whoring in his 19th and 20th years. [Chap. 57]
2633 **seven]** G [196] adds: diabolical succubae, each different from the other, having the forms
2638 **Walloons]** G [197]: Swabians ● PF chooses a nationality that would be more familiar to his readers
2639 **Franconian]** G [197] adds: a paragon of the whole country
sweet personages] G [197]: diabolical women
2642 **Chap. 54]** G [197]: [Chap. 58]
2643 **heir]** G [197] adds: and should lack for nothing
he] G [197]: Mephostophiles
2645 **in]** G [197] adds: the crypt of
2647 **having... deep]** G [197f]: there
2651 **of fire]** E
2651f **that... tormented]** G [198]: ghosts [*Gespenste*]
2653f **after his... servant]** G [198]: his servant has reported ● The G reading refers to the lost 'Wagner's life of Faustus'.
2657 **23rd... Chap. 55]** G [198]: last year. [Chap. 59] ◇ A1348–76, B1863–93
2659 **mind]** G [198] adds: at midnight
2662 **of Wittenberg]** G [199]: on Low Sunday
2664 **did.]** G [199] adds: and this Helena was of the same form as her he had raised for the students, with most beautiful, charming looks

2664 **one hour]** G [199]: a moment

2666–8 **if he... seeming]** E, in line with contemporary dogma forbidding the pregnancy of succubae

2669 **whom... named]** G [199]: at which Faustus rejoiced greatly and named him

2671 **matters]** † an O edit; '08 &c transmit the original

2672 **together.]** G [200] follows with a heading: Here follows the account of Doctor Faustus' dealings with his spirit and others during his 24th and final year

2674 **Chap. 56]** G [200]: [Chap. 60]

2675 **his]** † a sensible O edit

had a] G [200]: had raised a

2676 **to his servant]** E

2678f **so that... master's]** G [201]: he was a wicked, vagabond scamp who had formerly gone a-begging in Wittenberg

2680 **unhappiness]** ¶ knavishness (*OED* 2)

2684 **conversant]** ¶ familiarly associating (*OED* adj. 2)

2685 **garden]** G [201] adds: the which was next the Gansers' and Vitus Rodinger's house, near the Iron Gate in the Schergasse on the outer walls • PF omits these details as irrelevant to his readers; they were attacked as spurious by Lercheimer, who denied that Faustus ever had a house in Wittenberg

2685–9 **he gave... jollity]** ◇ A1268, B1778–82

2685f **ready money]** G [201]: rents

2686 **farm]** G [201] adds: worth 800 guilders, 600 guilders in ready cash

chain] G [201] adds: worth 300 crowns

2686–8 **and other... spend]** G [201]: which he had acquired at the courts, especially those from [202] the Papal and Turkish courts, worth up to a thousand guilders, but not much else in the way of household stuff for he did not spend much time at home but • cf. commentary to 1376–80

2691 **Chap. 57]** G [202]: [Chap. 61]

2693–7 **'I have... cunning']** dir. sp.; ¶ opened: revealed

2701 **well.]** G [203] adds: and turn to no one else

2701–3 **Further... thee]** E

2706f **'Art... him?]** dir. sp.

2708 **that he... ape]** rep. sp.

2712 **away]** G [204] adds: and you shall see no more of him

2713 **Akercock]** G [204]: *Auwerhan* [= meadow cock] [also at 2716] ¶ Aker: obsolete for acre, a field (*OED* acre. 1)

2716f **and if... help thee]** ‡ cf. John 14: 26: But that Comforter, which is the Holy Ghost, whom my Father will send in my name, he shall teach you all things, and bring all things to your remembrance, whatsoever I have told you (Geneva 1557)

2717 **so shall... world]** G [204]: for they will want this history of mine from you • The injunctions to Wagner are to provide provenance for the lost 'Wagner's life of Faustus', not for the Faust Book itself (cf. 2938–40)

2719 **Chap. 58]** G [205]: [Chap. 62]

2722 **Here... token]** G [205]: Then was Faustus tame for once ¶ token (*OED* sb. 1,5): indication of what was to come

2723–5 **the which... to die:** G [205]: who has received his judgment in prison and now awaits the death penalty

2730 **Chap. 59]** G [206]: [Chap. 63]

2733 **is... followeth]** G [206]: this is one of his written lamentations

2734f **sorrowful... in]** G [206]: presumptuous and unworthy heart who lures your companion members with you into the

2736 **gross]** coarse, i.e. imperfect. The sense is that a failure of intellect and a perverted will have endangered his physical body, which although innocent of itself, has enjoyed the rewards of Faustus' contract and must now share in the punishment (cf. 2739f)

2737f **what seizeth... life?]** G [206]: Of what do you accuse [*zeihestu*] my members that they have now nothing to expect but to be robbed of their life ‡ cf. Rom. 7: 23

2738 **Bewail]** G [206]: *beklagen* [probably corrupt for *klagen*, = accuse]

2739f **bewail... as I]** G [206]: [see prec.] accuse me, my senses, [207], for it was in my power to give or to take and to gratify you by my improvement

2740 **Envy and Disdain]** G [207]: Love and Hate ¶ envy: possibly as *OED* 2: active evil, mischief, but a more acceptable reading employs the modern sense, i.e. envy of the forbidden knowledge of the spirits and disdain for God's gifts

2741–3 **Ah whither... perish?]** G [207]: Oh Mercy and Revenge, why have you procured me such a reward, such shame? Oh Wrath and Pity, was I created human so that I myself should both occasion and endure the punishment which awaits me? ● 'by sufferance': by allowing Faustus the freedom of choice, God allows him to perish

2744 **prepared... myself]** i.e. self-occasioned

2747 **Chap. 60]** G [207]: [Chap. 64]

2750 **unmeasurable]** ¶ beyond due measure, inordinate
lamentable] G [208] adds: for me, a compassionate man
yet any] G [208]: a cruel

2751 **senseless... forgetfulness!]** G [208]: reason, wantonness, presumptuousness and free will! ● 'forgetfulness': i. e of his soul's safety cf. 206, 298, 350f

2753 **soul]** G [208] adds: making them as blind as thou art

2754 **in the... day]** E

2755 **heart]** G [208]: spirit
become... thee?] G [208]: thy perception ● 'knowledge': Christian knowledge, knowledge of God

2758 **that pierce... heart]** E

2762 **further.]** G [209] follows with a chapter [Chap. 65], omitted by PF, in which Mephostophiles mocks Faustus with a battery of proverbs. See Appendix 2.

2764 **Chap. 61]** G [213]: [Chap. 66]

2765–8 **how happy... darkness]** ◇ A1489–95, B2072–9

2766 **unreasonable]** ¶ lacking rational thought

2767 **feel any... doubts]** G [213]: have to toil any further ¶ doubts: fear

2769 **rest and peace]** G [214]: beauty and joy

2770f **pains... gnashing]** G [214]: restraint, scorn, trembling and quaking, pain, affliction, weeping and wailing and gnashing of teeth

2772 **me]** G [214] adds: and must endure eternal scorn from the saints

2773 **Mephostophiles... tell me]** cf. 655f

2775–7 **the twigs... punishment]** G [124]: chaff, wood and iron burn, one more readily than another, so do the damned in the furnaces of hell

2777–9 **Ah thou... quenched]** G [214]: O eternal damnation, kindled by the anger of God, composed of fire and heat and needing no stoking throughout eternity

2779 **I dwell in]** G [214]: one endure

2780f **torment... blubbering]** E, recalling 646 etc.

2783f **Ah that... last to]** G [215]: I would readily dispense with [*entberen*] heaven, if only I might • PF possibly misconstrued *entberen* to mean 'bear' § Atlas was punished for his rebellion against Zeus by being condemned to carry the heavens upon his shoulders; Faustus would prefer this temporal punishment, presumably because it would allow him time for full repentance. The mathematician and physician, Dr Richard Forster, applied the same simile to Dr Dee: 'Unless he re-interposes his Atlas-like shoulders, all [the mathematical disciplines] with the heavens of Copernicus and Rheinholdt will fall to ruin': cited in translation from *Ephemerides Meteorographicae* (London 1575), sig G4v, in French, p. 6

2785f **the which... me]** E

2789 **Where... hold]** G [215]: *Wo ist meine feste Burg?* [Luther] ¶ hold: stronghold, fort

2789f **Knowledge... not]** E, replacing G [215]: Where may I seek consolation? Not from God's blessed ones § Faustus' 'knowledge' is a perverted knowledge and cannot help him as true knowledge of God would. He also lacks the divine grace which would incline his soul to God

2790 **Him]** G [215]: them

2791 **but He... from me]** G [215]: I must cover my face before them

2793 **No, I... groanings]** G [215]: since my lamentations yield no consolation

2794 **and God... misdoings]** G [215]: Amen, amen

2795 **comfort... calamities]** G [215]: add to my injuries • PF uses 'comfort' ironically

2797 **Chap. 62]** G [216]: [Chap. 67]

2798 **come,]** G [216] adds: and even in the week appointed

2800f **against... appointed]** G [216]: on the next night ¶ against: at

2804f **it is... judgment]** G [216]: it is still a long time before you will be judged • Mephostophiles offers Faustus hope that he may be saved at the universal resurrection

2806 **thousand]** G [216]: hundred

2808 **for the]** G [217]: for you do not yet know what is ordained for you, and **promised]** G [217] adds: you a body and soul of steel

2817f **with him... banquet]** G [217]: their repast with him

2819 **dinner]** G [217]: lunch
2821 **rude]** ¶ coarse, inelegant (*OED* adj. 9)
2822 **supper]** G [218] adds: and spend the whole night with him
2822f **For. . due']** G [218]: for he had something important to tell them • 'victualler's due': the devil's due
2823 **And when... heads)]** mistrans. for G [218]: After they had dined and drunk their nightcap
2826f **and when... requested]** E
2828 **Chap. 63]** G [218]: [Chap. 68]
2832 **help of]** G [219] adds: none but
2836–40 **I must... actions]** E; ¶ wanted: lacked
2840–6 **I have... blood]** ◇ A494, B442; A1426–8, B1960–2
2842f **night... expect]** G [219]: the hour-glass stands before mine eyes and when it runs out I must be ready ¶ expect: await
2846 **proper]** ¶ own
2847 **friends... fellows]** E
2854 **lewd]** ¶ wicked
2862 **not to... lost]** ‡ Ezek. 18: 23; 33: 11
2872ff **bad Christian...]** † '08 &c suffer from a haplographic 2-line omission, cf. intro., p. 39
2873 **mercy]** G [221]: grace
2881 **knavery]** G [222] adds: vain curiosity [*Fürwitz*]
give] G [222]: place
2882 **unto... devil]** G [222]: in such danger
devil;] G [222] adds: they were deeply sorry for him
2882f **and never... to them]** E
2884–8 **Ah, friend... soul]** ◇ A1429f, B1964f
2885f **and the... God]** E
2888–94 **I durst... altogether]** ◇ A1431–3, B1966–70
2894–8 **Thus... enemy]** E, providing a fine peroration; ¶ purpose of amendment: intention to amend
2899 **to do... but]** G [223]: that, as nothing else was now to be expected, he should
2899ff **call upon... him]** ◇ A1444f, B1978f
2904 **being... deluded]** E
2906 **This they... hold]** G [223]: He told them that he wanted to pray but he couldn't bring himself to do so
2907 **he also... forgive]** ‡ Gen. 4: 13
2908f **filthy... blood]** G [223]: gross
2910 **prayed for]** G [224]: blessed
wept] G [224] adds: and embraced him
2912 **privy]** ¶ cognizant of
2912f **It happened... midnight]** ◇ A1499, B2083; B2101
2917 **out of doors]** G [224]: to another house
2920 **adders]** G [224] adds: and other venomous serpents ◇ A1506, B2090
2921 **cry for help]** ◇ B2104

2925 **found no]** † O transmits the exact translation, edited in '08 &c

2928 **pitiful and fearful sight]** † the '08 variant demonstrates that this was not the source text for '10

2932 **dashed... pieces]** G [225]: hanging loose ◇ B2095f

2934f **where he... tormented]** E

2936f **very sad... matter]** E

2941–3 **And you... Faustus]** E

2944f **before... dark]** G [226]: was henceforth so eerie ● before: before Helena and the child vanished away, i.e. while inhabited by the devil; G refers only to the haunting *after* Faustus' death, which persists for some time (cf. 2945 below) and is not restricted to a single occasion

2945f **The same... appeared]** G [226]: By night, Doctor Faustus would appear

2946 **lively]** ¶ as if living

2950 **whole]** G [226] adds: authentic

2952 **and high-minded]** G [227]: proud, curious and refractory

2953 **and to... vocation]** E, showing a Calvinist tendency

2958f **honour... prayer]** G [227]: serve Him and love Him with all our heart

2962f **and God's... glorified]** E

2963 **Amen.]** G [227] adds a verse from I Peter, 5: Be sober and watch, for your adversary the devil as a roaring lion walketh about, seeking whom he may devour. Whom resist, steadfast in the faith (Geneva, 1557)

2965 **Here followeth...]** the Register of Contents is exclusive to O and independent of G

APPENDIX I

Bibliography of the English Faust Book

This bibliography is restricted to editions of the EFB, excluding other treatments such as the Faustus Ballad, the verse treatment (cf. intro., n. 59) and the numerous eighteenth- and nineteenth-century abridgements and chap-books. For a critical study of the ballad, see Leba M. Goldstein: 'An Account of the Faustus Ballad', *The Library*, 5th Ser., 16 (1961), pp. 176–89

(a) *Editions to 1648*

[?1592] S (*STC*: wrongly collated as 10711) loc.: Shrewsbury School Library
THE / HISTORY OF / the damnable [l]ife, and / deserued Death of [D]octor / *Iohn Fa[u]stu[s]* / Newly imprinted, and [in] conuenient / *places imperfect matter a[mende]d: accor-*/ ding to the true Coppie p[rinte]d at / Franckfort and Trans[l]ate[d] into / English by P. F. Ge[nt] / Seene and allowed. / [Device: Mckerrow 290] [? printed by E. Allde ? for Edward White]
Imprint and portion of device missing. Single sheet only (sig. A), see Plate 2 and intro. pp. 35, 42.

1592 O (*STC* 10711) loc.: Brit. Lib (C. 27. b. 43) (see Plate 6)
THE / HISTORIE / of the damnable / life, and deserued death of /*Doctor Iohn Faustus,* / Newly imprinted, and in conueni-/*ent places imperfect matter amended:* / according to the true Copie printed / *at* Franckfort, *and translated into* / *English by* P. F. *Gent.* // Seene and allowed. / [Device: McKerrow 273] //
Jmprinted at London by Thomas Orwin, and are to be / solde by Edward White, dwelling at the little North / doore of Paules, at the signe of the Gun. 1592. //
4°. **BL**; 11 signatures: A-L.; A1: title; A2: A Discourse. . . etc.; L4v blank; paginated, with errors in sigs. A, C, and L: (erroneous paginations are here marked with an asterisk:
sig. A: title page, blank, [1],2,3,5*,4*,6
sig. C: 15,18*,19*,18,19,22*,23*,22
sig. L: 81*,80,81,80*, contents [1], contents [2], contents [3], blank;
the errors in signatures A and L are corrected in the contents register, those in signature C remain uncorrected.

Running header: [v:] The famous History / [r:] of Doctor Faustus
63 chapters. Chapter numbers follow chapter headings. C. 61 is not numbered.
Characteristic spellings: Beelzebub, Mahumet, Chamagosta.
Catch-words: C3: rea- D4: Kalendar HV: mad

1608 (*STC* 10712) loc.: Brit. Lib. (G. 1029)
THE / HISTORIE / OF / The Damnable Life, / *and deserued Death of Doctor* / Iohn Faustus. // *Newly imprinted, and in conuenient places, imperfect* / matter amended: according to the true Copie / printed at Franckfort, and translated into / English by P. F. Gent. / *Seene and allowed* / [ornament] /
LONDON / Printed by I. Windet, for Edward White, and are to be solde / at his Shop neere the little North doore of Saint / *Paules Church, at the Signe of the Gun.* / *1608* //
4° **BL**; unpaginated, no register of contents.
10 signatures: A-K. A1: Title; A2: A Discourse... etc.; last page of text is K3v
running header: sig. A: [v:] The famous Hystorie / [r:] of Doctor Faustus; the remaining signatures have: [v:] The famous Historie / etc.
Characteristic spellings: Belzebub, Mahomet, Glarigolds.
Catchwords: B3v: domini- F3: lãd G3: withal
Inserted as frontispiece in unique exemplar: a fine, contemporary engraving by Sichem, inscribed *Sichem Inven: sculp: et excudit*, showing Mephostophiles discoursing with Doctor Faustus before a background depicting scenes from the book (Faustus writing his pact, etc.). Possibly this was printed on K4 to be used as a wrap.

1610 (*STC* 10712.5) loc.: Christ Church, Oxford (A202/22a)
Title as 1608.
Imprint: *LONDON*, / Printed by *E. Allde*, for *Edward White*, and are to be solde at his Shop / neere the little North doore of Saint *Paules* Church, / at the Signe of the Gun. / 1610. /
description: as 1608; unique exemplar lacks top portion of K3

1618 (*STC* 10713) loc: Bodleian Lib. (Douce F. 202)
THE / HISTORYE / OF / The Damnable Life and / deserued Death of Doctor / *Iohn Faustus.* / Newly imprinted, and in conuenient places, im-/ perfect matter amended: according to the true / Coppy printed at *Franckfort*, and / translated into English by / P. F. Gent. // [ornament] / *LONDON.* / Printed by *Edw : All-de* for *Edward White*, and are to be sold at his / Shop neare the little North doore of St *Pauls Church*, / at the signe of the Gun. 1618 //
Description: as 1610

1622 (*STC* 10713.5). loc.: Brit. Lib. (C. 118. bb. 11)
THE / HISTORIE / OF / The Damnable Life and / deserued Death of Doctor / IOHN FAVSTVS. / Newly imprinted, and in conuenient places, im = / perfect matter amended, according to the true / Copie printed at *Franckfort*, and / translated into English / by P. P. Gent. // [device] / LONDON, / Printed by *William Iones* for T. P[avier]. and I. W[right]. / 1622.
4°, **BL**; unpaginated, no register of contents;
sigs. A–K; A1: title; A2: A Discourse... etc.; last printed page: K4 (missing in exemplar);
The device, a coat of arms within elaborate scroll-work, flanked by bouquets of flowers, is not listed in McKerrow.
Running header: The famous History / of Doctor Daustus. [and variants]

1636 (*STC* 10714) loc.: Huntington Lib.; Brit. Lib.: microfilm copy (Mic. A 577(10)); Folger;
THE / HISTORIE / OF / THE DAMNABLE / LIFE, AND DESERVED / DEATH OF DOCTOR / *JOHN FAVSTVS.* / Newly printed, and in conuenient places, imperfect / matter amended : according to the true Copie printed / at *Frankfort*, and translated into English, / By *P. R.* Gent. // [woodcut from 1604 quarto of *Dr F*] / Printed at London for *Iohn Wright*, and are to be sold at the Signe of the / *Bible* in *Giltspur-Street* without Newgate. 1636. //
Description: as 1622
Chapter numbers (Roman numerals) precede chapter headings.

1648 London 1648 (*STC*(w) 2151). Loc.: Brit. Lib. (C. 27. b. 44)
THE / HISTORIE / OF THE / DAMNABLE LIFE / AND DESERVED DEATH / OF / Doctor John Faustus. / Newly printed; and in convenient places imperfect matter a- / mended : according to the true Copie printed at *Frankford*; and / translated into English, by P. R. Gent. // [woodcut from 1604 quarto of *Dr F*] / Printed at *London*, for *Edward Wright*; and are to be sold at the Signe of the *Bible* in *Giltspur-street* without Newgate. 1648 /
Description: as 1636

(b) *SCR notices to 1640*

1596 Apr 5 entry to Edward White (cf. intro. p. 45). (Arber III. 63)
1620 Dec 13 assignment, Edward White to Thomas Pavier & John Wright. (Arber IV. 44)
1626 Aug 4 assignment of interest of Thomas Pavier by his widow, to Edmund Brewster and Robert Bird. (Arber IV. 164)
1634 Apr 20 assignment from Robert Bird to John Wright (Arber IV. 318)

(c) *Brief listing of editions post 1648*

The following all 4°, Black letter, sigs. A–K., with title:
The history of the damnable life etc. ... in convenient places impertinent matter amended... P. R. Gent...

1674 (*STC*(w) 2152) loc.: Magdalen Coll., Cambridge
For William Whitwood London 1674

[?1677] (*STC*(w) 2154) loc.: Brit. Lib. (113 c. 26)
For William Whitwood London [?1677: the bottom of the title page has been obliquely cut, probably during rebinding, and only the fragments of the top of the date remain, but the missing figures have been written in ink on A2, presumably when the cut was made. Subsequent repair of A1 occludes this written completion. (*STC* suggests ?1687)]
K4v° carries an advert for 'the second part'... 'to be sold by William Whitwood'
A 1677 edition (*For T. Sawbridge*) is reported in *The Term Catalogues*, Trinity, 1677, I. 285; not otherwise known, it may be identical with the above, since Whitwood and Sawbridge were business associates, cf. 1690 edition below

1682 (*STC*(w) 2153) loc.: Huntington Lib.
For Thomas Sawbridge London 1682

1690 (*STC*(w) 2154A) loc.: Yale University Lib.
Printed by W. H. for William Whitwood, and sold by T. Sawbridge London 1690 (listed *Term Cat.*, Trinity 1690, II. 326)

[1696] (*STC*(w) 2155) loc.: Brit. Lib. (C. 56 d. 30), Folger Lib.
Printed by W. O[nley] for J. Back London [1696]
listed *Term Cat.*, priced 6d, Michaelmas 1696, II. 607
This edition omits one of Faustus' lamentations (O c. 60)

[?1700] (*STC*(w) 2156) loc.: Brit. Lib. (G 1031); Bodleian Lib. (Malone 688)
Printed by C. Brown for M. Hotham London
Contents as for 1696 edition. Re-issued in 1742 in *Winter Evening Amusements*

APPENDIX 2

Translation of GFB c. 65 (absent from the EFB)

[209] *How the wicked Spirit pestered the sorrowing Faustus with strange and scornful witticisms and sayings.*

Following the above lamentation, Faustus' spirit Mephostophiles appeared, approached him and said: 'Because you knew full well what is written in the Bible, that you should pray only to God, serve Him and have no other gods but Him, neither to the left nor to the right, and because you have not done this but have tested your God, fallen away from Him, denied Him and committed yourself to us, body and soul, now you must keep your promise. And mark my rhymes:

'If aught you know, keep mum, / If all be well with you, then rest content, / [210] If aught you have, look after it. / Misfortune is swift to come, / So suffer in silence, endure alone, / Bewail your wretched fate to none. / It is too late, despair of God, / Your doom pursues you every day.

'Therefore, my Faustus, it isn't wise to eat cherries with great lords or the devil – they throw the stalks in your face, as you now see. On which account you would have done better to have kept your distance: a broad berth makes for a safer gallop, but your arrogant pony has thrown you. You despised the skills God gave you, you were not satisfied with them but invited the devil to be your guest, and for the past 24 years you have supposed all that glisters to be gold, believing all your spirit told you; and thus the devil has belled you as if you were a cat. Once you were a nobly fashioned creature, but then, roses held to the nose for long don't [211] last. You have had your supper and now you must sing your song. If you put off the fast until Good Friday, it is soon Easter.

'This is no idle promise you have made. Every sausage has two ends, and the devil's ice is thin for skating on. You have an evil nature and birds of a feather flock together. Did the cat ever stop chasing the mouse? Too much sharpening gives a jagged edge. The cook uses the ladle when it is new but when it is old he shits in it – try licking it then! Isn't it just the same with you? Once you were the devil's newest ladle but now he no longer uses you, for you could be bought for nothing in the market. If only you had shown a little forethought you would not have despised what God had given you. Again, how insolent you have been, my

Faustus! In all your dealings you have called yourself the devil's friend, so now prepare yourself. For God is Lord, [212] the devil but abbot or monk. Good never comes of arrogance. A jack-of-all-trades is master of none. He who seeks too much will end with too little. After you have played your game of skittles you must pick them up again. 35

'So take my lessons and sayings to heart (a heart well-nigh lost). You should not have put so much trust in the devil, for he is God's ape, a murderer and a liar. You should have been cleverer. Insult leads to injury. A man's life is soon done, and it costs so much to train him. It takes a clever landlord to play host to the devil. There is more to the dance than a pair of red shoes. 40

'If only you had kept your sight on God and had been satisfied with the gifts He had given you, then you would not have had to tread this measure. You ought not to have been so ready to do the devil's bidding and to believe in him, for he who is quick to trust is soon betrayed. Now [213] the devil wipes his chops and gets up from the table. You have given bond with your own blood and now the bond will 45 be wrung from you. You have let it all go in one ear and straight out the other.'

When the spirit had sufficiently carolled 'O Poor Judas', he disappeared and left Faustus alone, bewildered and melancholy.

APPENDIX 3

Concordance with *Doctor Faustus* A and B

Line references are from Greg. For the reverse concordance, see Commentary.

A	B	EFB line	key-words
12f	12f	20	born, Rhodes
14–16	14–16	22–6	Wittenberg, kinsman
18	17	42f	Doctor
19f	18f	38–42	excelling, theology
22	21	72	wings
24	23	28, 51, 71	devilish exercise
26f	25f	54	necromancy, magic
28	27	65	bliss
44–52	42–49	58f	physician
89		798	rend the clouds
111	106	2162f	spirits... please
136		44	fantasy
143	132	297	ravished
157	146	88	lions
251–5	234–8	81	circle, characters
260	243f	146f	Orientis princeps
260–3	244f	83–5, 98f	Mephostophilis, Beelzebub
262	246	93	quod tumeraris
269	253	118	Franciscan friar
281f	262f	131–5	wait... live
285–7	266–8	136–9	leave
295f	276f	152f	damned
307f	288f	146f	Lucifer, commander
309–13	290–4	414–18, 483–93	Lucifer's fall
330f	310f	796f	never... possess
338–40	318–20	131–5	Faustus' conditions
344f	324f	159–61	midnight

A	B	EFB line	key-words
358	338	73f	speculation
387	361	363	tear thee in pieces
438–43	390–5	162–6	needs be damned
472	420	192f	buy... soul
475	423	194f	own blood
494	442	2840–6	proper blood
497	444	237	blood... arm
503	450	242	fire
507	454	251	gives... soul
517–24	464–70	238f	homo fuge
528–31	476–9	304–6	delight, magic
533f	480	307f	receive this scroll
541–9	487–95	180–8	Faustus' conditions
550–7	496–502	244–61	pact
562	508	439–41	where is hell?
563	509	464	under the heavens
566	512	643–5	tortured
573	519	349	hell's a fable
577f	523f	559	given thy soul
580–2	525–8	349	old wives' tales
587	532	351f	wife
588	533	374–6	wanton, lascivious
590		361f	How, a wife?
591f		375	I will have one
599	540	357	ceremonial toy
601–3	542–4	396f	fairest courtesans
606	547	487–9	bright Lucifer
607	548	405–8	take this book
610	551	797f	thunder, lightning
612	553	1936f	men in armour
644	585	668–70	devil, pity
647	589	702–4	hardened
650f	591	533–5	knives, halters
658f	598f	95f, 297	ravishing, harp
662f	602f	771–5	astrology
671	612	789f	Saturn... Jupiter
675	615	818	East to West
694	636	859–61	who made the world
698f	640f	855f	bound, kingdom
702	644	865	Remember this
707	648	744	too late
709	650	864	tear, pieces
713	654	869–73	Enter Lucifer
716	657	869–73	lookst, terrible

A	B	EFB line	key-words
719	659	874f	come to fetch
720–2	660–2	878–80	injure, promise
730	669f	881–3	hell, pastime
735	675	955	creation
799–801	733–5	969f	see hell, midnight
802f	736f	943	book, turn
810–2	778f (558–60)	1067–70	Astronomy
814f	781f (562f)	1103–5	chariot, dragons
	783f	1144, 1212	clouds, sky
	785	1156	bright circle
	786f	1128	height, circumference
	789	1130f, 1151	East to West, swift
	790	1121, 1216	eight days
818	799 (566)	1330f	Pope, court
819	800 (567)	1348–51	feast
825f	806f	1258–60	Trier, not to be won
827f	808f	1265–7	Paris, River Main
830–6	811–16	1268–77	Naples, Maro's tomb
837–9	817–21	1280–9	Venice, Padua
853–9	836–45	1305–12	Rome, bridges, canons
860f	846f	1318f	pyramids, Africa
869	855	1348–51	Peter's feast
	870	1121, 1216	eight days
	876	1128–34	kingdoms of the world
	951	1450	basilisk
	1019	1421	o'er the Alps
887	1080	1358f	snatched the meat
892	1084	1358f	I'll ha't
	1086	1361	fetch me some wine
	1090	1363	lubbers
895–8	1095–100	1356f	ghost, Purgatory
898	1100	1372	lay... ghost
899–904f	1101–6	1351–3	box on the ear
908–10	1108–10	1372–4	bell, book and candle
914–29	1111–25	1375–80	friars' dirge
933		1700f	returned home
939–41		1744f	astrology, etc.
944		1838	Carolus the fifth
945		1841f	noblemen
1027	1161	1601	Constantinople
	1180	1602–4	great Turk's court
	1192	1849	wonder of the world
	1193–7	1856–77	progenitors, Alexander
	1202f, 1223f, 1228	1914f	sluggard, window

A	B	EFB line	key-words
1040–9		1848–53	Emperor, proof of skill
1055		1855f	content... command
1057–91	1264–8	1856–77	Emperor's request
	1284f	1878–80	no questions
1101	1292, 1295	1882f, 1892	Alexander, paramour
	1297–1307	1888–91	in mine arms
1102–5	1309–15	1901–3	wart
1111–5	1319–26	1917–19	knight, horns
1130	1360	1925f	transform him
	1371 etc.	1928	revenge
	1483 etc.	2588	army
1134–6		833	restless course
1143 etc.	1523 etc.	2065	horse-courser
1222	1571	2136	Duke of Vanholt
	1600–7	2085	load of hay
	1611–29	2065	horse-courser
	1641	2169	enchanted castle
1232–57	1646–74	2135	Duchess, grapes
	1758–69	2110	charm him dumb
1268	1778–80	2685–9	will, Wagner
1272	1783f	2264–8	belly-cheer
1275–1300	1785–1811	2358	Helen show
1302–41	1812–56	2450	Old Man, 2nd pact
1307f		2476	tears... filthiness
1314	1830, 1843	2466	what hast thou done
1318	1833	1033f	suicide
1324–6	1839f	2487–9	comfort
1330–2	1844–6	2491f	I do repent
1335–9	1849–54	2503–5	piecemeal, blood
1342–5	1857–60	2524f	torment, aged man
1348–76	1863–93	2657	thousand ships
1384f		2539	laughs... scorn
	1908–10	585f	over-reach the devil
	1911	225f	sauced with pain
1421–48	1955–80	2829ff	oration to the students
	1988–92	551–6	led thine eye
	1993	744; App. 2: 11f	too late
	2020f	652	burning forks
	2027	680f	poor starve
1462	2048	586–8	who pulls me down
1489–95	2072–9	2765–8	brutish beast
1506	2090	2920	adders and serpents
1515–7	2119–21	562–8	unlawful things

APPENDIX 4

Parallels with *The Most Famous History of the Learned Fryer Bacon* (M).

(a) Parallels with Marlowe's *Doctor Faustus*

(i) *The 'shoulder of mutton'*

M sig. A3^{r-v}: 'in came the Cook-wench, brought by a Spirit at the Window, with a Spit and a roasted Shoulder of Mutton on it'; cf. intro. p. 61

Dr F A367–9 (B348f): 'so hungry, that I know he would giue his soule to the Diuel for a shoulder of mutton, though it were blood rawe.'; A371f (B351f): 'I had neede haue it wel roasted, and good sawce to it'; B1164: 'will it please you to take a shoulder of Mutton to supper'

(ii) *Robin/Miles conjuring*

M sig. C3v: 'Miles . . . finding by chance his Master's Study Door open, got his Book, and to the top of the House he went with it, and there would needs conjure for Money. After he had read a few Charms, the Devil came in a frightful Shape . . . The Devil hereupon began to spit Fire in his Face, which made him run about the Leads like a mad Man, and the Devil bellowing after. . . . and upon Miles' Promise never more to meddle with any of his books. . .'

Dr F A949f (B745): *Robin*: . . . here I ha stolne one of doctor Faustus coniuring books'; A1012f: *Enter Mephostophilis: sets squibs at their backes: they runne about.*'; A1018f: 'good diuel forgiue me now, and Ile neuer rob thy Library more'

(iii) *the knight gives Bacon/Faustus the lie*

M sig. A2v: 'the knight. . . saying, Scholars and Travellers might lie by Authority'. . . 'Well, said the Gentleman of the Bed-Chamber, I doubt not but one will prove as true as the other.'

Dr F A1084f: '*Knight*: I mary master doctor, now theres a signe of grace in you, when you will confesse the trueth.'; A1095: '*Kn.* Ifaith thats as true as Diana turnd me to a stag.'

(iv) *threats of revenge*

M sig. A3: 'but here the Dog is, and I'll be revenged on him'; sig. A3v: 'though the Gentleman was much asham'd and confounded, to be thus exposed, still muttering revenge'... 'and [BACON] bid him have a Care how he gave a Scholar the lye again'.
Dr F A1116: *Kn*: Thou damned wretch, and execrable dogge'; A1129 (B1360): 'and sir knight, hereafter speake well of Scholers'; B1362–6: '*Ben.* Speake well of yee?... But an I be not reueng'd for this...';

(v) *punishment by mire and briars*

M sig. A2v: 'turning down a Bye lane, rode over Hedge and Ditch';
Dr F [horse-courser scene] A1160: ride him ouer hedge or ditch

M sig. A3: 'the Gentleman of the Bed-chamber came in puffing and blowing, all bemired and dirty, his Face and Hands scratched with Bushes and Bryers'; sig. C1v [Miles' punishment of the 3 thieves]: 'he led them through Quagmires, Bogs and Briars, ... until they were almost dead, with Weariness, Wet, Mire, and loss of Blood, by scratching in the Bushes.'
Dr F B1461: 'And hurle him in some lake of mud and dirt: ... dragge him through the woods, amongst the pricking thornes, and sharpest briers'; B1489ff. *Enter ... Benuolio, Fredericke, and Martino, their heads and faces bloudy, and besmear'd with mud and durt...*'; B1497: Halfe smother'd in a Lake of mud and durt'
(cf. also below, parallel with *The Tempest*)

(vi) *hell*

M sig. C2r: 'then said Bacon, Have you not heard of Hell? No, says [the Villain]; or if I have, I only take it for a Bugbear set up by you Priests, to frighten Children and Old Women.
D. F A573 (B519): 'Come, I thinke hell's a fable.'; A582 (B527): 'Tush these are trifles and meere olde wiues tales.'

M sig. C2r 'thereupon he conjur'd up the Ghost of Julius Caesar the Apostate, in a burning Chair, torn with fiery Whips and hot Pincers, by many fiends';
Dr F B2023f: 'this euer-burning chaire, Is for ore-tortur'd soules to rest them in.'

(vii) *wall of brass*

M sig. B1v: 'they would require that all the Seagirt Shores of England and Wales should be walled with Brass'; sig. B3: 'Hadst thou called me then, all England had been Walled with Brass to my immortal Fame.'
Dr F A120 (B115): 'Ile haue them wall all Iermany with brasse'

(b) Parallels with Shakespeare's *The Tempest* (Reference text: *The Riverside Shakespeare*, Boston (Houghton Mifflin) 1974).

(i) *Shapes with a banquet*

M sig. A3 [in Bacon's performance before the King and Queen]: 'there presently, to their great Amazement, ensued the most melodious Musick they had ever heard in their Lives... another kind of Musick was heard, and presently Dancers in Antick Shapes at a Masquerade... louder Musick was heard, and whilst that play'd, a Table was placed by an invisible Hand, and richly covered with all the Dainties that could be thought on; then he bid the King and Queen draw their Seats near, and partake of the Provisions he had provided for their Highnesses; which they did and all thereupon vanished... the Place was perfumed with all the Sweets of Arabia...'
Tempest III. iii. 17, s. d.: 'Solemn and strange music'; ibid., 19: 'Marvellous sweet music!'; s. d.: 'Enter several strange shapes, bringing in a banket; and dance about it with gentle actions of salutations; and inviting the King, etc., to eat, they depart.'; ibid., 21f: 'A living drollery. Now I will believe... that in Arabia...'; ibid., 49: 'I will stand to and feed'; ibid., 53, s. d.: 'the banquet vanishes'

(ii) *magic paralysis*

M sig. C2: 'Bacon... with the waving of his Wand, struck his Arm lame, so that he could not use his sword.'
Tempest III. iii, 66ff: 'If you could hurt, / Your swords are now too massy for your strengths, / And will not be uplifted.'; v. i. 60f: 'There stand, / For you are spell-stopp'd.'

(iii) *'pied piper' and mire and briers*

M sig. B2: [Miles] got him[self] ... a Tabor and Pipe to play...; sig. C1v: [Bacon] slipped an Inchanted Pipe into Miles' Hand... Miles began to play, and [the three thieves] to Dance, ... they followed him Dancing, as before, so that he led them through Quagmires... [etc. see above, parallels with *Dr F*]
Tempest IV. i. 175–84 [Ariel describes how he has led Caliban, Stefano and Trinculo]: 'Then I beat my tabor,... So I charm'd their ears / That calf-like they my lowing follow'd through / Tooth'd briers, sharp furzes, pricking goss, and thorns, / Which ent'red their frail shins. At last I left them / I'th'filthy-mantled pool beyond your cell, / There dancing up to th'chins, that the foul lake / O'erstunk their feet.'

(iv) *abjuration of magic*

M sig C4v: '[Bacon] burnt his Books... shut himself up in a Cell, where he lived two Years lamenting for his Sins, and dug the Grave he was Buried in with his own Nails, ... at two Years end he died a true Penitent...'
Tempest v. i. 50f: 'But this rough magic / I here abjure'; ibid., 311: 'And thence retire me to Milan, where / Every third thought shall be my grave'; Epilogue 13ff: 'Now I want / Spirits to enforce, art to enchant, / And my ending is despair, / Unless I be reliev'd by prayer.'

General index

Names of authors listed in the abbreviations on pp. xii–xv do not feature in this index unless specifically referred to in the text.

Abbreviations: FB: Faust books; EFB: English Faust Book; GFB: German Faust Book; F: Famous History; M: Most Famous History; n.: notes to introduction (pp. 72–87).

References in bold type e.g. **776**, are to line indicators in the commentary (pp. 185–245).

Textual index

Numbers enclosed by angle brackets refer to text lines, otherwise to page numbers.